# Palgrave Modern Legal History

Series Editors
Catharine MacMillan
The Dickson Poon School of Law
King's College London
London, UK

Rebecca Probert
School of Law
University of Exeter
Exeter, UK

This series provides a forum for the publication of high-quality monographs that take innovative, contextual, and inter- or multi-disciplinary approaches to legal history. It brings legal history to a wider audience by exploring the history of law as part of a broader social, intellectual, cultural, literary, or economic context. Its focus is on modern British and Imperial legal history (post 1750), but within that time frame engages with the widest possible range of subject areas.

More information about this series at
https://link.springer.com/bookseries/14681

Sarah McKibbin • Jeremy Patrick
Marcus K. Harmes
Editors

# The Impact of Law's History

What's Past is Prologue

*Editors*
Sarah McKibbin
University of Southern Queensland
Toowoomba, QLD, Australia

Jeremy Patrick
School of Law and Justice
University of Southern Queensland
Toowoomba, QLD, Australia

Marcus K. Harmes
University of Southern Queensland
Toowoomba, QLD, Australia

Palgrave Modern Legal History
ISBN 978-3-030-90067-0        ISBN 978-3-030-90068-7   (eBook)
https://doi.org/10.1007/978-3-030-90068-7

© The Editor(s) (if applicable) and The Author(s), under exclusive licence to Springer Nature Switzerland AG 2022
This work is subject to copyright. All rights are solely and exclusively licensed by the Publisher, whether the whole or part of the material is concerned, specifically the rights of translation, reprinting, reuse of illustrations, recitation, broadcasting, reproduction on microfilms or in any other physical way, and transmission or information storage and retrieval, electronic adaptation, computer software, or by similar or dissimilar methodology now known or hereafter developed.
The use of general descriptive names, registered names, trademarks, service marks, etc. in this publication does not imply, even in the absence of a specific statement, that such names are exempt from the relevant protective laws and regulations and therefore free for general use.
The publisher, the authors and the editors are safe to assume that the advice and information in this book are believed to be true and accurate at the date of publication. Neither the publisher nor the authors or the editors give a warranty, expressed or implied, with respect to the material contained herein or for any errors or omissions that may have been made. The publisher remains neutral with regard to jurisdictional claims in published maps and institutional affiliations.

Cover image: © DigitalVision Vectors / Getty Images

This Palgrave Macmillan imprint is published by the registered company Springer Nature Switzerland AG.
The registered company address is: Gewerbestrasse 11, 6330 Cham, Switzerland

# Foreword

This volume shows the variety of approaches currently adopted by scholars working on the law and legal institutions of England and Australia and it is one which convincingly demonstrates the continuing importance of legal history for the understanding of the legal institutions and legal doctrine of these two common law jurisdictions. Of the thirteen papers included in the volume two focus on specific individuals (the English eighteenth-century Attorney General Sir Dudley Ryder and the Australian twentieth-century High Court judge Albert Bathurst Piddington) but place them in their wider contemporary context by looking at the development of the office of Attorney General and Ryder's relationship with his governmental colleagues and by sketching in Piddington's prior and subsequent career and explaining the circumstances which led to Piddington being appointed but never sitting in the High Court. Four papers focus on English and Australian constitutional law and development. One looks at Lord Atkin's famous dissent in the 1942 case of *Liversidge v Anderson*, a case which challenged the arbitrary exercise of executive discretion to imprison indefinitely. It locates that dissent in its contemporary social and legal context and then traces the stages by which Atkin's dissenting opinion came to be accepted as the constitutional orthodoxy. A second provides an ambitious overview of UK constitutional history over the four decades down to 2019. It looks at some of the major changes of that period (increasing centralisation of governmental power under Margaret Thatcher, devolution in Scotland and Wales under Tony Blair, the decline of Cabinet government and the impact of the Brexit referendum) and

v

vi FOREWORD

their short and longer-term impact on the UK's unwritten constitution. A third paper suggests that the concept of path dependency may be a useful tool for understanding why some doctrines of Australian constitutional law have been able to change quite dramatically over time while others have remained pretty much the same and uses two specific areas of constitutional law to show how that works in practice. A fourth argues that modern lawyers need to understand the deeper normative values which underlay the 1867 Constitution Act of Queensland if they are to be given a modern meaning in allowing the allocation of property as wealth on just and principled lines. Two papers focus on aspects of the modern history of the legal profession in England and Australia. One looks at the representation of members of the English legal profession of an earlier era (and particularly of English barristers defending the accused) in British television series of the second half of the twentieth century as one of the ways in which a non-academic public acquires its knowledge of the workings of the legal profession in the past. The other looks at the restrictions on the promotion of the services of members of the legal profession in Australia and New Zealand prior to the 1970s and shows how that was an inheritance from prior history of the legal profession in England from the Middle Ages onwards. It then traces how and why they were removed but also shows that the removal of the restrictions has had relatively little impact on the way lawyers sell their services to their clients. Two papers are mainly concerned with the history of private law. One traces the very long-term change in the law of tort from strict liability to the allocation of liability on the basis of the defendant's fault and why it occurred. This starts in the Ancient World with the Code of Hammurabi and the Twelve Tables of ancient Rome but brings us down to the present day (and beyond). A second paper demonstrates the way in which the High Court of Australia from the 1980s onwards has shifted Australian private law in new directions by creatively invoking common law arguments derived from English legal history, showing just how important knowledge of that legal history can be for Australian lawyers. Two papers take the legal treatment and status of Australia's indigenous people (its First Nations) in the past and in the future as their topic. One looks at the first half century after the arrival of the first group of British colonists in 1788 and the arrival of English law in Australia and what evidence there is of the settlers coming to treat indigenous people during this period as being entitled to the protection of English law. A second makes a brave effort to utilise the example

FOREWORD    vii

of Magna Carta as a precedent for the acceptance of a version of legal pluralism which might provide a conceptualisation for the constitutional recognition of indigenous rights in Australia alongside the existing framework of Australian law and common law rights. One final chapter gives an overview of the history of biosecurity regulation in Australia and its successes (including the exclusion of phylloxera) and failures (the ill-advised introduction of the cane toad) and the lessons which can be learned from them.

This is a valuable collection of essays on English and Australian legal history which illustrates the strengths of a variety of approaches to the doing of legal history and their complementarity. It also helps to demonstrate the continuing value of legal history to a broader understanding of current law. It can be commended to not just students but also teachers of both law and history and practitioners.

All Soul's College, Oxford                                    Paul Brand

# CONTENTS

1 **Introduction**         1
Marcus K. Harmes, Sarah McKibbin, and Jeremy Patrick

2 **Politics and Profession: Sir Dudley Ryder and the Office of Attorney General in England, 1689–1760**     5
Wilfrid Prest

3 **Lord Atkin's Dissent in *Liversidge v Anderson*: Indecorously Orthodox?**     25
Karen Schultz

4 **The Challenges to the UK Constitution Since 1979 and Brexit**     49
Michael Mulligan

5 **The Age of Rumpole Is Past? Legal History on British Television**     65
Marcus K. Harmes, Meredith A. Harmes, and Barbara Harmes

6 **The History of Legal Marketing in Australia and New Zealand**     83
A. Keith Thompson

ix

## x CONTENTS

7  The Historical Development of the Fault Basis of Liability
   in the Law of Torts                                    105
   Anthony Gray

8  What Albert Did and What Albert Did Next: Albert
   Bathurst Piddington—The High Court Judge Who
   Never Sat                                              131
   A. S. Bell and James Monaghan

9  Path Dependency, the High Court, and the Constitution  155
   Jeremy Patrick

10 The Use and Misuse of Legal History in the High Court
   of Australia                                           179
   Warren Swain

11 Did the Early British Colonists Regard the Indigenous
   Peoples of New South Wales as Subjects of the Crown
   Entitled to the Protection of English Law?             201
   Gavin Loughton

12 Land, the Social Imaginary, and the *Constitution Act 1867*
   (Qld)                                                  239
   Julie Copley

13 The Good, the Bad and the Ugly: A Short History of
   Biosecurity Regulation in Australia                    257
   Noeleen McNamara

14 Legal Pluralism Past and Present: Magna Carta and a
   First Nations' Voice in the Australian Constitution    277
   Jason Taliadoros

Index                                                     301

# Notes on Contributors

**A. S. Bell** was appointed President of the New South Wales Court of Appeal in February 2019. His Honour was a dual University medallist at the University of Sydney and Vinerian Scholar at Oxford University, where he took a BCL and DPhil. He was a silk at the NSW Bar prior to his elevation to the Bench.

**Julie Copley** is Lecturer (Property and Construction Law) at the University of Southern Queensland and a PhD in Law candidate at the University of Adelaide. Admitted to legal practice, Julie has worked for Queensland's Parliament and Court of Appeal and in public and private sectors in legal research, legislative and legal policy roles.

**Anthony Gray** is Professor of Law and Associate Head (Research) at the University of Southern Queensland, Australia. His approximately 140 peer-reviewed articles have been published, many in leading law journals both in Australia and internationally, and he has completed numerous monographs within the past five years.

**Barbara Harmes** lectures in communication at the University of Southern Queensland, with a particular focus on international students. Her doctoral research focused on the discursive controls built around sexuality in late-nineteenth century England. Her research interests include cultural studies, postgraduate education and religion.

**Marcus K. Harmes** is Associate Director (Research) at the University of Southern Queensland College and teaches legal history in the law degree.

xii   NOTES ON CONTRIBUTORS

His articles have been published extensively in the fields of religious and political history, with a particular emphasis on British religious history and constitutional history.

**Meredith A. Harmes** teaches communication in the enabling programmes at the University of Southern Queensland in Australia. Her research interests include modern British and Australian politics and popular culture in Britain and America. Her most recent publication in the *Australasian Journal of Popular Culture* was on race and cultural studies on American television.

**Gavin Loughton** has practised as a solicitor in Canberra since 1994. Since 2009 he has been a senior executive lawyer in the Constitutional Litigation Unit of the Australian Government Solicitor. He is one of the co-authors of the second edition of Perry & Lloyd's *Australian Native Title Law* (2018).

**Sarah McKibbin** is Lecturer (Law) in the School of Law and Justice, University of Southern Queensland, and co-author of *A Legal History for Australia* (2021) with Marcus K. Harmes and Libby Connors.

**Noeleen McNamara** is an associate professor in the School of Law and Justice at the University of Southern Queensland, where she teaches environmental law, contract law and torts law. McNamara's research focus is on environmental law, natural resources law and mining.

**James Monaghan** practises as solicitor in the NSW Crown Solicitor's Office. He was previously a researcher at the High Court of Australia and the NSW Court of Appeal. He studied at the University of Sydney and obtained the degrees of Bachelor of Arts (Hons I and the University Medal) and Bachelor of Laws (Hons I).

**Michael Mulligan** is a teaching fellow in the Centre for International Studies & Diplomacy at the School of Oriental & African Studies, University of London. He has previously taught at the British University in Egypt and Lancaster University. His research interests include international law and legal and constitutional history, and his recent publications include work on piracy, extraterritoriality and the East India Company.

**Jeremy Patrick** is a lecturer in the School of Law and Justice, University of Southern Queensland, Australia. His multiple journal articles have been published on historical aspects in the area of law and religion, including constitutional religion clauses, blasphemous libel, and the legal regulation of fortune-telling and individual spirituality. He is the author of *Faith or Fraud: Fortune-Telling, Spirituality, and the Law* (2020).

**Wilfrid Prest** trained as a historian at Melbourne and Oxford, then taught history in Adelaide from 1966 to 2001, before moving to the Adelaide Law School. A second edition of his first book, *The Inns of Court Under Elizabeth I and the Early Stuarts*, is forthcoming from Cambridge University Press.

**Karen Schultz** is a lecturer at the Griffith Law School, Griffith University, and a solicitor of the Supreme Court of Queensland. Her background is in private practice, public sector research, and reform. Schultz's teaching and academic research is focused on legal theory, constitutional law, equity, and legal history.

**Warren Swain** is Deputy Dean at the Faculty of Law, the University of Auckland, New Zealand. He writes on contract and tort law and the history of private law and legal doctrine more generally. His books include *The Law of Contract 1670–1870*, and *Contract Law: Principles and Context*, with Andrew Stewart and Karen Fairweather, both published by the Cambridge University Press.

**Jason Taliadoros** works in the Deakin Law School, Deakin University, where he researches and teaches in the areas of torts, statutory compensation schemes, and legal history. His published works in these areas seek to identify patterns of thought in the law and the history behind them.

**A. Keith Thompson** is Professor of Law in the Sydney School of Law and Business at the University of Notre Dame Australia. He formerly practised as a partner (and as the marketing director) of a large law firm in Auckland and then as General Counsel for the Church of Jesus Christ of Latter-day Saints first through the Pacific and then the African Continent.

# LIST OF TABLES

| | | |
|---|---|---|
| Table 10.1 | Total citations of English legal classics by the High Court from 1903 to 2019 | 198 |
| Table 10.2 | Total citations of secondary legal historical literature by the High Court from 1903 to 2019 | 199 |
| Table 10.3 | Citation of English legal classics by High Court judges of ten or more | 200 |
| Table 10.4 | Citations of historical secondary literature by High Court judges of ten or more | 200 |

CHAPTER 1

# Introduction

*Marcus K. Harmes, Sarah McKibbin, and Jeremy Patrick*

"What's past is prologue." These words from Shakespeare's *The Tempest* are uttered by Antonio to explain why he and Sebastian are about to make the fateful choice of entering a conspiracy to commit murder.[1] If carried out, this bloodshed would be no rash act of momentary impulse, but a cold, calculated manoeuvre selected from among competing options. But premeditated murder—as dramatic and irrevocable a decision as a human can make—would be inexplicable without understanding everything that had come before. When Antonio makes this famous statement, he's attempting to answer the question: "why?" Why have he and Sebastian somehow reached the point where murder seems like the best choice?

[1] Act 2, Scene 1.

M. K. Harmes • S. McKibbin (✉)
University of Southern Queensland, Toowoomba, QLD, Australia
e-mail: Marcus.Harmes@usq.edu.au; Sarah.McKibbin@usq.edu.au

Jeremy Patrick
School of Law and Justice, University of Southern Queensland,
Toowoomba, QLD, Australia
e-mail: Jeremy.Patrick@usq.edu.au

© The Author(s), under exclusive license to Springer Nature
Switzerland AG 2022
S. McKibbin et al. (eds.), *The Impact of Law's History*, Palgrave
Modern Legal History,
https://doi.org/10.1007/978-3-030-90068-7_1

1

2    M. K. HARMES ET AL.

The question of "why?" is also the theme of this book. In *The Tempest*, Antonio's and Sebastian's conspiracy is foiled by a magical sprite and they're eventually forgiven for their actions—without any recourse to law. But for those of us without the good (or bad) fortune to live on a remote island ruled by a sorcerer, law forms the unavoidable parameters of what we can and can't do. Law delineates the boundaries of our freedoms, imposes the constraints of duties and responsibilities, and makes the final decision of how something as mundane as a tax dispute or as serious as a murder plot should be resolved. But the laws we have weren't the result of pure syllogistic logic, the inevitable march of progress, or even the system "working itself pure." Antonio's reference to the past providing prologue is meant to give Sebastian *context* to why murder had become a viable choice, but it was still that—a *choice*. Similarly, the laws that govern us exist because choices were made against the backdrop of a particular historical context that impacted what seemed ideal or feasible at the time.

This book explores the question of how historical developments in particular contexts have shaped the legal system we have today.[2] A cynic might add a second "why" to the first one, and ask even if we could learn why we have the laws we have, *why* should we care? A decade ago in "Why Legal History Matters"—a John Salmond Lecture delivered at the Victoria University of Wellington—Jim Phillips provided a clear and persuasive answer. Phillips wrote:

> [There are] four principal reasons why *legal* history especially matters: [1] legal history teaches us about the contingency of law, about its fundamental shaping by other historical forces; [2] legal history shows us that while law is shaped by other forces, it can be at the same time relatively autonomous, not always the handmaiden of dominant interests; [3] legal history, perhaps paradoxically, frees us from the past, allows us to make our own decisions by seeing that there is nothing inevitable or preordained in what we currently have; and [4] legal history exposes the presence of many variants of legal pluralism in both the past and the present.[3]

It would be easy to misunderstand these insights. When Phillips writes about the contingency of law, he's not saying that they arose at random or are necessarily arbitrary—just that every law arises in a historical context that limits and influences which of a myriad of possibilities are adopted.

---

[2] This collection arose out of a colloquium held by the University of Southern Queensland's Law, Religion, and Heritage Research Program Team in Toowoomba in May 2019.

[3] Jim Phillips, "Why Legal History Matters," *Victoria University Wellington Law Review* 41 (2010): 294–5.

Similarly, when he writes about legal history as a liberating force, these are not the words of a revolutionary hoping to cast off the past but are instead the words of a historian reminding us that once we understand why we have a particular law, we can make better decisions on whether to keep or change it. "Appreciating the message of contingency demystifies the law," writes Phillips, "removes history as authority in itself, and makes it possible for current students and practitioners to envisage other worlds, other ways of doing things."[4]

The present collection contains thirteen different ways of demonstrating that the past is but prologue when it comes to the law. The chapters that follow focus on England and Australia, two common law jurisdictions with obvious historical linkages to one another and show the diversity of methodologies that can fall under "legal history." Some zoom in to dissect a particular court opinion of great importance, some zoom out to show the sweeping changes in a particular area of law over the span of centuries, and others ask us to think about legal history in new ways—such as on television! For ease of reference, the editors have divided this book into four sections.

Section I looks at legal history in the context of England. Chapter 2 by Wilfrid Prest presents a fascinating exploration of the office of the Attorney General in England over the years 1689–1760. Karen Schultz in Chap. 3 jumps forward to 1940s wartime Great Britain in her analysis of Lord Atkin's dissent in *Liversidge v Anderson*. Chapter 4 by Michael Mulligan brings us up to the present with his analysis of changes to the English Constitution since 1979 and up through Brexit. Marcus, Meredith, and Barbara Harmes in Chap. 5 remind us that law isn't just for lawyers in their chapter on how English legal history is portrayed on the small screen.

Section II bridges the United Kingdom and Australia through two chapters on the development of the common law. First, Keith Thompson in Chap. 6 discusses the evolution of legal restrictions on lawyers' abilities to market their own services. Second, Anthony Gray in Chap. 7 traces how a general norm of strict liability for tort gradually gave way to the standard of negligence.

Section III focuses on the High Court of Australia. The Honourable Justice A. S. Bell and James Monaghan in Chap. 8 present the fascinating story of "the High Court judge who never sat." Jeremy Patrick in Chap. 9 speculates that the concept of "path dependency" is useful for understanding why some High Court decisions stand the test of time, and others are

---

[4] Ibid., 305. In this way, legal history holds some similarities to comparative law.

quickly uprooted. Warren Swain in Chap. 10 explores how English legal history has been used in High Court decision-making.

Section IV is about land and the peoples who have occupied it since time immemorial. Gavin Loughton in Chap. 11 writes a deeply researched and detailed examination of how the doctrine of *terra nullius* entered Australian law. Julie Copley in Chap. 12 discusses land in the context of Queensland's *Constitution Act 1867*. Noeleen McNamara in Chap. 13 concludes the section with a history of biodiversity regulation in the country. Jason Taliadoros in Chap. 14 discusses the Uluru Statement from the Heart in the context of the Australian Constitution and Magna Carta.

Taken together, these 14 chapters make an important contribution to showing how "what's past is prologue" when it comes to law. The importance of quality historical legal scholarship can hardly be overstated given how frequently legal history is invoked in everything from influential court decisions to the reports of law reform commissions and Parliamentary committees. Fortunately, there are signs that legal history is making a resurgence both in education and in scholarship. Law shapes the world around us, and the better we understand its past, the better we can decide on its future.

CHAPTER 2

# Politics and Profession: Sir Dudley Ryder and the Office of Attorney General in England, 1689–1760

*Wilfrid Prest*

## INTRODUCTION

While writing a chapter on the legal profession for the ninth (1689–1760) volume of the *Oxford History of the Laws of England* (*OHLE*), I was invited to deliver the 2019 Annual Plunkett lecture of the Francis Forbes Society for Australian Legal History. As a work of reference, the *OHLE* can only touch lightly on many topics. But since the Forbes Society lecture memorialises John Herbert Plunkett (1802–1869), a notable early Attorney General

---

Research for this chapter was supported in part by Australian Research Council Discovery Project DP160100265, "A New History of Law in Post-Revolutionary England, 1689–1760". I am grateful to Sabina Flanagan, Mark Neuendorf, and Larissa Reid for their kind assistance.

---

W. Prest (✉)
University of Adelaide, Adelaide, SA, Australia
e-mail: wilfrid.prest@adelaide.edu.au

© The Author(s), under exclusive license to Springer Nature Switzerland AG 2022
S. McKibbin et al. (eds.), *The Impact of Law's History*, Palgrave Modern Legal History,
https://doi.org/10.1007/978-3-030-90068-7_2

of New South Wales, it seemed that comparison between the roles of eighteenth-century English attorneys-general and their later Australian counterparts might provide a theme for my talk.

In the event, that proved a bit too ambitious. The best I could do, then and in this chapter on which it is based, was to outline how the English office of Attorney General developed up to and beyond the Glorious Revolution of 1688, surveying both the nature of the post and those who filled it under William and Mary, Anne, and the first two Hanoverian monarchs. Following that introduction I discuss the working life of Sir Dudley Ryder, England's second longest-serving Attorney General, uniquely documented in a massive autobiographical archive. Finally, turning to the present day, a brief conclusion attempts to highlight some elements of both change and continuity between the original English Crown law office and its modern Australian derivatives.[1]

## Attorneys General in General, 1689–1759

Crown law officers have a long history. Like their most powerful subjects, medieval English monarchs retained their own counsel and attorneys, appointed by letters patent to represent the interests of the crown in litigation, principally as officers of the court of Common Pleas. The first such recorded appointment was that of William Langley in 1315; more than a century later the same post came to be entitled "king's attorney general", and a little after that the first king's solicitor (later solicitor general) was appointed.[2] These personal legal representatives of the monarch received a token salary from the royal exchequer, but doubtless earned the bulk of their income from fees paid by litigants eager to retain the top legal talent of the day. For despite their titles, both the Attorney General and the solicitor general were invariably chosen from the ranks of the legal profession's "upper branch", which comprised both serjeants at law and *apprentici ad legum* (apprentices of the law), the benchers and utter-barristers of the four London inns of court. By the Tudor period these crown law posts provided a recognised fast-track to high judicial preferment, as well as

---

[1] The history of attorneys-general from early modern England to colonial and post-Federation Australia is a very large subject, to which Hanlon's 2008 thesis provides a comprehensive introduction, drawing in part on the work of Edwards (1964 & 1984); other useful surveys are provided by Holdsworth (1937), Melikan (1997), Lurie (2013) and Appleby (2016).

[2] Sainty, *Law Officers*, 41–2, 59–60. Holdsworth, *History*, vi. 458–72.

considerable wealth; in 1581 a future chief justice was prepared to abandon his theoretically superior rank as serjeant at law to accept appointment to the more influential and lucrative position of solicitor general to Queen Elizabeth.[3]

One main difference between early holders of the office of Attorney General and their later successors in both England and the British overseas empire was that during the fifteenth, sixteenth, and early seventeenth centuries they were summoned (along with the judges) to serve as advisors or assistants in attendance on the infrequent meetings of the House of Lords, rather than elected to sit in the equally occasional sessions of the House of Commons. Indeed, the crown's law officers were by no means universally welcomed in parliament's lower house. In part this may have reflected a conservative preference to maintain their traditional association with the House of Lords. More significantly, growing tensions between rulers and parliament aroused fears that the crown's legal representatives, once admitted to the Commons, would operate as agents of monarch, ministers, and the royal court, rather than independent advocates for the interests of their constituents and upholders of parliament's liberties and privileges. Hence election of the newly appointed Attorney General Francis Bacon for one of two seats recently attached to his alma mater Cambridge University was seriously questioned in the opening sessions of James I's 1614 parliament. The matter came to be resolved only by muddled compromise, which permitted Bacon to remain a member of that short-lived assembly, but determined that no future Attorney General might follow his example.[4] Despite the formal inability of any parliament to bind its successors, not until the appointment of the long-serving member for Oxford University, Sir Heneage Finch, a future Lord Chancellor, as Charles II's Attorney General in 1680 did another crown law officer take his place in the Commons.[5] Mutterings about Finch's successor Francis North, later Chief Justice of Common Pleas, who became Attorney General in 1673, on the grounds of "incapacity of sitting as a member of that House", were to no avail.[6] Yet none of the next four attorneys general between 1675 and 1689 were MPs.

---

[3] Baker, *Introduction* (2019), 175–6; Baker, *Serjeants* (1984), 531, *s.v.* Popham, John.

[4] Jansson, *Proceedings*, 30, 54, 55, 57, 58.

[5] Sainty, *Law Officers*, 46; Yale, "Finch, Heneage"; cf. Holdsworth, History, vi. 465.

[6] Ibid., n 7, quoting North, *Lives*, i. 113–14.

8    W. PREST

Even after the Dutch invasion of 1688 and James II's flight into exile ushered in the Glorious Revolution, it was not axiomatic that attorneys general should hold a seat in the lower house. Sir Edward Ward, whose two years in post from 1693 were concluded by promotion to the judicial bench as Chief Baron of the Exchequer, was never an MP. Nor was Sir Edward Northey during his first six-year term as Attorney General from 1701 to 1707, although he did sit for a Devonshire constituency after re-appointment to that office in 1710. But from now on the Attorney General was always an MP. If he did not already hold a parliamentary seat, he was either supplied with one from a pocket borough controlled by a friend of the ministry, or allocated Treasury funds with which to buy his own way into the unreformed House of Commons.

Why did this substantial change in policy and practice reverse the earlier parliamentary exclusion of attorneys-general? Before James II was replaced by his son-in-law William and daughter Mary in 1688–1689, parliaments had met infrequently, their summoning and dismissal entirely at the monarch's discretion. After November 1685 James II ruled without any parliament for four years, as had his elder brother Charles II from January 1681 until his death in February 1685. But there were parliamentary sessions every year from 1689 onwards, and these sessions extended significantly longer than ever before. So, parliament now became a predictably regular institution of government, not just an occasional political event. The novel frequency and duration of parliamentary sittings signified a resolution of the constitutional conflicts of the preceding century, a decisive shift of political advantage from monarch to parliament.

Yet even before 1688–1689, kings and their ministers had derived considerable benefit from enlisting the forensic skills and oratorical abilities of crown law officers in support of government men and measures—precisely the reason why leading members of James I's second parliament had sought to exclude future attorneys-general. But after the post-1688 shift in the constitutional centre of gravity, the active presence of attorneys and solicitors general no longer aroused the same level of mistrust and suspicion in the lower house, whose members soon enjoyed a greater sense of institutional self-confidence, much less fearful of ambitious monarchs than their predecessors had been. Nor were either ministers in place or politicians eager for power less appreciative of the assistance that crown law officers could provide, whether by way of expert response on legal issues raised in debate, or by clarifying the finer details of complex legislation. In 1756 William Pitt, angling to become prime minister, was plied with advice by fellow MPs urging the claims of Charles Pratt, the future Lord Camden, Chief Justice of Common Pleas, as prospective Attorney General. One wrote that "If you have the lead in the House of Commons, 'tis fit you should have at your elbow a lawyer of your own". Another claimed that with Pratt as Attorney General and another favoured candidate as solicitor general, "we shall out-lawyer" the opposition.[7]

Seventeen individual barristers became attorneys general, some for more than one term, under William III, Queen Mary, and Queen Anne (1689–1714), the last Stuart monarchs, and their early Hanoverian successors, George I and II (1714–1760). Only two were not promoted to the judicial bench after their term in office, and all but one of those promotions was to the upper tier of the judiciary, as chief justice of king's bench or common pleas, chief baron of the exchequer, and lord keeper or lord chancellor.[8] The exception goes to prove the rule. For Sir Robert Raymond's embarrassed inability to manage the final stage of the parliamentary bill of pains and penalties against his "old and intimate friend" Bishop Atterbury in 1724 led to his "abandon[ing] politics for the bench at the cost of becoming temporarily a mere puisne judge, an unprecedented step for an attorney general". However Raymond had only a year to wait before becoming one of three commissioners of the great seal on the resignation of Lord Chancellor Macclesfield, and two months later was promoted lord chief justice of king's bench.[9] Since most attorneys-general were clearly destined for the heights of their profession, it is scarcely surprising to find among this cohort a trio of titans, men who wielded major political influence as well as high judicial authority: John Lord Somers (1651–1716), Philip Yorke, first earl of Hardwicke (1690–1746), and William Murray, first earl of Mansfield (1705–1796).[10] In the two to three decades after 1688, when the rage of party ran very high, some attorney

[7] Pitt, *Correspondence,* i. 167, 179.

[8] Sainty, *Law Officers,* 47–8. Neither Sir Edward Northey nor Nicholas Lechmere, who succeeded him in 1718, secured a judgeship. Northey was removed from office shortly after expressing a view unfavourable to the king's claims over his son, the prince of Wales, and granted a pension of £1,500 p.a., equivalent to a puisne judge's salary: Handley, "Northey, Sir Edward". Beattie, *English Court,* 271; Foss, *Judges,* viii. 10. Lechmere, promoted by the Whig grandee Sunderland, seems to have been a victim of Walpole's return to power in April 1720, although he obtained a peerage the following year: Hanham, "Lechmere, Nicholas"; Sedgwick, "Lechmere, Nicholas".

[9] Cruickshanks, "Raymond, Sir Robert"; Lemmings, "Raymond, Robert".

[10] The standard biographies—by Sachse, Yorke, and Poser—are generally less rewarding than the briefer *ODNB* memoirs, by Handley, Peter D. G. Thomas, and Oldham respectively.

10    W. PREST

general's terms in office were very brief: a matter of weeks in the case of Sir Henry Pollexfen, who served William and Mary in that role from March 4 to May 6, 1689, and less than a year for Somers, who after appointment in May 1692 was made lord keeper in March 1693. Greater political calm and stability following the Hanoverian accession eventually made for more secure official tenure; thus, Philip Yorke became Attorney General in 1724 near the end of George I's reign, was re-appointed at George II's accession in 1727, and left the post only when promoted chief justices of king's bench in 1733. The longest-serving crown law officer during our period—and indeed down to the present day—was Sir Dudley Ryder, who remained in office from January 1737 until April 1754, a term of over 17 years. But length of service is not Ryder's sole claim to our attention in this context.

## DUDLEY RYDER AS ATTORNEY GENERAL

Born in 1691, the younger son of a well-to-do linen London draper and his wife, a barrister's daughter, Ryder was brought up a protestant non-conformist, attending a dissenting academy before going on to the universities of Edinburgh and Leyden (hence avoiding the religious tests which sought to restrict attendance at the two English universities to conformist Anglicans). But rather than following various relatives into the ministry, he was admitted in 1713 to the Middle Temple, and called to the bar six years later. We know little of his early legal career, although it may have been fostered by Peter King, another dissenting tradesman's son of an earlier generation and a former Leyden student, who became chief justice of common pleas and then lord chancellor in 1725, when Ryder migrated to Lincoln's Inn, where Chancery sat between law terms. King also possibly brought Ryder to the attention of Walpole's administration, which secured his election to parliament in 1733 for Tiverton, a government-controlled Cornish borough, shortly followed by appointment as solicitor general. He must have given overall satisfaction in that office, since he began his long service as Attorney General four years later.[11]

Although he ended his life and career as lord chief justice of king's bench, Ryder's standing as a lawyer and public figure do not place him on an equal footing with Somers, Hardwicke, and Mansfield. He has

---

[11] David Lemmings, "Ryder, Sir Dudley", *ODNB*. William Marshall, Ryder's maternal grandfather, was called to the bar in 1653: Baildon, *Black Books,* 426.

accordingly attracted little attention from biographers or historians.[12] Yet contemporaries held his legal skills in high regard. The aged Whig grandee John Hervey, first earl of Bristol, writing to his son about a potential law suit in 1748, emphasised that "I must recommend your taking the attorney general's opinion and advice in every step you make … [he] is justly and universally esteemed the oracle of our law".[13] Walpole himself recommended Ryder to his political successor Henry Pelham as "very able and very honest" while the prime minister's son thought Ryder "A man of singular goodness and integrity, of the highest reputation in his profession". After his sudden and unexpected death even King George II recorded his "very good opinion of Ryder (who had served me very long and very well)".[14] The king had indeed approved his chief justice's longheld wish to be elevated to the peerage, two years after his judicial promotion; but Ryder died the night before the process was complete, and it took a further 20 years for the honour to be extended to his only son.

Besides being a skilful lawyer and on occasion a powerful orator, Ryder was a prolific writer, even if very little of what he wrote appeared in print during his lifetime. Indeed, his first book only came out on the eve of World War II, nearly two centuries after his death, in the form of selections from a student diary he had kept between June 1715 and December 1716, while preparing for call to the bar. Since then some odd fragments of his legal and personal writings have also appeared in print, but the great bulk of his writing remain unpublished to this day. The reason is simple: Ryder's surviving case notes, copies of correspondence, journals, and memoranda are written in shorthand.

According to William Matthews, who transcribed and edited the earliest surviving diary, this 918-page manuscript uses a distinctive shorthand system, derived from one developed in the mid-seventeenth century by Jeremiah Rich, and similar to those favoured by other eighteenth-century diarists, including Lord Chancellor King. An early modern English invention, shorthand was used by pious church- and chapel-goers to record the text of sermons, and by legal practitioners and law students to capture the details of oral in-court proceedings. Besides improving the speed and accuracy with which the spoken word could be recorded, shorthand

---

[12] Thus one passing reference demotes Ryder to solicitor general in 1754: Harris, *Politics and the Nation*, 212.

[13] Hervey, *Letter Books*, iii. 351–2.

[14] Quoted Sedgwick, "Ryder, Dudley".

offered a concise method for capturing transient actions, emotions, and thoughts, together with a degree of privacy, excluding access by anyone other than the writer or someone familiar with the same shorthand system.[15]

But besides nosy contemporaries, shorthand can also deter later historians, who even if they possess the requisite key, might still hesitate before the effort required to decipher multiple shorthand manuscripts. Ryder's surviving shorthand archive constitutes an exceptionally large and revelatory historical source, containing the estimated equivalent of some four million words.[16] Thanks however to Arthur T. Vanderbilt (1888–1957), an American legal academic who ended his career as chief justice of New Jersey, a small part of this vast textual horde is now available to historians. Vanderbilt planned a biography of William Murray, the later Lord Mansfield, who before replacing Ryder as lord chief justice of king's bench had served alongside him as solicitor general. Alerted to the existence of Ryder's shorthand manuscripts by Matthews's edition of the student diary, Vanderbilt was fortunate enough to locate someone on the spot who could both read and transcribe material of potential interest for his proposed book. So far, these transcripts have been used mainly by North American scholars, although David Lemmings also consulted them for his monograph on eighteenth-century barristers and English legal culture, as well as Ryder's brief life for the *Oxford Dictionary of Biography*.[17]

The Ryder papers provide a unique first-person perspective on the working life of a long-serving crown law officer; nothing comparable seems to exist for any of his English predecessors or successors. Intended neither for publication nor perusal by anyone except himself (and possibly his son), they constitute a running score sheet of his thoughts and actions, or at least those he thought worth committing to paper. Although like

[15] Matthews, *Diary*, vii–viii. 6. Henderson, "*Swifte and Secrete*," 1–13.

[16] Perrin, "Shorthand Diaries," n. xix. The Harrowby Mss Trust, Sandon Hall, Stafford, ST18 0BZ, England, holds the original Ryder archive. Copies of typewritten transcripts from some of the shorthand originals are at Sandon Hall and in the libraries of the University of Chicago and Wesleyan University. I am indebted to Amanda Nelson, Wesleyan University archivist, David Lemmings, and James Oldham for facilitating access to this material, as also to Michael Bosson, the Sandon Hall archivist, for much helpful information about the Perrin transcripts.

[17] Hay, "Property, Authority," 28; Hay, "Death Penalty," 2, 41 n. 11; Langbein, "Shaping," 1–136; Oldham, "Ryder and Murray," 157–73; Lemmings, *Professors*; Lemmings, "Ryder, Sir Dudley".

# 2 POLITICS AND PROFESSION: SIR DUDLEY RYDER AND THE OFFICE...

others from Dissenting families he chose to conform outwardly to the established church to be called to the bar, Ryder's Nonconformist upbringing made him a prime candidate for keeping a personal journal or diary as a medium of self-examination and self-fashioning, a practice long advocated by humanist educators and zealous protestants. At the start of his first surviving diary, he noted his plan to follow the example of his friend Robert Whatley of the Inner Temple (a barrister later turned clergyman),

> who told me the other day of a method he had taken for some time of keeping a diary. And I now intend to begin the same method. ... I intend particularly to observe my own temper and state of mind as to my fitness and disposition for study, or the easiness or satisfaction it finds within itself and the particular cause of that or of the contrary uneasiness that often disturbs my mind. ... I intend also to observe my own acts as to their goodness or badness. ... I shall be able then to review any parts of my life, have the pleasure of it if it be well spent, if otherwise know how to mend it.[18]

The conscientious desire for self-improvement manifest in this prologue seems to have remained with the diarist all his life. At the age of 57, after some ten years as Attorney General, an entry for December 28, 1746, begins as follows:

> My defects are want of memory and resolution, the latter being in great measure the effect of the former. The former has many bad effects, and it is surprising that I have been able to rise so high in a profession that is generally supposed to require the contrary excellency. But in truth the defect don't appear so much in my profession as it does in conversation; the reason is because I come prepared to the former, but can seldom be in the latter. I would endeavour to rectify it as to the latter, and will [get] a plan that by keeping in mind may supply it.[19]

He goes on to list under numbered headings "the three ends of conversation", and how these may be obtained, by "1. acquiring the materials of conversation" and "2. The manner of using these materials". Such detailed logical analysis of everyday matters or problems is typical of Ryder's approach to all aspects of his life, at least as manifested in the

---

[18] Matthews, *Diary*, 29.

[19] "Diary of Sir Dudley Ryder, 1746–56," 10. A later entry (31, 23 September 1748) suggests that Ryder may have employed the "theatre of memory" mnemonic technique discussed by Yates, *Art of Memory*, chs 6–7.

14  W. PREST

transcriptions. His memoranda are often as much concerned with personal or family matters, including his large and growing accumulation of landed property and his state of health, as with the formal business of his office.[20]

## RYDER'S WORK AS ATTORNEY GENERAL

The first point to make about Ryder's attorney generalship is that it was not a full-time position, despite involving a multitude of tasks undertaken on behalf of George II and the ministry of the day. For Ryder, like earlier and later attorneys-general in England and indeed Australia until at least the late nineteenth century, was entirely free to accept briefs from private clients. A lucrative private practice was one reason why after Ryder's death the office of Attorney General was estimated to be worth no less than £7000 per annum, or well over £1m in today's money values, placing its holder among the top 200 families in terms of income in England and Wales at the end of George II's reign.[21]

That Ryder was accustomed to keep many balls in the air at any one time is demonstrated by an entry dated September 29, 1746, written at his home in Tooting, Surrey, south of London. He first notes having that day despatched "several cases" to London by post, and received four "G[uineas] relating to proceedings in Scotland", while reminding himself to acquire a new Testament in Greek with a Latin-Greek dictionary, and to ask "about the estate of the Duke of Chand[os]". The entry continues:

> To think whenever I send or go to London what I have to be done there under the following heads, vizt.: what relating to clothes; books to send or to be sent; relating to Nat. [Ryder's only son], his books, his clothes, playthings; to physic; relating to the Chancellor [Hardwicke], the Pelhams [Prime Minister Henry and his brother Thomas, duke of Newcastle], Sharp [possibly William Sharp, clerk of the privy council], others, and business in the North [aftermath of the '45 Jacobite rising]; to Solicitor General [William Murray]; to the rebels [Jacobite prisoners from the '45]; to provisions, wine, fish; to cases or briefs; to my houses in Hackney; to the horses,

---

[20] It is not clear how closely the arrangement and titles of the transcripts follow the original shorthand manuscripts at Sandon Hall, the former having been "separated into long documents and grouped into categories before being bound": email from Michael Bosson, September 19, 2019.

[21] Melikan, "Mr Attorney General," 44; Lindert and Williamson, "England's Social Tables," 396–8.

their hay, corn, saddles, bridles, harness; to the coach or chariot; to my will; to purchase of estate Littleshall; Hab[eas] Corp[us] Act [which remained suspended following the '45].

Ryder's official and public business was notably diverse. In 1746–1747 he was particularly concerned with the legal aftermath of the recent Jacobite rebellion and Prince Charles Stuart's abortive invasion, including decisions as to whether sufficient evidence existed to warrant prosecution of Jacobite prisoners, arrangements for trials, warrants for the execution of those condemned as traitors, management of their forfeited estates, and the drafting of legislation intended to disarm and "pacify" Scotland's highlands, including the abolition of heritable jurisdictions. These matters were complicated by differences between Scots and English law on the composition of juries, the descent of lands, and powers to arrest suspected rebels.[22] Another tricky question referred to Ryder from his Scottish equivalent, the Lord Advocate, concerned Lord Pitsligo, attainted under the name of Alexander Lord Pitsligo for raising a Jacobite regiment in 1745 (as he had also done in 1715), although his correct title was Alexander Lord Forbes of Pitsligo. Ryder maintained at some length that this misnomer did not void the attainder and consequent forfeiture of the Pitsligo estates, a position eventually upheld by the House of Lords, despite a contrary finding by Scotland's Court of Session in 1749.[23]

Britain's burgeoning empire and Continental military involvements also contributed to the variety of Ryder's official workload. His opinion was sought on colonial disputes, for example a "Reference from the Commissioners of Trade to self and Solicitor General of a letter from Mr Wentworth, governor of New Hampshire" who was in conflict with his representative assembly, also on complaints from the neutral Danes and Dutch over ships searched by the royal navy and privateers for enemy (French or Spanish) goods, and from the Levant Company about alleged damage to their trade caused by English privateering in the eastern Mediterranean.[24] Another major issue growing out of the war of the Austrian Succession was the controversial addition of all 12 common law judges to the "Lords Commissioners of Prize Appeals", in order to expedite the hearing of cases appealed from admiralty court judgments. Ryder

---

[22] "Legal and Political Diary of Sir Douglas Ryder, 1746–49," 1–32 *passim*.

[23] "Legal and Political Diary," 42–44; Pittock, "Forbes, Alexander".

[24] "Legal and Political Diary," 9, 19–20, 24–5, 32–3, 47–8, 49–51, 52, 55–6, 71.

16  W. PREST

and Murray were tasked by Hardwicke with overcoming opposition from at least half the judiciary to this administrative expedient, and eventually to draft legislation "to declare this commission good".[25] Other miscellaneous domestic matters on which he advised included quarantine measures against the spread of cattle disease, the "audacious behaviour" of smugglers in Sussex, miscellaneous riots and escapes of prisoners, and how the death of an archbishop might affect the Church of England's convocation.[26]

Ryder's self-recorded behaviour and sentiments suggest that he regarded his official role as entirely subject to the aspirations and policies of his political masters, the great men and ministers of the crown with whom he was in frequent contact: Prime Minister Robert Walpole, Walpole's successor Henry Pelham, Henry's brother the duke of Newcastle, and Lord Chancellor Hardwicke.[27] Ryder recounts several wide-ranging discussions with Walpole and Pelham traversing both foreign and domestic politics in general, and legal appointments in particular. On December 21, 1748, he noted receipt of Pelham's letter, enclosing another from Scotland's lord advocate, about the crown's rights over a rebel's landowner's estate. This followed a claim lodged before the Edinburgh Court of Session under a statute of the previous reign (1 Geo. I, st. 2, c. 20), whereby the forfeited lands of attainted Scottish subjects passed to the lairds from whom they held those lands, rather than to the crown. The lord advocate wanted to know whether to lodge an appeal against the court's interim judgment, and "Mr P desires me to give my opinion on this whole case not as Attorney General but as a friend and servant of the Crown". What exactly did Pelham mean or Ryder understand by this distinction?

Ryder tells us (or himself) that in response he "accordingly called on" the prime minister, to tell him that the legislation in question reached beyond the Jacobite rising of 1715 which called it into being, and thus "the present determination of the court of sessions [sic] was right as to that question, though I said I knew the Chancellor seemed to think formerly otherwise". While Hardwicke LC and Ryder AG were close

---

[25] Oldham, "Ryder and Murray," 161–4.

[26] "Legal and Political Diary," 3, 6, 9, 10, 16, 19, 22, 28, 36, 49, 52, 68, 71, 74.

[27] "The Later Diaries of Sir Dudley Ryder, Selected Transcriptions," 41, 44–5; "Diary of Sir Dudley Ryder," Part 4A, 2–3 (February 27, 1754), 9–10 (March 22, 1754), 12–13 (March 15, 1754).

contemporaries in age, the lord chancellor undoubtedly outranked the Attorney General; so, Pelham may well have expected that Ryder would wish to avoid open dissent from Hardwicke's expressed opinion. Otherwise, it is hard to know what message Pelham sought to convey, unless he was simply insisting that the importance of the issue under consideration demanded that the Scottish court's ruling be overturned, regardless of any legal niceties. Yet in the remainder of his answer Ryder first showed himself to be quite well aware of pragmatic considerations, maintaining that "the advantage to the Crown by the continuance of some other clauses in the Act might be probably equal to the inconvenience by the continuing this clause". Then his final point neatly resolved the legal problem, for "there is an objection to the judgment of the lords of session which none of the parties in Scotland seemed to be aware of". This followed from the fact that the treason for which the recent Jacobite rebels had been attainted was levying war against Crown. But that was "not the treason mentioned in that Act", which comprised only corresponding with, remitting money to, or otherwise "adhering" to the Pretender. Hence "the Act seems not applicable to the present case".[28] Subsequent entries indicate that Ryder, Chancellor Hardwicke, and Solicitor General Murray agreed on an immediate appeal, the latter two endorsing Ryder's final point—which however proved superfluous, as the Scottish court eventually rejected the claim on other grounds.[29]

A more prominent case concerned the cat-and-mouse prosecution in 1748–1749 of Dr John Purnell, Vice-Chancellor of Oxford University, for alleged leniency towards undergraduate Jacobitism. James Oldham's exposition of this episode makes clear Ryder's somewhat equivocal role. For despite consistently urging Hardwicke and Newcastle not to proceed due to the weakness and likely loss of their case, over a 14-month period he twice complied with ministerial directives to file an *ex officio* information against Purnell in King's Bench, subsequently entering a *nolle prosequi*, so that "after a very heavy Expense with which an innocent man has been saddled, the Prosecution is at last dropped", to quote the young William Blackstone, an unsympathetic contemporary observer.[30]

---

[28] "Legal and Political Diary," 56–7.
[29] Ibid., 57–8.
[30] Oldham, "Ryder and Murray," 164–73; Blackstone, "*Letters*," 8.

## Conclusion

The most obvious difference between the office of Attorney General in mid-eighteenth-century England and its modern equivalents is one of scale: whereas Dudley Ryder seems essentially to have operated as a sole practitioner, assisted by a few of his own clerks, attorneys general in both England and Australia are today ministerial heads of large government departments, holding formal responsibility to parliament for the administration of various state agencies with legal or quasi-legal functions, staffed by civil (England) or public (Australia) servants. No doubt the growth of the modern state with its associated bureaucratic apparatus made it inevitable that attorneys general would become large-scale administrators, overseeing many government agencies and departments. In Australia at both Commonwealth and state level they are now always members of parliament, ministers of the crown, and usually if not invariably members of cabinet. Much the same applies in England and Wales, except that there by long-standing convention (briefly interrupted in the early twentieth century) attorneys-general are not formally part of the executive and do not sit in cabinet, the better to emphasise the segregation of their independent legal functions from party-political influence.[31] The office tends to have a more overtly political profile and a wider range of administrative responsibilities in Australia than England. This may be partly because the former English office of lord chancellor with its wide-ranging legal and ministerial functions and powers was never replicated in the Australian colonies. Moreover, even before the coming of responsible government, attorneys-general like J. H. Plunkett in New South Wales were serving as appointed members of the governor's executive council, thus playing a vital role in the formulation of policy, as well as tendering advice on various legal matters (including judicial and other professional promotions) and representing the Crown in litigation. Once having gained this influential position, successive attorneys-general tended to accumulate additional ministerial portfolios, not necessarily of a particularly legal nature. Thus, in the 1930s R. G. Menzies served simultaneously as Attorney General of Victoria and Minister of Railways, while in the 1970s Garfield Barwick was both Commonwealth Attorney General and Minister for External Affairs. The distinctive Australian development of the office of solicitor general as a statutory non-parliamentary position (whereas in England both Attorney

---

[31] Edwards, *Law Officers*, chs. 9–11.

General and solicitor general continue to sit in parliament and share ministerial responsibilities, although the former still outranks the latter) may also have encouraged both commonwealth and state attorneys-general to adopt a more partisan and overtly political role than their English counterparts. [32]

Yet the nature and extent of an Attorney General's autonomy with respect to his or (more recently, her) legal role, especially the launching of criminal prosecutions, has long been a matter of controversy and tension. In eighteenth-century England, Dr Melikan maintains, law and politics proved an "uneasy combination" for those holding the office of Attorney General. This was partly because lawyers tended to treat the post as merely a convenient rung on the steep ladder leading to the highest ranks of the judiciary, while many non-lawyer MPs resisted any suggestion that they were not as well qualified as professional lawyers to determine policy matters, including those with significant legal content or ramifications.

In post-Federation Australia what Dr Hanlon has characterised as the "orthodox view" maintains that attorneys general should always act as independent agents, upholding fundamental legal principles and the rule of law before any party or political considerations. But a contrary body of opinion holds that attorneys-general in no way differ from other incumbents of ministerial office, being bound by the same principle of collective responsibility for government actions and policy. So, if conflict should occur between their legal duties and the political best interests of the government in which they serve, they must either persuade their ministerial colleagues to follow the appropriate legal path, or simply resign.[33]

The origins of the "orthodox view" are not clear. It has been claimed to derive from an eighteenth-century distinction between two different concepts of the monarch whom the Attorney General served: the crown, or the monarch's immortal "body-politic" on the one hand, and the natural body of the reigning king or queen on the other.[34] But if eighteenth-century attorneys general did see themselves as bound to uphold the law of the realm whatever the political cost to those currently administering the kingdom on the crown's behalf, they seem not to have documented

---

[32] Appleby, *Solicitor General*, chs. 2–3.

[33] Melikan, "Mr Attorney General," *passim*. Hanlon, thesis, 10–11; Edwards, *The Attorney General*, chs 3, 11–12; in addition to examples cited there, see Hancock, *Tom Hughes*, chs. 10–11, for another recent Federal Attorney General who exemplified the "orthodox view". See also La Forgia, "Attorney General".

[34] Lurie, "Attorney-General," 125–33.

that conviction. Dudley Ryder's attempts to persuade his political masters for or against particular courses of legal action appear to have been largely motivated by a pragmatic wish to avoid ineffective or otherwise undesirable outcomes, whether prosecutions based on insufficient evidence to secure conviction, or legal instruments which might not ensure the achievement of a desired goal.[35] The hierarchical nature of eighteenth-century English politics and society was a further reason for Ryder's essentially subordinate role. He appears to have been regarded by his aristocratic masters—who were also very much his social superiors—as a high-grade functionary whose professional advice should be taken seriously, but not accorded conclusive status (reminiscent of the famous adage ascribed to Winston Churchill although evidently coined by the Irish writer George William Russell or *AE*, that experts should be "on tap, not on top").[36] Apart from his relatively modest family origins, even Ryder's personal deportment and physique may have encouraged this attitude. Thus, a doggerel verse portrait from 1745 depicts him patronisingly characterised by Hardwicke LC (in the persona of "Lord Paramount"):

> Then Lord *Paramount*, singling little Sir Dud,
> Said, tho' for his Post he was proper and good,
> Yet if he rose higher he'd sink in the Scene,
> And his Figure and Aspect are rather too mean.[37]

Ryder's workmanlike approach, together with his self-confessed "fears of displeasing or offending [the] Chancellor or other great men", and thereby risking the lucrative post which had enabled him to "raise an estate", underpinned his remarkably extended term as crown law officer.[38] So notwithstanding his reputation in elite Whig circles as an expert legal craftsman, it is scarcely surprising that contemporaries of a different political persuasion viewed his career as wholly opportunistic and unprincipled. A mock-epitaph published after Ryder's death portrays a man

> Whose love of Money
> Was only exceeded
> By his Lust of Punishment:
> Form'd by Nature for all the Chicanery

---

[35] Lurie, 142–5.

[36] https://quoteinvestigator.com/2019/01/26/expert/ (accessed July 5, 2021).

[37] M. Morgan, *The Processionade* (1745), 7.

[38] "Diary of Sir Dudley Ryder, 1746–56," 75, 94.

> Of the Law,
> By unwearied application
> To his own Interest,
> By prostituting his Conscience,
> And
> A true time-serving Spirit ....
> From the basest Original,
> He acquired the immense Sum
> Of Three Hundred Thousand Pounds
> And wriggled himself into the Post
> Of Att------ G------.[39]

From there, it was claimed, Ryder's "slavish Obedience to M[inisteria]l Mandates" earned him promotion to lord chief justice. Despite the blatant personal/political animus and rhetorical exaggeration of this indictment, Ryder's own shorthand writings do reveal a distinct preoccupation with the acquisition of land, money, and social status. At the same time, they also display a psychologically vulnerable human being, afflicted with hypochondria, "despondency and uneasiness", seeking to "disperse the gloom which speeds so often over me in the night".[40] Perhaps such distress was one way in which tensions between political and professional imperatives might affect a particularly conscientious and driven Attorney General. But in the absence of evidence—which of course may exist, but has yet to be unearthed—that his English and Australian counterparts and successors suffered from similar problems, Ryder's case can hardly be solely explained in terms of occupational risk.

## BIBLIOGRAPHY

### MANUSCRIPT SOURCES

1. Perrin transcripts, originally from Sandon Hall, Staffordshire, manuscript shorthand notebooks of Sir Dudley Ryder: Box 317, Arthur T. Vanderbilt papers, Special Collections & Archives, Wesleyan University, Connecticut.
2. 'Diary of Sir Dudley Ryder, 1746–56'
3. 'Legal and Political Diary of Sir Douglas Ryder, 1746–49'
4. 'The Later Diaries of Sir Dudley Ryder, Selected Transcriptions' (c. 1726–1754)

---

[39] Anon., *Epitaph.*
[40] "Diary of Sir Dudley Ryder, 1746–56," 75, 76.

## Articles, Books and Reports

1. [Anon.], *Epitaph for Sir D----y R----r, Kn---t.* [broadsheet] London?: 1756.
2. Appleby, Gabrielle, *The Role of the Solicitor-General: Negotiating Law, Politics and the Public Interest.* Oxford: Hart, 2016
3. Baildon, William P. ed. *The Records of the Honourable Society of Lincoln's Inn. The Black Books Vol. III.* London: Lincoln's Inn, 1899.
4. Baker, John Hamilton. *An Introduction to English Legal History*, 5th edn. Oxford: Oxford University Press, 2019.
5. ———. *The Order of Serjeants at Law.* London: Selden Society, 1984.
6. Beattie, John M. *The English Court in the Reign of George I.* Cambridge: Cambridge University Press, 1967.
7. Blackstone, William. *The Letters of Sir William Blackstone, 1644–1780.* W. Prest ed. London: Selden Society, 2006.
8. Cruickshanks, Eveline. 'Raymond, Sir Robert (1673–1733)'. In https://www.historyofparliamentonline.org/volume/1715-1754/member/raymond-sir-robert-1673-1733.
9. Edwards, John Ll. J. *The Law Officers of the Crown.* London: Sweet and Maxwell, 1964.
10. ———. *The Attorney General, Politics and the Public Interest.* London: Sweet and Maxwell, 1984.
11. Foss, Edward. *The Judges of England*, 9 vols. London: Longman, 1848–64.
12. Hancock, Ian. *Tom Hughes QC.* Sydney: Federation Press, 2016.
13. Hanham, A. A. 'Lechmere, Nicholas, Baron Lechmere (1675–1727)'. *ODNB,* 2004. https://doi.org/10.193/ref:odnb/16262.
14. Handley, Stuart. 'Northey, Sir Edward (1652–1723)'. ODNB, 2004. https://doi.org/10.1093/ref:odnb/20330.
15. Hanlon, Fiona. 'An Analysis of the Office of Attorney-General in Australia'. Unpublished PhD thesis, University of Melbourne, 2008.
16. Harris, Bob. *Politics and the Nation: Britain in the Mid-Eighteenth Century.* Oxford: Oxford University Press, 2002.
17. Hay, Douglas. 'Property, Authority and the Criminal Law'. In *Albion's Fatal Tree: Crime and Society in Eighteenth-Century England.* New York: Pantheon Books, 1975.
18. ———. 'Writing about the Death Penalty'. *Legal History* 10 (2006): 35–52.
19. Henderson, Frances. '"Swifte and Secrete Writing" in Seventeenth-Century England and Samuel Shelton's *Brachygraphy*'. *Electronic British Library Journal* (2008): article 5.
20. Hervey, John. *Letter Books of John Hervey, First Earl of Bristol*, 3 vols, ed. S. H. A. Hervey. Wells: Ernest Jackson, 1894.

21. Holdsworth, William Searle. *A History of English Law* 16 vols. 2nd edn. London: Methuen, 1932–66.
22. Jansson, Maijja ed. *Proceedings in Parliament 1614 (House of Commons)*. Philadelphia: American Philosophical Society, 1988.
23. La Forgia, Rebecca. 'Attorney General, Chief Law Officer of the Crown: But where is the law?' *Alternative Law Journal*, 28 (2003): 163–8.
24. Langbein, John H. 'Shaping the Eighteenth-Century Criminal Trial: A View from the Ryder Sources'. *University of Chicago Law Review*, 50 (1983): 1–136.
25. Lemmings, David. *Professors of the Law*. Oxford: Oxford University Press, 2000.
26. ———. 'Raymond, Robert, first Baron Raymond (1673–1733)'. *ODNB*, 2006. https://doi.org/10.1093/ref:odnb/23207.
27. ———. 'Ryder, Sir Dudley (1691–1756)'. *ODNB*, 2009. https://doi.org/10.1093/ref:odnb/24394.
28. Lindert, Peter H. and Williamson, Jeffrey. 'Revising England's Social Tables 1688–1812', *Explorations in Economic History* 19 (1982): 385–408.
29. Lurie, Guy. 'The Attorney-General in Eighteenth-Century England'. 18 *The Journal Jurisprudence* (2013): 125–46.
30. Matthews, William. *The Diary of Dudley Ryder 1715–1716*. London: Methuen, 1939.
31. Melikan, R. A. 'Mr Attorney General and the Politicians'. *Historical Journal* 40 (1997): 41–69.
32. [Morgan, Macnamara] *The Processionade: In Panegryi-Satiri-Serio-Comi-Baladical Versicles. By Porcupinus Pelagius*. London: M. Cooper, 1745
33. North, Roger. *The Lives of the Right Hon. Francis North...Dudley North and...John North*. 3 vols. Edited by Augustus Jessop. London: Bell, 1890.
34. Oldham, James. 'The Work of Ryder and Murray as Law Officers of the Crown'. In *Legal Record and Historical Reality*, 157–73. Edited by Thomas G. Watkin. London: Hambledon Press, 1989.
35. Perrin, Keith L. 'Sir Dudley Ryder's Shorthand Diaries'. https://www.historyofparliamentonline.org/volume/1715-1754/survey/vi-Notes
36. Pitt, William. *Correspondence of William Pitt, Earl of Chatham*, 4 vols. Edited by William Stanhope Taylor and John Henry Pringle. London: John Murray, 1838–40.
37. Pittock, Murray G. H. 'Forbes, Alexander, fourth Lord Forbes of Pitsligo (1678–1762)'. *ODNB*. 2006. https://doi.org/10.1093/ref:odnb/9813.
38. Poser, Norman S. *Lord Mansfield: Justice in the Age of Reason*. Montreal: McGill-Queen's University Press, 2013.
39. Sachse, William L. *Lord Somers: a Political Portrait*. Manchester: Manchester University Press, 1975.
40. Sainty, John. *A List of English Law Officers, King's Counsel and Holders of Patents of Precedence*. London: Selden Society, 1987.

41. Sedgwick, Romney R. 'Lechmere, Nicholas (1675–1727)'. In https://www.historyofparliamentonline.org/volume/1715-1754/member/lechmere-nicholas-1675-1725.
42. Sedgwick, Romney R. 'Ryder, Dudley (1691–1756'. In https://www.historyofparliamentonline.org/volume/1715-1754/member/ryder-dudley-1691-1756.
43. Yale, David E. C. 'Finch, Heneage, first earl of Nottingham (1621–1682)', ODNB, 2004. https://doi.org/10.1093/ref.odnb/9433
44. Yates, Frances, *The Art of Memory*. London: Routledge, 1999.
45. Yorke, Philip C. *The Life and Correspondence of Philip Yorke, Earl of Hardwicke and Lord High Chancellor of Great Britain*, 3 vols. Cambridge: Cambridge University Press, 1913.

CHAPTER 3

# Lord Atkin's Dissent in *Liversidge v Anderson:* Indecorously Orthodox?

*Karen Schultz*

## PROLOGUE

Lord Atkin's dissent in *Liversidge v Anderson* (1942)[1] has had a powerful afterlife: its arresting delivery was the prologue to its continuing impact. It remains in the Anglo-Australian legal imaginary as a turning point that heralds the common law's reframing of aspects of the exercise of executive discretion. Lord Atkin's dissent has been embraced in the legal and public imagination as a rejection of arbitrary detention and rule by decree—it recognises executive discretion's consequences for individual liberty. Equally, Lord Atkin's dissent has been a conversation point for the question of decorum in common law judicial writing as its prose continues to be read as including a dose of indecorum. The question of its indecorous orthodoxy remains a live issue—it is this chapter's ultimate focus.

---

[1] *Liversidge v Anderson* [1942] AC 206, 225ff (Atkin LJ).

---

K. Schultz (✉)
Griffith University, Brisbane, QLD, Australia
e-mail: k.schultz@griffith.edu.au

© The Author(s), under exclusive license to Springer Nature          25
Switzerland AG 2022
S. McKibbin et al. (eds.), *The Impact of Law's History*, Palgrave
Modern Legal History,
https://doi.org/10.1007/978-3-030-90068-7_3

26    K. SCHULTZ

In the modern day, *Liversidge v Anderson* is infamous for its majority decision, but celebrated for the substantive aspects of Lord Atkin's dissent. Four of its Law Lords, in construing the notorious Regulation 18B, were aware of the potential for judicial power to scrutinise executive detention's "drastic invasion of the liberty of the subject",[2] but neglected to exercise this judicial power. Instead, they considered that Regulation 18B's recitation of the executive's "reasonable cause to believe" in a threat to "public safety" and "defence of the realm" rendered the exercise of its discretion to detain as effectively unchallengeable. By contrast, the fifth Law Lord, Lord Atkin, embraced the principle of the judicial scrutiny of the exercise of this discretion. Ultimately, his dissent has been favoured as the orthodox substantive approach in modern common law. But questions remain as to its formal orthodoxy—the decorum of its style and delivery.

Anglo-Australian common law dissent is enabled by decorum—the decorum of consensus but the propriety of recognising the value of voicing opposing judicial views in a final appellate case. A substantively contentious dissent, if it ultimately becomes orthodox, may illustrate "what's past is prologue", but a formally contentious dissent may remain notorious. This chapter explores the impact and decorum of Lord Atkin's celebrated dissent in *Liversidge v Anderson*, the infamous, wartime public law case. First, examples of the staging of Lord Atkin's dissent are offered to highlight its wartime context and embedding in the Anglo-Australian imagination. Second, the substantive orthodoxy of Lord Atkin's reasoning is considered—its adoption in modern-day precedent illustrates how the common law's past is prologue. Third, formal aspects of Lord Atkin's dissent are sketched—its references to executive-minded judges, English legal history, and Humpty Dumpty's meaning have been variously perceived as indecorous. Finally, in weighing the impact of Lord Atkin's dissent and the question of its indecorous orthodoxy, this chapter endorses decorum's unquestionable value but offers, subject to caveats, that suppressing diverse judicial voices would itself be indecorous in subverting the critical functions of common law dissent and the rule of law.

---

[2] *Liversidge v Anderson*, 251 (MacMillan LJ).

## Staging

*Liversidge v Anderson's* contemporary wartime staging was located in two agonistic landscapes—World War II Britain pockmarked by the Blitz, and the Appellate Committee's split decision that oscillated between executive discretion's objective and subjective tests. Recent Anglo-Australian "stagings" of Lord Atkin's dissent include an actual theatrical representation and a Supreme Court Library of Queensland Exhibition. This lime-lighting of Lord Atkin's dissent illustrates the currency of law's (English) history, and the relevance of this dissent's continued reference and use.

*Liversidge v Anderson's* contemporary wartime staging foregrounds the context of war's force and executive secrecy, and World War II Britain's dire restrictions on individual liberty. During the Blitz from September 1940 to May 1941, the British public and armed forces endured catastrophic destruction, relentless damage to property, and agonising loss of life from the Luftwaffe's ceaseless aerial bombing campaign of civilian targets. The Blitz's lightning raids rained projectiles of death, targeting London and industrial cities, and contributing to the hothouse climate of suspicion and "high anxiety" of "the risk of German collaborators in the United Kingdom".[3] Judges took judicial notice of the "import of words like Fifth Columnists and Quislings".[4] In this climate, Regulation 18B's enactment conferred extraordinary executive power and expressed a statutory suspicion. For, at this "low point" in wartime,[5] there was a daily expectation of imminent German invasion: "Hitler's armies had conquered the nation states of Europe from the Spanish border to central Russia"; and the British army's destruction in the fall of France heralded "the gravest national crisis in the life of anyone alive".[6]

Coincidentally, the national emergency context directly affected *Liversidge v Anderson's* hearing and actual delivery by the Appellate Committee, the Lords of Appeal in Ordinary.[7] In wartime London, emotions were running high; *Liversidge v Anderson* concerned issues that attracted a public audience, particularly the issue of "legitimis[ing] the

---

[3] Tom Bingham, "The Case of *Liversidge v Anderson*: The Rule of Law Amid the Clash of Arms," *The International Lawyer* 43 (2009): 34.

[4] *Liversidge v Anderson*, 265 (Wright LJ).

[5] Geoffrey Lewis, *Lord Atkin* (Oxford: Hart Publishing, 1999), 132 ("low point"); Bingham, "*Liversidge v Anderson*," 35 ("very low point").

[6] Bingham, "*Liversidge v Anderson*," 34.

[7] Bingham, "*Liversidge v Anderson*," 34.

detention of British subjects, without trial".[8] Moreover, in the Blitz's aftermath, on Monday 3 November 1941, the Law Lords delivered their judgments not in their usual House of Lords Chamber, but in the King's Robing Room at Westminster. This re-staging was a wartime accommodation—the House of Lords Chamber was now occupied by the members of the House of Commons following the destruction of the Commons Chamber in the Blitz.[9] The Law Lords' oral delivery of their judgments highlights the issue of audience—the publicity and media comment attending Lord Atkin's dissent was notable.[10] One of Lord Atkin's daughters, Elizabeth, who had accompanied her father to the oral delivery, reported that when Lord Atkin began reading his judgment, there was a stirring: counsel who appeared "asleep or dead" suddenly enlivened; Valentine Holmes, counsel for the Crown, "beg[a]n to smile".[11] Moreover, *Liversidge v Anderson* received national newspaper attention on Tuesday 4 November 1941, with the headlines beginning late Monday. Lord Atkin's daughter Elizabeth, returning home via the Underground, reported the large headline—"Judge likens court to Star Chamber".[12] But it was Lord Maugham's sensational letter to *The Times* criticising Lord Atkin's dissent, and then his speech to the House of Lords, that ratcheted up this dissent's immediate impact and attracted supportive media attention.[13]

Innovatively, the recent staging and public representations of Lord Atkin's dissent attest to its continuing impact in the legal and cultural imagination, and continue to enliven the significance of law's past for the present. In 2015, Lord Atkin's dissent inspired the staging of a one-act play, *Regulation 18B—No Free Man*, acclaimed in England and Wales.[14] Scott Wright, its playwright, focused not only on fictionally representing Lord Atkin's writing of his dissent, but on the dramatic potential of the Court's personal and intellectual conflict—that is, the case's impact on Lord Atkin's friendship with Lord Wright, both sitting in *Liversidge v*

---

[8] AW Brian Simpson, "Rhetoric, Reality, and Regulation 18B," *Denning Law Journal* 3 (1988): 124.

[9] Bingham, "*Liversidge v Anderson*," 35.

[10] Bingham, "*Liversidge v Anderson*," 37.

[11] Lewis, *Lord Atkin*, 143.

[12] Lewis, *Lord Atkin*, 143.

[13] Lewis, *Lord Atkin*, 144–47.

[14] Scott Wright, *Regulation 18B—No Free Man* (2015) (http://www.regulation18b.com/). Note the publicity: https://www.graysinn.org.uk/calendar/regulation-18b-no-free-man; http://www.regulation18b.com/

*Anderson*. The play's publicity promoted the case's historic drama, contemporary significance, and continued relevance for long-held common law principles. Effectively, Lord Atkin's dissent was constructed as a metaphor for courageous struggle against the government's clampdown on individual liberty, and against the threat of arbitrary detention. Moreover, the timing of the play's premiere in 2015 highlighted the resonance of Lord Atkin's dissent with cultural understandings of Magna Carta. For 2015 marked the 800th anniversary of the Great Charter, itself an icon of the protection of individual liberty embedded in the Anglo-Australian legal imaginary.[15]

Equally, marking the 150th anniversary of Lord Atkin's birth in Queensland in 2017, the Supreme Court Library of Queensland curated a public Exhibition as a physical and online installation celebrating his common law legacy,[16] and founded an annual "Lord Atkin Lecture". The Exhibition recognised Lord Atkin's Australian roots from his birthplace in Brisbane and early life in country Queensland; it reflected on his family's influence, given his reform-oriented, politician father[17] and the remarkable women in his life. Additionally, it featured cameos of Lord Atkin's "towering judgments"[18] in cases where he was a key player—his majority judgment in *Donoghue v Stevenson* (1932),[19] and his dissent in *Liversidge v Anderson* (1941). From this Exhibition's public "staging", the enduring impact of Lord Atkin's dissent continues to be experienced in the public imagination.

## PLAYERS

*Liversidge v Anderson's* players include its judicial cast, and its protagonists. Its principal judicial cast comprised its five sitting Lord Lords; the Lord Chancellor was not sitting but had an interesting role at the

---

[15] Jonathan Ames, "Scott Wright's Play Depicts a Clampdown on Liberty," *The Times* (London), July 9, 2015.

[16] Supreme Court Library of Queensland, "Lord Atkin: from Queensland to the House of Lords," Exhibition, Supreme Court Library of Queensland, Brisbane (November 28, 2017 to present), https://legalheritage.sclqld.org.au/exhibitions/lordatkin

[17] Peter Applegarth, "Lord Atkin: Principle and Progress," *Australian Law Journal* 90 (2016): 712ff; Peter Applegarth, "Robert Atkin: Founding Father of Social Justice," *The Australian*, January 22, 2016.

[18] Applegarth, "Lord Atkin," 711.

[19] *Donoghue v Stevenson* [1932] AC 562.

30   K. SCHULTZ

judgment's point of delivery. In addition to Lord Atkin, the four sitting Lord Lords were all of roughly similar vintage: Lord Maugham and Lord Romer were born in 1866, Lord Wright in 1869, and Lord Macmillan in 1873. The Lord Chancellor, Lord Simon, born in 1873, offered views on the decorum and impact of Lord Atkin's dissent. Lord Atkin was the sole dissentient in this Court. Born on 28 November 1867, he was a few weeks from his 74th birthday when he delivered his dissent; he died three years later. Appointed a Lord Justice of Appeal in 1919, and a Lord of Appeal in Ordinary in 1928 styled Baron Atkin of Aberdovey, Lord Atkin not only had long judicial experience in the highest British courts but was renowned for his revolutionary majority judgment in *Donoghue v Stevenson* (1932). In that "celebrated judgment in a landmark decision",[20] he was "playing the role of 'demolisher of precedent'";[21] his judgment was a "quintessentially modernist text" that has engrossed lawyers' imaginations.[22] Lord Atkin's dissent, a decade later in *Liversidge v Anderson*, ultimately has had a similar impact, but its contemporary impact was conditioned by the contention surrounding its split decision.

*Liversidge v Anderson's* eponymous protagonists in this "legal morality tale"[23] were Robert Liversidge, the detainee, and Sir John Anderson, the Home Secretary or Secretary of State,[24] who exercised the executive discretion to detain. Liversidge was an assumed name for Jacob "Jack" Perlzweig, a British citizen with Russian-Jewish immigrant parentage[25] and a "curious" past.[26] A "somewhat shadowy and mysterious figure",[27] Liversidge was associated, apparently unintentionally, with a conspiracy to defraud in his early life in the late 1920s,[28] and hence acquired a police

[20] HP Lee, "Of Lions and Squeaking Mice in Anxious Times," *Monash University Law Review* 42 (2016): 2.

[21] Lee, "Lions and Squeaking Mice," 3.

[22] Honni van Rijswijk, "Neighbourly Injuries: Proximity in Tort Law and Virginia Woolf's Theory of Suffering," *Feminist Legal Studies* 20 (2012): 40.

[23] Bingham, "*Liversidge v Anderson*," 33.

[24] This chapter uses "Home Secretary" generally to describe this executive role, but "Secretary of State" to reflect extracts from statutory, judicial, or official material.

[25] AW Brian Simpson, *In the Highest Degree Odious: Detention Without Trial in Wartime Britain* (Oxford: Oxford University Press, 1994), 333.

[26] Simpson, *Highest Degree Odious*, 336.

[27] Tom Bingham, *Lives of the Law: Selected Essays and Speeches: 2000–2010* (Oxford University Press, 2011) 203.

[28] Simpson, *Highest Degree Odious*, 333.

file.[29] Later however, Liversidge redeemed himself. Prior to serving "with outstanding success" as a Pilot Officer in the Royal Airforce Volunteer Reserve from 1939, and then as an Intelligence Officer at a Fighter Command,[30] he "engaged in various successful business enterprises".[31] Coincidentally, he apparently had "connection with British Intelligence in the 1930s".[32] On Simpson's summation, not only was Liversidge a "loyal citizen[ ] who ... ought never to be detained",[33] but the prosecution case was "very close" to a detention order created in "bad faith".[34]

Liversidge's "detainer" in name, Anderson, later Lord Waverley, was regarded as having a consistently "remarkable" administrative career—"in Ireland and in Bengal he became familiar with detention".[35] From May to August 1940, Anderson directed the issue of 1428 detention orders.[36] The warrant for Liversidge's arrest on 24 April 1940 formally issued on Anderson's order; Liversidge was detained in Brixton Prison on 28 May 1940.[37] The detention order's initial recital averred the Home Secretary's "reasonable cause to believe" that Perlzweig alias Liversidge was a "person of hostile associations". However, the detention order lacked any accusation of criminal conduct. What, then, were the actual reasons for Liversidge's detention? The autobiography of Liversidge's counsel, Pritt KC, recollects three specific grounds: Liversidge's engagement in commercial frauds; his engagement with suspected enemy agents; and his Jewish heritage.[38] When Simpson's assiduous archival research from government departments uncovered the "Reasons for Order"[39]—a reduced

[29] Simpson, *Highest Degree Odious*, 334.
[30] Simpson, *Highest Degree Odious*, 335 ff.
[31] Simpson, *Highest Degree Odious*, 334.
[32] Simpson, *Highest Degree Odious*, 335.
[33] Simpson, *Highest Degree Odious*, 333.
[34] Simpson, *Highest Degree Odious*, 421.
[35] Simpson, *Highest Degree Odious*, 28–29, n 96.
[36] Bingham, "*Liversidge v Anderson*," 34; RFV Heuston, "*Liversidge v Anderson* in Retrospect" *Law Quarterly Review* 86 (1970): 42.
[37] Simpson, *Highest Degree Odious*, 338 (28 May 1940); Simpson, "Rhetoric, Reality," 136 (28 May 1940); Bingham, "*Liversidge v Anderson*," 34 (29 May 1940).
[38] Lewis, *Lord Atkin*, 132, 133 n 5, citing DN Pritt QC, *From Right to Left* (1967); the complete citation is Denis Nowell Pritt, *The Autobiography of D N Pritt, Part 1; From Right to Left* (London: Lawrence & Wishart, 1965); Heuston, "*Liversidge v Anderson*," 66; Tom Bingham, "Mr Perlzweig, Mr Liversidge, and Lord Atkin" in *The Business of Judging: Selected Essays and Speeches* (Oxford: Oxford University Press, 2000), 211, 219. Note that the third ground on Pritt's recounting was "being the son of a Jewish Rabbi".
[39] Simpson, *Highest Degree Odious*, 339; Simpson, "Rhetoric, Reality," 139.

version of the prosecution brief undisclosed to detainees[40]—eight specific grounds were revealed for Liversidge's internment. Two themes dominated: Liversidge's history of false particulars and identities; and Liversidge's early association with fraudsters. Only the penultimate ground—Liversidge's alleged association with "Germans" and "German Secret service" associates[41]—had any conceivable relevance to Regulation 18B's requirement of the detainee's "hostile associations".

Ultimately, on 14 March 1941, Liversidge sued for damages for false imprisonment, as opposed to habeas corpus.[42] His application requesting particulars of the grounds of Anderson's "reasonable cause to believe" was unsuccessful. Liversidge continued to appeal the refusal of his request up the judicial hierarchy, leading to the litigation's final staging in the Appellate Committee.

## ACT I: SUBSTANCE AND ORTHODOXY

The judicial treatment of the substance of *Liversidge v Anderson* is critical to assessing the impact of law's history—modern-day Anglo-Australian precedent rejects the majority judgments and adopts Lord Atkin's dissent. To illustrate this turnaround, essential points of the substance of the majority judgments will be first outlined below and then the Anglo-Australian interment or burial of the majority judgments, and acclamation of Lord Atkin's dissent, will be sketched.

Moving first to the substance of *Liversidge v Anderson's* judgments, at first glance, the case concerned the issue of whether a subjective or objective test governed Regulation 18B's interpretation. But the issue was larger: it was a "simple one of statutory construction but with profound consequences for individual liberty".[43] While the case has been considered a test of the performance of the judiciary's claimed role as the "guardian of British liberty against the over-mighty executive",[44] the judiciary has been perceived to be an unenthusiastic guardian; for Simpson, the majority judgments better represent the reality of Regulation 18B's unreviewable

---

[40] Simpson, *Highest Degree Odious*, 89; Simpson, "Rhetoric, Reality," 133.

[41] Simpson, *Highest Degree Odious*, 339. Note that the first ground mentions his Russian parentage and his father's name (and appends "a Jewish Rabbi" as a coda).

[42] Simpson, *Highest Degree Odious*, 353 ff.

[43] Gerard Carney, "Lord Atkin: his Queensland Origins and Legacy," in *Supreme Court History Program Yearbook 2005* (Supreme Court Library of Queensland, 2005), 33, 54.

[44] Simpson, *Highest Degree Odious*, 352.

executive discretion, and Lord Atkin's dissent unconvincingly attempts to promote the traditional judicial role in a legal order that permits this discretion.[45] Yet Lord Atkin did not advocate unlimited judicial scrutiny of the non-judicial arms of government—instead, he recognised Parliament's unlimited powers to grant executive discretion, but argued that Regulation 18B was not expressed so expansively.[46]

Regulation 18B was enacted pursuant to the *Emergency Powers (Defence) Act 1939*. It was a government control purporting to respond to growing national security concerns in the lead-up to war, and to secure public safety, defend the realm, maintain public order, and enable the war's efficient prosecution. But its passage was controversial. Its initial draft empowered the Home Secretary to direct any person's detention "if satisfied" that their detention was necessary to prevent action that was "prejudicial to the public safety or the defence of the Realm". Following House of Commons' debate,[47] the initial draft was amended on 31 October 1939, so opening the debate to objective and subjective constructions of Regulation 18B's executive discretion. The amended draft empowered the Home Secretary to direct any person's detention, if the Home Secretary "has reasonable cause to believe [that] person to be of hostile origin or associations, or to have been recently concerned in acts prejudicial to the public safety or the defence of the Realm". In September 1941, in Liversidge's final appeal to the Appellate Committee, argument addressed whether the Home Secretary's exercise of discretion—his "reasonable cause to believe"—was judicially reviewable. Specifically, could this "reasonable cause to believe", as required by Regulation 18B, be discharged by the Home Secretary's subjective view (requiring only the exercise of good faith) or by an objective view (requiring the demonstration and weighing of facts). The Court split.

*Liversidge v Anderson*'s majority upheld the so-called subjective standard. While the majority judgments differ in their mix and emphases, there are points of commonality in their approaches.[48] For instance, Lords Maugham and Romer stressed that executive discretion cannot be judicially reviewable;[49] Lords Macmillan and Wright emphasised that the stan-

---

[45] Simpson, *Highest Degree Odious*, 363.

[46] *Liversidge v Anderson*, 239 (Atkin LJ); Lewis, *Lord Atkin*, 133.

[47] Lewis, *Lord Atkin*, 147ff.

[48] Susan Kiefel, "Judicial Courage and the Decorum of Dissent," Selden Society Lecture, Supreme Court of Queensland (November 28, 2017), 2.

[49] *Liversidge v Anderson*, 220 (Maugham LJ), 279 (Romer LJ).

dard of reasonableness for Regulations 18B's "reasonable cause to believe" was a subjective test.[50] A brief expansion will illustrate various key points. For Lord Maugham, the presiding judge, executive discretion was not amenable to "criticism and control of a judge in a court of law".[51] He adduced four points to support his construction that legally admissible "external fact[s]" were not necessary to trigger the Home Secretary's executive discretion: controlling the detainee was a matter for executive discretion; hearsay was sufficient for exercising executive discretion; extreme confidentiality or prejudice attended the potential information; and safeguards existed for exercising executive discretion, including the Home Secretary's answerability to Parliament. For Lord Macmillan, Regulation 18B "introduces a personal, not an impersonal requirement" to the Home Secretary's "reasonable cause of belief";[52] interpretation of emergency legislation should "promote ... its efficacy for the defence of the realm".[53] For Lord Wright, the "liberty of the subject" was clearly in issue, but Regulation 18B's statutory use of the adjective "reasonable" only connoted that the Home Secretary did not "lightly or arbitrarily" invade the subject's liberty.[54] Finally, for Lord Romer, the "crucial question" is whether the Home Secretary can be "compelled to disclose grounds"; neither the legislature nor Regulations 18B's framers intended the judiciary to be the "ultimate judges" on detention orders.[55]

By contrast, Lord Atkin's dissent upheld the objective standard as the antidote—the anti-virus—to the intellectual vice of the "virus of subjectivism".[56] He held that the words "reasonable cause to believe" imposed an objective standard of reasonableness on the Home Secretary's belief; a subjective belief was insufficient for the "unconditional power of imprisonment"[57] authorised by Regulation 18B. For Regulation 18B's words had "only one meaning"[58]—an objective meaning. Hence, the

[50] *Liversidge v Anderson*, 251 (MacMillan LJ), 270 (Wright LJ).

[51] *Liversidge v Anderson*, 220 (Maugham LJ).

[52] *Liversidge v Anderson*, 251, 248 (MacMillan LJ).

[53] *Liversidge v Anderson*, 252 (MacMillan LJ).

[54] *Liversidge v Anderson*, 260, 268 (Wright LJ).

[55] *Liversidge v Anderson*, 277, 281 (Romer LJ).

[56] Simpson, "Rhetoric, Reality," 151; *Liversidge v Anderson*, 247 (Atkin LJ). Note Lord Atkin's description of the Court of Appeal being "infected with the 'subjective virus'".

[57] *Liversidge v Anderson*, 247 (Atkin LJ).

[58] *Liversidge v Anderson*, 244 (Atkin LJ).

Home Secretary's "reasonable cause to believe" in a person's "hostile associations" had to be ascertained objectively—that is, factually.

In persuasively constructing his dissent, Lord Atkin used analytic strategies and techniques classically aligned with common law reasoning. Doctrine, precedential and statutory examples, and illustrations and analogies are interwoven within his argument. For instance, he expressly listed 13 examples of arrest powers,[59] and then 23 examples of statutory discretionary powers;[60] he deployed these illustrations of statutory language to argue that Regulation 18B intended an unconditional, irreviewable, executive discretion.[61] In addition, Lord Atkin argued by analogy to illustrate the issue of "false logic" fuelling the majority judgments.[62] To indicate that Regulation 18B did not intend an unconditional detention power and that its "reasonable cause to believe" had to be conditioned on objective facts, he employed a "broken ankle" analogy. Was the established fact of a broken ankle the same as simply thinking that one has a broken ankle? He answered, persuasively at least for Allen,[63] that "reasonable cause to believe" in a detainee's "hostile associations" requires the objective reality or fact of hostile associations to be established, not simply a subjective thought of hostile associations to exist. Next, to underline that Regulation 18B's words had "only one meaning", Lord Atkin deployed a series of illustrations. His "clash of arms" illustration[64] was a point of departure from Cicero's remark, "*inter arma enim silent leges*".[65] He declared that "amid the clash of arms, the laws are not silent"; instead, the laws "speak the same language" regardless of wartime or peacetime.[66] Hence, laws are not to be interpreted or understood differently in wartime. In classic common law form, this illustration supplemented the substance of his argument—it was functional, not simply a flourish. The decorum otherwise in Lord Atkin's dissent will be addressed separately, below.

---

[59] *Liversidge v Anderson*, 229ff (Atkin LJ).

[60] *Liversidge v Anderson*, 233ff (Atkin LJ).

[61] *Liversidge v Anderson*, 229ff, 233ff (Atkin LJ); Heuston, "*Liversidge v Anderson*," 35.

[62] Simpson, "Rhetoric, Reality," 151.

[63] Carleton Kemp Allen, "Regulation 18B and Reasonable Cause," *Law Quarterly Review* 58 (1942): 234.

[64] *Liversidge v Anderson*, 244 (Atkin LJ).

[65] "For in times of war the laws are silent."

[66] *Liversidge v Anderson*, 244 (Atkin LJ).

36   K. SCHULTZ

Moving to the historical treatment of *Liversidge v Anderson's* substance, Lord Atkin's dissent was ultimately vindicated[67] and the majority judgments were finally interred.[68] The contemporary groundswell of support for Lord Atkin's dissent gradually gained traction in the highest Anglo-Australian courts. Substantively, Lord Atkin's dissent reflects Antonio's famous line in Shakespeare's *The Tempest*, "what's past is prologue", in representing an introduction or turning point to orthodoxy; it offers a context for, and reaction to, arguments concerning untrammelled or unreviewable executive discretion that have since been addressed to courts. This turning point was clearly heralded in Britain in 1951, when a similarly phrased Ceylon regulation was in issue. Lord Radcliffe, delivering the Privy Council's advice, recognised that this analogous "reasonable cause to believe" phrase must be intended as "a condition limiting the exercise of an otherwise arbitrary power".[69] Then, in 1964, Lord Reid doubted the majority judgments when he described *Liversidge v Anderson* as "this very peculiar decision of this House";[70] he restricted it to its wartime context. Ultimately, in 1980, the death blow was delivered in another "reasonable cause" case.[71] There, Lord Diplock, with reference to the 1941 wartime staging, declared that it was time "to acknowledge that the majority of this House in *Liversidge v Anderson* were expediently and, at that time, perhaps, excusably, wrong and the dissenting speech of Lord Atkin was right"; Lord Scarman held that *Liversidge v Anderson* "need no longer haunt the law".[72] In similar vein, in 1984, Lord Scarman forthrightly declared, "The classic dissent of Lord Atkin ... is now accepted ... as correct", not only in terms of Regulation 18B's construction, but "in its declaration of English legal principle".[73]

Joining the ultimate adoption of Lord Atkin's dissent, Australia's High Court has upheld its language protecting the subject's liberties but has extended this protection to peacetime. In 1990, the Mason High Court unanimously upheld "Lord Atkin's famous, and now orthodox dissent in *Liversidge v Anderson*";[74] hence, a statutory prescription of "reasonable

---

[67] Carney, "Lord Atkin," 55; Applegarth, "Lord Atkin," 749.

[68] Lewis, *Lord Atkin*, 132.

[69] *Nakkuda Ali v Jayaratne* [1951] AC 66, 77 (Radcliffe LJ).

[70] *Ridge v Baldwin* [1964] AC 40, 73 (Reid LJ).

[71] Bingham, "Mr Perlzweig," 220.

[72] *R v IRC; ex parte Rossminster* [1980] AC 952, 1025 (Scarman LJ), 1011 (Diplock LJ).

[73] *Khera v Secretary of State for the Home Department* [1984] AC 74, 110.

[74] *George v Rockett* (1990) 170 CLR 104, 112.

grounds" for a suspicion or belief demands the "existence of facts … sufficient to induce that state of mind in a reasonable person". The words were held to create an objective test concerning a reasonable person's conclusion in the circumstances, not the decision-maker's subjective mental state. The Court observed that this factual requirement "opens many administrative decisions to judicial review and precludes the arbitrary exercise of many statutory powers".[75] Similarly, in 2017, when examining an analogous statutory phrase—"reasonable grounds for believing"—Justice Gageler's dissent endorsed Lord Atkin's dissent. In the prologue to his "powerful" judgment,[76] Justice Gageler elevated personal liberty as the foremost common law right,[77] and unpacked the relation between subjective and objective elements of belief. In his view, the statutory phrase requires three interlinked elements for the exercise of executive discretion: the decision-maker's "actual subjective belief"; the formation of the belief "by reference to objective circumstances"; and objective circumstances "sufficient to induce that state of mind in a reasonable person".[78]

This snapshot of Anglo-Australian authority instances the common law's backward- and forward-looking character.[79] Notably, Lord Atkin's dissent is not simply a case of history repeating or of the past replaying—its initial staging in wartime has been expanded to applying its reasoning in peacetime. Instead, it is a case where the past has signalled a turning point from deficient oversight of detention practices, and from inadequate institutional recognition of the rule of law's promotion of individual liberties.

## ACT II: FORM AND DECORUM

Equally critical to an assessment of the impact of law's history is the form or style of Lord Atkin's dissent. It is "as powerful an example of the rhetorical common law judicial opinion" as exists in the Law Reports[80]—it deploys form and substance to destroy the majority arguments. Yet Lord

[75] *George v Rockett*, 112.
[76] Julian R Murphy, "Unreviewable Police Powers? The Reliance on Past Policing Experience in *Prior v Mole*," *Indigenous Law Bulletin* 8 (2017): 20.
[77] *Prior v Mole* (2017) 261 CLR 265, 277 (Gageler J).
[78] *Prior v Mole*, 278 (Gageler J).
[79] Janet McLean, "Ideologies in Law Time: The Oxford History of the Laws of England," *Law & Social Inquiry* 38 (2013): 747.
[80] Simpson, "Rhetoric, Reality," 151.

Atkin's references to the risk of executive-minded judges, English legal history, and Humpty Dumpty's meaning have been perceived as formally contentious or indecorous—that is, as betraying the judicial disposition, character, or delivery. These three references are located in two of the three paragraphs of Lord Atkin's peroration on Liversidge's appeal.[81] The references did not endear Lord Atkin to his colleagues; one reference spurred Lord Maugham's unprecedented extra-judicial rebuke of Lord Atkin's dissent. To examine this issue of form, the general formal or stylistic features of Lord Atkin's dissent will be first examined, followed by the three contentious references.

Regarding its general formal features, Lord Atkin's dissent proceeds from a statement of the case's importance, to theme and method, to illustration and analysis, and then full-circle to the theme—this return was invested with irony and a "dose of ridicule".[82] Of a piece with judgment-writing styles in 1941, Lord Atkin did not rehearse secondary academic material; this instanced, perhaps, the "living authors" rule in operation.[83] His dissent's deceptively simple English has been regarded as "powerfully expressed and beautifully written"[84]—it is a "vigorous but dispassionate dissection" of the majority.[85] As *Liversidge v Anderson* concerned the statutory interpretation of Regulation 18B's prescription of a "reasonable cause to believe", Lord Atkin's theme was the "plain and natural meaning";[86] his key argument was that Regulation 18B required objective fact to ground the belief, not subjective belief. Throughout his judgment, he nested this key argument within the larger issues of the subject's liberty, and the judiciary's duty to uphold liberty. Next, Lord Atkin detailed his method of adducing "innumerable" examples and illustrations. He later explained, by letter to Lord Simon, that his aim was to "destroy" the "legal ground[s]" of the majority's arguments[87]—hence, the "weight of examples was and

---

[81] *Liversidge v Anderson*, 244–45 (Atkin LJ). Note that, to his reasons in the Liversidge appeal, Lord Atkin appended his reasons in the Greene appeal, disposing of two cases in the one judgment.

[82] Lewis, *Lord Atkin*, 139.

[83] Susan Kiefel, "The Academy and the Courts; What Do They Mean to Each Other Today?" *Melbourne University Law Review* 44 (2020): 451, 452.

[84] Bingham, "*Liversidge v Anderson*," 36.

[85] Michael Kirby, "On the Writing of Judgments," *Australian Law Journal* 64 (1990): 699.

[86] *Liversidge v Anderson*, 228 (Atkin LJ).

[87] Lewis, *Lord Atkin*, 139.

was intended to be crushing".[88] Coincidentally, the gravitational force of the lists of examples evidences the industry and consideration invested in Lord Atkin's dissent; it was not a continuous tract of impassioned prose. Lord Atkin executed his argument by analysing the illustrations and deploying analogies, all the while interweaving statements of principle. Finally, "he restated his theme"[89] and underlined it with what were perceived to be three contentious references that were targeted by contemporary critics for their perceived indecorum.

The three contentious references in Lord Atkin's dissent were to executive-minded judges, English legal history, and Humpty Dumpty's meaning, respectively. First, the reference to executive-minded judges emerged from Lord Atkin's declaration of his "apprehension" of the "attitude of judges who on a mere question of construction, when face to face with claims involving the liberty of the subject", demonstrate that they are "more executive minded than the executive".[90] Here, he critiques a judicial approach that adopts a liberty-restricting interpretation by allowing an "unnatural", "subjective construction" of Regulation 18B's language. This reference particularly wounded Lord Chief Justice Caldecote. By letter to Lord Atkin, he expressed his upset with what he perceived to be the general "criticism" of, and aspersion on, judges who had previously offered conclusions aligned with *Liversidge v Anderson*'s majority judgments—for instance, he had so concluded in two earlier judgments.[91] Lord Atkin's letter in response mollified Lord Chief Justice Caldecote: he emphasised that his judgment contained "no criticism of judges generally" nor "imputation of subservience to the Executive"; his focus was instead on the *Liversidge v Anderson* majority who had "adopted this unnatural construction".[92]

Second, the reference to English legal history emerged from Lord Atkin's musing that Crown counsel's arguments during the appeal "might have been addressed acceptably to the Court of King's Bench in the time of Charles I".[93] Commentators have advised[94] that Lord Atkin was likely

---

[88] Lewis, *Lord Atkin*, 136.
[89] Lewis, *Lord Atkin*, 137.
[90] *Liversidge v Anderson*, 244 (Atkin LJ).
[91] Lewis, *Lord Atkin*, 140–41.
[92] Lewis, *Lord Atkin*, 141–42.
[93] *Liversidge v Anderson*, 244 (Atkin LJ).
[94] GW Keeton, "*Liversidge v Anderson*," *Modern Law Review* 5 (1942): 162 ff; Lewis, *Lord Atkin*, 154ff.

40  K. SCHULTZ

channelling *Darnel's Case* (1627)[95] where the Court of Kings Bench notoriously refused bail for five English knights arrested via the royal prerogative—the case ultimately signalled an impasse in the executive's power-grab and imposition of detention. This reference excited Lord Maugham to publish an unexpectedly indecorous letter, "War and Habeas Corpus", to *The Times* on Thursday 6 November 1941.[96] Hence, while Lord Maugham was absent from the judgments' oral delivery by apparent oversight, his voice emerged three days later in the newspapers. Extracting Lord Atkin's reference to English legal history, he repudiated its relevance to the Home Secretary's counsel (the Attorney General and Valentine Holmes), claiming that the Bar's traditions and ethics rendered counsel powerless to respond to "so grave an animadversion".[97] Lord Maugham followed with a speech to the House of Lords, claiming that his letter meant to "protect" counsel from any perceived "pain and perhaps professional injury" in Lord Atkin's "offensive remark", although he caveated that he may have "misunderstood Lord Atkin's meaning";[98] Lord Maugham's speech was equally a platform for deflecting criticism that he had "lost dignity" as a result of his newspaper comments.[99] By contrast, Lord Atkin continued a dignified public silence but recorded, by letter to his daughter Nancy, that this "unprecedented" and "unpardonable" attack suggested Lord Maugham's "nervous strain".[100] The irony of Lord Maugham's praying in aid the "traditions of the Bar" for his own indecorous actions cannot be overstated; its lack of credibility is underlined by recognising that judicial condemnation of counsel's arguments is not "necessarily directed against the counsel" acting on instructions.[101]

Third, the reference to Humpty Dumpty's "meaning" emerged from Lord Atkin's extraction of well-known text from Lewis Carroll's *Through the Looking Glass*, the sequel to *Alice's Adventures in Wonderland*.[102] Here, in a "dose of ridicule", Lord Atkin deploys Humpty Dumpty's dialogue with Alice in order to represent the "only one authority ... [that] might

[95] *Darnel* (1627) 3 How St Tr 1.

[96] *Liversidge v Anderson*, 244 (Atkin LJ).

[97] Lewis, *Lord Atkin*, 143.

[98] Lewis, *Lord Atkin*, 146.

[99] Lewis, *Lord Atkin*, 146.

[100] Lewis, *Lord Atkin*, 143, 144.

[101] Heuston, "*Liversidge v Anderson*," 45.

[102] Lewis Carroll, *Through the Looking Glass*, Chapter VI; *Liversidge v Anderson*, 245 (Atkin LJ).

justify the suggested method of construction" of the majority judgments. For Humpty Dumpty's approach to language allows judges unlimited control and mastery when deducing the meaning of words. By contrast, Lord Atkin was clear in his method of construction—"The words have only one meaning". He drilled the point that the Executive was attempting to argue for a subjective construction of statutory words that latterly had an objective construction. This reference instilled particular anxiety in the Lord Chancellor, Lord Simon, upon reading the draft judgment. By letter to Lord Atkin, he suggested the removal of the Humpty Dumpty reference. Lord Simon questioned whether the "very amusing citation" was "necessary"—literary allusion could "enliven[ ]", but "neither the dignity of the House, nor the collaboration of colleagues, nor the force of your reasoning would suffer from the omission".[103] Lord Atkin's letter in response outlined his method for dismissing the majority's subjective construction of Regulation 18B—"I consider that I have destroyed it on every legal ground" and hence it was "fair to conclude with a dose of ridicule". Lord Atkin assured his "highest esteem for [his] colleagues" but repeated his strong feelings on the twin questions of the subject's liberty and the Court's impartial duty. He expressly rejected Lord Simon's suggestion that he was ridiculing or "wounding" his colleagues ("I have not the slightest intent to ridicule") and repudiated any suggestion that the "dignity of the House will suffer".[104] This prompted Lord Simon's follow-up on judgment day, 3 November 1941, reiterating his preference for "omit[ting] the jibe", whilst referencing Lord Atkin's confirmation of the "dose of ridicule".[105]

Lord Atkin's formal and stylistic choices did not endear him to his colleagues—he was "cold shouldered",[106] and his "vivid prose had mortifying consequences" for his subsequent "encounters" with colleagues.[107] However, from these three contentious references in 1941, the perception of indecorum has, in twenty-first-century Australia, been distilled to the final reference. It remains to consider the live issue of the indecorous orthodoxy of Lord Atkin's dissent.

[103] Lewis, *Lord Atkin*, 139.

[104] Lewis, *Lord Atkin*, 139–40.

[105] Lewis, *Lord Atkin*, 140.

[106] Bingham, "Mr Perlzweig," 212.

[107] Michael Kirby, "Literature in Australian Judicial Reasoning," *Australian Law Journal* 75 (2000): 603; Stephen Sedley, "When Judges Sleep," *London Review of Books* (June 10, 1993).

## ACT III: DECORUM AND IMPACT

Is Lord Atkin's dissent an example of indecorous orthodoxy? Clearly, in Anglo-Australian law, it now represents the orthodox substantive approach to unreviewable statutory discretions that recite a "reasonable cause to believe". The impact of Lord Atkin's dissent is unquestionable—its substantive vindication marked the turning point to a new orthodoxy. But substance is interwoven with form, and style can contribute to a judgment's impact and reception. Hence, the decorum of Lord Atkin's dissent continues as a twenty-first-century point of debate. But the debate has narrowed from the three contentious references to one only—the reference to Humpty Dumpty's meaning.

Lord Atkin rarely dissented,[108] and his reputation "len[t] the dissent an authority"—"reputation is inevitably an aspect of subsequent citation and influence".[109] Clearly, "great dissents" can be delivered by judges who are not labelled serial "Great Dissenters", but who are frequently in the majority as "intellectual leaders of the court".[110] When weighing or measuring decorous language and delivery, a critical question is whether a judgment's form, style, and rhetoric contribute to its reasoning, or merely colour, inflate, or decorate it.[111] The substantive strength of Lord Atkin's dissent is revealed at the level of style; his principled reasoning, laden with examples and illustrations, builds to a crescendo where the principles are re-asserted in his peroration on Liversidge's appeal, and are pinpointed by the three contentious references. This crescendo's striking language fortifies the statements of principle—it catches the audience's attention, cementing the importance of Lord Atkin's strong arguments on the twin questions of the subject's liberty and the Court's impartial duty. Throughout his dissent, Lord Atkin attempted to logically dissect and dismiss the majority judgments that he considered were fallaciously embracing this "era of 'subjective' cause"[112]—the fallacy was their interpretation of Regulation 18B as requiring only the Home Secretary's subjective belief.

---

[108] Lewis, *Lord Atkin*, 176.

[109] Andrew Lynch, "Introduction—What Makes a Dissent 'Great'?" in Andrew Lynch (ed), *Great Australian Dissents* (Cambridge: Cambridge University Press, 2016), 1, 10.

[110] Lynch, "Dissent 'Great'?" in Andrew Lynch (ed), *Great Australian Dissents* (Cambridge: Cambridge University Press, 2016), 1, 10.

[111] Desmond Manderson, "Literature in Law—Judicial Method, Epistemology, Strategy, and Doctrine," *University of New South Wales Law Journal* 38 (2015): 1305.

[112] *Liversidge v Anderson*, 241 (Atkin LJ).

Lord Atkin's dissent was decorous in its direct references to colleagues: "the noble Lords"; "my noble and learned friend Lord Wright"; and "my noble friend Lord Macmillan".[113] But an indirect reference to colleagues— the reference to Humpty Dumpty's meaning—remains a live issue. Was this remark unnecessary or rhetorically effective? Put differently, was Lord Atkin necessarily critiquing his colleagues' method of interpretation, or was he unnecessarily ridiculing his colleagues and derogating from the judiciary's dignity? To address this, there follows a brief consideration of common law dissent's value and functions, and then an equally brief assessment of twenty-first-century Australian critique of Lord Atkin's reference to Humpty Dumpty's meaning and the impact of Lord Atkin's dissent.

In terms of dissent's value and functions, the common law has clearly recognised the "prerogative to write separately"[114] together with decorum's unquestionable value in maintaining collegiality and efficiency. The institution of dissent is an "integral feature" to common law adjudication[115] and an "act of independence".[116] Dissent effects three broad critical functions: ensuring the judiciary's core capabilities in a democratic society; benefiting the adjudicative process by clarifying majority reasoning, and affirming both the process's integrity and the judiciary's independence; and developing and advancing the law by facilitating progression and change.[117] Dissent's specific roles include that it signifies integrity, embodies democratic ideals, clarifies the law, and forecasts the law in its "appeal to the brooding spirit of the law".[118] Admittedly, consensus norms can affect whether a dissent is considered valuable or necessary; they illustrate a nexus between a court's guiding institutional practice and purpose, and can have the effect of "cabining the number of dissents".[119] But collegial

---

[113] *Liversidge v Anderson*, 241, 244, 246 respectively (Atkin LJ).

[114] Ruth Bader Ginsburg, "The Role of Dissenting Opinions," *Minnesota Law Review* 95 (2010): 3.

[115] John Alder, "Dissents in Courts of Last Resort: Tragic Choices?" *Oxford Journal of Legal Studies* 20 (2000): 221.

[116] Kiefel, "Decorum of Dissent," 8.

[117] Andrew Lynch, "Dissent: The Rewards and Risks of Judicial Disagreement in the High Court of Australia," *Melbourne University Law Review* 27 (2003): 725–26, 737.

[118] Joe McIntyre, "In Defence of Judicial Dissent," *Adelaide Law Review* 37 (2016): 439, 433, quoting Charles Evans Hughes, *The Supreme Court of the United States; Its Foundation, Methods, and Achievements: An Interpretation* (New York: Columbia University Press, 1928), 66.

[119] Harvard Law Review, "From Consensus to Collegiality: The Origins of the 'Respectful' Dissent," *Harvard Law Review* 124 (2011): 1305, 1309.

dissenting has been identified as an "immensely attractive alternative to consensus jurisprudence" and as integral to the "larger, truth-seeking institutional dialogue";[120] hence, the judicial choice of dissent is expected to comport with common law conventions of restraint and decorum. Anglo-Australian dissent has received increased scholarly attention from 2000 in Britain (when dissent and its "constitutional role" received "little discussion" in the English law and literature[121]), and from 2003 in Australia (when dissent "attract[ed] direct consideration only sporadically"[122]). However, immediately from its publication, Lord Atkin's dissent attracted various British views on its three contentious references. For instance, Heuston characterised these references as so "passionate", even verging on the wildly rhetorical, that it appeared that an "explosion" had occurred in Lord Atkin's mind.[123] By contrast, Lewis recorded that the "extreme", "extravagant" language employed in Lord Atkin's dissent heightened its interest,[124] and former Lord Chief Justice Bingham applauded Lord Atkin's dissent as "eloquent and courageous".[125]

In terms of twenty-first-century Australian critique, extra-judicial views have variously characterised Lord Atkin's reference to Humpty Dumpty's meaning. For Justice Kirby, Lord Atkin's "brilliant dissent" contained this "powerful allusion" and "persuasive image";[126] this reference illustrated judicial irony's dangers, but its "vivid language" and "vigorous expression" contributed to "captur[ing] the attention of law commentators and judges".[127] By contrast, for Justice Applegarth, "an unfortunate feature" in Lord Atkin's "brilliant judgment" was the "unnecessary swipe at his colleagues with his humiliating reference"; the executive-minded judges reference was stinging, but the Humpty Dumpty reference was "unnecessarily provocative, and destructive of the collegiality" that defines properly functioning appellate courts.[128] Similarly, for Chief Justice Kiefel, there was

---

[120] Harvard Law Review, "Consensus to Collegiality," 1305, 1320.

[121] Alder, "Dissents," 221.

[122] Lynch, "Dissent," 724.

[123] Heuston, "*Liversidge v Anderson*," 36, 37 ("explosion").

[124] Lewis, *Lord Atkin*, 132, 154.

[125] Bingham, *Lives of the Law*, 203, citing *R v Inland Revenue Commissioners*, 1011.

[126] Kirby, "Literature," 603, 612, 613; Justice Kirby was appointed to the High Court of Australia from 1996 to 2009.

[127] Kirby, "Writing of Judgments," 699.

[128] Applegarth, "Lord Atkin," 712, 746. Note Justice Applegarth's description of it causing "unnecessary offence": 744.

detectable "disdain in the tone of Lord Atkin's dissent", and discourtesy and annoyance;[129] literary allusions may be questionable in judgments, but a judgment's ridicule of judicial colleagues is impermissible as it "cannot but detract from the authority of the court".[130] Both Chief Justice Kiefel and Justice Applegarth endorsed the propriety of Lord Simon's attempted intervention in Lord Atkin's dissent. On their view, a senior judicial colleague (here the Lord Chancellor) can properly suggest revision of reasons in order to preserve the Court's institutional dignity and consideration to colleagues.[131] However, Chief Justice Kiefel's caveat concerning the irrelevance of judges' "hurt feelings"[132] signals why Lord Atkin did not consider that his dissent lacked decorum—his attention was fixed on "upholding old traditions of justice" and on rejecting the majority's "strained and ultra-legal construction".[133] As he outlined, his three contentious references were introduced not to personally attack judicial colleagues, but to dismiss the majority's methods of construction. Hence, they were not tangential formal flourishes, but supplements to principled reasoning, legal clarity, and democratic values. While the Humpty Dumpty reference ran to ridicule, it was not vituperative—it was a well-known literary allusion concerning meaning.

Finally, in terms of an assessment of impact, what does it mean for Lord Atkin's dissent to be indecorously orthodox? Clearly, it has seized the imagination substantively and formally, and its substantive approach has been upheld. In the emotive wartime context, its strongly reasoned principles and normative statements combined with the force and interpretive potential of vivid language. In modern times, Lord Atkin's dissent offers a judicial illustration of "what's past is prologue"[134]—it indicates how, in the Janus-faced common law, the past is the literary, legal gateway to the present and future. However, Lord Atkin's dissent continues to be read as including indecorous language. Judicial views on this issue of decorum have evident and significant weight; they particularly illustrate institutional norms and perceptions. Equally, Lord Atkin considered that his language only targeted the majority's collective method of construction, not their

---

[129] Kiefel, "Decorum of Dissent," 3, 5, 10.

[130] Kiefel, "Decorum of Dissent," 6–7, 10. Chief Justice Kiefel refers to Justice Isaacs's use in 1930 of *The Taming of the Shrew*.

[131] Kiefel, "Decorum of Dissent," 4; Applegarth, "Lord Atkin," 746. Contrast Bingham, "Mr Perlzweig," 216.

[132] Kiefel, "Decorum of Dissent," 10.

[133] Lewis, *Lord Atkin*, 140.

[134] William Shakespeare, *The Tempest*, Act II Scene 1.

personal capacities. The forthrightness of Lord Atkin's prose can be explained by the wartime context, his clear views on construction, and the deep liberties at stake. Moreover, the institution of dissent is itself a testament to freedom of conscience and expression; in promoting public confidence in judicial integrity, dissent is a "quality control and safety valve", and a "powerful tool of external accountability".[135] Evidently, decorum is an interpretive space in the discursive regime of common law dissent. Vivid prose, with its allusive interpretability, risks being perceived as indecorous; its intended delivery and meaning may diverge from its received meaning. But vivid prose can contribute to reasoning's strength or impact—Lord Atkin's aim was to safeguard the subject's liberties.

## Epilogue

Lord Atkin's celebrated dissent continues to be influential—it is now the principal reason for reading *Liversidge v Anderson*.[136] As a "dissent vindicated by history",[137] its form and style combine with its substance to offer a compelling reference point in the legal imagination for the impact of law's history. In point of substance, Lord Atkin's dissent has been central to the modern-day construction of "reasonable cause to believe" discretions. However, in point of form, Lord Atkin's language in three contentious references has spurred differing views as to its decorum. Extra-judicial views have addressed the decorum of the one reference of Lord Atkin's dissent that remains a live issue in twenty-first-century Australia—the reference to Humpty Dumpty's meaning. This chapter endorses both the substantive orthodoxy of Lord Atkin's dissent and decorum's unquestionable value. Equally, the view is offered, subject to caveats, that suppressing diverse judicial voices would itself be indecorous in subverting the critical functions of common law dissent and the rule of law. An imperative guiding Lord Atkin's dissent was the common concern with law's "correct and coherent development"[138]—his dissent has had a central role in this development. Despite the continued views of its indecorum, the impact of the reasoning and rhetoric of Lord Atkin's dissent is signalled by its status as a historical reference point in the Anglo-Australian legal imagination.

[135] McIntyre, "Defence of Judicial Dissent," 440, 445.
[136] Simpson, "Rhetoric, Reality," 151.
[137] Applegarth, "Lord Atkin," 712.
[138] Kiefel, "Academy and the Courts," 448.

## REFERENCES

1. Alder, John. "Dissents in Courts of Last Resort: Tragic Choices?" *Oxford Journal of Legal Studies* (2000) no. 20, 221.
2. Allen, Carleton Kemp. "Regulation 18B and Reasonable Cause" *Law Quarterly Review* (1942) no. 58, 232.
3. Ames, Jonathan "Scott Wright's Play Depicts a Clampdown on Liberty" *The Times* (9 July 2015).
4. Applegarth, Peter. "Lord Atkin: Principle and Progress" *Australian Law Journal* (2016) no. 90, 711.
5. Applegarth, Peter. "Robert Atkin: Founding Father of Social Justice" (*Australian*, 22 January 2016).
6. Bingham, Tom. "Mr Perlzweig, Mr Liversidge, and Lord Atkin" in *The Business of Judging: Selected Essays and Speeches*. Oxford University Press, 2000.
7. Bingham, Tom. "The Case of *Liversidge v Anderson*: The Rule of Law Amid the Clash of Arms" *The International Lawyer* (2009) no. 43, 33.
8. Bingham, Tom. *Lives of the Law: Selected Essays and Speeches: 2000–2010*. Oxford University Press, 2011.
9. Carney, Gerard. "Lord Atkin: his Queensland Origins and Legacy." In *Supreme Court History Program Yearbook 2005*. Supreme Court Library of Queensland, 2005, 54.
10. Dyzenhaus, David. "Intimations of Legality Amid the Clash of Arms" *International Journal of Constitutional Law* (2004) no. 2, 244.
11. Ginsburg, Ruth Bader. 'The Role of Dissenting Opinions' *Minnesota Law Review* (2010) no. 95, 1.
12. Harvard Law Review. "From Consensus to Collegiality: The Origins of the 'Respectful' Dissent" *Harvard Law Review* (2011) no. 124, 1.
13. Heuston, RFV. "*Liversidge v Anderson* in Retrospect" *Law Quarterly Review* (1970) no. 86, 33.
14. Keeton, GW. "*Liversidge v Anderson*" *Modern Law Review* (1942) no. 5, 162.
15. Kiefel, Susan. "Judicial Courage and the Decorum of Dissent", Selden Society Lecture, Supreme Court of Queensland (28 November 2017).
16. Kiefel, Susan. "The Academy and the Courts; What Do They Mean to Each Other Today?" *Melbourne University Law Review* (2020) no. 44, 447.
17. Kirby, Michael. "Literature in Australian Judicial Reasoning" *Australian Law Journal* (2000) no. 75, 602.
18. Kirby, Michael. "On the Writing of Judgments" *Australian Law Journal* (1990) no. 64, 691.
19. Lee, HP. "Of Lions and Squeaking Mice in Anxious Times" *Monash University Law Review* (2016) no. 42, 1.
20. Lewis Carroll, *Through the Looking Glass*, Chapter VI.
21. Lewis, Geoffrey. *Lord Atkin*. Hart Publishing, 1999.

48 K. SCHULTZ

22. Lynch, Andrew. "Dissent: The Rewards and Risks of Judicial Disagreement in the High Court of Australia" *Melbourne University Law Review* (2003) no. 27, 724.
23. Lynch, Andrew. "Introduction – What Makes a Dissent 'Great'?" In *Great Australian Dissents*. Edited by Andrew Lynch. Cambridge University Press, 2016.
24. Manderson, Desmond. "Literature in Law – Judicial Method, Epistemology, Strategy, and Doctrine" *University of New South Wales Law Journal* (2015) no. 38, 1300.
25. McIntyre, Joe. "In Defence of Judicial Dissent" *Adelaide Law Review* (2016) no. 37, 431.
26. McLean, Janet. "Ideologies in Law Time: The Oxford History of the Laws of England" *Law & Social Inquiry* (2013) no. 38, 746.
27. Murphy, Julian R. "Unreviewable Police Powers? The Reliance on Past Policing Experience in *Prior v Mole*" *Indigenous Law Bulletin* (2017) no. 8, 18.
28. Sedley, Stephen. "When Judges Sleep" *London Review of Books* (10 June 1993).
29. Shakespeare, William. *The Tempest*, Act II Scene 1.
30. Simpson, AW Brian. "Rhetoric, Reality, and Regulation 18B" *Denning Law Journal* (1988) no. 3, 123.
31. Simpson, AW Brian. *In the Highest Degree Odious: Detention Without Trial in Wartime Britain*. Oxford University Press, 1994.
32. Supreme Court Library of Queensland, "Lord Atkin: from Queensland to the House of Lords" Exhibition, Supreme Court Library of Queensland, Brisbane (28 November 2017 to present). (https://legalheritage.sclqld.org.au/exhibitions/lordatkin).
33. van Rijswijk, Honni. "Neighbourly Injuries: Proximity in Tort Law and Virginia Woolf's Theory of Suffering" *Feminist Legal Studies* (2012) no. 20, 39.
34. Wright, Scott. *Regulation 18B – No Free Man* (2015) (http://www.regulation18b.com/).

Cases

1. *Darnel* (1627) 3 *How St Tr* 1.
2. *Donoghue v Stevenson* [1932] AC 562.
3. *George v Rockett* (1990) 170 CLR 104.
4. *Khera v Secretary of State for the Home Department* [1984] AC 74.
5. *Liversidge v Anderson* [1942] AC 206.
6. *Nakkuda Ali v Jayaratne* [1951] AC 66.
7. *Prior v Mole* (2017) 261 CLR 265.
8. *R v IRC; ex parteRossminster* [1980] AC 952.
9. *Ridge v Baldwin* [1964] AC 40.

CHAPTER 4

# The Challenges to the UK Constitution Since 1979 and Brexit

*Michael Mulligan*

## INTRODUCTION

In his Richard Dimbleby address of 1976 the former, and latter, Lord Chancellor Lord Hailsham referred to the possibility of 'elective dictatorship' inherent in the parliamentary sovereignty which is the cornerstone of the unwritten British Constitution.[1] Over forty years later, in October 2019, this precept of parliamentary sovereignty was assailed on many fronts; by the government of the day that had prorogued parliament, by the UK Supreme Court rulings on political matters such as that

---

[1] Quintin Hogg, 'Elective dictatorship,' Lecture, *The Listener*, BBC, 21 October 1976. Ironically, Mr Hogg was notably quiet on the issue of elective dictatorships when he was Lord Chancellor in the Conservative Party government from 1979 to 1987. Under the leadership of Margaret Thatcher, the Conservatives won resounding parliamentary majorities in the 1983 and 1987 elections.

---

M. Mulligan (✉)
University of London, London, UK
e-mail: mm881@soas.ac.uk

© The Author(s), under exclusive license to Springer Nature Switzerland AG 2022
S. McKibbin et al. (eds.), *The Impact of Law's History*, Palgrave Modern Legal History,
https://doi.org/10.1007/978-3-030-90068-7_4

proroguing, and by the withdrawal from the European Union and the strictures of the European Court of Human Rights.

Lord Hailsham's claim of elective dictatorship came at a time when the political consensus was predicated on a Keynesian economic model that had been followed by successive governments after 1945.[2] Ironically, there were already winds of change blowing that promised to bring challenges to that consensus. Britain's joining the European Economic Community in January 1973 had profound ramifications for the legal, constitutional, and economic future of the UK. As early as 1974 Lord Denning, the Master of the Rolls, had referred to European law 'flowing swimmingly through the rivers and estuaries of England' imbued with a primacy over English law passed in the Parliament.[3] In 1976, the humiliation of the British government taking a loan from the International Monetary Fund forced an economic re-evaluation which sowed the seeds for the monetarist revolution that was to take place under Margaret Thatcher. But even to a conservative and unionist such as Lord Hailsham, subsequent events would be of real concern. Today, Scotland has a devolved government intent on achieving full independence; courts have been accused of adopting a political agenda, and the country is arguably a more divided society than at any time since the nineteenth century.

The central argument of this chapter is that the change from a political to a legal discourse has coincided with, and has been influenced by, the constitutional changes that have occurred since 1979. In the absence of substantive discussion of economic and social choices, there has been a reliance on the invocation of slogans such as the need to 'take back sovereignty' or the goal of 'levelling up' without any true debate about what these terms are meant to achieve and, more importantly, how.

The issue of Brexit and how it has played out over the last five years has highlighted many of the constitutional anomalies which exist in the case of the UK having an 'unwritten' constitution.[4] The purpose of this chapter is

---

[2] The economic policies over governments between 1945 and 1979 were often said to be 'Butskellite' in their nature. The term was derived from the successive Labour and Conservative Chancellors of the Exchequer from 1950 to 1955, Hugh Gaitskell and Rab Butler. At the heart of the policy was a belief in government intervention in the economy to maintain full employment by means of demand management with the government acting as a conduit between employers and the trade unions

[3] *Bulmer v Bollinger*, 1 Ch 401, [1974] 3 WLR 202, [1974] 2 All ER 1226.

[4] The 'unwritten' constitution moniker is misleading as in effect there are several constituent parts to the UK constitution, namely, the *Bill of Rights 1688*, the *Acts of Union* of 1707,

4 THE CHALLENGES TO THE UK CONSTITUTION SINCE 1979 AND BREXIT   51

to demonstrate how some of the problematic aspects encountered since 2016 first emerged after 1979. Among the issues discussed here are the constitutional reforms enacted by the Blair government, the decline of Cabinet government, and the changing nature of the relationship between the executive, legislature, and judiciary in the UK. Some of the key examples discussed in the chapter will be devolution of Scotland, and Wales, the incorporation of the European Convention on Human Rights, and the decision to go to war in Iraq in 2003. The malaise is also evident in a fragmentation of political identity that had traditionally been associated with the main political parties in the UK. The decline in political participation and the employment of referenda (in the case of Scottish independence and Brexit) has led, according to Lord Sumption, to majority-based democracy exacerbating the 'fissiparous' nature of democracy.[5]

## THE BRITISH CONSTITUTION AND THE SOVEREIGNTY OF PARLIAMENT

At the heart of any debate about the challenges faced by the British constitution is the notion that Parliament is sovereign in that it can enact and repeal any laws it sees fit do to do so. The doctrine of parliamentary sovereignty attributes to Parliament a law-making power which is legally unlimited. In accordance with A.V. Dicey's famous two principles, the House of Commons, House of Lords, and the Queen can together 'make or unmake any law whatever', and no court or any other body can override the legislation which is produced.[6] In purely descriptive terms, the 'doctrine of parliamentary sovereignty is a principle which facilitates politics through law'.[7] Without a written constitution and a clear separation of powers, a simplified view of how Britain was governed would be that the parliament made laws, the executive ensured those laws were enforced, and the judiciary resolved disputes about the meaning and application of those laws. In reality, the situation was more complex. As a consequence of the residuary powers vested in the Crown by virtue of the Royal

*Magna Carta*, the *Human Rights Act 1998*, and the now repealed *European Communities Act 1972*.

[5] Jonathan Sumption, 'In Praise of Politics,' Lecture, *The Reith Lectures*, BBC, 1 June 2019.

[6] A.V. Dicey, *Introduction to the Study of the Law of the Constitution* (8th ed.; London: Macmillan, 1915) 37–38.

[7] Michael Gordon, 'Parliamentary Sovereignty and the Political Constitution(s): From Griffith to Brexit', *King's Law Journal* 30, no. 1 (2019): 133.

Prerogative, the executive had a large degree of discretion in respect of certain areas such as foreign affairs. Though the judiciary's role was seemingly to apply the laws passed by parliament in the context of particular disputes, there was in fact a consistent body of judge-made law—common law—that was a well-established aspect of British constitutional history.

What has laid bare certain problematic aspects of the constitutional arrangement has been the sense that a more penetrating light has been shone on some of the contradictions that were inherent in perpetuating the notion of parliamentary sovereignty at a time when the axiom was less secure than perhaps once thought. From the 1940s onwards, there had been a slow but seemingly inevitable expansion of judicial review by English courts of the exercise of governmental powers at national and local levels (powers often based on Acts of Parliament).[8] The limitation on the exercise of executive action placed by the court in *Entick v Carrington* had gradually been extended to actions of government that are identified as irrational.[9] Through the European law of the Court of Justice (ECJ) and the European Convention on Human Rights (ECHR), there was an incursion of European laws into the English legal system. Nevertheless, because of the foundation stone of parliamentary sovereignty, British governments had an extremely deep and wide-ranging law-making capacity. Compared to the limitations on legislative power (and legislative oversight of executive power) built into the US Constitution, British executive power was considerable.

## The Thatcher Government

The Conservative government of Margaret Thatcher from 1979 to 1990, as with Ronald Reagan's administration from 1981 to 1989 in the US, overturned the post-Second World War economic consensus. In doing so they embedded the ideals of free market economics as the dominant

---

[8] A great contribution was made to the development of British administrative law by Lord Greene in the cases *Carltona Ltd v Minister of Works* [1943] 2 All ER 560 (CA) and *Associated Provincial Picture Houses Ltd. v. Wednesbury Corp* [1948] 1 KB 223.

[9] *Entick v Carrington* (1765) EWHC KB J98. The subject of judicial scrutiny of executive action has recently been subject to much criticism from members of the government of Boris Johnson. The much heralded analysis of judicial review, the so-called Faulks Review, nevertheless steered clear of any call to curtail existing recourse to judicial review in its current form. Frances Gibb, 'Lord Faulks interview: Has judicial review gone too far?', *The Times,* 10 September 2020.

discourse in the UK and US, a consensus which remains despite the problems that became apparent in the 2007 economic crisis and its aftermath.

Under the vagaries of the British 'first past the post' electoral system, the landslide victory of the Conservative government of 397 seats in the 1983 election was based on just 42.9% of the overall votes cast. In contrast, the defeated Labour Party and Social Democratic Party-Liberal Alliance garnered 53% of votes but together won only 232 seats. The Thatcher government continued and accelerated certain centralising tendencies of successive British governments. Under Mrs Thatcher local government was often perceived, rightly so, as troublesome centres of political opposition to the government. The highest profile case was that of the Greater London Council (GLC). The GLC was eventually abolished in 1985, but it had already had its wings clipped in the controversial case *Bromley London Borough Council v Greater London Council.*[10] There, the House of Lords stated that a levy imposed on transport in Bromley to subsidise fares in poorer parts of London was illegal.

*Bromley* is best understood in the context of the control of tax raising powers. In the 1980s, the Conservative government followed a policy of curtailing the ability of local government to raise local taxes; with this curtailment came less ability to exercise powers over other areas of government. Instead, decision making in a wide range of areas was increasingly brought into the domain of central government, from planning applications to education (with the advent of the national curriculum) to policing. The issue of tax would be Margaret Thatcher's undoing as the attempt to impose a new form of local tax, the community charge or poll tax, was rejected first in Scotland then the rest of the UK. The backlash against the tax arguably led to her removal as prime minister. Nevertheless, its replacement, the Council tax, was itself problematic. It was subject to capping and, as of 2021, had not been adjusted to reflect house price inflation since 1991. This meant that the taxes imposed on some of the most expensive real estate in Europe were derisory when compared to taxes on incomes.[11] The consequence of this were two-fold: (1) local government was deprived of a lever for exercising autonomy over local political developments; and (2) decision making and regional economic inequalities were exacerbated.

[10] [1982] 1 All ER 129.

[11] John Ferguson & Jennifer Hyland, 'Super-rich London homeowners pay less Council Tax than hard-working Scots families', *Daily Record*, 23 February 2020

## The Blair Government

The Labour government which was elected in a landslide after 1997 therefore faced a dilemma. It was not willing to challenge the essential economic principles of the previous Conservative government but looked to constitutional innovation to give substance to its reforming agenda. There were several threads which it would weave to create the web of problems faced by later governments—problems that mirrored issues arising under the Thatcher government. Indeed, in many ways the Blair government was a continuation of Thatcherism. As Vernon Bogdanor notes:

> The 1997 general election was a triumph not only for Tony Blair but also for Margaret Thatcher. It was her final triumph in that it enshrined that Thatcherism would survive a change of government. Indeed, Labour was seen as safe to entrust with power only after it had fully accepted the broad outlines of Thatcherism.[12]

Faced with a seemingly settled economic consensus inherited from the Thatcher and Major administrations, the Blair government looked to constitutional adjustment to justify its 'reforming agenda'. As Bogdanor elaborates:

> One consequence of New Labour's acceptance of the Thatcherite dispensation was the growth of a new consensus on social and economic policy. The main differences between the parties in the 1997 general election lay not in their answer to the question 'how should the economy be managed?' but in their answer to a quite different question--did the British constitution need radical reform?[13]

These reforms included devolution for Scotland (and to a lesser extent, Wales) and the Good Friday peace process in Northern Ireland which necessarily allowed a greater degree of involvement in its affairs by the Republic of Ireland. The devolution of Scotland has had several foreseen, at least by certain of its opponents, consequences, and some unseen. It has not negated the move towards full independence. Yet, it is also clear that Scotland and Wales have both acquired an acuter sense of the damage

---

[12] Vernon Bogdanor 'Labour and the Constitution; Part I: The Record' in *New Labour in Power: Precedents and Prospects*, ed. Tim Bale & Brian Brivati (Taylor & Francis, 1998), 111.

[13] Ibid.

wrought by an inequality born out of changes to the UK economy since 1979. However, whilst Scotland has continued to see membership of the European Union as vital to its future independence and economic model, Wales still has a considerable pro-Brexit majority. In Northern Ireland a majority vote to remain part of the European Union has been overridden with the result that Irish unity looks a more likely prospect in the next 20 years than at any time in the last 100 years since the partition of Ireland in 1921.

In the English regions a certain degree of devolution was heralded by the introduction of city mayors, first in London with Ken Livingstone in 2000 and after in other cities. These positions have increasingly attracted high-profile candidates such as Andy Burnham in Manchester and Andy Street in Birmingham. However, the extent of their powers, and their autonomy from central government, is constrained by the limitation on their ability to levy taxes and their lack of input into decision making in cases such as the high-speed train link known as High Speed Two (HS2).

Another significant reform was made in respect of the Palace of Westminster and the second chamber of parliament, the House of Lords. As Bogdanor has observed:

> The House of Lords Act of 1999 has removed all but 92 of the hereditary peers from the House of Lords, as the first phase of a wider reform of that body. The *Constitutional Reform Act* of 2005 has restructured the historic office of Lord Chancellor, establishing a new Supreme Court and removing its judges from the House of Lords. The head of the judiciary will now be the Lord Chief Justice, not the Lord Chancellor, and the Lord Chancellor will no longer be the Speaker of the House of Lords. Instead, the House of Lords chooses its own Lord Speaker. All this goes toward creating a system of separation of powers in Britain.[14]

What the Labour government saw as part of the problem was that the UK constitution was underpinned as much by conventions as by separation of powers. The situation worked because the actors involved understood the extent of the powers vested in, but also the limitations, of their offices.[15] For example, for over 100 years the role of Lord Chancellor had

---

[14] Vernon Bogdanor, 'The Historic Legacy of Tony Blair', *Current History*, March 2007, 101.

[15] As the British lawyer Cyril Radcliffe noted: 'Constitutional forms and legal systems are very well in their way, but they are the costumes for the men who wear them'. Lord Radcliffe, *The Problem of Power* (London: Collins, 1958), 33.

bewildered constitutional experts, insofar as the individual was simultaneously a member of the Cabinet (part of the executive), head of the judiciary, and presiding officer of the House of Lords, the second chamber of the legislature! Despite this apparent breach of the principle of separation of powers, the position had worked, with there being several notable examples of the office being held by leading legal and *political* figures (such as Lord Gardiner, Lord Mackay, and Lord Hailsham) who understood the fundamentally nuanced interpretation of the post required by the appointee. The position of Lord Chancellor was downgraded when in 2003 the Labour government made clear its objective to establish a supreme court so as to remedy the apparent constitutional anachronism of the highest court in the UK being the Judicial Committee of the House of Lords, the second legislative chamber.

Nevertheless, the separation of powers remained an important issue especially considering the increasingly 'presidential' nature of the office of prime minister. The role of the prime minister only really came into being in the early twentieth century. Though the position of First Lord of the Treasury and the primary minister of the Crown had existed since Robert Walpole assumed the office in 1721, the prime minister was by convention primus inter pares of the various ministers who constituted the cabinet, the executive that ran the government which the First Lord of the Treasury chaired. In his *Law of the Constitution* written in 1885, A.V. Dicey set himself the task of establishing the principle behind the practice of government. His first principle was the sovereignty of parliament, his second, the rule of law, and third, the force of convention, where he showed how the personal will of the monarch had gradually transformed into parliamentary prerogatives carried out by ministers, called 'conventions'. Dicey noted that 'The important point is that these conventions ran counter to the rule of law: [The rule of law] means, in the first place, the absolute supremacy or predominance of regular law as to the influence of arbitrary power, and excludes the existence of arbitrariness, of prerogative or even of wider discretionary authority on the part of government.'[16] By the late nineteenth century Dicey conceded that in practice, these powers were 'exercised by a Cabinet who are really servants, not of the Crown, but of a representative chamber which in its turn obeys the behests of the electors'.[17]

---

[16] Dicey, *An Introduction*, 202.
[17] Dicey, *An Introduction*, 312.

By the late twentieth century prime ministers such as Thatcher and then Blair were increasingly side-lining cabinet in favour of bilateral relations with individual ministers according to particular circumstances. The apotheosis of this arrangement, or the nadir, came with the decision to go war in Iraq in 2003. The decision was largely taken, according to accounts in the numerous inquiries, by Blair in conjunction with a small number of advisers and selected ministers, and then presented to the cabinet as essentially a fait d'accompli (especially since troops were being activated by the selected ministers after having first provided assurance to their commanders on the ground that the action was in adherence with international law). The decision to wage war based on a dubious legal and factual basis was made despite opposition from within the country, opposition which of course grew after the reasons given for going to war were shown to be falsehoods. The war in Iraq also highlighted the considerable powers that remained as part of the Royal prerogative. Though the prime minister took the decision to go to war to a vote in the House of Commons, largely to substantiate the legitimacy of his decision, the prerogative power of the Crown meant that he did not need to do so.

The Iraq war and subsequent MPs' expenses scandals signify a certain break down of the constitutional model that had underpinned the British constitution.[18] Under the convention of responsible government, ministers were to be responsible for the policies that were implemented by civil servants and there was to be a clear line of accountability. However, under Tony Blair, and his successors, ministerial responsibility was tested to destruction with civil servants often being held responsible for failures in the application of government policy.[19] Certain influential observers have therefore looked to constitutional reform to provide a more systematic system of checks and balances.[20] This call is somewhat undermined by the

---

[18] That is not to say that these conventions have not broken down in the past. There is, for instance, the example of the Suez Crisis. However, that led to the resignation of Prime Minister Anthony Eden and considerable reflection on Britain's place in the world.

[19] This has been evident in the recent resignation of the Cabinet Secretary Mark Sedwill and the somewhat bizarre scene of the Home Office being subject to allegations about institutionalised bullying.

[20] According to Philip (now Lord) Sales, 'it might assist the rational development of the law for separation-of-powers-type analysis to be brought more to the forefront of the reasoning of the courts, so that the competing interests and policy considerations are balanced more explicitly and within a coherent intellectual framework'. Philip Sales 'Act of State and the Separation of Powers' *Judicial Review* 11, no. 1 (2006): 97.

fear that changes to the constitutional balance may have the effect of tugging at the delicate fabric of the constitution without a realisation of how interwoven and mutually dependent each individual thread is.

The already complex and subtle intricacies of the British constitution were further complicated by the incorporation of the European Convention on Human Rights into English law. This Act placed a further degree of emphasis on the sovereignty of parliament at the heart of the UK constitution and the laws that stemmed from it. With the growth of judicial review of the legality of governmental actions since the 1960s it was apparent that the doctrine of the sovereignty of parliament would be contradicted by the propagation of natural rights enshrined in the European Convention on Human Rights.[21]

## THE EUROPEAN CONVENTION ON HUMAN RIGHTS

The locus of debate about the relationship between the executive and judiciary has largely been focused on the influence of the European Convention on Human Rights (ECHR). The ECHR has often been conflated with the EU though it is a separate commitment and the signatories to the ECHR include states that are outside the EU. Of course, it is often repeated that one of the principal drafters of the convention was the British lawyer David Maxwell-Fyfe, who was Attorney General, Home Secretary, and Lord Chancellor in Conservative governments between 1945 and 1962. With its origins in the aftermath of the Second World War, the ECHR does share some of the same characteristics and intent as the EU. It is the product of one of Europe's darkest hours when law was contorted and promulgated in a manner which underpinned and facilitated the policies of the Nazi regime in Germany and beyond. At the ECHR's very core is the notion of certain unassailable human rights. The convention was incorporated into British law through the *Human Rights Act 1998*. The consequences of incorporation of this act in English law have led to criticism from certain quarters, most notably former justice of the Supreme Court, Lord Sumption. Lord Sumption has asserted that the Act, particularly Article 8 of the European Convention of Human Rights dealing with protection of privacy and family, has brought issues that have traditionally

---

[21] As early as the case of *Ridge v Baldwin* (1965) AC 40, Lord Evershed had pointed to the notion that the invocation of a claim to natural rights or justice could be a means of trumping parliamentary sovereignty.

been within the domain of the legislature into that of the judiciary.[22] Lord Sumption's criticism mirror, to a certain extent, the same criticisms made by Justice Antonin Scalia of the US Supreme Court that in effect, the courts are intruding into areas of that are essentially questions which should be addressed by political debate and legislation.[23]

If one were to compare the resort to judicial interpretation of legal and moral issues with previous *political* debates about these issues, then the Labour government of 1964–1970 is informative. At the direction of Roy Jenkins, the Home Secretary from 1965 to 1967, that government introduced legislation that notably liberalised British law in respect of individual rights, abolished the death penalty, and curtailed censorship. Whether or not later governments, or indeed the general population, agreed with these developments, they did not seek to repeal them.

## IMMIGRATION

The issue of immigration was one of the most contentious issues during the years of the Labour government after 1997. The largest influx of migrants came from Eastern Europe after the accession of Poland, Czech Republic, and Hungary in 2004. There was very little debate about this level of migration in the UK and the debate was framed by certain assumptions. Firstly, that this was a necessary acceptance of EU rules on freedom of movement. Secondly, that debates about immigration were tinged with the issue of racism. In fact, both assumptions were incorrect. Both France and Germany had introduced transitory arrangements for the influx of migrant workers. In the latter case the main driver of immigration was the demand for immigrant labour from indigenous British businesses.

The issue of immigration has flittered in and out of political discourse and debate in the UK for over fifty years (at least since the *Commonwealth Immigration Act 1968*). However, a strong argument was made by politicians on all sides of the political spectrum[24] that immigration was necessary to fill job vacancies where there was little appetite for the work involved. Additionally, a necessary consequence of the notion of *Pax*

---

[22] Jonathan Sumption, *Trials of the State: Law and the Decline of Politics* (London: Profile Books, 2019).

[23] Justice Scalia ventured that the legality of issues such as abortion and the death penalty were not ones that should be determined by reference to their constitutionality per se, but rather political questions to be determined by the *body politic* at a particular time.

[24] With exceptions such as Enoch Powell who were outside the political mainstream.

*Britannica* was that citizens of the British Empire were citizens of Britain. Humanitarian justifications were also invoked at times; many Ugandans of Asian descent arrived in the UK after they expelled from their homes by Idi Amin in 1972. The fair mindedness of the vast majority of the British people in the past has been demonstrated by these examples which make the lack of discussion over the post-2004 migration even more marked.

## BREXIT AND THE 2019 ELECTION

The result of the 2016 Brexit referendum was a victory for the 'Vote Leave' campaign. This campaign was underpinned by a strong call for a reclamation of British sovereignty seemingly lost to the EU.[25] What followed was a puzzling interregnum in which the tugging of the threads of the British constitution laid bare the contradictory conventions at the heart of British sovereignty, and the fundamental assumptions that such sovereignty resides with Parliament. An early that arose in the aftermath of the Brexit referendum was whether the UK required an Act of Parliament to be passed for the UK to withdraw from the EU or whether this could be done by the government merely stating it would withdraw. The subsequent case of *Miller* confirmed that a parliamentary vote was required.[26]

The attempted proroguing of the parliament by the government of Boris Johnson was another one of these contradictions. In this second *Miller* case, the Supreme Court availed itself of the opportunity to examine the extent of the prerogative powers in respect of the executive suspending Parliament for political reasons.[27] Though the court found there was no authority to do so, the repercussions were rendered null by the subsequent parliamentary election in December 2019 that handed the incumbent Conservative government, which had undertaken the prorogation, a healthy eighty-seat majority.

Yet, the nature of the referendum that had first instigated this course of action was itself an anomalistic incident in British political history. It was a

[25] As Guglielmo Verdirame points out, the notion that the sovereign would remain inert while sovereign powers were relocated was shattered with the UK's June 2016 referendum on EU membership. The Leave campaign's slogan 'Take Back Control' captured the classical conception of sovereignty as authority and will. Guglielmo Verdirame 'Sovereignty' in *Concepts for International Law: Contributions to Disciplinary Thought*, ed. Jean D'Aspremont and Sahib Singh (Cheltenham, UK: Edward Elgar, 2019), 835.

[26] *R (Miller) v Secretary of State for Exiting the European Union* [2017] UKSC 5.

[27] *R (Miller) v Prime Minister* [2019] UKSC 41.

# 4 THE CHALLENGES TO THE UK CONSTITUTION SINCE 1979 AND BREXIT 61

legalistic, binary answer to a non-binary political question—that is, to what extent should Britain be part of the EU and bound by EU law? This question was made more complicated by the conflating of issues of EU law with those concerned with Britain's obligations under the European Convention of Human Rights, most notably in the sphere of criminal law. Brexit therefore was subject to different interpretations; did it mean Britain remaining part of the European Single Market? Did it mean a total break from Europe?

At the same time, in order to guarantee that European institutions would be able to work after the eastern enlargement in 2004 (when ten new countries joined the fifteen existing member states), many areas of decision making were shifted from unanimity to qualified majority voting. That essentially meant that individual countries lost their veto power over decisions in the EU. While this was a necessary step to avoid a complete institutional deadlock, it nevertheless signified a major shift of sovereignty from the national to the European level.

This outmoded conception is exacerbated by the highly centralised nature of the UK. Britain is one of only a few countries in Europe in which the political, financial, and cultural centres of the country coincide in the capital city. This has led British citizens to mistake the effect of national centralisation for one of European centralisation. Decisions were not taken locally, but not because of the EU, but because of Westminster.[28] The decision over Brexit can therefore be seen in a wider context—people who had been deprived of a voice in decision making over economic, planning, and social questions were allowed a say over the future of the UK's relationship and, having been told for forty years that the reason for the deprivation of their input was the EU, chose to reject continuing membership of that institution.

---

[28] The predominance of London, and in particular the City of London to the British economy, is symptomatic of this centralisation, as are decision making processes. For instance, the presumption in favour of land development for business use. For example, the *Planning and Compulsory Purchase Act 2004* was described by Simon Jenkins as part of 'the most centralised planning regime in the free world'. Simon Jenkins, 'This is an open invitation to developers to try their luck', *The Guardian* (6 December 2006).

## CONCLUSION

The decision to leave the European Union in 2016 and subsequent victory for Boris Johnson's government in the 'Get Brexit Done' election of December 2019 seem to have settled certain issues. The re-election of the Conservative government lent a sheen of legitimacy to its actions. However, even then the most difficult issues were left to be resolved at a later date with the COVID-19 pandemic interregnum further postponing progress on such matters as the border between Northern Ireland and the Irish Republic. Johnson's success was based on winning over northern 'red wall' seats previously loyal to Labour that had most voraciously voted for leave. It was these voters who are now most keen to see how 'levelling up' will be manifested, most notably in the redistribution of economic opportunity from the prosperous south to the poorer north. The lack of debate over political and economic questions, leaving such issues as planning laws and migration to be decided as legal matters, has led to a certain *lassitude*: the economic model followed by successive governments has highlighted the role of the 'market' as opposed to state intervention, but that dichotomy has been blurred by the huge level of state spending, especially on transport infrastructure projects such as Crossrail in London. Governments have also largely emphasised 'consumer welfare' at the expense of competition. The result was that the British economy has developed oligopolistic tendencies, with the favoured oligopolies receiving much political favour. In retrospect, the last two decades have been bookended by the harsh consequences of easy political choices; the bursting of a credit bubble that underpinned economic growth to 2007 and the inadequacies that resulted from a decade of economic austerity laid bare by the COVID-19 pandemic. There has also been greater emphasis on the potential for corruption as a result of this uncomfortably close nexus between government and certain business activities.

The developments in the constitution of the UK since the 1970s have led to a greater scrutiny of the conventions that have underpinned the unwritten Constitution for many centuries. Recent crises have witnessed a shift from the *political* to the *legal*. Political parties, as in the US, are increasingly not mass-member movements, but vehicles of particular, notably corporate, interests.[29] Post-Brexit it may be that the UK itself may

---

[29] In Britain, as in the US, this has led to elections becoming increasingly dependent on who has the largest war chest. It has also led to questions about who are funding political

# 4 THE CHALLENGES TO THE UK CONSTITUTION SINCE 1979 AND BREXIT 63

look very different. A second Scottish referendum and a referendum on a union between Northern Ireland (two propositions that were near unthinkable twenty years ago) are readily discussed. The recent issues of Brexit and the ruinous economic impact of the COVID-19 pandemic have highlighted the necessity of dealing with these issues head-on.[30]

The Johnson government has now focused on the 'politicisation' of the UK Supreme Court and the unfettered access to judicial review. The Conservative election manifesto in 2019 stated that the incoming Conservative government 'would "update" administrative law to ensure a "proper balance" between individual rights, national security, and effective government. The manifesto also said that the government would ensure that judicial review 'is not abused to conduct politics by another means or to create needless delays'.[31] This incursion by the executive into judicial concerns seems to ignore the argument for a separation of powers, but does reflect growing unease over the legalisation of certain political issues. The temptation to ascribe legal answers to political questions has an ignominious history.[32] Nevertheless, the usurpation of judicial considerations by the executive is equally fraught. Within a constitution that is as subtle and somewhat fragile as the UK's, the consequences of pushing too far in one direction or another could be profoundly damaging.

---

parties. In the US this has become a key issue in the debate about the nexus between law and politics. See *Citizens United v. Federal Election Commission*, 558 U.S. 310 (2010).

[30] The opaque nature of the British constitution and the relationships between the constituent parts of the UK have been laid bare by Brexit. As Raphael Behr notes in relation to the Brexit agreement signed between the UK and Europe 'To concede on the principle that any part of the UK is subject to European regulatory standards—the compromise he (Boris Johnson) signed to avoid a land border on the island of Ireland—would be to admit that a portion of sovereignty was conceded in the negotiations'. Raphael Behr, 'British politics is still drunk on Brexit spirit, and Boris Johnson won't call time', *The Guardian* (15 June 2021).

[31] Raphael Hogarth, 'Judicial Review' *Institute for Government*, last updated 9 March 2020, https://www.instituteforgovernment.org.uk/explainers/judicial-review

[32] There is, for example, the *Dred Scott* decision of the US Supreme Court. President James Buchanan purposefully allowed the Supreme Court to adjudicate on the question of slavery in the states, but despondency over the Court's decision to uphold slavery's legality precipitated the Civil War. See *Dred Scott v Sandford*, 60 U.S. (19 How.) 393 (1857).

CHAPTER 5

# The Age of Rumpole Is Past? Legal History on British Television

*Marcus K. Harmes, Meredith A. Harmes, and Barbara Harmes*

## INTRODUCTION

In 2016, members of the English bar were seen with well-thumbed copies of Sally Smith's new biography of the famous and flamboyant Edwardian barrister, Marshall Hall.[1] Although Hall died almost a century ago, Smith's biography is not the first time he's risen (figuratively) from the dead. The 1934 British drama film *The Great Defender* focused on a barrister called Sir Douglas Rolls, but was closely based on Marshall Hall, not least on his reputation as the great defender but also on other biographical and legal details such as health problems and the trial of an artist for murder. Marshall Hall also inspired the barrister character in Alfred Hitchcock's

[1] Sally Smith, *Marshall Hall: A Law unto Himself* (London: Wildy, Simmonds and Hill Publishing, 2016).

M. K. Harmes (✉) • M. A. Harmes • B. Harmes
University of Southern Queensland, Toowoomba, QLD, Australia
e-mail: Marcus.Harmes@usq.edu.au

© The Author(s), under exclusive license to Springer Nature
Switzerland AG 2022
S. McKibbin et al. (eds.), *The Impact of Law's History*, Palgrave
Modern Legal History,
https://doi.org/10.1007/978-3-030-90068-7_5

65

1947 court drama *The Paradine Case*. In 1989, his life and courtroom theatrics were brought back to life in the television series *Shadow of the Noose* which made him the central character and, occasionally, he has appeared as a character in other period dramas involving his court cases.

Why however would his life be of appeal and interest to his modern successors and what is learnt from the dramatisation of the legal past, notably the courtroom drama? Visions of legal history made in modern television are eclectic and extensive including, besides *Shadow of the Noose*, *Witness for the Prosecution* (in the 1957 film and 1982 and 2016 television adaptations of the Agatha Christie play set in the 1950s), *The Rivals of Sherlock Holmes* (broadcast 1971–1973 and set in the Victorian and Edwardian eras), *Lady Killers* (broadcast 1980–1981 set over several time periods), *Inspector Morse* (specifically the 1998 Victorian-set episode "The Wench is Dead") and *Garrow's Law* (broadcast 2009–2011 and set in the eighteenth century). Even programmes that, at the time of their production were set in the present day, now seem products of an earlier age such as *Rumpole of the Bailey* (1975, 1978–1992) and *Everyman*'s 1977 recreation of the *Gay News* blasphemous libel trial. Nostalgia can and should be critiqued, but its emergence in television, in biography and in the hands of members of the legal professional also merits interpretation. In an era when the UK Ministry of Justice is criticised by the Bar Council for "airbrushing" the barrister out of history (see below) and comprising a more general lament that the age of the characterful advocate is past, this chapter considers the range, meaning, impact and potency of a legal history of the defending barrister evoked by popular culture.

While scholarly attention has been paid to law and lawyers on British television and more often American and European television that have examined the many hundreds of film and television programmes about the law, lawyers and court cases, less specifically has been noted on legal history on the small screen, especially examining dramas set in the past.[2] Law and popular culture and law and film and television scholarship are still emergent areas, as is the field of popular legal studies, with a strong series of interpretations and theoretical perspectives appearing since the 1980s,

---

[2] See: Michael Asimow, *Lawyers in Your Living Room!: Law on Television* (American Bar Association, 2009), 209; Steve Greenfield, Guy Osborn and Peter Robson, *Film and the Law: The Cinema of Justice* (London: Hart Publishing, 2010); Peter Robson and Jennifer L Schulz, *A Transnational Study of Law and Justice on TV* (London: Hart Publishing, 2019).

but often with attention to American fictional lawyers.[3] British programmes about the law have received considerably less academic attention than American drama. Horace Rumpole, the titular and central character in *Rumpole of the Bailey* is the only fictional lawyer to have attracted a level of academic attention comparable to American counterparts including Perry Mason (from the same-titled drama series), Ben Matlock in *Matlock*, Ally McBeal (titular character of the American drama series), Arnie Becker in *L.A. Law*, Denny Crane in *Boston Legal* and Jack McCoy in *Law and Order*.[4] This chapter will focus on three drama series set in the legal past of the eighteenth century, nineteenth century and turn of the twentieth, and the twentieth century before modernisations to justice took place such as the abolition of the Assizes in 1972 and the creation in 2006 of the Ministry of Justice in place of the Lord Chancellor's Department.[5] It is notable that to date no drama writer or producer has elected to make a series about the life and career of the jurist Sir Edward Coke (1552–1634), even though Coke intersects with many high-water marks of religious and constitutional drama of the sixteenth and seventeenth centuries and is perhaps the most celebrated jurist in the history of English law. Coke did appear as a character in the Hollywood costume drama *The Private Lives of Elizabeth and Essex* in 1939 and in *The King's Bounty*, an episode of *ITV Television Playhouse* in 1957 but these are sparse appearances in the overall total of both period drama and legal drama. However other controversial historical lawyers have been the centrepiece of drama. The swashbuckling character of William Garrow, a lawyer equally as controversial as Coke, featured as the title character in *Garrow's Law*, set in and around the Old Bailey in the Georgian period. Sir Edward Marshall Hall, more glamorous than Garrow but also famous in his time, was the central character in *Shadow of the Noose*, based on Marshall Hall's criminal defence trials at the turn of the nineteenth and twentieth centuries. Both Garrow and Marshall

---

[3] Peter Robson and Jessica Sibley, "Introduction," in *Law and Justice on the Small Screen* (Hart Publishing 2012), 1; Richard K. Sherwin, "Law in Popular Culture," in *Blackwell Companion to Law and Society*, ed. Austin Sharat, 105 (Oxford: Blackwell Publishing, 2004).

[4] Ross E. Davies, "The Popular Prosecutor: Mr. District Attorney and the Television Stars of American Law", *Green Bag* 16 (2012): 63; Jason Bainbridge, "'Sexy Men in Wigs': *North Square* and the Representation of Law on British Television," *Journal of British Cinema and Television* 6, no. 1 (2009): 85.

[5] Graham Gee, Robert Hazell, Kate Malleson, and Patrick O'Brien, *The Politics of Judicial Independence in the UK's Changing Constitution* (Cambridge: Cambridge University Press, 2015), 43.

68   M. K. HARMES ET AL.

Hall, as doughty defenders with faith in the plea of "not guilty", provided aspects of the characterisation of the fictional barrister Horace Rumpole. Rumpole in general seems a somewhat tatty anachronism even in the world of the Inns of Court and the criminal bar, where time moves more slowly, and he is apt to dwell on his own legal history, including the long-ago case of the Penge Bungalow Murders. More specifically though, the first season of the *Rumpole of the Bailey* television series took place in the recent legal past, showing cases from earlier in Rumpole's career and therefore when historic aspects of the legal system were still in place, including judges who were old enough to have sentenced men to death and barristers going out on the Assizes.

## THE HISTORY OF LAW ON BRITISH TELEVISION

A trial lends itself to drama. What the legal historian John Langbein calls the "crisp" organisation of prosecution and defence, as well as the wide and often colourful array of people, the rising action leading to a verdict and possibly a conviction, are all elements of the structure and clarity of a trial that adapt to the diegesis of a television drama.[6] The law also easily evokes the past, particularly on the small screen and especially if there is a depiction of the English legal system. The dark panelled court rooms, the outmoded but enduring wigs and gowns of the judges and barristers, and the general air of fustiness that can prevail allow the law on screen to seem historic.

Among early television crime dramas, *Boyd QC* (ITV, 1956–1964) was set in the present day consistent with the period of the production, but the barristers' chambers and the panelled courtroom, plus the timeless wigs and gowns, gave the proceedings a more old-fashioned appearance.[7] Actual historical cases formed the substance of *On Trial* (ITV, 1960), bringing the legal past to life. With scripts based on available trial records, including actual speeches used as dialogue, the cases ranged widely in type and period. The late seventeenth-century trial of Spencer Cowper for murdering the Quaker woman Sarah Stout brought Stuart-era justice

[6] John Langbein, *The Origins of Adversary Criminal Trial* (Oxford: Oxford University Press, 2003), 259.

[7] Peter Robson, "Developments in Law and Popular Culture: The Case of the TV Lawyer," in *Representations of Justice*, eds. Antoine Masson and Kevin O'Connor, 81 (New York: Peter Lang, 2007).

onto the screen. Other famous historical defendants including Oscar Wilde in his 1895 trial for gross indecency and Sir Roger Casement for treason in 1916 were featured in episodes.[8] Beyond the normal civilian common law courts, military justice also appeared in the episode about the court martial and execution of Admiral John Byng in 1757. Like *Boyd QC* after it, the producer and writer aimed to achieve a documentary format. In *Boyd QC* that included having the barrister's clerk serve as a narrator, breaking the fourth wall of television and speaking about the events on screen directly to the audience.

Similarly, in *On Trial* the dramatisation of the historical events in the courtrooms was narrated for the watching television audience, the voice of the narrator breaking in on events and reinforcing for the audience the fact that they were watching a reconstruction. In addition, the Irish journalist Brian Inglis, then the editor of the *Spectator*, provided commentary. In this way, the writing, production and the fabric of drama itself served to make the past a prologue. Viewers, far from being able to be absorbed by 60 minutes of period drama, were repeatedly brought back to the present day; the technology of the television production in allowing the recording of the first-person narrative to be heard along with the expert commentary from Brian Inglis, interspersed with the drama and history, a modern intrusion into the past while explaining the historical events for the present day.

More conventional drama that did not have intrusions into the fourth wall or expert commentary breaking in on the diegesis nonetheless showcased English legal history. Anthology series including *Lady Killers* (1980–1981), about notorious female killers including Ruth Ellis and Marie Marguerite Fahmy, and *The Rivals of Sherlock Holmes*, provided ongoing spaces on television for historic scenes of courtroom activity, as did occasional programmes such as *Witness for the Prosecution* (1982). A striking use and understanding of legal history appears in the 1964 episode of *The Avengers* called *Brief for Murder*. Set in and around Lincoln's Inn and the Old Bailey, *Brief for Murder* begins disorientingly for regular viewers with main characters John Steed and Cathy Gale at odds bitterly and violently, a breakdown in their relationship that then turns fatal. In actuality, the crime fighters are investigating two elderly solicitors, the Lakin brothers, who, after many years of obscurity have suddenly begun to produce briefs for a barrister with entirely unbeatable evidence and

---

[8] *R v Casement* [1917] 1 KB 98; *Wilde v. Queensberry* (1895) and *R v Wilde* (1895).

guidance for cross-examination. As the episode progresses, it emerges that the elderly solicitors have in fact virtually weaponised legal history, using their vast knowledge of old cases, including some from the eighteenth century or earlier, to create crimes that their clients can enact and get away with because of their defence briefs. The setting evokes the past, as their chambers in Lincoln's Inn are a characteristically book-lined space and bowler-hatted lawyers walk around the precincts, but with the additional import that the weighty volumes on the shelves are not dusty and unused but contain the legal historical content giving them inspiration for modern crimes. The volumes are gleefully plundered and old cases such as a "Rex v Mascot" from 1895 and "Rex v Norrie" from the 1831 Dorset Assizes, provide methodologies for modern murder. *Brief for Murder* is an entertainingly one-off use of the legal past in the legal present on British television and the characters themselves express a sense of historical awareness, proclaiming they will, through using the past, be making legal history themselves.

The lives and actions of lawyers, especially members of the bar and judges, have long maintained a place in television production and schedules following these 1950s and 1960s productions. Even when set in the present day, in line with the date of production, many legal dramas have a recognisable identity as "heritage television".[9] The wigs and gowns are in their own distinctive way a period dress from a costume drama, and the courtrooms and barristers' and judges' chambers are created by set and production designers to appear as historic spaces. Series such as *Rumpole of the Bailey* included location shooting in the gardens and courtyards of the Inner and Middle Temple and *Garrow's Law* around Old College in Edinburgh, to evoke the Georgian Old Bailey. Judge John Deed, the central character in the eponymous television programme, is a judge in the modern period but presides from the bench in a gloomy gothic courtroom. *Kavanagh QC* was about James Kavanagh, a senior member of the criminal bar whose chambers, Riverside, were charming and old-world Georgian rooms in the Inns of Court. Television production design in fact insists on a degree of historicity in courtrooms and court infrastructure that is not matched by reality. Historically many court proceedings took place in improvised surroundings such as the great halls of castles or town

---

[9] Peter Robson, "Lawyers and the Legal System on TV: The British Experience," *International Journal of Law in Context* 2 (2007): 340.

guildhalls and many crown court and magistrates court buildings are modern not the panelled, gothic spaces created for television courtrooms.

Not only setting and design but also content could bring legal history onto the screen. Notably, the reconstruction in an episode of *Everyman* (a BBC religious affairs programme) of the *Gay News* blasphemy trial reinforced that the actual trial had been a relic of archaic blasphemy laws that were in time repealed.[10] The first blasphemy cases since 1921, *Whitehouse v Lemon* in 1977 and then *R v Lemon*, were brought by Mary Whitehouse based on the common law offence of blasphemy.[11] In the *Everyman* episode, the judge Alexander King-Hamilton, the morality campaigner Mary Whitehouse and the barristers John Mortimer, Geoffrey Robertson and John Smyth were portrayed by actors, and the script foregrounded the legal argument by the *Gay News* defence barristers that the blasphemy law was, by 1977, an archaic relic in the legal system.

While productions set in the modern day may be, *ipso facto*, heritage television because many legal trappings are so inherently historic, actual period dramas have also brought the law on screen. That has included bringing onto television screens historic aspects of the law that are now defunct, such as the more unruly trial procedures and now obsolete ranks such as the serjeants at law. Prime sources are literary adaptations of Victorian novels including Charles Dickens' *Pickwick Papers*, dramatised by the BBC in 1985 with scenes in the Court of King's Bench of two serjeants at law in a breach of promise case. Similarly, the historical sequences of a trial in "The Wench is Dead", an instalment of the *Morse* series, like Josephine Tey's *The Daughter of Time*, involved a modern but unwell detective re-examining a historic crime.

## The First Defender: *Garrow's Law*

To move from this wider survey of the legal past on television to specific instances, the earliest in terms of the legal past is the dramatisation of cases defended by William Garrow. Unlike Horace Rumpole but like Edward Marshall Hall, William Garrow was an actual person. However, unlike

---

[10] Clive Unsworth, "Blasphemy, Cultural Divergence, and Legal Relativism," *Modern Law Review* 58 (1995): 658.

[11] *Whitehouse v Lemon* [1979] 2 WLR 281; *R v Lemon* [1979] AC 617, 664; Reid Mortensen, "Blasphemy in a Secular State: A Pardonable Sin," *UNSW Law Journal* 17, no. 2 (1994): 411.

Marshall Hall, he lived long enough ago for the dramatisation of his life and court cases to be blurred between reality and drama and to be partly fictionalised. *Garrow's Law* could pick and choose aspects of his career to foreground. *Garrow's Law* (BBC, 2009–2011) recreated the Georgian court room antics of Sir William Garrow (1760–1840) in the Old Bailey. It did so selectively but began with largely true to life dramatisation of Garrow's professional origins in his humble education (not at a public school) and his professional association with the solicitor John Southouse. As the first episode of the first season begins, the young and ambitious Garrow is watching cases in the Old Bailey while aspiring to be part of the action.

The series portrays Garrow as a very Rumpole-like outsider, not only through his principled decision to defend the poor and vulnerable rather than accept briefs to prosecute, but also because of his tendency to annoy figures of authority from the aristocracy to judges and the Attorney General. Viewers of the series would therefore appreciate Garrow's courage and technical adroitness as an advocate, his innovative courtroom strategies and his humble career origins but would little guess that the real-life Garrow had before him a glittering career safely in the bosom of the establishment as a King's Counsel, member of parliament, judge, privy councillor, as well as a successful career as a prosecuting barrister not a defender. Garrow died in 1840 having had multiple honours lavished on him and many career successes, an establishment status eschewed in the television series.

These points of emphasis are understandable on the part of makers of a television drama which need to make a long and complex life conform to the demands of dramatic structure, pacing and character development. However these points of emphasis are also where the nostalgic interest lies and where Garrow, as recreated and resurrected by television, provides a meaningful prologue to the legal present. As noted, in episode one of season one, Garrow is only an observer not a participant in the trials taking place in the Old Bailey courtroom presided over by Judge Francis Buller, played by an actor on screen but who was an actual puisne judge in both the King's Bench and the Court of Common Pleas.[12] Giving a patina of historical actuality, Garrow interacts on screen with other actual historical

---

[12] Edward Foss, *The Judges of England: With Sketches of Their Lives, and Miscellaneous Notices Connected with the Courts at Westminster, from the Time of the Conquest*, Volume 8 (London: John Murray, 1864), 252.

figures including the Tory statesman Sir Arthur Hill, the barrister John Silvester and the businessman philanthropist John Julius Angerstein, most of whom are turned into antagonists for the sake of drama, therefore emphasising Garrow's crusades for justice.[13] Some of Garrow's briefs also involve crimes that actually took place, including the attacks of the "London Monster" in 1788 and the 1781 Zong Massacre on board a slaving ship, but the drama also intrudes the fictionalised Garrow into actual cases where the actual Garrow had not been involved. These include the trial of the Captain of the *Zong*, which did take place in historical actuality but which did not involve William Garrow.

The three series of *Garrow's Law* follow contours laid down by legal historian J.M. Beattie's 1991 *History Today* article "Garrow for the Defence".[14] Beattie noted Garrow's enduring fame into the nineteenth century, and through his article in this academic but popular journal sought to give new impetus to Garrow's reputation and career achievements. As the television series would later do, Beattie wove Garrow's career into the fabric of Georgian criminal justice including biased judges and untrustworthy thief takers, explaining the gradual significance of a defence barrister with a well-prepared brief and the willingness to cross-examine prosecution witnesses. Beattie also valorised Garrow for his many critics and enemies from the Prince of Wales downwards, again reinforcing the narrative emphasis in *Garrow's Law* which in each episode pitted Garrow not only against a prosecution case but also against many influential detractors seeking to influence the administration of criminal justice through covert and subtle means.

## The Great Defender: Marshall Hall

This chapter began with reference to Sally Smith's biography of Edward Marshall Hall, a barrister (appointed King's Counsel in 1898 and knighted in 1917) whose career spans the Victorian to Edwardian eras. Like the fictional Rumpole and the actual Garrow, Hall is chiefly associated with a career taking on defence not prosecution briefs including defending apparently hopeless cases. Like Rumpole and unlike Garrow, he obtained success at the bar but did not achieve a judgeship. Marshall Hall's reputation

---

[13] Allyson May, "Advocates and Truth Seeking in the Old Bailey Courtroom," *Journal of Legal History* 26 (2005): 84.

[14] John Beattie, "Garrow for the Defence," *History Today* 41, no. 2 (1991): 9.

remained high into the twentieth century. Edward Marjoribanks published his *Life of Marshall Hall* in 1929 and the criminologist Edgar Lustgarten included him among the major advocates he acclaimed in his study *Defender's Triumph* in 1951, specifically studying his defence of Robert Woods in the "Camden Town Murder".[15] Hall was judged not only the handsomest man at the bar but also one of the handsomest in England. Although no recording survives (including sadly his lost BBC performance as a serjeant at law from Charles Dickens' *The Pickwick Papers*), sources unanimously describe him as possessed of a magnificent speaking voice. On television, he has therefore been played by actors noted for commanding a resonant and even beautiful speaking voice, including Robert Stephens in *Ladykillers: Murder at the Savoy Hotel* in 1980 and Jonathan Hyde starring in *Shadow of the Noose*.

Smith concluded her own biography with some reflections on how Hall, who died in 1927, would most likely have relished the era of social media. In court, he was adept at encapsulating his line of defence in short, telling comments that could easily have translated to tweets had he lived a century later.[16]

But in suggesting that Marshall Hall may have enjoyed or at least accommodated the social media age, Smith focused on Hall's capacity to turn a whole case into one or two vivid points. Yet there were other aspects of his advocacy, aspects most relevant to bringing his life and cases onto the television screen as period drama. At the other end of the spectrum from the short and vivid, Hall could hold an audience, which for him could include jurors, the judge, the crowds in the public gallery and a massive newspaper reading public, spellbound for a lengthy period. Long speeches, extensive cross-examinations and a compelling performance made Hall the apotheosis of the era when trials, for their entire length, could command a rapt audience willing to concentrate for a lengthy period. Marshall Hall also spoke of his awareness of the importance of creating atmosphere and virtually taking on a host of different characters, now the defendant, now a member of the jury, and his performances could culminate with applause from his audience in the gallery.[17] Far from being

---

[15] Edward Marjoribanks, *Famous Trials of Marshall Hall* (London and New York: Penguin, 1950); Edgar Lustgarten, *Defender's Triumph* (London and New York: Wingate, 1951), 81–144.

[16] Smith, *Marshall Hall*, 249.

[17] Thomas Grant, *Court Number One: The Old Bailey Trials that Defined Modern Britain* (London: John Murray, 2019).

a harbinger of social media pithiness, Marshall Hall spoke rapidly but at great length, thinking nothing of delivering a three or four-hour speech. These characteristics, of speechifying, electrifying interactions between advocates, judges and witnesses, and copious amounts of speech, easily modulate to period drama. That point is especially pertinent to the BBC's *Shadow of the Noose*, the 1989 mini-series about Marshall Hall and some of his more famous cases. The programme's production context, and the style and technology defining 1980s television drama made on videotape, means the series is largely static and dialogue driven. Videotape, harder to edit than film, results in drama contingent on talk to maintain interest rather than action filmed around a location, and videotaped drama is a medium particularly suitable for the long court room scenes or the conferences in Marshall Hall's chambers that make up most of the action in each episode. These included some of his notable cases including the "Camden Town Murder", in which he defended the artist Robert Wood and the "Body in the Trunk" case, defending the prostitute, Marie Hermann. The eight episodes which comprise the series in fact dramatise a variety of cases from his career, including libel actions as well as murder, although some of his most notable cases including the "Green Bicycle" and the "Brides in the Bath" are omitted. The scripts take few liberties with the cases, faithfully re-using the actual words of the transcripts, and give due emphasis to Marshall Hall's sensational cross-examinations and closing speeches. They are also at pains to portray his humanity, including a commitment to hopeless cases.

## THE OTHER GREAT DEFENDER: RUMPOLE

Horace Rumpole is a fictional aggregate of many sources of inspiration. Permanently a junior barrister and never a silk or head of chambers, Rumpole shares Marshall Hall's and Garrow's reputation as a defender, but lacks their social and professional esteem, as progression to head of chambers, silk or even a relatively minor circuit judgeship all elude Rumpole. John Mortimer's experiences at the bar provided a range of analogues and inspirations for Rumpole and his colleagues and the down at heel barrister had a literacy ancestor in another of Mortimer's fictional lawyers, Morgenhall in *The Dock Brief*.[18] Other actual barristers fuelled Mortimer's imagination including James Burge QC and Jeremy

[18] John Kidwell, "The Dock Brief," *Legal Studies Forum* 25 (2001): 290.

Hutchinson QC, Lord Hutchinson, defender of the spy George Blake, the model Christine Keeler, and publishers of works including *Fanny Hill* and *Lady Chatterley's Lover*.[19] In *Voyage Round My Father*, dramatised on television in 1982, Mortimer had also created scenes of his father's Edwardian legal practice, a world evoked on screen by barristers in spats and scandalous divorce cases. His cases had a prominence and cachet that Rumpole's mostly did not, although Rumpole's defence in the wartime Penge Bungalow Murders was a notable case (within the fictional universe of John Mortimer's stories) and in one story (*Rumpole and the Official Secret*) Rumpole came up against the secret services and even appeared before the Lord Chief Justice, an echo of Hutchinson's cases including Blake's and the ABC Case. Related to John Mortimer's collections of short stories, Thames Television's *Rumpole of the Bailey* was in production from 1978 to 1992, but the first years were set back in time from the year of production and recounted cases from somewhat earlier in Horace Rumpole's life.

The historical setting is signalled by the features of legal history brought onto the screen. The programme's original producer, Irene Shubik, likened the appearance of the lead actor Leo McKern (once costumed in a shabby gown and disintegrating wig) to a nineteenth-century legal caricature by George Cruikshank (and sounding like Dr Johnson).[20] These resonances to the legal past are further evoked on screen. Elderly judges in pince-nez or with monocles, and old enough to be have been appointed before a compulsory retirement age and when the death penalty was still in force, are still sitting on the bench. Rumpole travels on the Assizes, which had in reality ended in 1972, before the production commenced. At times the programme reinforced the more historic features of Rumpole's setting and practice by the jarring juxtaposition of modern law with the historic. For example in the episode *Rumpole and the Fascist Beast* (1979), Rumpole defends a racist politician who has been charged under the *Race Relations Act*, presented as a modern piece of legislation intruding into Rumpole's legal universe where he appealed to timeless principles espoused by Voltaire for the freedom of speech.[21] Even more timeless are the key

---

[19] John Whitworth, "Rumpole of the Bailey, an Anarchist at Heart", *Quadrant* (2016): 93; *Guardian*, November 14, 2017.

[20] Irene Shubik, *Play for Today: The Evolution of Television Drama* (Manchester University Press, 2000), 186.

[21] *Race Relations Act 1965* (UK).

items of Rumpole's legal philosophy. Professing to be a lawyer who knows very little law, Rumpole instead builds cases based on broad and immemorial privileges, chiefly the Magna Carta of 1215, the presumption of innocence, lyrically described on several occasions as the "golden thread" running through English justice, and the rules of evidence.[22] Rumpole chides his colleagues for their ignorance of common law and the Magna Carta and finds the world of civil law uncongenial for its technicalities.[23] Adduced from these broad if rather vaguely applied legal sources is Rumpole's overarching legal philosophy to plead not guilty and to offer a robust defence of his clients.

## Barristers to the Rescue? Or Barristers Needing Rescue?

These three series bring the legal past back to life, raising the question of what points they sought to make about the past for the present, and what type of nostalgia they sought to evoke for the legal past. The critical factor for all three dramas is that there is a *barrister* hero at the heart of each. Each is a flawed hero in some way, from Garrow's impetuosity, Marshall Hall's professional arrogance and Rumpole's many minor failings and his career shortfalls, but as champions of pleading not guilty and doughty champions of their clients they stand forth distinctively against other hostile forces.

Between them, Garrow, Marshall Hall and Rumpole bring onto the screen a traditional legal configuration of defence and prosecution counsel briefed by instructing solicitors and appearing on behalf of clients. This long-standing arrangement, recognisable from many other television programmes, is one significantly not referred to or recognised in recent Ministry of Justice guidelines intended for everyday use and broad consumption which, according to critics from the bar, "airbrushed" barristers out of the descriptions it provided of how a crown court trial would proceed.[24] The Ministry of Justice itself would not be an institution familiar to Garrow, Marshall Hall and Rumpole, its 2007 creation making it a

---

[22] Paul Bergman, "Rumpole's Ethics," *Berkeley Journal of Entertainment and Sports Law* 1, no. 2 (2012): 119.

[23] In the episodes *Rumpole and the Old, Old Story* (broadcast 1987) and *Rumpole and the Bubble Reputation* (broadcast 1988).

[24] *The Times*, October 11, 2019.

recent addition to the English legal hierarchy. One critic of the Ministry of Justice guidelines, Bar Council chairman Richard Atkins QC, crucially linked the absence of barristers to history, arguing that "to effectively airbrush out of history the role of barristers in the criminal courts is incomprehensible".[25] According to the Law Society's own *Gazette*, "Barristers are mentioned just twice in the four-part guide. Solicitors are mentioned in every section of the pamphlet." The omissions from these guides in fact stand in direct challenge to the narrative emphasis in *Garrow's Law*, and the way Beattie had reconstructed his career in *History Today*, in which Garrow appeared as partly or even largely responsible for creating a space and role for the defence counsel in trial procedures. Garrow, Marshall Hall and Rumpole would also not have recognised the subsuming of the Lord Chancellor's duties and role by the Secretary of State for Justice. After comprehensively reviewing his life and career for her biography, Sally Smith QC also pinpointed other aspects of the modern bar and legal system which Marshall Hall may have found puzzling and uncongenial. One was the controversial Quality Assurance Scheme for Advocates (QASA), an accrediting process for advocates to be overseen by judges. The QASA was challenged in the Supreme Court and ultimately abandoned in 2017, and bar chair Andrew Langdon QC said on its demise: "The birth of the Quality Assurance Scheme for Advocates (QASA) was not celebrated by many and its death will be mourned by fewer". To its critics, the notion of judges assessing and accrediting advocates was inherently problematic "because it risked placing both advocates and judges in a problematic position, given their respective roles during a trial". Smith though was more succinct and direct in predicting what Marshall Hall would have thought of the idea: "One of the things Marshall Hall was famous for was being indescribably offensive to judges. So I don't think he'd think much of the idea of being assessed by judges. I think he'd treat it with contempt."[26] This antipathy to judges unites Garrow, Marshall and Rumpole, an attitude to authority concomitant with their unswerving commitment to the importance of a defence barrister. Although, as noted

[25] Jemma Slinga, "'Incomprehensible' MoJ Guides Airbrush Barristers Out, Says Bar Council," *The Law Society Gazette*, October 11, 2019, https://www.lawgazette.co.uk/news/incomprehensible-moj-guides-airbrush-barristers-out-says-bar-council/5101780.article

[26] Quoted in Catherine Baksi, "Legal Hackette Lunches with Sally Smith QC", June 20, 2016, *Legal Hackette's Brief* https://legalhackette.com/2016/06/20/legal-hackette-lunches-with-sally-smith-qc/

above, the earlier Rumpole episodes were set in the past as per the date of production, later episodes noted and disparaged changes that were proposed and which threatened the centuries of continuity in the legal profession. For example, in *Rumpole and the Summer of Discontent* (broadcast 1991), barristers, judges and clerks are all upset at threatened modernisation, including attempts to bring in judges from the ranks of solicitors and modernising practices and efficiencies in chambers. The episode speaks to a theme recurring in the series of an attachment to the legal past as a bastion against change, change which in Rumpole's view is intended to water down the importance of defence barristers and weaken the presumption of innocence.

The character and opinions of Horace Rumpole in particular surface in nostalgic and often conservative discourse. For the *Telegraph* columnist Nigel Farndale, the fictional Rumpole was a cherishable English archetype on a par with Bertie Wooster, the creation of P.G. Wodehouse and an equally nostalgic figure. According to Farndale, when Rumpole "first emerged as a comic creation in the mid-Seventies, there was a real-life Rumpole in almost every set of chambers. But you don't see many of them around today."[27] Rumpole and the values he espoused are woven into other conservative discourses. The *Daily Mail* columnist Richard Littlejohn hailed the character's inherent crustiness, refusal to move with the times and his attachment to the presumption of innocence, but also suggested that Rumpole should also put his talents to work in prosecuting "the entire political class" with "murdering Brexit". Writing at a point in 2019 when the Brexit negotiations were again stalled, Littlejohn associates the fictional character and its values with a notably right-wing political discourse.[28] Conservatism though can also be a theme that resonates with a concern that once surely established principles of justice are weakening. As noted above, while professing ignorance of the law, Rumpole spoke in powerful if somewhat vague terms of the rule of law, the presumption of innocence and the liberties enshrined in Magna Carta. These preoccupations resonate with lawyers concerned that the "golden thread" of the presumption of innocence is diluted by bail and plea bargaining. The Australian jurist Justice Terry Connolly (of the Supreme Court of the Australian Capital Territory) invoked Rumpole to articulate concerns that the burden of proof was challenged and subverted "as Parliaments around

[27] *Telegraph*, March 27, 2016.
[28] *Daily Mail*, April 12, 2019.

Australia increasingly intervene to reverse the presumption in favour of bail, or indeed to expressly provide that bail is not an option for certain offences, and as studies show an increasing tendency for increased rates of remand in custody". Against these trends, Justice Connolly found in Rumpole a conservative but constructive evocation of what ought to be a universally understood principle.[29]

The televisual adventures of Garrow, Marshall Hall and Rumpole also evoke nostalgia for a type of legal personality and performance that now seems lost. Marshall Hall may also, had he lived a century later, found his style of advocacy outmoded and the current condition of the bar dispiriting. Hall's style may also have drawn a mixed response. The Australian High Court justice Virginia Bell suggests more flamboyant oratory at the bar is not only outmoded but gives an unfair advantage to male advocates.[30] Conversely, the lawyer and columnist Marcel Berlins laments "must modern barristers be so boring", certainly a complaint that would never have applied to Marshall Hall's advocacy.[31] Berlins in fact uses Marshall Hall and his American counterpart Clarence Darrow as instances of earlier and more electrifying courtroom performers. The impact Marshall Hall had on the atmosphere of a courtroom and trial is documented in accounts of his advocacy. Sally Smith finds in Marshall Hall an early but meaningful instance of "total advocacy"; as Smith explains, that includes the barrister's self-belief that their case is winnable.[32] In Marshall Hall's case it also meant totally inhabiting the mental and emotional worlds of the jurors, the judges and the defendants and ensuring that a dramatic entrance into the courtroom signified to everyone within that he was entering, anticipating that he would pull off the impossible and win.[33] The jurist Lord Birkett noted a "tightening of the tension, an air of expectation" when a trial involved Marshall Hall or his equally famous contemporary Sir Edward Carson. John Mortimer, Rumpole's creator, knew of the impact created by a "flurry of solicitors and learned juniors" who formed the backdrop for Marshall Hall's performances. The nostalgia

[29] Terry Connolly, "Golden Thread or Tattered Fabric: Bail and the Presumption of Innocence," Paper presented to the Law Council of Australia National Access to Justice and Pro Bono Conference 2006, Melbourne, August 11–12, 2006.

[30] *Lawyers Weekly*, August 13, 2012.

[31] *Guardian*, July 13, 2009.

[32] Smith, *Marshall Hall*, 249.

[33] Andrew Watson, *Speaking in Court: Developments in Court Advocacy from the Seventeenth to the Twenty-First Century* (London: Palgrave Macmillan, 2019), 165.

inherent in the courtroom dramatics of former barristers is not only for a style of flamboyant oratory but a level of professional recognition now unthinkable. Sally Smith's biography of Marshall Hall notes the theatrical character of the trials. Writing of one of his most celebrated and macabre cases, the so-called Brides in the Bath murders, she characterises it as "a murder trial so gothic as to be almost farcical with a title which would have looked just as suitable up in lights".[34] It was certainly, as she suggests, just as entertaining as any West End production. Similarly, Lord Birkett lamented the decline in the public and professional profile of great barristers, stating "the fashionable divorce suit, the sensational libel action, the great murder trial—they are no longer the dramatic events that once occupied public attention to the exclusion of almost everything else".[35]

## An Australian Coda

With its legal system and divided profession inherited from England, Australia has produced fictional barristers on television. The character Cleaver Greene from the series *Rake* at one point sarcastically refers to a fellow barrister as "Rumpole". It is the only moment of acknowledgement in *Rake* of the British series, but John Flood notes the many parallels between the fictional barristers. Neither has achieved professional success, being stuck as junior counsel rather than taking silk, both have somewhat shambolic careers and lives, and a healthy disrespect for the pompous. Acknowledging differences as well, not only between Cleaver and Rumpole but broadly between Australian and British society, Flood nonetheless pinpoints the importance of the fictional barrister as an analogue to centuries of professional practice.[36] However, Greene is clearly modern. While in court he wears the timeless gown, wig and jabot and as a barrister is connected to centuries of professional continuities. However, on screen his life in contemporary Sydney is devoid of the historical fustiness of Rumpole's chambers and Greene's myriad personal issues are sharply contemporary, including problems with loan sharks and clubs. *Rake* brings

---

[34] Smith, *Marshall Hall*, 155. The "Brides in the Bath" case was the Old Bailey trial of George Joseph Smith in 1915.

[35] Quoted in J. H. Fazan, "The Decline of the Trial as a Public Event", *South African Law Journal* 101, no. 2 (1984): 365, 366.

[36] John Flood, "Rake and Rumpole: Mavericks for Justice—Purity and Impurity in Legal Professionalism," in *Law, Lawyers and Justice Through Australian Lenses*, ed. D. Weinert, Karen Crawley and Kieran Tranter (London: Routledge, 2020).

onto screen a wigged and gowned barrister, echoing *Garrow's Law*, *Shadow of the Noose* and *Rumpole of the Bailey* but has brought the life and work of a barrister to dynamic existence in a way that disconnects the profession from its past to a large extent. The British television shows brought the legal past into the televisual present (at the date of production) and conveyed significant messages. These barristers cherished the presumption of innocence and wanted their clients to not only plead not guilty but be found not guilty. But these values were inherently historic, and these values seemed to link to the past more than the present. As such, names such Rumpole's could be linked to conservative opinions and the great defenders seemed to belong to a vanished age and a vanishing professional identity, making the updated barrister of *Rake* an intriguing revision of this legal past.

CHAPTER 6

# The History of Legal Marketing in Australia and New Zealand

*A. Keith Thompson*

## INTRODUCTION

Until the 1980s, lawyers were restricted from advertising their services in a variety of ways including by legislation, subordinate law society regulation and common law rules against 'maintenance' and 'champerty'. But the advent of anti-trust legislation in Australia and New Zealand in the 1970s led to questioning of the traditional view that legal advertising was gauche and unbecoming of those engaged in a profession. The following analysis of business practice also called into question the ancient view that professional legal practice was something completely different from any other business or trade. At the same time, marketing was being developed as a separate academic discipline within business schools and the associated research revealed that marketing was not simply advertising. There were many other ways in which business goods and services could and had been

A. K. Thompson (✉)
The University of Notre Dame Australia, Sydney, NSW, Australia
e-mail: keith.thompson@nd.edu.au

© The Author(s), under exclusive license to Springer Nature     83
Switzerland AG 2022
S. McKibbin et al. (eds.), *The Impact of Law's History*, Palgrave
Modern Legal History,
https://doi.org/10.1007/978-3-030-90068-7_6

marketed to consumers for centuries though very few had previously been the subject of concentrated objective analysis.

This chapter traces the history and nature of the marketing of legal services. It begins with a summary of the origins of the legal profession and then notes the restrictions on the promotion of legal services that existed in both Australia and New Zealand in the early 1980s and how those were broken down in the following decades. I then discuss how marketing is academically understood in business schools and suggest that the development of those definitions is incomplete. I explain that, while marketing is no longer understood as the mere production of goods or their sale once those goods leave the factory, it now also includes services and the sale of both has to be integrated into a holistic business strategy. I also observe that our understanding is likely to undergo further development in the twenty-first century as contemporary ideas of corporate social responsibility condemn some traditional marketing practices. I suggest that future definitions of marketing will focus on sustainable and responsible marketing practice that avoids abusive methods. I also identify soft legal skills and the development of legal doctrine as particular contributors to the rise, establishment and continuing relevance of the legal profession.

The chapter concludes that lawyer confidence in the written and spoken word remains the profession's greatest marketing tool. Because competence and confidence continue to be promoted by word of mouth, the relaxation of previous restrictions on other promotional methods have had little impact on the way lawyers do marketing.

## The Origins of the Legal Profession and the Marketing of its Services

I begin with a summary of the history of the legal profession and its ancient medieval practices to provide context for the marketing of legal services in the present. That is important considering the conclusion that, notwithstanding technological and other advances, because of the nature of legal skills and services many of the profession's undocumented marketing practices remain the most effective.

In England, a legal profession was not born until wealthy landowners delegated their responsibility to attend court to respected deputies, who became known as 'attorneys', an outgrowth of earlier and less useful

## 6 THE HISTORY OF LEGAL MARKETING IN AUSTRALIA AND NEW ZEALAND    85

representatives known as 'responsalis'. From the time of Henry II (1133–1189, reigned 1154–1189), as now, attorneys were given power to bind their principals within clear bounds.[1] A little later, perhaps as early as the reign of Henry III (1207–1272, reigned 1216–1272), 'narratores' were appointed to tell the plaintiff's tale in court without slip.[2] But perhaps the most significant event in the development of the profession came in 1292 when a royal writ was sent to Mettingham CJ and his fellows of the Common Bench which read:

> Concerning attorneys and learners ('apprentices') the Lord King enjoined Mettingham and his fellows to provide and ordain at their discretion a certain number, from every county, of the better, worthier and more promising students ... and that those so chosen should follow the court and take part in its business; and no others.[3]

According to Plucknett, the most remarkable features of this writ were "its policy of putting legal education under the direction of the court and its promise to successful students of a monopoly on practice".[4] This writ also suggests the lobbying that the early common law profession did during the reign of Henry II. For though legal learning had been a part of clerical training under the direction of the archbishops of Canterbury from "the darkest ages", those clerical schools had been closed in London in 1234 by royal edict.[5] Maitland and Plucknett assert that hired lawyers were seen as a parasitic phenomenon and that view was confirmed when the king excluded them from the Exchequer in 1297.[6]

Concern about growing lawyer numbers seems to have resulted in the suggestion that proper education, placed in the hands of the judges who knew the common law, would best protect the public from the

---

[1] T. F. T. Plucknett, *A Concise History of the Common Law* (Boston: Little, Brown and Company, 1956), 216.

[2] Plucknett, *A Concise History*, 216–17.

[3] Plucknett, *A Concise History*, 217–218. See also A Harding, *A Social History of English Law* (Baltimore: Penguin Books, 1966), 170.

[4] Plucknett, *A Concise History*, 218.

[5] Plucknett, *A Concise History*, 219.

[6] Plucknett, *A Concise History*, 219. Plucknett cites F. W. Maitland, *Select Pleas in Manorial Courts* (London: Bernard Quaritch, 1889), 136 where lawyers were said to have 'invaded' those courts.

## 86 A. K. THOMPSON

incompetence to which they objected. However, the king's exclusion of professional pleaders (early common law lawyers) from the Exchequer in 1297 confirms that their monopoly on representation was not yet universal.

Plucknett also points out that the assignment of common law legal education to the courts, rather than the universities, enabled the development of a uniquely English form of practice by excluding continental Romanesque ideas.[7] Holdsworth balances that picture by explaining that civil and canon lawyers were trained at Oxford from the end of the twelfth century and at Cambridge from slightly later. He confirms that this control of civil and canon law education was equivalent to that which the Inns of Court secured over training in the common law.[8] The canon lawyers had their monopolies in different places and it was doubtless they who had lobbied for the exclusion of the common lawyers from the Exchequer in 1297. Holdsworth suggests civil and canon law education before the sixteenth century led to "place and preferment" for "men who hoped to win honour and wealth by gaining posts ... which could only be held by clerics and canonists".[9] In the sixteenth century, however, Henry VIII sponsored and systematised civilian practice in:

1. The ecclesiastical courts ....
2. The region of diplomacy, where the principles of the new international law were being rapidly evolved.
3. The Court of Admiralty which was ... the court where the Law Merchant was being principally administered ....
4. The numerous arbitrations ordered by the Council in which points of foreign maritime or commercial law were involved.
5. Cases brought before Star Chamber, the Chancery, or the Court of Requests, which involved the discussion of principles outside the rules of the common law.
6. Many miscellaneous questions which arose in the conduct of the business of the State.

---

[7] Plucknett, *A Concise History*, 220.

[8] W. S. Holdsworth, *A History of English Law*, 3rd ed., vol. 4 (New York: Little Brown and Co., 1923), 228–29.

[9] Holdsworth, *History of English Law*, 231–32.

7. The courts of Constable and Marshal, and the two universities.[10]

Maitland qualified that view of civilian ascendancy when he observed that the clergy and civilian lawyers trained at Oxford and Cambridge:

[w]ere not the only learned men in England, the only cultivated men, the only men of ideas. Vigorous intellectual effort was to be found outside the monasteries and universities. These [common] lawyers are worldly men, not men of the sterile caste; they marry and found families, some of which become as noble as any in the land; but they are in their way learned, culti-vated men, linguists, logicians, tenacious disputants, true lovers of the nice case and the moot-point. They are gregarious, clubable men, grouping themselves together in hospices which become schools of law, multiplying manuscripts, arguing, learning and teaching ... the great mediators between life and logic, a reasoning, reasonable element in the English nation.[11]

In due course, the 'narratores' or pleaders, who were the ancestors of the barristerial side of the profession, became 'serjeants-at-law'.[12] Plucknett has further explained the status of the serjeants:

The tempting coincidence that serjeanty was a tenure, that lawyers got 'fees', and did fealty to their 'lords', need not prove that serjeants were feu-dally provided with land, although the word 'serjeant' does seem to imply a rather more permanent relationship of employment than is usually the case with the ordinary litigant and his counsel.[13]

What it also expresses is that these early lawyers had carved out for themselves a tenure akin to the wealthy, but a tenure that did not rely upon land.[14] As they advised the great upon the management of their affairs, they came to have a social place with them. By the end of the four-teenth century, the serjeants had so consolidated their position as to be in complete control of the legal profession:[15]

[10] Holdsworth, *History of English Law*, 238.
[11] Y.BB. Edward II (Selden Society), I, lxxxi.
[12] Plucknett, *Concise History*, 221. See also Harding, *Social History*, 172.
[13] Plucknett, *Concise History*, 221.
[14] Plucknett, *Concise History*, 221.
[15] Plucknett, *Concise History*, 223.

## 88  A. K. THOMPSON

[T]he bench and the leaders of the bar; the junior practitioners (who have developed out of the old class of apprentices) are outside the guild but under its supervision ... the judges are all members of the order of serjeants, and serjeants alone can be heard in the principal court, that of Common Pleas.[16]

### *Legal Dress as a Marketing Tool*

The mystique of the serjeants was magnified by their grand attire. While Plucknett says that English judicial costume is not of ecclesiastical origin,[17] the robe was as effective in setting apart the legal profession as it was the clergy. As ordinary people nowadays expect to pay more for the engagement of a Queen's Counsel, so the fees charged by the serjeants-at-law were magnified upon appointment. Plucknett likened the creation of a serjeant to a king's coronation, with seven days of celebratory proceedings, including the distribution of liveries and gold rings in profusion.[18] Hargreaves-Mawdsley has affirmed that grand legal costumery was one way that European rulers freed themselves from ecclesiastical influence. Hence kings clothed their judges in finery

that any noble might envy ... legal dress ... [was] considered ... vital to preserve the dignity of the law ... because a robe c[ould] produce the detached dignity which military uniform or court dress cannot. Where ... the long costume was abandoned as a result of revolutionary or 'enlightened' governments, it was later reassumed.[19]

But in sixteenth-century England, the guilds regulated legal dress "to ensure that it was dignified, but also so that it conveyed the special character of the common law as compared with other European systems of law".[20] While that originally meant robes of a sad colour worn by men

---

[16] Plucknett, *Concise History*, 223.

[17] Plucknett, *Concise History*, 224.

[18] Plucknett, *Concise History*, 223.

[19] W. N. Hargreaves-Mawdsley, *A History of Legal Dress in Europe Until the End of the Eighteenth Century* (Oxford: Clarendon Press, Oxford, 1963), 2–3.

[20] R. McQueen, "Of Wigs and Gowns: A Short History of Legal and Judicial Dress in Australia," *Law Context: A Socio-Legal Journal* 16 (1999): 31–32.

6 THE HISTORY OF LEGAL MARKETING IN AUSTRALIA AND NEW ZEALAND    89

without beards or long hair to show their Englishness,[21] fashionable wigs were introduced from France after the Restoration with the original white coif of point lace then worn on top or "recessed into the crown of judicial wigs".[22] Thus while the English legal profession may have been required to studiously avoid the reception of things Roman from the continent, they were not above selective imitation when it suited their purpose. According to McQueen, the black silk robes of King's Counsel were "simply a manifestation of their association with the royal court":

> [T]he foppish style adopted by these counsel being but an extension of the form of dress adopted by gentlemen-commoners at the time in order to distinguish themselves from the common rabble.[23]

### The Inns of Court as Legal Guilds

Another way in which those who practised law were set apart from others was by the requirement that they be members of a legal guild before they could do so. The Inns of Court were the legal guilds. They exercised considerable influence over legal education, legal dress and the nature of legal practice. The Inns were the legal guilds that settled the learning required of apprentices[24] and developed English legal dress in accord with English sumptuary laws from 1509.[25]

Guild statutes in England date back to the eleventh century and have Germanic and Scandinavian origin where tribes made covenants for mutual support including in plunder and war.[26] In England their first manifestation appears to have been in fraternal religious orders which were copied in feudal agreements to protect against invasion. Civil lawyers appear to have fleshed out these covenantal ideas in their concepts of *collegium*,

---

[21] McQueen, "Of Wigs and Gowns," 32 where McQueen quotes Peter Goodrich, *Oedipus Lex: Psychoanalysis, History, Law* (Berkeley and Los Angeles: University of California Press, 1995), 88–89.

[22] McQueen, "Of Wigs and Gowns," 33–35.

[23] McQueen, "Of Wigs and Gowns," 38 citing Hargreaves-Mawdsley, *Legal Dress*, 85–87.

[24] Plucknett, *Concise History*, 217–20.

[25] McQueen, "Of Wigs and Gowns," 32.

[26] L. Brentano, *On the History and Development of Gilds and the Origins of Trade-Unions* (London: Trubner and Co., 1870), lxvii.

## 90   A. K. THOMPSON

*corpus* and *corporation*, which also existed in early Roman codes.[27] Epstein suggests that the revival of Roman law in the twelfth century popularised these civil law corporate concepts[28] and made them available to common lawyers, so that it was a small step for common lawyers to register their own collective existence when they felt the need for brotherhood like other crafts. Epstein also explains the way that the idea of guild monopoly grew:

> Once the king conceded the right to have a guild, the guild was no longer voluntary, in the sense that one had to join in order to practice the craft in London. The London weavers were not the only group to approach the King seeking legal recognition; Henry II had founded the rights of the merchant guilds in Lincoln and Winchester and granted a charter to the corvesars and cordwainers (cobblers) of Oxford.[29]

It is thus fair to surmise that the concept of guild monopoly was very much alive as the legal profession and its Inns were being established. But we can draw more from Epstein's European guild history, including the insight that the Normans brought with them commercial and business practices from their empire in France and Italy and their written records of contractual arrangements. While Norman reliance on written records varied from place to place, legal knowledge and practice kept pace with increasing commercial reliance "on records to settle disputes".[30] Those 'Roman' practices likely included a "coherent framework for apprenticeship and work contracts"[31] since apprenticeship is "an old French term that slipped into English usage".[32]

Epstein has also written that the "guilds found canon lawyers to be unexpected but strong allies in defending the legitimacy of corporate status" and that Sinabaldo Fieschi, Pope Innocent IV (1195–1254, reigned 1243–1254), was one of the strongest of those advocates because he

---

[27] Steven A. Epstein, *Wage and Labour Guilds in Medieval Europe* (Chapel Hill and London, The University of North Carolina Press, 1991), 228.

[28] Epstein, *Wage and Labour Guilds*, 57.

[29] Epstein, *Wage and Labour Guilds*, 59.

[30] Epstein, *Wage and Labour Guilds*, 63.

[31] Epstein, *Wage and Labour Guilds*, 73.

[32] Epstein, *Wage and Labour Guilds*, 65.

understood the realities of urban economics.[33] Epstein has also observed that the clergy had their own reasons "for defending private associations and liberties that did not flow down from the state or secular authority",[34] but that "[j]urisprudence lent its voice ... to defending the guild as a spontaneous institution, and by legitimizing self-interest as somehow just, some jurists provided a counterargument against those who claimed that self-interest was base and often harmed a more noble common good".[35]

On the Continent, it is clear that the members of early guilds turned to lawyers and notaries for help in making laws.[36] What is interesting in light of the spread of the guild concept through Europe and to England during Lopez's commercial revolution[37] is that it took some time before the European guilds sought external authority for the grant of their status.[38] In England however the very earliest guild organisations of which there is record show grants by the King—notifying the relevant local authorities that legal control over membership and a corporate monopoly had arisen by virtue of a royal charter to the guild concerned.[39] Both in Europe and in England, the arguments used to justify monopolies against self-interest arguments were framed in terms of quality through control and the economic need of the sphere of influence.[40] Epstein has therefore observed that "[t]he artisans of Chartres and London were capable of responding to the challenges of competition and a commercial revolution by strategies of their own devising".[41]

Such justifications were also adopted by English common lawyers as soon as we find them collected around the Inns of Court. These had a

[33] Epstein, *Wage and Labour Guilds*, 81.

[34] Epstein, *Wage and Labour Guilds*, 82.

[35] Epstein, *Wage and Labour Guilds*, 82.

[36] Epstein, *Wage and Labour Guilds*, 82.

[37] Epstein, *Wage and Labour Guilds*, 63. See also R. Lopez, *The Commercial Revolution of the Middle Ages 950–1350* (Cambridge: Cambridge University Press, 1976).

[38] Such guilds, as for example in Bologna, devised methods other than civic authority or statutory legal power to enforce the monopolies they sought, but essentially forced people into their guilds "by their own weight as employers": Epstein, *Wage and Labour Guilds*, 85.

[39] As, for example, to the weavers in London during the reign of Henry II. Epstein, *Wage and Labour Guilds*, 58.

[40] See Epstein's citation of the London cappers' response to cheap German imports after 1270: Epstein, *Wage and Labour Guilds*, 88–89.

[41] Epstein, *Wage and Labour Guilds*, 86.

guild spirit from the earliest times since they excluded different portions of the 'greater profession'.[42] There was at one time a great multiplicity of these Inns, including the Inns of Court, ten Inns of Chancery, Serjeants' Inn and, for the civilians, Doctors' Commons. The creation of the Scriveners Company in the early seventeenth century demonstrates the continuing evolution of the monopolistic legal guild idea, but there were other factors pressing upon the legal guilds as well. The Tudor direction of civil education to the English universities was one of those and the formation of modern law societies was prefigured by both a 1728 Statute[43] which required that a practising solicitor must have completed five years' apprenticeship before enrolment, and the 1739 statute commanding formation of a voluntary "Society of Gentlemen Practisers of the Law and Equity".[44] In 1831, this later Society was merged with others[45] into "The Society of Attorneys, Solicitors, Proctors and others, not being Barristers, practising in the Courts of Law and Equity of the United Kingdom", known for short as "The Incorporated Law Society". It continued until 1903 when it formally became "The Law Society" although the modern exams for admission date to the *Solicitors Act 1877* (UK).

The Guilds always exercised control over their membership including over personal conduct, and the lawyer guilds were no exceptions. In the Inns of Court, these controls came to constitute ethical rules, were extended by the common law itself and were carried forward into the statutes and subordinate regulation that succeeded the rules of the Inns from the nineteenth century.

---

[42] Those members of the Inns who became Serjeants at a later date had to resign from the Inns of Court before taking up their new offices. Later the scriveners obtained their own separate charter from James I for what was called "The Scriveners Company or Guild" because they were not eligible and did not belong to any of the Inns of Court: E Jenks, *A Short History of English Law* (Boston: Little Brown and Co., 1913), 204. Further we note that in the early eighteenth century, attorneys and solicitors were themselves excluded from the Inns of Court and Chancery, after which time Jenks notes that the traditional strength and identity of those Inns decay rapidly: Jenks, *Short History*, 205.

[43] Attorneys and Solicitors Act 1728, 2 Geo II, c 23.

[44] Jenks, *Short History*, 206.

[45] Jenks, *Short History*, 207.

## Touting, Maintenance and Champerty

While I have not been able to date the origins of the 'touting rule', the *Oxford English Dictionary* confirms that the word is of much more recent origin than the profession itself. That is, the idea that 'touting' means unbecoming self-promotion is no older than the late seventeenth century.[46] But the prohibition of direct self-advancement in a legal professional is older and responded to behaviour that was discouraged by the leaders of all the Inns from their origin. The common law rules against maintenance and champerty similarly manifest the imprint of collegial discipline within the Inns of Court but there are few records to substantiate. However, Sir Edward Coke's commentary upon maintenance in the third volume of his *Institutes* in the early seventeenth century shows that these principles were well established by the early seventeenth century. He wrote that

> [m]aintenance, manutenentia, is derived of the verb manutenere, and signifieth in law, a taking in hand, bearing up or upholding of quarrels and sides, to the disturbance or hindrance of the common right; Culpa est rei se immiscere ad se non pertinenti; and is twofold, one in the country, and another in the court. For quarrels and sides in the court, the statutes have inflicted grievous punishments.

> But this kind of maintenance of quarrels and sides in the country, is punishable only at the suit of the king, as it has been resolved. And this maintenance called manutenentia or manutentio ruralis, for example, as to take possessions, or keep possessions, whereof Littleton, sect 701, speaketh, or the like.[47]

The courts were concerned to prevent people not personally involved in civil claims from supporting them, and this principle extended to criminalising those who supported (maintained) robbers and heretics. Champerty, from the Old French word *champart*, had more specific reference to those who funded lawsuits on the basis that they would receive a share of the

---

[46] See, for example, "Tout", *Oxford English and Spanish Dictionary, n.d.*, https://en.oxforddictionaries.com/definition/tout

[47] J H Thomas, *A Systematic Arrangement of Lord Coke's First Institute of the Laws of England* (Philadelphia: Alexander Towar, 1836), 425 https://books.google.com.au/books/about/A_Systematic_Arrangement_of_Lord_Coke_s.html?id=6ewyAAAAIAAJ&redir_esc=y

94    A. K. THOMPSON

proceeds of the litigation if it was ultimately successful. The concept is a precursor to the modern practice of litigation funding which, unlike historical champerty, is seen as having social utility to the extent it enables impoverished litigants to advance socially just causes. Both practices were illegal under ethical rules in England, Australia and New Zealand until the concept of legal monopoly came under pressure from anti-trust legislation beginning in the 1970s.

When consumer protection advocates lobbied for legislation that outlawed trade practices that limited competition, professional bodies including law societies in Australia and New Zealand did not realise that some of their professional rules would also come under pressure to reform. All the professional standards imposed on lawyers by legislation and law societies were said to be justified by the need to ensure holistic professional practice standards. But it did not take long before consumer advocates insisted that fixed scale charges for conveyancing were anti-competitive, although it was more difficult to argue against the requirement that all lawyers be licensed to ensure service quality for consumers. It is to these more recent changes that this chapter now turns.

## LEGAL ADVERTISING

In New Zealand, those rules were liberalised and legal advertising was first allowed in November 1984 and there were further changes a year later.[48] Earlier experimentation with modern marketing methods included large law firms issuing client newsletters to cross-market new services to existing clients.[49] In Australia, the validity of the 2002 regulations were challenged in *APLA Ltd v Legal Services Commissioner (NSW)* in 2005[50] even though most advertising restrictions had been removed in 1994.[51] In that 2005

---

[48] New Zealand Law Society, "Using the Airwaves to Promote Legal Services," *LawTalk*, no. 825 (August 16, 2013), https://www.lawsociety.org.nz/news/lawtalk/issue-825/using-the-airwaves-to-promote-legal-services/

[49] Auckland law firm, Fortune Manning was in the vanguard of such promotion and issued its first *Legal Letter* in December 1982.

[50] *APLA Ltd v Legal Services Commissioner (NSW)* (2005) 224 CLR 322.

[51] The *Legal Profession Amendment (Advertising) Regulation* 2002 (NSW) modified the *Legal Profession Regulation 1994* (NSW) issued under the *Legal Profession Act 1987* (NSW). The 2002 Amendment inserted a new Part 7B into the 1994 Regulation headed "Advertising of Personal Injury Services". As Gummow J explained in the *APLA case*, "[c]lause 139 ...

# 6 THE HISTORY OF LEGAL MARKETING IN AUSTRALIA AND NEW ZEALAND 95

case, the plaintiffs argued that the new ban on advertising was inconsistent with the implied freedom of political communication under the *Australian Constitution* to the extent that it interfered with public awareness of the legal services available in personal injury cases. The High Court held that the legal services in issue were not inherently political matters and so the continuing ban on advertising did not offend the implied constitutional freedom. But the restrictions in issue were lifted in New South Wales in 2015.[52] From that date onwards, legal marketing became subject to the same regime that applies to all other commercial activity under the *Australian Consumer Law* including its well-known prohibition on misleading and deceptive conduct. However, despite its recent legality in Australia and New Zealand, direct advertising has not become popular in the profession as a whole and for the present remains the preserve of personal injury lawyers. And the perception that reliance on direct marketing including advertising is unprofessional may be part of the reason why some believe that personal injury lawyers bring the profession into disrepute.[53]

I now discuss the development of marketing as a scientific discipline during the twentieth century so that the innovation and imagination of medieval lawyers and their successors in practice can be appreciated.

---

placed restrictions on the advertising of legal services in relation to personal injury, but advertisements published in printed publications or publicly exhibited in buildings or on any street or public place were generally permissible" (at 387). As Gleeson CJ and Heydon J had earlier explained citing the NSW Premier's Ministerial Statement when introducing the 2002 personal injury advertising restrictions, they were designed to prevent "[e]lements in the legal profession" from encouraging the view "that litigation is the way to resolve disputes" (at 343).

[52] When the *Legal Profession Uniform Law Application Act 2014* (NSW) took effect from 1 July 2015, it omitted clause 24 of the *NSW Legal Profession Regulation* which had prohibited the advertising of legal services connected with personal injury claims and the parallel prohibition (clauses 74–80) in the *NSW Workers Compensation Regulation 2003* was removed at the same time: http://www.olsc.nsw.gov.au/Documents/LPUL-impact-on-PI_COL_May2015-accessible.pdf

[53] See, for example, Brian O Sutter, "Overcoming the Stigma of Personal Injury Law", n.d., *All Injuries Law Firm* https://www.allinjurieslawfirm.com/blog/overcoming-the-stigma-of-personal-injury-law. See also Smiley Law Firm, "Stigma of Hiring a Personal Injury Attorney", July 5, 2021 https://www.smileyinjurylaw.com/stigma-of-hiring-an-injury-attorney/

## The Evolution of Marketing
## as an Academic Discipline

Historically, the market evolved as a place where the exchange of goods was transacted. It was originally the place of the transaction, but the meaning of the word 'market' has evolved considerably. According to the *Oxford English Dictionary* again, there are now at least ten different meanings (some of which are only what we might call nuances in meaning) of the word 'market', including the place of exchange (twelfth century or earlier), the legal authority from the King or a feudal lord to hold a market there (twelfth century), buying and selling at that market as manifest in the term 'marketing' (sixteenth century), the opportunity to buy and sell in economics (seventeenth century), and the use of the word market as a prefix as in 'market-place' or 'market-driven' (eighteenth century).

The first exchanges that took place in the market were exchanges of goods for goods. As society became more sophisticated and specialised, these exchanges were facilitated by intermediate units of currency. In lay minds, the words 'selling' and 'advertising' have become synonyms for the word 'marketing' in some contexts but refer to specialised aspects of 'the marketing concept' or 'the marketing mix' as those two terms have been used in business schools in universities since the mid-twentieth century. 'Marketing' is the term that has been chosen to represent those aspects of a transaction which extend it beyond the simple transaction, and 'marketing' has come to connote the integration of all the resources of an enterprise into one united whole to achieve a profit or other objective.[54] Hence 'marketing' is more than just selling or advertising. It refers to a comprehensive concept that encompasses all the activities of the enterprise which are designed to ensure that the exchange takes place and includes the forward planning involved in ensuring the exchange satisfies wants and needs. The concept of 'marketing' now includes both the engineering of a product, the planning of a service and the research that seeks to understand the customer's wishes. 'Marketing' can even include the education the enterprise commissions to stimulate customer desire in the first place. Marketing thus encompasses selling, advertising, demographic,

---

[54] See, for example, William J. Stanton, *Fundamentals of Marketing*, 7th ed. (New York: McGraw-Hill College, 1984), 7. See also Neil H. Bordern, "The Concept of the Marketing Mix" in *Science in Marketing*, ed. George Schwartz (New York: John Wiley, 1964) and James G. Hutton, "Integrated Relationship-Marketing Communications: A Key Opportunity for IMC," *Journal of Marketing Communications* 2, no. 3 (1996), 192–93.

psychological and economic research, as well as production and distribution. Stanton defines it as follows:

> As business people have come to recognise that marketing is vitally important to the success of any firm, an entirely new way of business thinking—a new philosophy—has evolved. It is called the marketing concept, and it is based on three fundamental beliefs:
>
> 1. all company planning and operations should be customer-oriented;
> 2. the goal of the form should be profitable sales volume, and not just volume for the sake of volume alone;
> 3. all marketing activities in a firm should be organisationally coordinated.

In its fullest sense, the <u>marketing concept</u> is a philosophy of business that states that the customer's want/satisfaction is the economic and social justification for a firm's existence. Consequently, all company activities must be devoted to finding out what the customer wants and then satisfying those wants, while still making a profit over the long run (emphasis in original).[55]

This realisation that marketing must be an all-encompassing project if an enterprise is to succeed did not dawn on business until late in the twentieth century.[56] The seeds of the realisation were sown during the Industrial Revolution, but the number of functions that had to be integrated to ensure enterprise success was a late realisation. The earliest markets arose when the producers of goods and services understood they could produce more than they needed for their own consumption and that others wanted or needed their surplus. That understanding was developed during the Industrial Revolution from the eighteenth century onwards when some specialist producers developed the skills to mechanise their production. Thereafter the word 'want' developed a new meaning altogether. Deeper twentieth-century marketing insight followed a production-only orientation after the First World War and subsequent Great Depression. Manufacturers could not afford to make product if consumers could not afford to buy that product. Manufacturers also realised that idle stock did

---

[55] Stanton, *Fundamentals of Marketing*, 12. See also Michael J. Etzel, Bruce J. Walker and William J. Stanton, *Marketing*, 11th ed., (New York: The McGraw-Hill Companies, Inc., 1997), 11.

[56] Stanton, *Fundamentals of Marketing*, 13–18.

not generate profit. The excesses of the following 'hard-sell' era were then moderated by the advent of the product liability lawsuit at the same time as ideas of coordination, integration and product differentiation dawned. Most recently coordination, integration and differentiation have been modified by the ethical requirement that no enterprise can survive and prosper if it does not act in a socially and environmentally sustainable way.

Practical insights into the relationships between individual and corporate human nature and the environmental consequences of commerce insist that the development of marketing as an academic discipline is not yet complete. Future development will include differentiation between good marketing and bad marketing with new good and bad differences dictated by changing social norms.[57] Bad marketing currently includes corporate planning that disregards long-term environmental damage, and boardroom decisions that approve substance addiction as a legitimate repeat business strategy. Bad marketing in the future is likely to include practices that disregard evolving measures of corporate social responsibility, and legislatures will pass laws against such practices as a matter of public policy.

In the context of a marketplace where consumer law principles outlaw all kinds of monopoly and closed shop practices, the final part of this essay will discuss the other ways in which lawyers traditionally marketed their services and whether those methods will also have to change if future lawyers are to prosper economically. The discussion that follows will also identify what legal marketing techniques are timeless.

## Historical Approaches to the Marketing of Legal Services

The primary legal marketing tools of the past were the establishment of a monopoly on the provision of legal services followed by the promotion of unique competences and skill levels. Because I have discussed where the idea of monopoly came from above, I do not revisit it here. But the related entrenchment of skilled advocates in the lives and business of the wealthy

---

[57] See, for example, Etzel, Walker and Stanton, *Marketing*, 11–16 where those authors discuss the advent of both a 'Societal Marketing Concept' and the need for modern companies to instil 'an Ethical Orientation' to survive in business in the twenty-first century.

and influential facilitated the reputation and political influence of the most successful legal practitioners of the past.

## Soft Legal Skills

It was not just the courtroom competence and articulation of the most famous lawyers that was valued by their wealthy patrons and clients; their insight and dexterity in crafting compromises made good lawyers of the past irreplaceable. The canon lawyer, Ivo of Chartres (d.1 115), proposed that the investiture power struggle between the Church and medieval kings might be resolved if church officials invested new bishops with ring and staff after those bishops had been elected in the presence of the king so that his presence was still felt and his will known in those appointments.[58] Similarly, fifty years later when the continuing jurisdictional wrangle between church and state was adjusted in England by the *Constitutions of Clarendon* (1164) so that Henry II was consulted before his tenants-in-chief could be excommunicated, it was unheralded lawyers who crafted the underlying ideas into legal instruments. The excesses of the Peasants' revolts in France and Switzerland[59] in 1381 were also avoided in England in its own Peasants' revolt because of silent reforms that adapted the law to new social conditions.[60]

## Legal Doctrines

The rising legal profession also entrenched patterns and doctrines into English administrative and political practice and two of the doctrines provided the profession with brilliant marketing opportunities. There are others,[61] but discussion of these two will demonstrate the point. The

---

[58] Plucknett, *Concise History*, 14. Henry I accepted this compromise rather than risk excommunication during a period when the Church had achieved political ascendancy.

[59] Jenks, *Short History*, 320–21.

[60] Plucknett, *Concise History*, 34.

[61] Bernard Brown cites Hayek and Kamenko as authority for the proposition that "law's most vital latent achievement has been its generation of a methodology which confers on it an internal coherence and a distinctive character independent of social-political plans that their promoters would have it uncritically serve". Such "internal coherence" has certainly relied upon its almost religious adherence to rules that transcend the players who grace any legal arena: B. J. Brown, "Light on Latent Effects of Law," *New Zealand Universities Law Review* 10, no 1 (1982): 1, 16.

100 A. K. THOMPSON

doctrines chosen for this purpose are *stare decisis* also known as the doctrine of precedent, and the canons of statutory interpretation. Both doctrines are so well established that it is no longer possible to raise questions about their legitimacy. They are an assumed part of legal system. While they are generally accepted because they are believed to simplify process and increase certainty in society, that is not always true.

## *Precedent*

The doctrine of precedent did not have a statutory genesis and its beginning cannot be traced to any one case. It grew out of concepts that seemed efficient and because there was an expectation that like cases would be decided alike.

In English common law, the judge's task is "to [find] the general rule applicable to the particular case … [but] it does not conceive the rule as being applicable directly by simple deduction. It works forward from the particular to the general"[62] and accordingly "the English judge has to search for [the general principle] in the learning and dialectic"[63] of others. "Thus [the judge] is always reasoning inductively, and in the process he is said to be bound by the decisions of tribunals higher than his own."[64] This idea in English law and the hierarchical court structure that it has seeded did not originate in a moment but by the time of Chief Justice Bereford (died 1326) counsel were already being advised "that unless they can 'distinguish' his precedent, they cannot succeed".[65]

However, the signal step towards our modern doctrine of precedent was the increasing reliability of the law reports to which Coke alluded when he said that "[o]ur book cases are the best proof of what the law is".[66] While the variability of reporting quality slowed the evolution of the doctrine of precedent, the final steps in the evolution of the doctrine of precedent in the nineteenth century were the systematisation of law reporting, the hierarchical restructuring of the courts, and the exclusion of lay lords from judicial functions in the House of Lords.

[62] CK Allen, *Law in the Making*, 7th ed., (Oxford: Oxford University Press, 1964), 162.

[63] Allen, *Law in the Making*, 162.

[64] Allen, *Law in the Making*, 162.

[65] Allen, *Law in the Making*, 194 where Allen quotes from the Year Books (*Halstedd v Graveshale* Y.B.2 & 3, Ed 11 (S.S. ii), 53, 54 and *Bernake v Hontalt* Y.B. 3 Ed 11 (S.S. iii), 60).

[66] Allen, *Law in the Making*, 207 where Allen cites from Coke on Littleton (*The First Part of the Institutes of the Laws of England*) at 2549.

## 6 THE HISTORY OF LEGAL MARKETING IN AUSTRALIA AND NEW ZEALAND 101

The marketing advantage which accrued to the benefit of the profession from the development of the doctrine of precedent was its emphasis on the relative certainty of the law and the respect in which common law judges should be held because of their commitment to that certainty. For though there have always been perceptions of injustice, the reliability of the law remains because it can be right, and injustice can be attributed to human weakness somewhere else than in the law itself or its doctrine of precedent. While there is no direct benefit to individual modern lawyers from the certainty that flows from the common law's reliance on the doctrine of precedent, the understanding of the certainties in law that individual lawyers acquire through their training and experience is attractive to the public who do not understand them. All lawyers benefit from the stability that law is perceived to contribute to society. But those who rise to the top of the profession and especially those who are recognised as experts by their peers can ask more their services than those with lesser reputations.

### *Statutory Interpretation*

Though critics have observed that judges use statutory interpretation to achieve whatever result they want,[67] we would do a "grave injustice" to the "great majority" of judges if we did not accept they were "honestly trying to find the mode of interpretation which they believe to be consistent with their duty".[68] Originally, the king's judges were intimate with the king's legislating council and knew their intention when passing statutes. As distance grew and government powers were separated, personal requests for clarification became impractical and judges were obliged to interpret the words provided in the statute strictly because they assumed the king meant what he had written.[69] Statutes were no longer suggestions of policy. But it was not this initial separation of powers (judicial from those executive and legislative) that enabled the judiciary to develop statutory interpretation as a check on abuses in other fields of societal administration. Judicial discretion which was the product of intimate familiarity with the king's person and personality gave way to logic, and the grammar

---

[67] Allen, *Law in the Making*, 526 citing John Willis, "Statutory Interpretation", *Canadian Bar Review* 16 (1938): 1.

[68] Allen, *Law in the Making*, 526.

[69] Plucknett, *Concise History*, 333. See also Allen, *Law in the Making*, 445.

and the internal context of an Act could be used as an aid in the difficult task of interpretation. In the course of time, there were so many rules that a judge could pick and choose the result he wanted,[70] but they were also rules that only someone properly trained in their nuance could understand and use in court. And this doctrine has contributed to lay fear about participating in litigation or commerce without appropriate legal advice. Once again, individual lawyers, who become expert in statutory interpretation and particularly those whose specialty is recognised by their peers, can demand higher fees for their services than those with lesser reputations.

## Conclusion

Legal marketing has not needed to change much in the last one hundred years despite advances in technology and the removal of monopoly in commercial law. The most successful lawyers are still those whose competence is promoted by word of mouth and whose skills lie in their first-hand knowledge of the law, and their ability to explain it and advocate a client's position effectively. While other professions may have found larger profits and succeeded in moving in on what was once lawyer monopoly space, they have generally done so by engaging lawyers in their businesses rather than by having legal work done by other professionals.[71] Even though the concepts of maintenance and champerty are no longer well understood and have in part been superseded by regulated funding that enables public interest litigation, the idea that direct advertising is gauche remains and has not become established practice except in the personal injury space. To the extent that other forms of promotion of legal reputation are taking off, they are only new in the sense that the old messages are being passed along in modern ways by the same people. That is, public relations (PR) releases and social media endorsement at base are arguably just a modern take on the personal referral of the thirteenth century.

While there are and will continue to be new ways to market legal services as communication technologies develop, I submit that the core

---

[70] Plucknett, *Concise History*, 334.

[71] See discussion of current marketing efforts by the so-called Big Four accounting firms in Jonathan Derbyshire, "Big Four Circle the Legal Profession," *Financial Times*, November 15, 2018, https://www.ft.com/content/9b1fdab2-cd3c-11e8-8d0b-a6539b949662

element in the marketing of legal services will be communicating competence to the legal services consumer. By itself, direct advertising is unlikely to inspire the levels of trust which have always been critical in long-term relationships between lawyers and business clients involved in continuing business activity as opposed to once in a lifetime personal injury litigation or occasional conveyancing.

CHAPTER 7

# The Historical Development of the Fault Basis of Liability in the Law of Torts

*Anthony Gray*

## INTRODUCTION

As I write in the third decade of the twenty-first century, the law of torts is dominated by the tort of negligence.[1] Though one of the youngest torts, it has grown exponentially since the landmark decision in *Donoghue v Stevenson*,[2] where a generalised duty of care was recognised. Most tort cases now involve negligence claims. Negligence now occupies territory previously held by other torts, and their future has become clouded given this overwhelming growth. Negligence is the classic example of a fault-based tort. It is fundamental to a negligence claim that the plaintiff demonstrate that the defendant breached a duty of care the latter owed to the former. A

---

[1] Tony Weir, "The Staggering March of Negligence," in *The Law of Obligations: Essays in Celebration of John Fleming*, ed. Peter Cane and Jane Stapleton (Oxford: Clarendon Press), 97.

[2] [1932] AC 562.

---

A. Gray (✉)
University of Southern Queensland, Ipswich, QLD, Australia
e-mail: Anthony.Gray@usq.edu.au

© The Author(s), under exclusive license to Springer Nature Switzerland AG 2022
S. McKibbin et al. (eds.), *The Impact of Law's History*, Palgrave Modern Legal History,
https://doi.org/10.1007/978-3-030-90068-7_7

105

breach inevitably involves considerations of fault and blame. The law seeks to determine in what circumstances a defendant should be liable for injuries or loss they caused to another. In the realm of negligence, this is shown by proving that the defendant is at fault; in other words, that they should be legally considered to be to blame for the plaintiff's loss.

The law did not always fasten upon concepts of fault and blame as the basis for civil liability, and in some pockets of the law of torts, still does not. There remains an uneasy conflict in the law of torts between fault-based torts, and non-fault-based torts, though over time the scales of justice have tilted heavily towards a requirement that fault be shown as a basis for civil liability. For the purposes of discussion, a 'non-fault-based tort' will henceforth be referred to as 'strict liability'. This is taken to mean liability in the absence of fault. Defences may be available. It thus differs in meaning from 'absolute liability'. It is the purpose of this chapter to consider how and when (and, relatedly, why) this tilt towards fault-based liability occurred.

## ANCIENT HISTORY: STRICT LIABILITY

The earliest records of formal legal systems provide evidence of acceptance of principles of strict liability. Evidence appears in the *Code of Hammurabi* (circa 1900 BC), *Assyrian Code* (circa 1500 BC) and, in Roman times, the *Twelve Tables* (circa 450 BC) and *Lex Aquilia* (circa 287 BC). What unites these legal sources is a principle that one person is liable to pay another compensation if they *cause* them loss or injury. Causation is the fundamental principle. Fault or culpability is not referred to in these sources. What also unites these legal sources is an evident desire to provide a remedy for a person wronged by another to avoid what is often referred to as the 'blood feud'.[3] In early times, a person who believed they had been wronged by another would seek 'revenge' (typically physical) against the person believed to have caused the wrong. Those who crafted these ancient legal documents were typically seeking to assuage the person aggrieved through the payment of compensation to them, to reduce the likelihood that they would cause a breach of the peace in seeking to exact revenge. In other

---

[3] Wex Malone, "Ruminations on the Role of Fault in the History of the Common Law of Torts," *Louisiana Law Review* 33 (1970): 1; Francis Bowes Sayre, "Mens Rea," *Harvard Law Review* 45 (1932): 977, 979; Jeremiah Smith, "Tort and Absolute Liability: Suggested Changes in Classification," *Harvard Law Review* 30 (1917): 248.

# 7 THE HISTORICAL DEVELOPMENT OF THE FAULT BASIS OF LIABILITY... 107

words, it was part of an attempt to 'civilise' society. The system was financially generous in not enquiring as to the culpability or otherwise of the person said to be responsible. Obviously, it is easier to obtain compensation if it is not a pre-condition to obtaining it that the claimant proves another was at fault for their loss.

However, the situation evolved. By the second century AD, Roman law did have regard to the *culpa* of the defendant in determining whether the defendant should be required to pay the plaintiff compensation.[4] The mere fact of *injuria* or *damnum* was no longer sufficient. This is also reflected in Gaius' *Institutes*. Essentially, within the space of 600 years, Roman law had evolved from a strict liability model to one where fault was important in determining whether a defendant should be held civilly liable for wrongdoing. In other words, the generosity of the strict liability model and its rationale of preserving the peace was eventually determined not to outweigh the possible injustice involved when the culpability or otherwise of the defendant was ignored, as the original system did. The desire for justice was stronger than the need for social control over the aggressive instincts of some in society.

## MIDDLE AGES: STRICT LIABILITY

There is evidence of strict liability underpinning the English legal system. Alfred 16 was clear that a defendant who injured another with a spear, regardless of intent or fault, was liable to compensate the victim. And the *Leges Henrici Primi 1118* (Eng.) Chapter 8 s 6 notes *qui inscienter peccat scienter emendet*; in other words, the person who commits wrong unknowingly must pay for it knowingly. At this point, the mental position of the defendant, in terms of whether they intended or ought to have known that their actions would or might injure the plaintiff, was irrelevant in determining their liability for the plaintiff's injury.

A classic example of strict liability principles is contained in the famous *Case of Thorns* (1466).[5] The case involved simple facts: the defendant's bushes growing onto the property of the plaintiff. The defendant entered the plaintiff's property to attempt to retrieve the bushes and thorns attached to them and in doing so caused some damage to the plaintiff's

---

[4] David Ibbetson, "How the Romans Did for Us: Ancient Roots of the Tort of Negligence," *University of New South Wales Law Journal* 26 (2003): 477.

[5] *Hull v. Orynge* (1466) B & M 327 (KB).

property. There was no evidence that the defendant had been negligent. In finding the defendant liable for the damage caused to the plaintiff's land, a majority of the judges expressed themselves in terms of strict liability. Brian J stated that 'though a man doth a lawful thing, yet if any damage do thereby befall another, he shall answer for it, if he could have avoided it'. He added that 'where a man does a thing, he is held to do it in such a way that through his act no prejudice, or damage, shall happen to others'. Littleton J expressed a similar view, stating that 'if a man is damaged he ought to be recompensed ... if your cattle come on my land and eat my grass, notwithstanding you come freshly and drive them out, you ought to make amends for what your cattle have done'.

These sentiments are typically interpreted to approximate a strict liability view. The position of Littleton J is clearer—he makes clear with his example that one who owns cattle will be liable for the damage the cattle cause, even where the owner has taken reasonable steps to avoid or mitigate the damage. This is basically a liability without fault position. Brian J also tends to this view, requiring that a person doing an act not do prejudice or damage to others, although he recognises a possible exception that liability only exists where the defendant 'could have avoided it'. This is perhaps an allusion to the doctrine of 'inevitable accident'. There is evidence that courts did not find a defendant liable in cases where the plaintiff was injured as a result of 'inevitable accident', though scholars differ sharply on the meaning of this phrase. Some view it as analogous to non-negligence,[6] some said it was entirely independent of a negligence standard[7] and others say it is somewhere between strict liability and fault-based liability.[8]

## Sixteenth, Seventeenth and Eighteenth Centuries: Strict Liability

The English courts recognised strict liability in particular categories of case. These categories include cases of common carriers, where a defendant was contracted to carry the goods of the plaintiff, and the goods were

---

[6] David Kretzmer, "Transformation of Tort Liability in the Nineteenth Century: The Visible Hand," *Oxford Journal of Legal Studies* 4, no. 1 (1984): 74–76.

[7] Percy H. Winfield, "The History of Negligence in the Law of Torts," *Law Quarterly Review* 42, no. 2 (April 1926): 194.

[8] Stephen G. Gilles, "Inevitable Accident in Classical English Tort Law," *Emory Law Journal* 43, no. 2 (Spring 1994): 576.

damaged in transit. In such cases, it was established that the plaintiff had a valid case against the defendant, even in the absence of any proof of negligence on the defendant's part.[9] Interestingly, this example of the application of strict liability was limited to common carriers of goods, not carriers of people.

Evidence of the strictness with which an innkeeper's liability to guests suffering property damage or personal injury whilst staying at the inn appears in the mid-fourteenth century,[10] and is evident in the seventeenth and eighteenth.[11] Strict liability for the consequences of fire was also evident. The tort of cattle trespass was strict, and this strictness would extend to loss caused by the owner or keeper of a wild animal, in respect of damage the animal might cause. The classic decision in 1705 in *Tenant v Goldwin* would confirm the strictness of the liability in nuisance, for interference with the property rights of another.[12] And in the 1681 personal injury case of *Lambert v Bessey*,[13] the court report concludes that civil liability did 'not so much regard the intent of the actor, as the loss and damage of the party suffering'. The Court provided an example: 'if a man assault me and I lift up my staff to defend myself, and in lifting it up hit another, an action lies against me, and yet I did a lawful thing. And the reason of all these cases is because he that is damaged ought to be recompensed.' These cases reflect a strict liability approach, where the negligence of the defendant (or otherwise) is irrelevant to liability; the issue is whether the defendant caused the plaintiff loss.

## DEVELOPMENT OF FAULT AS THE BASIS OF LIABILITY

Though many examples of strict liability have been provided, there is also evidence that the courts were considering fault in determining civil liability. Now, it is possible that the legal system was quietly taking into account for centuries the issue of the defendant's blameworthiness for the plaintiff's injury or loss. Some legal historians have argued that, when assessing particular cases, juries were in fact taking into account whether, in their view, the defendant's conduct was sufficiently blameworthy so as to

---

[9] *Rich v. Kneeland* (1613) Cro. Jac. 330; 79 ER 282.

[10] *Navenby v. Lascelles* (1368) B & M 552, 554.

[11] *Calye's Case* (1604) 8 Co. Rep. 321; 77 ER 520; *Bennett v. Mellor* (1793) TR 273; 101 ER 154.

[12] *Tenant v. Goodwin* (1705) 2 Ld. Raym. 1089, 1092; 92 ER 222, 224.

[13] *Lambert v Bessey* (1681) Sir T. Raym. 467, 467; 83 ER 244, 244.

## 110   A. GRAY

warrant legal remedy.[14] Of course, although an interesting argument, it is not really possible to know the truth, given the secrecy surrounding jury deliberations. All that can really be said is that there is suspicion that fault was being considered by at least some juries hearing civil matters, but the argument cannot be taken much further than that, due to the dearth of evidence on the record.[15]

However, focusing on the available *explicit* evidence, we see in the *Case of Thorns* (1466) in the judgment of Choke J a remark that the defendant might avoid liability if they could show they had done all they reasonably could to avoid the injury or loss caused to the plaintiff. Though the word 'negligence' was not used, the sentiment is clear that a more sophisticated inquiry might be called for, other than the mere fact that the defendant caused the plaintiff injury.

Two seventeenth-century cases are pivotal. The first is *Weaver v Ward*.[16] The plaintiff was a soldier injured accidentally by another soldier during horseplay. The defendant's defence was that it was an accident, for which he should not be held responsible. The Court expressed the view that 'no man shall be excused of a trespass ... except it may be judged utterly *without his fault*' (my emphasis), explaining that:

> As if a man by force take my hand and strike you, or if here the defendant had said that the plaintiff ran across his piece when it was discharging, or had set forth the case with the circumstances, so as it had appeared to the court that it had been inevitable, and that the defendant had committed no negligence to give occasion to the tort.

It must be conceded that it is not entirely clear the sense in which the judge used the word 'fault' and used the word 'negligence'; it is certainly

---

[14] David Ibbetson, *A Historical Introduction to the Law of Obligations* (Oxford: Oxford University Press, 1999), 58–63.

[15] Robert J. Kaczorowski, "The Common-Law Background of Nineteenth-Century Tort Law," *Ohio State Law Journal* 51 (1990): 1169–70: "Charles Wigmore and John Baker and S Milsom argued that as early as the sixteenth century fault or negligence was a factual circumstance plaintiffs had to prove before juries would find defendants guilty. These authors have suggested that the defendant's negligence may have become relevant if he pleaded the general issue of 'not guilty' and tried to explain his actions by explaining the circumstances to the jury. However, lacking records of trial proceedings and jury deliberations, conclusive evidence supporting this view is non-existent and hence the view itself will never advance beyond an unprovable hypothesis".

[16] (1616) Hob. 134, 135; 80 ER 284, 284.

## 7 THE HISTORICAL DEVELOPMENT OF THE FAULT BASIS OF LIABILITY... 111

the case that the words 'negligence' and 'neglect' have been used throughout legal history to mean something different to what they would generally be understood to mean in legal circles today.[17] That conceded, it does seem to suggest a move away from liability in all cases where the defendant caused the plaintiff injury, and towards an enquiry as to the precise circumstances, and the defendant's culpability (if any) for injuries caused to the plaintiff.

The other pivotal case is *Mitchil v Alestree*.[18] Here the defendant's employee brought the defendant's horse to a common. The horse escaped from the employee, causing injury to several members of the public. An action against the employee failed, but an action against the defendant succeeded. In so finding, the Court concluded, 'it was the defendant's fault, to bring a wild horse into such a place where mischief might probably be done, by reason of the concourse of people'.[19] Wylde J said it was similar to a situation where a defendant owner of a horse left the stable door open, allowing the animal to bolt. Twisden J agreed that a person who owned a tame fox would not be liable if the animal escaped, and then resumed its 'wild' nature. Though the judgments are very brief, they seem to suggest an intention to limit a defendant's civil liability to cases where they were blameworthy and culpable for the loss caused to the plaintiff—per the example of Wylde J, where the defendant had left open the stable door. Twisden J did not think it just to hold the previous owner of an animal liable, merely because it had escaped. Legal historian Baker traces the birth of the tort of negligence to this case, with fault at its heart.[20]

### OTHER INFLUENCES FAVOURING FAULT-BASED LIABILITY OVER STRICT LIABILITY

There were at least three other influences that served, whether by accident or by design, to tilt the balance in the civil law away from strict liability and in favour of fault-based liability. I will now discuss these in some detail.

---

[17] George P. Fletcher, "Fairness and Utility in Tort Theory," *Harvard Law Review* 85 (January 1972): 556–58.

[18] (1676) 1 Vent. 295; 86 ER 190. See also *Michell v. Allestry* (1685) 3 Keb. 650; 84 ER 932.

[19] (1676) 1 Vent. 295, 295; 86 ER 190, 190.

[20] J. H. Baker, *An Introduction to English Legal History* (London: Butterworths, 2002), 411.

## The Forms of Action, Including Development of the Action on the Case

The forms of action originally focused on the type of harm done, rather than the circumstances in which it was committed. So, for example, the writ of trespass *vi et armis* was, for historical reasons, concerned with the question whether the defendant committed violence in the course of committing the alleged trespass. Other aspects of their behaviour, including whether their conduct was blameworthy or culpable, were not generally considered. Further, the writ of trespass did not permit the plaintiff to discuss much detail as to the events giving rise to the action. They would basically claim that the defendant's actions had caused them injury or loss. The focus was on proving that the defendant had done an act, and that this act had caused the plaintiff injury or loss. In turn, the defendant was strictly limited in how they could respond to the issued writ. They could deny they committed the act, or that the act caused the plaintiff loss. They might argue they should not be held responsible because the injury to the plaintiff was 'inevitable'. They could not specifically argue that they should not be held liable because they were not at fault. If they effectively wanted to argue this, they would simply respond 'not guilty' to the writ. The matter would then be heard in court, and the jury would determine whether the plaintiff's claim should succeed. Of course, it is possible that in determining this, jurors did take account of the culpability or otherwise of the defendant's actions. However, we cannot know this, as acknowledged earlier.

With the advent and development of the action on the case, the opportunity increased for more detail of the events to be placed on the record. Initially, introduction of the action on the case in the late fourteenth century did not have a lot of influence on the law, but this action grew exponentially in popularity in the late seventeenth century for various reasons, including potentially higher damages, longer limitation periods and vicarious liability on employers. The action on the case was essentially a fault-based jurisdiction, so as it grew in popularity, courts became more likely to expressly consider the defendant's culpability or otherwise when assessing liability.[21]

---

[21] Ibbetson, "How the Romans Did For Us," 499.

## Developments in Criminal Law

Obviously, at one time what we now consider to be criminal law was part of civil law. Those who had committed what we would now regard as criminal acts would pay compensation to the victim. Over time, a separate branch of law known as the criminal law developed. Within this nascent realm, at least two different influences in this context were important. The first was Bracton, highly steeped in Roman law. He was aware that Roman law took account of the *animo* (mind) and *voluntate* (intent) of one accused of breaching the criminal law, and he argued that English law should adopt this position. Further, the ecclesiastical courts considered the moral culpability of those accused of breaching the laws administered in that jurisdiction.

There is academic discussion of a 1368 decision where the court apparently distinguishes civil and criminal liability.[22] The plaintiff claimed his goods were stolen while he was staying at an inn. He brought action against the innkeeper. The innkeeper denied responsibility, claiming the premises had been soundly constructed, the plaintiff's room was secure and he was not to blame for the theft. The plaintiff sought an order to arrest and jail the defendant. The Court refused to do this, on the basis the defendant was not at fault. It recognised the injustice of subjecting a person to a criminal sanction in the absence of moral wrongdoing. It ordered the defendant to pay the plaintiff financial compensation for their loss. The case demonstrates how criminal law separated from civil law, in considering the question of the moral blameworthiness of the defendant's activity, while at this time the civil law did not, particularly in relation to the liability of innkeepers. Yearbooks of the late fifteenth and early sixteenth centuries reflect the importance of intention in the criminal law,[23] and it appears in the writing of Matthew Hale.[24]

Judicial affirmation of this difference in approach between the criminal law and civil law appears in *Lambert v Bessey* where the Court notes:

---

[22] Morris S. Arnold, "Accident, Mistake, and Rules of Liability in the Fourteenth-Century Law of Torts," *University of Pennsylvania Law Review* 128 (December 1979): 372. The case referred to appears at YB Pasch. 42 Edw. 3, f. 11, pl. 13, 42, Liner Assisarum, f. 260, pl. 17 (1368).

[23] Sayre, "Mens Rea," 990–91.

[24] Matthew Hale, *Pleas of the Crown*, trans. (London: Atkyns and Atkyns, 1682), 38.

If a man assault me and I lift up my staff to defend myself and in lifting it up hit another, an action lies by that person, and yet I did a lawful thing ... and the reason is because he that is damaged ought to be recompensed. But otherwise it is in criminal cases, for there actus non facit reum, nisi mens sit rea.[25]

It is suggested that these developments in the criminal law, in time, impacted the civil law. As Pollock and Maitland note, the quantum of compensation in the civil realm began to depend on the particular facts, rather than the mere fact of injury, and the defendant's intention became important in determining the amount of compensation payable.[26]

### *Statutory Reform*

Statute influenced the development of the civil law towards a fault basis through at least two mechanisms, direct and indirect. First, the legislature directly reformed the law pertaining to some of the particular categories of cases mentioned above where strict liability had become established. So, for instance, the strict liability attaching to common carriers in respect of goods carried was curtailed by the *Carriers Act 1830* (UK), which limited a carrier's liability to circumstances where the customer had declared the value of goods being transported and permitted the carrier to charge customers a fee based on recouping the costs of insuring the item. In the context of innkeepers too, the harshness of strict liability was curtailed by limiting the quantum of damage for which the defendant would be held responsible in the absence of fault.[27]

The other effect was more indirect. Various statutes empowered companies and government bodies to construct infrastructure. This was particularly prevalent during the Industrial Revolution of the early to mid-nineteenth century. Inevitably, the construction of this infrastructure, such as railway lines, roads, canals and dams, would increase the risk of accidents through which victims could be injured. The question arose as to the liability, if any, of those who constructed or owned such infrastructure for the accidents such construction caused, either during the construction phase or once the infrastructure was operational. The issue was

[25] (1681) Raym. Sir. T 421, 423; 80 ER 220, 221.
[26] Frederick Pollock and Frederic Maitland, *Before the Time of Edward I*, vol. 2 of *The History of English Law* (Boston: Little, Brown and Company, 1895), 469.
[27] *Innkeepers Act 1863* (UK).

the interpretation of the statute under which such work had occurred, which generally enabled it to occur by declaring it to be 'lawful' for such activity to be conducted. How did this affect, if at all, the liability position of the entity empowered to conduct the activity? These statutes were typically silent as to the liability position of the company or body that constructed, owned or managed the infrastructure.

The courts arrived at the position that where a plaintiff was injured as a result of the construction or working of such infrastructure, the company or body that constructed it should not be held liable on a strict liability basis. In such cases, the plaintiff would need to show there had been negligence in the construction, maintenance or use of such infrastructure in order to succeed.[28] This approach covered a large number of cases and gave increased impetus towards a fault basis of liability, as opposed to a strict liability basis, in areas of civil liability beyond the context of infrastructure construction or management. Interestingly, another example of this approach to statutory interpretation in the context of fault or strict liability appears in a judgment by Brett J in *Hammond v The Vestry of St Pancras*.[29] It should be noted that Brett J, a decade later as Master of the Rolls, would (in dissent) advocate a generalised duty of care in the tort of negligence,[30] a suggestion which would become law, and the broad foundation of negligence, more than 50 years later. Back in *Hammond* in 1874, Brett J stated:

> It would seem to be to be contrary to natural justice to say that parliament intended to impose upon a public body a liability for a thing which no reasonable care or skill could obviate. The duty may notwithstanding be absolute: but, if so, it ought to be imposed in the clearest possible terms ... where the language used (in the legislation) is consistent with either view (strict liability or fault-based liability) it should not be construed as to inflict a liability unless the party sought to be charged has been wanting in the exercise of due and reasonable care in the performance of the duty imposed.[31]

In summary, statutory developments would, both directly and indirectly, provide an impetus towards a fault basis of liability. Not surprisingly,

---

[28] *Vaughan v. Taff Vale Railway* (1860) 5 H & N 679; 156 ER 667, applying *Rex v. Pease* (1832) 4 B & Ad. 30; 110 ER 366.

[29] (1874) LR 9 CP 316.

[30] *Heaven v. Pender* (1883) 11 QBD 503, 509.

[31] *Heaven v. Pender*, 322 (Denman J took a similar position).

116    A. GRAY

some of the judges who sought to interpret statutes to only make defendants liable for infrastructure that caused another injury or damage in cases of proven negligence argued for these principles to be applied on a much broader scale.

In sum, as the Industrial Revolution transformed United Kingdom society, so it impacted the law of that jurisdiction. It exponentially increased the sheer volume of interactions among people, and exponentially increased industrial and commercial development, greatly expanding the potential for an organisation or person to (inadvertently) cause injury or loss to another or interfere with their rights. This placed great pressure on the legal system, increasing the quantum of cases, and varying the circumstances in which a defendant might suffer loss and demand compensation from those whom they claimed to be responsible. The exponential development of the action on the case facilitated these claims, as did the impact that criminal law had on civil law. The courts also responded by tightening their interpretation of legislation, reducing the likelihood that a person injured as a result of the construction or working of infrastructure could obtain compensation. By the mid-nineteenth century, many forces were aligning to direct the law of torts in the direction of a fault basis of liability, away from its strict liability roots.

## BACK TO THE FUTURE: *RYLANDS V FLETCHER* STRICT LIABILITY

An unusual thing then happened. The United Kingdom legal system again appeared to re-assert principles of strict liability. This occurred in the (in)famous decision in *Rylands v Fletcher*. The simple facts involved the plaintiff and defendant as neighbouring property owners. Water escaped from a reservoir on the defendant's property onto that of the plaintiff, flooding an underground shaft and damaging their mine. There was no evidence that the reservoir had been constructed or maintained negligently. Although the Court of Appeal found the defendants were 'free from all blame', it nevertheless held them liable.[32] It purported to base the cause of action in strict liability. In a classic passage, Blackburn J for the Court held that:

> We think that the true rule of law is that the person who, for his own purposes, brings on his lands and collect and keeps there anything likely to do mischief if it escapes, must keep it at his peril, and if he does not do so, is

[32] *Fletcher v. Rylands* (1865) LR 1 Ex. 265 (CA).

7 THE HISTORICAL DEVELOPMENT OF THE FAULT BASIS OF LIABILITY... 117

prima facie answerable for all the damage which is the natural consequence of its escape. He can excuse himself by shewing that the escape was owing to the plaintiff's default, or perhaps that the escape was the consequence of vis major, or the Act of God ... the general rule seems, on principle, just. The person whose grass or corn is eaten down by the escaping cattle of his neighbour, or whose mine is flooded by the water, from his neighbour's reservoir, or whose cellar is invaded by the filth of his neighbour's privy, or whose habitation is made unhealthy by the fumes and noisome vapours of his neighbour's alkali works, is damnified without any fault of his own, and it seems but reasonable and just that the neighbour, who has brought something on his own property which was not naturally there, harmless to others so long as it is confined to his own property, but which he knows to be mischievous if it gets on his neighbour's, should be obliged to make good the damage which ensues if he does not succeed in confining it to his own property ... the case that has most commonly occurred, and which is most frequently to be found in the books, is as to the obligation of the owner of cattle which he has brought on his land, to prevent their escaping and doing mischief. The law as to them seems to be perfectly settled from early times; the owner must keep them at his peril, or he will be answerable for the natural consequences of their escape (emphasis added).[33]

The phrase 'at peril' is a typical short-hand way of referring to strict liability. An appeal against this decision to the House of Lords was dismissed. Two Lords delivered judgments. Lord Cranworth stated:

In considering whether a defendant is liable to a plaintiff for damage which the plaintiff may have sustained, the question in general is not whether the defendant has acted with due care and caution, but whether his acts have occasioned the damage ... and the doctrine is founded on good sense. For when one person, in managing his own affairs, however innocently, damages another, it is obviously only just that he should be the party to suffer.[34]

This passage reads as a rejection of fault-based liability, Lord Cranworth denying that the question was whether the defendant acted with due care and caution, a fundamental question when issues of negligence are being considered.

---

[33] *Fletcher v. Rylands*, 279–280 (Blackburn J, for Willes Keating Mellor Montague Smith and Lush JJ).

[34] *Rylands v. Fletcher* (1868) LR 3 AC 330, 341.

118    A. GRAY

It is somewhat difficult to reconcile this apparent reversion to principles of strict liability at the highest judicial levels in the United Kingdom with the developments in the common law alluded to earlier, which appeared to be demonstrating a move towards fault-based liability. Possible explanations might include that in the years leading up to the *Rylands* decision, there had been dam failures resulting in the deaths of many, and victims' families sometimes found it difficult to obtain compensation because of the difficulty in proving negligence.[35] It might also reflect the fact that the law often traditionally favoured property interests over personal safety, and this was a way to safeguard interference with property interests, making them actionable in the absence of fault.[36]

It may be that the architects of the *Rylands v Fletcher* decision understood it to herald a fundamental principle applicable to fields beyond the immediate context in the case. This principle might be applied in situations involving 'dangerousness'. This argument is partly undercut by the fact that the chief architect of the doctrine in *Rylands*, Blackburn J, himself later seemed to resile from the suggestion. In any event, concepts such as 'not naturally there' and 'knows it is liable to do mischief if it escapes' proved to be fatally uncertain, resulting in fine distinctions that became increasingly difficult to rationalise and justify. In *Read v J Lyons and Company*,[37] the House of Lords denied that *Rylands* stood for any broad, far-reaching principle of tort law in relation to 'dangerous' activity. Later in *Cambridge Water Co v Eastern Counties Leather Co*,[38] it would re-interpret the decision as an example of the tort of private nuisance. Even so, this has not made the principle any easier to explain, as the House of Lords demonstrated with its highly unsatisfactory decision in *Transco Plc v Stockport Metropolitan Borough Council*.[39] The decision was eventually

---

[35] A. W. B. Simpson, "Legal Liability for Bursting Reservoirs: The Historical Context of Rylands v. Fletcher," *Journal of Legal Studies* 13 (June 1984): 251–52.

[36] G. H. L. Fridman "The Rise and Fall of Rylands v. Fletcher," *Canadian Bar Review* 34, no. 7 (August–September 1956): 813.

[37] [1947] AC 156.

[38] [1994] 2 AC 264.

[39] [2004] 2 AC 1. The decision is unsatisfactory for many reasons, which I elaborate upon in my book Anthony Gray, *The Evolution from Strict Liability to Fault in the Law of Torts* (Oxford, Hart Publishing, 2021), 91–96. Essentially, the dissatisfaction comes from apparent attempts to resurrect strict liability (Lord Bingham), attempts to relate liability to insurability (Lord Hoffmann), attempts to retro-fit concepts of control onto *Rylands* (Lord Hobhouse), and consideration of whether the defendant's use of the land was 'reasonable'

7 THE HISTORICAL DEVELOPMENT OF THE FAULT BASIS OF LIABILITY... **119**

abandoned by the Australian High Court,[40] but somewhat unexpectedly, it had the most influence on the law in the United States, where its philosophy continues to be reflected in the *Restatements (Torts)*.[41]

Whether or not *Rylands* was intended to reorient the law of torts back towards a strict liability position, the fact is that it was not successful. Key decisions late in the nineteenth century after *Rylands*, such as *Holmes v Mather*[42] and *Stanley v Powell*[43] re-asserted the primacy of fault in the personal injuries context. Somewhat ironically, it was Baron Bramwell in the Court of Exchequer in *Holmes* who re-asserted the importance of fault-based liability on the concept of reasonable care: 'for the convenience of mankind in carrying on the affairs of life, people as they go along roads must expect, or put up with, such mischief as reasonable care on the part of others cannot avoid'.[44]

This is ironic because it was Baron Bramwell in the original decision in *Rylands* who advocated (admittedly, in the context of damage to property rather than personal injury) strict liability. The rationale for favouring strict liability in respect of property interests, but fault-based liability in respect of personal injuries, was never articulated. And further, Blackburn J, the architect of the strict liability principle in the Court of Appeal in *Rylands*, seemed to adopt a fault basis of liability in relation to the public nuisance case of *Tarry v Ashton*.[45] Full realisation of the generalised duty of care based on fault in the context of personal injuries,[46] damage to property[47] and purely economic loss[48] would follow.

(Lord Scott), and whether the loss resulted from actions of the defendant that were planned or were gradual and invisible (Lord Walker).

[40] *Burnie Port Authority v. General Jones Pty Ltd* (1994) 179 CLR 520.

[41] *Restatement (First) of Torts*, American Law Institute (1938), s 520; *Restatement (Second) of Torts*, American Law Institute (1977), ss 519–20; *Restatement (Third) of Torts*, American Law Institute (1998), s 20(a).

[42] (1875) LR 10 Ex. 261.

[43] [1891] 1 QB 86 (Denman J).

[44] *Holmes v. Mather*, 267.

[45] (1876) 1 QBD 314, 319: 'if there were a latent defect in the premises, or something done to them without the knowledge of the owner or occupier by a wrongdoer, such as digging out the coals underneath and so leaving a house near the highway in a dangerous condition, I doubt ... whether or not the occupier would be liable. But if he did know of the defect, and neglect(ed) to put the premises in order, he would be liable. He would be responsible to this extent, that as soon as he knew of the danger he would be bound to put the premises in repair or pull them down.'

[46] *Donoghue v. Stevenson* [1932] AC 562.

[47] *Sedleigh-Denfield v. O'Callaghan* [1940] AC 880.

[48] *Hedley Byrne v. Heller and Partners* [1964] AC 562.

## Philosophical Debate: Strict Liability Versus Fault Liability

It is only in more recent times that scholars have attempted to provide a philosophical justification for their adherence to either strict liability or fault-based liability. Somewhat frustratingly, justifications typically do not appear in judgments, leaving others to guess as to the underlying reasoning for particular positions in court decisions.

That having been said, much of the scholarship favouring the imposition of strict liability in the past 50 years or so has focused on notions of 'enterprise risk'.[49] This is the idea that a business enterprise should have allocated to it costs reasonably associated with the running of it. This is said to be economically efficient—if a particular business has 'too few' costs attributed to it, it will produce more than is economically efficient; conversely if the particular business has 'too many' costs attributed to it, it will produce less than is economically efficient. The key question in this reasoning is which costs should be allocated to the particular business. The terminology here varies, but typically the concept of 'characteristic' risk is used. If a loss is a materialisation of a risk that is 'characteristic' of a particular business, then the theory goes that the loss should be allocated to that business. Of course, this begs the question of what a 'characteristic' risk is. For example, is the failure of infrastructure, for example a dam or a railway line, a 'characteristic risk'? In the case of an educational institution, is the possibility that a teacher might abuse a student a 'characteristic risk'. This theory suffers from the indeterminacy of key concepts it uses. Further, it appears to justify allocating these losses to the business on the basis that the business derives all the benefit from the business activity; therefore, it should bear all of the risks. However, this is simplistic—of course, there are many beneficiaries of particular business activity, apart from the owner or owners of the business. They include employees and their families, their customers and clients, and all members of the community in terms of taxation revenue on business profits.

Other justifications for the imposition of strict liability have been on the basis that a business (typically, but not now always, the nature of the defendant) is in a better position to 'distribute' the risks associated with

---

[49] Frederick Pollock, *Essays in Jurisprudence and Ethics* (London: Macmillan and Co., 1882), 122.

## 7 THE HISTORICAL DEVELOPMENT OF THE FAULT BASIS OF LIABILITY... 121

particular activity.[50] It might do this by insuring against the event, by pricing its services to account for the risk, for example. However, again the argument is somewhat simplistic. We would need to know more about the availability of insurance, and the terms on which it is available, to draw any definitive conclusion about the extent of 'distributability'.[51] The orthodox view is that the law does not take into account the availability of insurance in determining legal rules, or outcomes reached as a result of those rules.[52] And the extent to which a given business might be able to 'pass on' these costs to customers is another complicated question involving economic concepts such as elasticity of demand for the product, as well as other aspects of the particular market into which the particular business supplies.[53] Thus, it would need to be a case-by-case assessment considering the precise economic and market circumstances of the defendant. This makes it an unpromising context into which to place unbending legal rules that defendants are liable for all losses relating to accidents that are 'characteristic' of their business.

It is also sometimes claimed that strict liability will effect deterrence. For example, McLachlan J, for the Supreme Court of Canada, in *Bazley v Curry*[54] opined that a major policy argument in favour of vicarious liability (a type of strict liability) was:

> Deterrence of future harm. Fixing the employer with the responsibility for the employee's wrongful act, even where the employer is not negligent, may have a deterrent effect. Employers are often in a position to reduce accidents and intentional wrongs by efficient organisation and supervision. Failure to take such measures may not suffice to establish a case of tortious negligence directly against the employer. Perhaps the harm cannot be shown to have been foreseeable under negligence law. Perhaps the employer can avail themselves of the defence of compliance with the industry standard. Or perhaps the employer (complied) with the standard of reasonable care ... (however) beyond the narrow band of employer conduct that attracts direct

---

[50] Howard C. Klemme, "The Enterprise Liability Theory of Torts," *University of Colorado Law Review* 47, no. 2 (Winter 1976): 153.

[51] C. Robert Morris Jr., "Enterprise Liability and the Actuarial Process--The Insignificance of Foresight," *Yale Law Journal* 70, no. 4 (March 1961): 586.

[52] *Lister v. Romford Ice and Cold Storage Co Ltd* [1957] AC 555, 576–77 (Viscount Simonds).

[53] Guido Calabresi, "Some Thoughts on Risk Distribution and the Law of Torts," *Yale Law Journal* 70 (March 1961): 523.

[54] [1999] 2 SCR 534.

liability in negligence lies a vast area where imaginative and efficient administration and supervision can reduce the risk that the employer has introduced into the community. Holding the (defendant liable) may … encourage (them) to take such steps, and thus to reduce the risk of future harm.[55]

McLachlin J had also noted that 'the employer is often in the best position to spread the losses through mechanisms like insurance and higher prices, thus minimizing the dislocative effect of the tort within society'.[56]

With great respect, these arguments are unconvincing. It is difficult to reconcile the two positions. First, it is said that businesses are in a position to redistribute the losses, so they in effect do not pay them. Then it is also claimed that businesses will be deterred by the threat of strict liability. Presumably, they are deterred because they would be liable to pay compensation to an injured party under a strict liability standard. How can a doctrine be lauded on the basis that: (a) the business upon which the liability is imposed will not pay the loss; and (b) the business upon which the liability is imposed will pay the loss. The positions are contradictory.

Of course, a position in favour of fault-based liability would attract philosophical support from adherents of corrective justice such as Ernest Weinrib. Weinrib would argue that the law of torts should operate to correct a wrong. A wrong means that someone has committed an action that the law regards as wrongful. On this view, the mere fact that the defendant caused the plaintiff loss would not be sufficient. The defendant would also need to have committed an action or omission that the law regards as wrongful, such as the breach of an identified duty of care.

Other notable adherents of a fault-based standard of liability were academic turned Supreme Court justice Oliver Wendell Holmes Jr and Allan Beever. Holmes noted:

The undertaking to distribute losses simply on the ground that they resulted from the defendant's act would not only be open to these objections (lack of public benefit) but … to the still graver one of offending the sense of justice. Unless my act is of a nature to threaten others, unless under the circumstances a prudent man would have foreseen the possibility of harm, it

[55] *Bazley v. Curry*, 554–55.
[56] *Bazley v. Curry*, 554.

# 7 THE HISTORICAL DEVELOPMENT OF THE FAULT BASIS OF LIABILITY... 123

is no more justifiable to make me indemnify my neighbour against the consequences than to make me do the same thing if I had fallen upon him in a fit, or to compel me to insure him against lightning.[57]

Similarly, Allan Beever noted of the strict liability approach:

The loss model (assumes) that the causing of loss is wrongful, at least prima facie ... the model maintains that tort law is most fundamentally concerned with loss ... of course, practicalities demand that not all losses can be compensated. Thus, control mechanisms must be introduced to constrain liability. There is a deep problem with this view; far deeper than its inability to provide an adequate account of the law ... the problem is that the loss model is based on notions inconsistent with the reality of the human condition. Given human nature and the world in which we find ourselves, causing loss to others is a fact of life ... building into one's understanding of law that notion that things are even prima facie unjust unless they are otherwise is, frankly, otherworldly. It is reality denyingly utopian; the result of failing to look the human condition in the eye. If loss is an evil, then life itself is evil, and living a life with one's eyes open to the consequences is an act of intentional evil ... the loss model is not merely wrong; it is pathology.[58]

The other major benefit of a duty of care/breach and fault basis liability, as opposed to a strict liability approach, is its flexibility. It permits decision makers to take all circumstances into account, including what both the plaintiff and defendant did or did not do, the context in which the events took place, and all other relevant circumstances. This is a much more sophisticated analysis than a simple question of whether the defendant's actions or omissions caused loss to the plaintiff. It is surely more likely to lead to just outcomes to take account of all of the circumstances surrounding an event, as opposed to the mere fact that one person caused another loss. It is appreciated that by taking into account all of the circumstances of the case and basing decisions on the basis of reasonableness, this may produce some uncertainty in application, and result. It is less certain than a simple question of causation. That accepted, justice is messy, and may on occasion be uncertain. Certainty in law is extremely difficult, if not impossible, to attain.

---

[57] Oliver Wendell Holmes, *The Common Law* (Boston: Little, Brown and Company, 1881), 60.

[58] Allan Beever, *A Theory of Tort Liability* (Oxford: Hart Publishing, 2016), 18.

124　A. GRAY

There is also the suggestion that the certainty apparently provided by strict liability is elusive. We cannot know, but it is sometimes argued that in the middle ages juries were in reality taking into account the fault or blameworthiness of defendants, in determining whether they should be legally liable for the injury or loss they caused to the plaintiff. While we cannot know the truth of what happened in the jury room, many scholars believe that juries were in fact considering fault in making their decisions. If true, it perhaps suggests the inevitability of fault-based considerations in determining liability. It marries with common sense. It marries with most people's intuitive sense of justice. It must be a fact-specific determination, not the unthinking application of fixed rules. And participants in the legal system, whether they are jurors or judges, will one way or the other act in ways that protect this flexibility—whether it be jurors taking into account fault in a supposedly strict liability system, whether it be acquitting defendants who might be technically guilty of a crime but where they might believe, for example, that the mandatory penalty attaching to such a crime is unjust. Experience has surely taught us the folly of hard, fixed rules in the law that are insensitive to the factual scenario in which it is sought to apply them, scenarios which demand flexibility, not inflexibility. In the end, a fault-based liability system is better able to achieve this.[59]

## Unfinished Business

Notwithstanding the explosive growth of fault-based negligence, anomalies remain in the law of torts on the question of strict liability versus fault. There is a highly unsatisfactory situation within the law of nuisance. Nuisance was traditionally considered to be a tort of strict liability. However, in many, if not most, cases ostensibly involving nuisance claims, interferences with property rights, the court decides the matter on the basis of negligence principles, even when it is purporting to apply nuisance principles. It considers whether the defendant was guilty of blameworthy behaviour in determining whether they have committed the tort of nuisance. The concept of 'reasonable user' in the law of nuisance has inevitably invited in general discussion of the 'reasonableness' of the defendant's behaviour, drawing the nuisance discussion perilously close to, if not

---

[59] For more discussion, see Anthony Gray, *Vicarious Liability: Critique and Reform* (Oxford: Hart Publishing, 2018), chs 5–7 and Gray, *The Evolution from Strict Liability to Fault in the Law of Torts*, chs 5–6.

entering into, the territory of negligence.[60] Some argue that the concept of 'reasonable user' in nuisance differs from the 'reasonableness' in negligence,[61] but this argument wears a bit thin when one reads the judgments and sees the extensive intermingling of principle.[62] Elsewhere, I have argued that the time has come to subsume the tort of nuisance into the law of negligence.[63] This has already occurred in respect of the tort of public nuisance. It should also occur in respect of the tort of private nuisance, in my view. The tort of nuisance clearly predates the tort of negligence, but the exponential, explosive growth of the latter has left the former redundant. At the very least, its strict liability ancestry is an anachronism.

Similar complexity attends the torts of defamation and libel. In its very earliest iterations in the ecclesiastical courts, there was evidence that malice (clearly analogous to fault) was required in order to bring action. As defamation moved into the common law courts the strictness of its liability became more apparent. Examples include the *De Libellis Famosis* decision of 1606,[64] where (in)famously it was determined that truth was no defence to a libel action, and *R v Woodfall*, where Lord Mansfield determined that 'whatever a man publishes, he publishes at his peril'.[65] Obviously, the phrase 'at peril' is a classic description of strict liability. This was again

---

[60] *Sedleigh-Denfield v. O'Callaghan* [1940] AC 880; *Torette House Pty Ltd v. Berkman* (1940) 62 CLR 637. Scholars have noted the confusing conflation of nuisance and negligence in this case: Conor Gearty, "The Place of Private Nuisance in a Modern Law of Torts," *Cambridge Law Journal* 48, no. 2 (1989): 237; John Murphy, *The Law of Nuisance* (Oxford: Oxford University Press, 2010), 17. See F. H. Newark, "The Boundaries of Nuisance," *Law Quarterly Review* 65, no. 4 (October 1949): 486–87.

[61] Classically, P. H. Winfield, "Nuisance as a Tort," *The Cambridge Law Journal* 4, no. 2 (1931): 198.

[62] Maria Lee, "What is Private Nuisance?" *Law Quarterly Review* 119 (2003): 303: 'in a number of instances, the courts have certainly, whilst calling the action private nuisance, emphasised the importance of the conduct of the defendant, and analysed the issues in the language of negligence ... the argument that negligence-type fault is required in certain cases addressed under private nuisance has apparently been accepted by the courts. Even if the courts describe the question in terms of private nuisance, or say that it does not matter which tort is used, the claim is essentially fault-based, and rests on negligence.'

[63] Anthony Gray, "The Evolution from Strict Liability to Negligence: When and Why? Part 1," *Australian Law Journal* 94, no. 8 (2020); Anthony Gray, "The Evolution from Strict Liability to Negligence: When and Why? Part 2," *Australian Law Journal* 94, no. 9 (2020).

[64] (1606) 5 Co Rep 125; 77 ER 250.

[65] (1770) 5 Burr 2776.

126    A. GRAY

evident in *E Hulton & Co v Jones*.[66] There the defendant (apparently unwittingly) wrote a fictional poem concerning a character Artemis Jones. There was a real Artemis Jones, who did not take kindly to the poem, and sued for defamation. The House of Lords noted it made no difference in determining liability whether the defendant acted intentionally or accidentally.

The harshness of these traditional rules of defamation has been noted.[67] In part, the strictness has been ameliorated by defences which take into account the reasonableness of the defendant's behaviour, particularly in the context of innocent dissemination.[68] On occasion, the court has recognised that one set of facts may give rise to both defamation and negligence claims, recognising that the tort of defamation may become less important over time as a result of the tension between the two.[69] Descheemaeker has noted the infusion of fault-based principles into strict liability defamation.[70]

So too in relation to the supposed strict liability tort of trespass. We have seen an increasing infusion of fault-based negligence principles, particularly in relation to defences. So, for example, the defence of self-defence considers whether the defendant's response was reasonable. In relation to the exigencies of everyday life, the court also considers the reasonableness of the defendant's behaviour, judged against community standards and expectations. In trespass to land cases too, courts have considered the question of fault, and the blameworthiness (if any) of the

[66] [1910] AC 20, 23–24.

[67] Tony Weir, "The Staggering March of Negligence," 115: 'if there is one tort which would have benefited from the introduction of the rules of negligence, it is defamation'.

[68] *Emmens v. Pottle* (1885) 16 QBD 354; *Defamation Act 1996* (UK) s 1(1). Eric Descheemaeker, "Protecting Reputation: Defamation and Negligence," *Oxford Journal of Legal Studies* 29 (2009): 630 describes the offer to make amends in s 4 of that Act as 'an excellent example of the imposition of a negligence standard of liability on the law of defamation'.

[69] *Spring v. Guardian Assurance Plc* [1995] 2 AC 296, 337 (Lord Slynn), 346 (Lord Woolf).

[70] Eric Descheemaeker, "Protecting Reputation," 639–40: 'over the course of the past century, the English law of defamation has seen a massive, if typically under-recognized, infiltration of the principles of negligence in a tort which had previously been defined … in isolation from it. This can be taken to reflect the law's growing dissatisfaction with the modern paradigm of defamation. This paradigm is that liability for injuring someone's reputation unjustifiably is ordinarily strict … there seems to be a gradual convergence towards negligence-culpa as the standard of liability.'

defendant's actions.[71] This has led commentators to declare that the traditional tort of trespass is (or should be regarded as) obsolete.[72]

In sum, although these three torts of nuisance, defamation and trespass were traditionally considered to be 'strict', in each of them courts have found that strict liability is not sufficient to deliver justice, and notions of fault have found their way in, whether in the concept of 'reasonable user' and consideration of fault issues in nuisance cases, and in respect of defences in the area of defamation and trespass. These torts have become somewhat chameleon-like, with a history of strict liability, but a development that incorporates fault elements. It is not something that adds to the intellectual coherence of tort law.

## Conclusion

The common law of tort has evolved substantially away from a strict liability approach towards a fault-based approach. While there are traces of this from the seventeenth century, the Industrial Revolution sped up this evolution substantially, aided by the development of the action on the case, developments in criminal law and statutory provision. An apparent attempt to re-calibrate the common law back to strict liability in *Rylands* would eventually founder. A fault basis of liability is superior because it better enables courts to consider all of the circumstances of a particular scenario in determining whether or not a defendant should be liable for causing the plaintiff injury or loss. It judges the defendant's behaviour against the standards of the community and questions of reasonableness, a more nuanced and sophisticated inquiry than application of strict liability principles would permit. Though the common law has come a long way, vestiges of strict liability remain in the torts of nuisance, defamation and

---

[71] *Chic Fashions (West Wales) v. Jones* [1968] 2 QB 299, 315 (CA) (noting that the action for trespass to land did not traditionally involve questions of blameworthiness on the defendant's part, before continuing) 'the development of the common law in the last thirty years, however, has tended towards equating civil liability with conduct which right-minded men in contemporary society would regard as blameworthy and towards protecting those who act reasonably in intended performance of what right-minded men would deem a duty to their fellow men'.

[72] Christine Beuermann, "Are the Torts of Trespass to the Person Obsolete? Part II: Continued Evolution," *Tort Law Review* 26 (2018): 17. See similarly M. A. Millner, "The Retreat of Trespass," *Current Legal Problems* 18, no. 1 (1965): 30 and Peter Handford, "Intentional Negligence: A Contradiction in Terms?" *Sydney Law Review* 32 (2010): 61–62.

trespass, though even in these supposedly strict liability torts, fault considerations continued to arise. It would be better for the law of torts to make a clean break entirely from its strict liability origins, rather than be forced to import in fault considerations to torts that are (at least notionally) strict in nature. The history of the law of torts must not be permitted to continue to shackle its present and future.

## REFERENCES

1. Arnold, Morris S. 1979. Accident, Mistake, and Rules of Liability in the Fourteenth-Century Law of Torts. *University of Pennsylvania Law Review* 128: 361–378.
2. Baker, J. H. 2002. *An Introduction to English Legal History.* 4th ed. London: Butterworths.
3. *Bazley v. Curry* [1999] 2 SCR 534 (Can.)
4. Beever, Allan. 2016. *A Theory of Tort Liability.* Oxford: Hart Publishing.
5. *Bennett v. Mellor* (1793) TR 273; 101 ER 154.
6. Beuermann, Christine. 2018. Are the Torts of Trespass to the Person Obsolete? Part 2: Continued Evolution. *Tort Law Review* 26: 6–17.
7. *Burnie Port Authority v. General Jones Pty Ltd* (1994) 179 CLR 520.
8. Calabresi, Guido. 1961. Some Thoughts on Risk Distribution and the Law of Torts. *Yale Law Journal* 70: 499–553.
9. *Calye's Case* (1604) 8 Co Rep 321; 77 ER 520.
10. *Cambridge Water Co. v. Eastern Counties Leather Co.* [1994] 2 AC 264.
11. *Carriers Act 1830* (UK).
12. *Chic Fashions (West Wales) v. Jones* [1968] 2 QB 299.
13. *De Libellis Famosis* (1606) 5 Co. Rep. 125; 77 ER 250.
14. *Defamation Act 1996* (UK).
15. Descheemaeker, Eric. 2009. Protecting Reputation: Defamation and Negligence. *Oxford Journal of Legal Studies* 29: 603–641.
16. *E Hulton & Co v. Jones* [1910] AC 20.
17. *Emmens v. Pottle* (1885) 16 QBD 354.
18. *Fletcher v. Rylands* (1865) LR 1 Ex. 265 (CA).
19. Fletcher, George P. 1972. Fairness and Utility in Tort Theory. *Harvard Law Review* 85: 537–73.
20. Fridman, G. H. L. 1956. The Rise and Fall of Rylands v. Fletcher. *Canadian Bar Review* 34: 810–824.
21. Gearty, Conor. 1989. The Place of Private Nuisance in a Modern Law of Torts. *The Cambridge Law Journal* 48: 214–42.
22. Gilles, Stephen G. 1994. Inevitable Accident in Classical English Tort Law. *Emory Law Journal* 43: 575–646.

## 7 THE HISTORICAL DEVELOPMENT OF THE FAULT BASIS OF LIABILITY... 129

23. Gray, Anthony. 2020. The Evolution from Strict Liability to Negligence: When and Why? Part 1. *Australian Law Journal* 94: 614–630.
24. ———. 2020. The Evolution from Strict Liability to Negligence: When and Why? Part 2. *Australian Law Journal* 94: 699–708.
25. ———. 2021. *The Evolution from Strict Liability to Fault in the Law of Torts.* Oxford: Hart Publishing.
26. ———. 2018. *Vicarious Liability: Critique and Reform.* Oxford: Hart Publishing.
27. Hale, Matthew. 1682. *Pleas of the Crown.* London: Atkyns and Atkyns.
28. *Hammond v The Vestry of St Pancras* (1874) LR 9 CP 316.
29. Handford, Peter. 2010. Intentional Negligence: A Contradiction in Terms. *Sydney Law Review* 32: 29–62.
30. *Heaven v. Pender* (1883) 11 QBD 503.
31. *Hedley Byrne v. Heller and Partners* [1964] AC 562.
32. *Holmes v. Mather* (1875) LR 10 Ex. 261.
33. Holmes, Oliver Wendell, Jr. 1881. *The Common Law.* Boston: Little, Brown and Company.
34. *Hull v. Orynge* (1466) B & M 327 (KB).
35. Ibbetson, David J. 1999. *A Historical Introduction to the Law of Obligations.* Oxford: Oxford University Press.
36. ———. 2003. How the Romans Did for Us: Ancient Roots of the Tort of Negligence. *University of New South Wales Law Journal* 26 (2): 475–514.
37. *Innkeepers Act 1863* (UK).
38. Kaczorowski, Robert J. 1990. The Common-Law Background of Nineteenth-Century Tort Law. *Ohio State Law Journal* 51: 1127–1200.
39. Klemme, Howard C. 1976. The Enterprise Liability Theory of Torts. *University of Colorado Law Review* 47: 153–232.
40. Kretzmer, David. 1984. Transformation of Tort Liability in the Nineteenth Century: The Visible Hand. *Oxford Journal of Legal Studies* 4: 46–87.
41. *Lambert v Bessey* (1681) Sir T Raym. 467; 83 ER 244.
42. Lee, Maria. 2003. What is Private Nuisance? *Law Quarterly Review* 119: 298–325.
43. *Lister v. Romford Ice and Cold Storage Co Ltd* [1957] AC 555.
44. Malone, Wex S. 1970–1971. "Ruminations on the Role of Fault in the History of the Common Law of Torts." *Louisiana Law Review* 31: 1–44.
45. *Michell v. Allestry* (1685) 3 Keb. 650; 84 ER 932.
46. Millner, M. A. 1965. "The Retreat of Trespass." *Current Legal Problems* 18: 20–38.
47. *Mitchil v Alestree* (1676) 1 Vent. 295; 86 ER 190.
48. Morris, C. Robert Jr. 1961. Enterprise Liability and the Actuarial Process—The Insignificance of Foresight. *Yale Law Journal* 70: 554–602.
49. Murphy, John. 2010. *The Law of Nuisance.* Oxford: Oxford University Press.

130  A. GRAY

50. *Navenby v. Lascelles* (1368) B & M 552.
51. Newark, F. H. 1949. The Boundaries of Nuisance. *Law Quarterly Review* 65: 480–490.
52. Pollock, Frederick and Frederic Maitland. 1895. *History of English Law before the Time of Edward I.* Boston: Little, Brown and Company.
53. Pollock, Frederick. 1882. *Essays in Jurisprudence and Ethics.* London: Macmillan and Co.
54. *R v. Woodfall* (1770) 5 Burr. 2776.
55. *Read v. J Lyons and Company* [1947] AC 156.
56. *Restatement (First) of Torts,* American Law Institute (1938).
57. *Restatement (Second) of Torts,* American Law Institute (1977).
58. *Restatement (Third) of Torts,* American Law Institute (1998).
59. *Rex v. Pease* (1832) 4 B & Ad. 30; 110 ER 366.
60. *Rich v. Kneeland* (1613) Cro. Jac. 330; 79 ER 282.
61. *Rylands v. Fletcher* (1868) LR 3 AC 330.
62. Sayre, Francis Bowes. 1932. Mens Rea. *Harvard Law Review* 45: 974–1026.
63. *Sedleigh-Denfield v. O'Callaghan* [1940] AC 880.
64. Simpson, A. W. B. 1984. Legal Liability for Bursting Reservoirs: The Historical Context of Rylands v. Fletcher. *Journal of Legal Studies* 13: 209–264.
65. Smith, Jeremiah. 1917. Tort and Absolute Liability: Suggested Changes in Classification. *Harvard Law Review* 30: 241–62.
66. *Spring v. Guardian Assurance Plc* [1995] 2 AC 296.
67. *Stanley v. Powell* [1891] 1 QB 86.
68. *Tarry v. Ashton* (1876) 1 QBD 314.
69. *Tenant v. Goodwin* (1705) 2 Ld. Raym. 1089; 92 ER 222.
70. *Torette House Pty Ltd v. Berkman* (1940) 62 CLR 637.
71. *Transco Plc v. Stockport Metropolitan Borough Council* [2004] 2 AC 1.
72. *Vaughan v. Taff Vale Railway* (1860) 5 H & N 679; 156 ER 667.
73. *Weaver v. Ward* (1616) Hob. 134; 80 ER 284.
74. Weir, Tony. 1998. The Staggering March of Negligence. In *The Law of Obligations: Essays in Celebration of John Fleming,* ed. Peter Cane and Jane Stapleton, 97–138. Oxford: Clarendon Press.
75. Winfield, P. H. 1931. Nuisance as a Tort. *The Cambridge Law Journal* 4: 189–206.
76. ———. 1926. The History of Negligence in the Law of Torts. *Law Quarterly Review* 42: 184–201.

CHAPTER 8

# What Albert Did and What Albert Did Next: Albert Bathurst Piddington—The High Court Judge Who Never Sat

*A. S. Bell and James Monaghan*

### INTRODUCTION

Albert Bathurst Piddington (Bathurst after the place of his birth) holds the dubious honour of being the only judge appointed to the High Court of Australia who never in fact sat on a case. More than a century has passed since the controversy surrounding his appointment and his subsequent decision to resign his commission as a puisne justice of the High

---

This chapter is adapted from an address given at the Law Faculty Dinner at St Paul's College, University of Sydney, on 2 September 2019.

---

A. S. Bell
Supreme Court of New South Wales, Solicitor, Sydney, Australia

J. Monaghan (✉)
Solicitor, Sydney, Australia

© The Author(s), under exclusive license to Springer Nature 131
Switzerland AG 2022
S. McKibbin et al. (eds.), *The Impact of Law's History*, Palgrave
Modern Legal History,
https://doi.org/10.1007/978-3-030-90068-7_8

Court—yet these events linger in our constitutional imagination, resurfacing from time to time in discourse concerning judicial appointments.[1]

Piddington may be best known now for his brief stint on the High Court, but it was just one season among many in a fascinating life. He lived through dynamic years of change, including the birth of the Commonwealth of Australia. He also, it would seem, enjoyed life to the full, and was forever intellectually curious and engaged.

This chapter has two aims. First, by following Piddington's life from his education through to his later cases and death, the chapter contextualises the one act—stepping down from the High Court—for which he is remembered. Second, the chapter highlights aspects of Piddington's life and career other than his appointment to and resignation from the High Court. Exploring these aspects of the man reveal the contemporary resonance of some of his labours, while also serving as a corrective to the tendency to reduce a rich life to a single episode.

## EARLY LIFE AND UNIVERSITY DAYS

Born to a clergyman in Bathurst on 9 September 1862,[2] Piddington moved around a great deal as a child. His schooling began at Cleveland Street Infants, followed by a short time at Newcastle Public School, a stint at Goulburn Public School, and a brief appearance at Newington College. According to Piddington's memoir, when he arrived at Newington, he was placed in the highest form in everything except Latin: a truant disposition in Goulburn had seen him attending more to the cattle sales than his conjugations. He therefore found himself in a beginners' Latin class with older divinity students. On his own account, "the tyrannical old Headmaster, unable to cane men of twenty-one or twenty-two, used to come down from his dais and cane me."[3] Understandably incensed, the young Piddington ran away for three days. His father, in Goulburn, telegraphed the President of the College, the Reverend Joseph Horner

---

[1] Stephen Gageler, "Judicial Appointment," *Sydney Law Review* 30, no. 1 (2008): 158; Rebecca Ananian-Welsh et al., *The Tim Carmody Affair: Australia's Greatest Judicial Crisis* (Sydney: NewSouth Books, 2016), 54–55.

[2] Graham Fricke, *Judges of the High Court* (Melbourne: Century Hutchinson, 1986), 77.

[3] Albert Bathurst Piddington, *Worshipful Masters* (Sydney: Angus & Robertson, 1929), 146–47.

## 8 WHAT ALBERT DID AND WHAT ALBERT DID NEXT: ALBERT BATHURST... 133

Fletcher, saying "Inform the police, search the river; if absconded, punish severely."[4]

Once located (and duly flogged), Piddington was, as they say, "withdrawn" from Newington at the end of the quarter.[5] He was sent to live on a station near Yass run by a Mr. J. F. Castle. There, he encountered a less brutal pedagogical style, and spent five months on the land, growing in his love of learning.[6] He would later write that:

> I owe Mr. Castle a great debt for taking, out of pure kindness towards the family, a young incorrigible as the guest not of his house and table only but of his rich mind and warm heart. But for him I should probably have never entered the Elysian fields, as they proved to be under [Professor Charles] Badham's later guidance, of foreign literature, and he made bearable a sentence of banishment from all schoolmates which first made me realize that school was not a place to run away from.[7]

From Yass, Piddington won a scholarship to Sydney Grammar School at age 14. After a few years there, he came to the University of Sydney and to St. Paul's College.

When he arrived at St. Paul's College in 1880, it was a much smaller place than it is now: in his first year, he was one of just seven undergraduates at the College, then under the wardenship of the Reverend William Hey Sharp.[8] In 1882, Piddington, Philip Street, and Andrew Macansh were all students at St. Paul's. In his history of the College, *Hearts and Minds*, Alan Atkinson writes that, in November of that year, Piddington and Macansh organised a petition complaining about food at breakfast and demanding the Steward's dismissal. Professor Atkinson continues:

> Then, late at night ... all three were together in their nightshirts in Macansh's room ..., singing to the combined melody of fire-irons, fender, concertina and French horn. "The Warden," said Piddington, "came in and ordered us to our rooms. Macansh invited us to stay as his guests. The Warden insisted. Macansh objected on grounds of jurisdiction under the by-laws." ... "Your

---

[4] Ibid., 147.
[5] Ibid., 148.
[6] Ibid., 150–59.
[7] Ibid., 158–59.
[8] University of Sydney, *The Sydney University Calendar 1880–81* (Sydney: Gibbs, Shallard & Co., 1881), 104–5, https://calendararchive.usyd.edu.au/Calendar/1880/1880-1.pdf

only power in a student's room, Macansh informed [Warden] Sharp, "is to order the removal of objectionable pictures from the walls. These gentlemen are not objectionable pictures, and what's more, they're not on the walls."[9]

Professor Atkinson records that Council dealt with this rebellion by tightening up the rules about suspension and expulsion. Of the three reprobates, one, Piddington, was to be appointed to the High Court; a second, Philip Street, was to become the eighth Chief Justice of New South Wales.

Later at the Bar, perhaps inspired by Macansh, Piddington would run a similarly ambitious argument regarding jurisdiction, trying to persuade the Supreme Court of New South Wales that the Court of Arbitration—established under the *Industrial Arbitration Act 1901* (NSW)—was not subject to the Supreme Court's supervisory jurisdiction. In response to Piddington's argument, Stephen ACJ rather pointedly remarked: "My only wonder is that anyone could be found to argue that this Court has been deprived of its most salutary jurisdiction to intervene in cases of this kind."[10]

At University, Piddington's scholarly gifts bloomed. He excelled in the matriculation exam and won scholarships and prizes each year.[11] At the end of 1883, he completed his BA with First Class Honours and the University Medal for Classics. He was outgoing and gregarious. As a 20-year-old, he attended a 22-course dinner for 150 guests—including judges and politicians—at Sydney Town Hall to mark the 70th birthday of Professor Badham, renowned Professor of Classics at Sydney University. Piddington was amongst the last four to leave in the company of the 33-year-old Edmund Barton. Piddington recorded that he "ate every

---

[9] Alan Atkinson, *Hearts and Minds: St. Paul's College, Sydney University, 1815–2016* (Sydney: UNSW Press, 2017), 150–51.

[10] *Hotel, Club, Restaurant and Caterers' Employees' Union v The Caterers' and Restaurant Keepers' Association* (1903) 2 AR (NSW) 196, 197.

[11] In the matriculation exam, he received first class honours in Classics and Mathematics, and was 'Distinguished' in Natural Science. In 1880, he was awarded the Hunter Baille Bursary No 2 and University Scholarship for General Proficiency (in Arts). In 1881, he was awarded the Lithgow Scholarship (for proficiency in classics) and a Prize Book in Classics. In 1882, he was awarded the Cooper Scholarship No 1 (for classical literature). And in 1883, together with the medal, he was awarded the University Prize for the BA Examination (Classics). See *The Sydney University Calendar* for the years: 1880–1, 1881–2, 1882–3, 1883–4, and 1884.

course, and afterwards walked home to St. Paul's College, treading (but treading firmly) on air all the way."[12]

Upon graduation, he stayed on at the College as Assistant Classical Lecturer[13] and Vice-Warden.[14] He also took up a post as a member of the first staff of Sydney High School—now Sydney Boys High School but then located in Castlereagh Street—where his intellectual gifts and passion for teaching attracted the admiration of students and staff alike.[15]

In 1887, he took a leave of absence to travel to Europe on a grand tour, visiting Professor Badham's old Oxford College, Wadham (hence, and inevitably, "Badham of Wadham").[16] He also travelled to Leiden in the Netherlands to call on one of Badham's academic colleagues, the ancient Greek scholar, C. G. Cobet and thence to Bonn in Germany where, apparently, "instead of seeking to make an impression as an academic he enthusiastically joined university students in noisy revelry."[17]

Upon his return, he continued to teach, lecturing evening students in English. And while he never abandoned his love of letters—indeed, on his death, Sir Robert Garran would write that literature was his first love—Piddington pivoted at this point, turning from academic pursuits towards the public square.[18] Taking up law, in 1889 he served as William Windeyer's Associate at the Supreme Court of New South Wales and, on 17 September 1890 aged 28, was called to the Bar.[19]

---

[12] Piddington, *Worshipful Masters*, 6. See also Robert Lehane, *William Bede Dalley: Silver-Tongued Pride of Old Sydney* (Charnwood, ACT: Ginninderra Press, 2007), 257–58.

[13] University of Sydney, *The Sydney University Calendar 1883–4* (Sydney: Gibbs, Shallard & Co., 1884), 145, https://calendararchive.usyd.edu.au/Calendar/1883/1883-4.pdf

[14] University of Sydney, *The Sydney University Calendar 1884* (Sydney: Gibbs, Shallard & Co., 1884), 154, https://calendararchive.usyd.edu.au/Calendar/1884/1884.pdf

[15] Morris Graham, *A. B. Piddington: The Last Radical Liberal* (Kensington, NSW: UNSW Press, 1995), 3.

[16] Piddington, *Worshipful Masters*, 12–14.

[17] Graham, *A. B. Piddington*, 4.

[18] Sir Robert Randolph Garran, "A. B. Piddington, M.A., K.C.," *ALJ* 19, no. 3 (1945): 69.

[19] Michael Roe, "Piddington, Albert Bathurst (1862–1945)," in *Australian Dictionary of Biography* (Melbourne: MUP, 1988).

## LAW AND POLITICS AT THE TURN OF THE CENTURY: FEDERATION AND ARBITRATION

During his first few years at the Bar in Denman Chambers, then located at 182 Phillip Street in Sydney, he continued to be involved in academic life, lecturing at the University, producing an annotated edition of extracts from Milton's *Paradise Lost*,[20] and serving as an examiner for the Junior Public Examination.[21] In 1894, at age 31, he felt a pull to political life, and ran for office in the Legislative Assembly in the electorate of Tamworth, having been invited by the Freetrade Association of Tamworth to be its candidate. He lost the 1894 election to a former Premier, Sir George Dibbs, but in the general election the following year, then aged 32, Piddington ran again and secured the seat.[22] Upon election, according to one historian, he declared that:

> He would support with his best efforts all fair and just requests, but as he was more than just the local member, "one representative of a people and of a colony," he would have to consider the interests of the whole colony. He would recommend deserving persons regardless of their politics. People now "demanded sincerity, straightness and earnestness" from their politicians.[23]

Piddington came to politics at a time when the question of federation was being hotly debated. He was supportive of federation, and eager to work for the establishment of a strong, flexible national government, founded on majoritarian democracy.[24] He did not consider, however, that the draft Commonwealth Constitution Bills that came out of the

---

[20] Early in his career at the Bar, Piddington was the plaintiff in proceedings in the Supreme Court—though he did not represent himself. He sought an injunction prohibiting publication of a book by George Thornton which he alleged infringed his copyright in relation to his edition of the Milton selections. The Chief Judge in Equity, Justice Owen, dismissed Piddington's motion for an injunction, holding that the two books substantially differed. The reason the two collections contained the same extracts from *Paradise Lost* is that those extracts were set texts for University examinations; Piddington had in fact set them. See *Piddington v Philip* (1893) 14 LR (NSW) Eq 159.

[21] Graham, *A. B. Piddington*, 4.

[22] L. F. Crisp, *Federation Fathers* (Melbourne: MUP, 1990), 129; Graham, *A.B. Piddington*, 12.

[23] Graham, *A. B. Piddington*, 12.

[24] Crisp, *Federation Fathers*, 130.

1897–1898 Convention and the 1899 Premiers' Conference would establish a national government of this character, and so was vocal in his criticism of them, both in and out of Parliament[25]—so much so that his opponents "interpreted his initials [A. B.] as 'Anti-Bill', and christened his brother, W. H. B. Piddington, 'Will Have Bill'."[26]

Piddington's core complaint about the draft bills was that they contained a fundamental incompatibility, trying to hold together the British system of responsible government with a US-style bicameral national legislature. On his view, the incompatibility arose out of the fact that, in the British system, the government is ultimately responsible to the lower house, being the house that represents the interest of the people. Where there is a second chamber in other Westminster systems, it "does not possess an insuperable veto … [and represents] the *same interest* [as the first chamber]—that of the nation at large."[27] In US-style federalism, however, the Senate represents a different interest to that of the House of Representatives—namely, that of the states. Piddington feared that the Convention bills, in failing to clearly specify the chamber to which the government was responsible and in giving the Senate power to refuse supply, were making the mistake "of giving [our] solar system two suns."[28]

He campaigned strenuously against the draft bills and, even after he lost his seat in the 1898 general elections, he campaigned in the press and in public addresses. In June 1899, speaking in Tamworth against the bill that had emerged from the Premiers' Conference earlier that year, Piddington said:

> I shall oppose the Bill, because a year's reflection has only made me more convinced that this is a measure which makes majority rule forever impossible for Australia. It denies to Australians the birthright of all men of British birth—the power of the purse. It puts heavy and needless burdens of taxation on the shoulders of those least able to bear them. It carries within it the germs of financial chaos and bitter heart-burnings between

[25] Ibid.

[26] Garran, "A. B. Piddington," 69.

[27] New South Wales, *Parliamentary Debates*, Legislative Assembly, 27 May 1897, 698, quoted in Crisp, *Federation Fathers*, 132.

[28] Albert Bathurst Piddington, *Popular Government and Federation* (Sydney: Angus & Robertson, 1898), 10–12.

State and State in the demoralising scramble for the Federal surplus. It breathes the very spirit of provincialism and sets up a mockery of true nationhood. It makes responsible government impossible because it gives the Government two masters—the House and the Senate. As the final stroke of injustice to all Australians yet born and yet to be born, it denies to us the fundamental privilege of all free people, the right by majority vote to amend our Constitution according to our needs whenever, like every other human instrument, its faults become visible in the onward march of time.[29]

Piddington's rhetoric gives a sense both of his intellect and of the depth of his concern: he thought the draft bills did the people of Australia a serious disservice, giving the interests of abstract governmental entities, the States, priority over the interests of ordinary people. One can also see that he was a nationalist.

By royal proclamation, the *Commonwealth of Australia Constitution Act 1900* commenced on 1 January 1901, and the Commonwealth was established. It is unlikely that Piddington was satisfied with the form that the *Constitution* took. But he had lost that argument and turned to other things.

Another statute, given assent at the close of 1901,[30] would set the course of much of Piddington's professional life for the next few decades. The *Industrial Arbitration Act 1901* (NSW) opened a new field of legal work for practitioners like Piddington. The Act provided for the registration and incorporation of employer unions and employee unions, and it created a new court: the Court of Arbitration. The Act was intended to encourage collective bargaining and, where such bargaining failed, the Court could hear and determine industrial disputes.[31]

The new system was beset with various problems, largely on account of employers who "frustrated the system by encouraging the registration of bogus unions, refusing to register their own associations and using legal representation to slow down procedures and increase

---

[29] *Tamworth Observer*, June 17, 1899, quoted in Crisp, *Federation Fathers*, 136.

[30] New South Wales, *Parliamentary Debates*, Legislative Assembly, 10 December 1901, 4070.

[31] *Industrial Arbitration Act 1901* (NSW) s 16. Graham, *A. B. Piddington*, 34.

[employee] union costs."[32] The employers also pursued proceedings in the Supreme Court and the newly formed High Court on points concerning the Court of Arbitration's jurisdiction.[33] Those proceedings had the effect of undermining the finality of the Court of Arbitration's decisions.

Piddington was not a partisan in these disputes between labour and capital. While it is true that he acted for employee unions far more regularly than he did for employer unions,[34] Piddington was, at least initially, primarily a barrister taking advantage of the opening of a new legal market. The difficulties that the new industrial system faced were unfortunate for workers but produced work for lawyers.

The *Industrial Arbitration Act 1901* (NSW) contained a sunset clause and, when it lapsed, the *Industrial Disputes Act 1908* (NSW) took its place. That Act and its successors were beset by plenty of difficulties[35]—but, for Piddington, the 1908 Act created opportunities to chair wage boards.[36] In that capacity, Piddington became a respected, but largely non-partisan, player in industrial law matters. His early involvement in that sphere would see him come to play significant roles in what we would now call industrial relations, as well as in shaping welfare policy. In 1911, by now 49 years of age, the Labor government in New South Wales appointed him Royal Commissioner, tasking him with inquiring into whether there was a labour shortage at the time, the working conditions of women and children, and the cause of a decline in apprenticeships.[37] This was the first of many commissions he would receive.

---

[32] Greg Patmore, *Australian Labour History* (Melbourne: Longman Cheshire, 1991), 110.

[33] See, for example, *Hotel, Club, Restaurant and Caterers' Employees' Union v The Caterers' and Restaurant Keepers' Association* (1903) 2 AR (NSW) 196 (Supreme Court of New South Wales); *Re Clancy* (1903) 3 AR (NSW) 6 (Supreme Court of New South Wales); *Re Clancy* (1904) 3 AR (NSW) 206 (High Court of Australia).

[34] Graham, *A. B. Piddington*, 35.

[35] See, for example, Patmore, *Australian Labour History*, 111–113.

[36] David Ash, "Albert Bathurst Piddington," *Bar News* (Summer 2009–10): 48.

[37] Roe, "Piddington, Albert Bathurst (1862–1945)"; Graham, *A. B. Piddington*, 43.

# 140    A. S. BELL AND J. MONAGHAN

## THE HIGH COURT: APPOINTMENT AND RESIGNATION

By 1912, though not appointed silk, Piddington had appeared in the High Court 26 times,[38] on 18 occasions unled or leading.[39] These suits spanned diverse areas of law including constitutional and administrative cases, statutory interpretation cases concerning the rights of public servants, cases about Crown Lands, tort and contract matters, and some criminal law as well.

[38] *Clancy v Butchers' Shop Employees Union* (1904) 1 CLR 181; *Borough of Tamworth v Sanders* (1904) 2 CLR 214; *Crowley v Glissan [No 2]* (1905) 2 CLR 744; *Miller v McKeon* (1905) 3 CLR 50; *Tindal v Calman* (1905) 3 CLR 150; *Sweeney v Fitzhardinge* (1906) 4 CLR 716; *Greville v Williams* (1906) 4 CLR 694; *Goldsborough, Mort and Co Ltd v Larcombe* (1907) 5 CLR 263; *Hazleton v Potter* (1907) 5 CLR 445; *O'Keefe v Williams* (1907) 5 CLR 217; *Mitchell v Scales* (1907) 5 CLR 405; *Merchant Service Guild of Australasia v Archibald Currie & Co Pty Ltd* (1908) 5 CLR 737; *Doodeward v Spence* (1908) 6 CLR 406; *Williams v Macharg* (1908) 7 CLR 213; *Sobye v Levy* (1909) 9 CLR 496; *Knowles v The Council of the Municipality of Newcastle* (1909) 9 CLR 534; *Australian Agricultural Co v Municipality of Newcastle* (1910) 10 CLR 391; *Mason v Commonwealth* (1910) 10 CLR 655; *R v Commonwealth Court of Conciliation and Arbitration; Ex parte Whybrow & Co* (1910) 11 CLR 1; *Wingadee Shire Council v Willis* (1910) 11 CLR 123; *O'Keefe v Williams* (1910) 11 CLR 171; *Osborne v Commonwealth* (1911) 12 CLR 321; *De Britt v Carr* (1911) 13 CLR 114; *Union Bank of Australia Ltd v Rudder* (1911) 13 CLR 152; *Colon Peaks Mining Co (NL) v Wollondilly Shire Council* (1911) 13 CLR 438; *Sendall v Federal Commissioner of Land Tax* (1911) 12 CLR 653.

[39] *Clancy v Butchers' Shop Employees Union* (1904) 1 CLR 181 (Piddington for the respondent); *Miller v McKeon* (1905) 3 CLR 50 (Piddington, J Young with him, for the respondent); *Tindal v Calman* (1905) 3 CLR 150 (Piddington for the respondent); *Greville v Williams* (1906) 4 CLR 694 (Piddington, Hammond with him, for the appellant); *Goldsborough, Mort and Co Ltd v Larcombe* (1907) 5 CLR 263 (Piddington, Waddell with him, for the respondent); *O'Keefe v Williams* (1907) 5 CLR 217 (Piddington, HM Stephen with him, for the respondent); *Mitchell v Scales* (1907) 5 CLR 405 (Piddington for the appellant); *Doodeward v Spence* (1908) 6 CLR 406 (Piddington for the respondent); *Williams v Macharg* (1908) 7 CLR 213 (Piddington for the appellant); *Sobye v Levy* (1909) 9 CLR 496 (Piddington for the applicant); *Knowles v The Council of the Municipality of Newcastle* (1909) 9 CLR 534 (Piddington for the respondent); *Australian Agricultural Co v Municipality of Newcastle* (1910) 10 CLR 391 (Piddington, Blacket with him, for the respondent); *Mason v Commonwealth* (1910) 10 CLR 655 (Piddington, Wise KC and Ferguson with him, for the defendant); *Wingadee Shire Council v Willis* (1910) 11 CLR 123 (Piddington and Pike for the appellants); *O'Keefe v Williams* (1910) 11 CLR 171 (Piddington and HM Stephen for the respondent); *De Britt v Carr* (1911) 13 CLR 114 (Piddington and Coffey for the respondent); *Union Bank of Australia Ltd v Rudder* (1911) 13 CLR 152 (Piddington and Thomson for the respondent); *Sendall v Federal Commissioner of Land Tax* (1911) 12 CLR 653 (Piddington and JA Browne for the respondent).

8 WHAT ALBERT DID AND WHAT ALBERT DID NEXT: ALBERT BATHURST...    141

In late 1912, Billy Hughes—then the Attorney General in the Fisher Labor government—had the opportunity to fill three seats on the High Court. The first vacancy was a result of the death of Justice O'Connor; the other two were products of the *Judiciary Act 1912* (Cth), which expanded the number of puisne justices of the High Court from four to six, creating the bench of seven justices (including the Chief Justice) that we still have today.

The early constitutional jurisprudence of the Court, shaped in large part by the original three justices—and especially the first Chief Justice, Sir Samuel Griffith, a former Premier of Queensland—had favoured the preservation of the pre-federation powers of the States over the expansion of Commonwealth power.[40] On this point, it is important to remember that it was not until 1920 that the Court, in the *Engineers' Case*,[41] would take a profoundly textualist turn in constitutional interpretation, eschewing reliance on the reserved powers doctrine.

Hughes did not share the states-rights sympathies of the original three justices. Accordingly, given the opportunity, he was keen to appoint someone who might favour Commonwealth power over that of the States. He appointed Frank Gavan Duffy K.C. from the Victorian Bar—a safe choice from the perspective of the profession,[42] and a conservative one constitutionally: in the *Engineers' Case*, Gavan Duffy J would be alone in dissent.[43] Hughes also appointed Charles Powers, the Commonwealth Crown Solicitor. Though formally admitted as a barrister and solicitor in Queensland, Powers had primarily practised as a solicitor, and had never

---

[40] Anne Twomey, "The Knox Court," in *The High Court, the Constitution and Australian Politics*, eds. Rosalind Dixon and George Williams (Port Melbourne, Vic: CUP, 2015), 98, 101–2.

[41] *Amalgamated Society of Engineers v Adelaide Steamship Co Ltd* (1920) 28 CLR 129 ('*Engineers' Case*'). The extent to which Griffith CJ, Barton and O'Connor JJ had developed the Court's early jurisprudence on the relationship between Commonwealth and State power as a bloc was evident in the majority judgment in the *Engineers' Case*, where Knox CJ, Isaacs, Rich and Starke JJ (Isaacs J delivering the judgment) said at 150: "Though [the doctrine of 'implied prohibition' has been] subsequently reaffirmed by three members of this Court, it has often been rejected by two other members of the Court, and has never been unreservedly accepted and applied." It is clear that the "three members" are the original three, while the "two other members" are Isaacs and Higgins JJ, the fourth and fifth justices appointed to the High Court.

[42] Geoffrey Sawer, *Australian Federalism in the Courts* (Melbourne: MUP, 1967), 65; Fricke, *Judges of the High Court*, 78.

[43] Fricke, *Judges of the High Court*, 66.

appeared before the High Court as an advocate.[44] On that account, his appointment was poorly received by the press and, perhaps more importantly, by the Sydney and Melbourne Bars.[45]

For his third choice, Hughes was considering Piddington, having admired the individualism that he had displayed in the debates leading up to the passage of the *Commonwealth Constitution*. It is also likely that Hughes looked favourably on Piddington's enthusiasm in the 1890s for a strong and flexible national government.[46] He wanted to be sure, however, as to what Piddington's views were on the balance of power between the Commonwealth and the States. At the time that Hughes was considering his appointment, Piddington was in Europe. Among other things, Piddington had been attending the International Eugenics Congress with his wife Marion.[47] Because of his absence, Hughes approached Piddington's brother-in-law, Dowell O'Reilly, seeking to discern Piddington's views on Commonwealth power. O'Reilly did not know, but cabled Piddington on 2 February 1913, writing: "Confidential most important know your views commonwealth versus state rights very urgent O'Reilly."[48]

Piddington received the message on his way back from Europe and replied saying: "In sympathy with supremacy of Commonwealth powers."[49] This was duly communicated to Hughes who, satisfied with the response, informally offered Piddington a seat on the bench. Somewhat concerned about the propriety of his earlier telegram, Piddington wired Hughes from Colombo on 14 February, saying: "If with complete independence [on] validity questions shall accept Do not hesitate to withdraw offer if you wish, wire again Freidrich der Grosse [the ship he was on] and I will reply officially grateful anyhow Piddington."[50]

Hughes was happy with this conditional acceptance and told the public that Piddington was to take up a seat on the bench. On 17 February, in

---

[44] Ibid., 70–2.

[45] Ibid., 80; Brian Galligan, *Politics of the High Court: A Study of the Judicial Branch of Government in Australia* (St Lucia, Qld: University of Queensland Press, 1987), 93.

[46] Crisp, *Federation Fathers*, 130.

[47] Roe, "Piddington, Albert Bathurst (1862–1945)."

[48] Telegram from Dowell O'Reilly to A. B. Piddington, Papers of A. B. Piddington, National Library of Australia, MS 1095/12.

[49] Telegram from A. B. Piddington to Dowell O'Reilly, Papers of A. B. Piddington, National Library of Australia, MS 1095/13.

[50] Telegram from A. B. Piddington to W. M. Hughes, Papers of A. B. Piddington, National Library of Australia, MS 1095/18, MS 1095/20.

## 8 WHAT ALBERT DID AND WHAT ALBERT DID NEXT: ALBERT BATHURST... 143

response to Piddington's concerns about independence, Hughes wrote to Piddington saying, "There are no conditions—except that you keep alive as long as you possibly can: Even this need not be put in writing."[51] In due course, the Governor-General issued a commission,[52] and preparations commenced for Piddington's swearing-in.

Piddington received many letters congratulating him on his appointment from friends, other judges and lawyers, and from former students. One such student, a solicitor called Ernest Henry Tebbutt, wrote to Piddington, "as an old High School boy, one who sat under you, and enjoyed and profited from your fine tuition."[53]

Unfortunately, not everyone received Powers' and Piddington's appointments so warmly. The Sydney and Melbourne Bars both resolved not to offer the customary congratulations to the new appointees.[54] The opposition to Piddington's appointment was not primarily political: the public did not know of his ill-advised telegram recording his Commonwealth sympathies. Rather, the objection was simply that Piddington lacked experience and standing in the profession, and that others would be better suited to high judicial office. *The Argus*, a Melbourne-based paper, summed up the feelings of the profession, saying:

> Mr Piddington has been sufficiently long in practice in New South Wales to justify his being elevated to the bench of the District Court (not to speak of the State Supreme Court), provided that his knowledge and ability had equipped him with the requisite qualifications. His name has never been mentioned in connection with any considerable legal post in his own State. His status in the profession is, to put it mildly, only moderate; yet he has been called to a Bench which will decide appeals from State judges who are, in knowledge of law, immeasurably his superiors. Not only so, but he is to hear arguments upon constitutional problems by lawyers beside whose attainments his own shrink into absurd insignificance. It is little wonder that such men feel not only dismayed and indignant, but affronted, by the choice of the Labour Ministry.[55]

---

[51] Letter from W. M. Hughes to A. B. Piddington, Papers of A.B. Piddington, National Library of Australia, MS 1095/29.

[52] Commonwealth, *Commonwealth of Australia Gazette*, No 17, 8 Mar 1913, 541.

[53] Letter from Ernest Henry Tebbutt to A. B. Piddington, Papers of A.B. Piddington, National Library of Australia, MS 1095/82.

[54] Fricke, *Judges of the High Court*, 81.

[55] *The Argus (Melbourne)*, Mar 13, 1913, 12.

144    A. S. BELL AND J. MONAGHAN

*The Bulletin* was even more forthright:

Piddington was, till W.M. Hughes discovered him last week, a more or less obscure junior, with a modest, in fact, insignificant practice. Setting aside the K.C.'s, it would be easy to name half a dozen men at the N.S. Wales Bar, and many at the Bar in other States, who are immeasurably his superiors. His personal character is, of course, unimpeachable. On the other hand he is one of the last whom a colleague would select as the possessor of a judicial mind. He possesses no sense of legal proportion. His intellect is, forensically speaking, of the perverse and pedantic order. He was a "coach" for years, and the mark of the schoolmaster is still on him in plain figures.[56]

Though the Governor-General had issued his commission, Piddington had not yet been sworn in. Faced with this criticism, and after taking advice from Sir William Cullen, the Chief Justice of New South Wales, and his friend Sir Edmund Barton, Piddington resigned his commission on 24 March 1913.[57] A Sydney paper, *The Sun*, noted that the New South Wales Bar Council was "elated" at the "capitulation of Mr Piddington on the eve of his swearing-in."[58]

Hughes was deeply disappointed by Piddington's choice and, turned on him, later describing Piddington as having "resigned from his great office like a panic-stricken boy."[59] Geoffrey Sawer read Piddington's response in similar terms, judging that he "was terrified into immediate resignation by the screams of rage which his appointment elicited from the reactionary Melbourne and Sydney bars."[60]

[56] *The Bulletin (Sydney)*, Feb 20, 1913, 8.

[57] Fricke, *Judges of the High Court*, 81–2; Geoffrey Sawer, *Australian Federal Politics and Law 1901–1929* (Melbourne: MUP, 1956), 105–6. Piddington is not the only Australian judge to have resigned without being sworn in. Keith Mason records that Julian Salomons was appointed Chief Justice of New South Wales on 12 November 1886 and resigned just 16 days later on 27 November without being sworn in: Keith Mason, *Lawyers Then and Now: An Australian Legal Miscellany* (Annandale, NSW: Federation Press, 2012), 84–5.

[58] "Mr Piddington's Withdrawal," *The Sun (Sydney)*, Mar 25, 1913; Papers of A. B. Piddington, National Library of Australia, MS 1095/137.

[59] Quoted in Fricke, *Judges of the High Court*, 82.

[60] Sawer, *Australian Federalism in the Courts*, 65. Note, however, that in an earlier and slightly longer treatment of the same episode, Sawer presents a more nuanced view, writing: "It seems probable that Piddington's resignation was induced not only by his scruples concerning the exchange of cables, but also by the hostile reception from the legal profession in Melbourne and Sydney." Sawer, *Australian Federal Politics and Law*, 106.

8 WHAT ALBERT DID AND WHAT ALBERT DID NEXT: ALBERT BATHURST... 145

That reading of things may be right—the criticism of Piddington's appointment was, after all, bitterly expressed, and it would be natural enough to feel somewhat intimidated as a result. But we should also recall that Piddington was a man of high principle—and from the debates over Federation, known to be. A few months after his resignation, he was appointed King's Counsel. When he announced his appointment before the High Court, according to the *Sydney Morning Herald*,[61] Barton ACJ:

> depart[ed] so far from the practice of the Court as to say that the Court welcomes your accession to the rank of King's Counsel with more feeling from the fact that you were recently one of its members, and resigned your commission as a Justice in this Court under circumstances which nobody who knows you can doubt evinced motives of the highest honour and most delicate feeling.

Whatever motivated his resignation, Piddington has the peculiar distinction of being the only High Court judge never to have sat on a case (although a decision he made as President of the Inter-State Commission was appealed to the High Court in 1915).[62] Though he gave up the high office of a justice of the High Court, Piddington went on to do much more in his long life, including 22 further appearances in the High Court in the years spanning 1923–1938.[63]

---

[61] *Sydney Morning Herald*, May 10, 1913, 19. Egon Kisch would later write in his memoir, *Australian Landfall*, that Piddington had resigned his position "because of a personal view regarding a point of duty": Egon Kisch, *Australian Landfall* (South Melbourne: Macmillan, 1969), 64.

[62] *New South Wales v Commonwealth* (1915) 20 CLR 54 ("*The Wheat Case*").

[63] *Spain v Union Steamship Company of New Zealand Limited* (1923) 32 CLR 138 (Piddington KC, Collins with him, for the appellant); *Russell v Wilson* (1923) 33 CLR 538 (Piddington KC, Delohery with him, for the appellant); *Spain v Union Steamship Company of New Zealand* (1923) 33 CLR 555 (Piddington KC, Collins with him, for the appellant); *Pickard v John Heine & Son Ltd* (1924) 35 CLR 1 (Piddington KC, Sherwood with him, for the appellant); *Hillman v Commonwealth* (1924) 35 CLR 260 (Piddington KC and Collins for the appellant); *Burwood Cinema Ltd v Australian Theatrical and Amusement Employees' Association* (1925) 35 CLR 528 (Piddington KC, Cantor with him, for the respondent); *Jumna Khan v Bankers & Traders Insurance Co Ltd* (1925) 37 CLR 451 (Piddington KC, Newell and KA Ferguson with him, for the appellant); *Clyde Engineering Company Limited v Cowburn* (1926) 37 CLR 466 (Piddington KC, Cantor with him, for the respondents); *New South Wales v Commonwealth* (1926) 38 CLR 74 (Piddington KC and Browne KC, McKell with them, for the plaintiffs); *Williams v Commissioner for Road Transport and Tramways (NSW)* (1933) 50 CLR 528 (Piddington KC, Herron and Curlewis with him, for

## WHAT ALBERT DID NEXT

In April 1913, the New South Wales Government appointed Piddington Royal Commissioner again, instructing him to inquire into the administration of the *Industrial Arbitration Act 1912* (NSW), an Act that had substantially failed to address problems with the *Industrial Disputes Act* of 1908. Not long after, in August 1913, the federal government, then led by Joseph Cook, appointed him the Chief Commissioner of the Inter-State Commission. Irony abounded in the sense that it was widely thought that Billy Hughes himself personally aspired to this appointment.[64] That a man of Hughes' ambition held such aspirations is an indication of the Commission's perceived status at the time.

Though now a constitutional artefact, the Inter-State Commission is in fact provided for in s 101 of the *Constitution* in mandatory language:

> There shall be an Inter-State Commission, with such powers of adjudication and administration as the Parliament deems necessary for the execution and maintenance, within the Commonwealth, of the provisions of this Constitution relating to trade and commerce, and of all laws made thereunder.

During the Convention debates, it was contemplated as a body equal in importance to the High Court. It was, in effect, to be an economic High Court whose principal focus would be on inter-state trade and commerce, it being recalled that the great controversy that the founding fathers

---

the appellant); *R v Carter; Ex parte Kisch* (1934) 52 CLR 221 (Piddington KC, Parsonage with him, for the applicant); *R v Wilson; Ex parte Kisch* (1934) 52 CLR 234 (Piddington KC for the applicant); *R v Fletcher* (1935) 52 CLR 248 (Piddington KC, Farrer with him, for the applicant); *MacDonald v The King* (1935) 52 CLR 739 (Piddington KC, Farrer with him, for the applicant); *R v Dunbabin* (1935) 53 CLR 434 (Piddington KC, Farrer with him, for the applicant); *R v Brislan* (1935) 54 CLR 262 (Piddington KC, Evatt and Farrer with him, for the applicant); *The Seamen's Union of Australasia v Commonwealth Steamship Owners' Association* (1936) 54 CLR 626 (Piddington KC, De Baun with him, for the applicant); *Mercer v Commissioner for Road Transport and Tramways (NSW)* (1936) 56 CLR 580 (Piddington KC, RM Kidston with him, for the appellant); *R v Paterson; Ex parte Purves* [1937] ALR 144 (Piddington KC, Farrer with him, for the applicant); *McDonald v Victoria* (1937) 47 CLR 274 (Piddington KC and Farrer for the plaintiff); *Brunker v Perpetual Trustee Co (Ltd)* (1937) 59 CLR 140 (Piddington KC, McKillop with him, for the appellant); *Werrin v Commonwealth* (1938) 59 CLR 150 (Piddington KC, O'Sullivan and Farrer with him, for the plaintiff).

[64] Graham, *A. B. Piddington*, 63.

needed to grapple with was the diametrically opposed views in various colonies surrounding free trade and protectionism. The disputes which still exist today between the States as to water rights were precisely the kind of disputes that the Inter-State Commission was designed to resolve.[65]

So also, s 92 of the *Constitution*—a section the interpretation of which bedevilled the High Court in over 140 cases up until its 1988 decision in *Cole v Whitfield*[66]—was meant to be administered by the Inter-State Commission (as opposed to the High Court), which was authorised to "adjudicate" upon disputes arising in inter-state trade or commerce.[67]

Piddington's appointment as the inaugural President or Chair of the Inter-State Commission, unlike his earlier appointment to the High Court, was not apparently the subject of similar criticism.[68] As a man who had taken an enormous interest in politics, the birth of the nation, the federal system and matters that we would today describe as economics, it was a very significant appointment. This time, however, it was not Piddington's appointment personally which caused a difficulty but the very creation of the Inter-State Commission itself, notwithstanding that it is provided for in the *Constitution*.

In a landmark decision in 1915, in which the High Court split 4:2 on the relevant point, and which smacks of institutional rivalry, a majority of the Court effectively held that the Inter-State Commission, as it had been established, was a "toothless tiger."[69] Part V of the *Inter-State Commission Act 1912* (Cth) had purported to confer judicial powers on the Commission—so that it could exercise its constitutional role of

---

[65] Andrew Bell, "The Missing Constitutional Cog: The Omission of the Inter-State Commission," *Bar News* (Summer 2009–10): 59–60. See also Stephen Gageler, "Chapter IV: The Inter-State Commission and the Regulation of Trade and Commerce under the Australian Constitution," *PLR* 28 (2017): 208–9.

[66] (1988) 165 CLR 360.

[67] Bell, "The Missing Constitutional Cog," 60; Andrew Bell, "Inter-State Commission," in *The Oxford Companion to the High Court of Australia*, eds. Tony Blackshield, Michael Coper, and George Williams (South Melbourne: OUP, 2001), 353, 354. See also Andrew Bell, "The Elusive Promise of the Inter-State Commission," in *Encounters with Constitutional Interpretation and Legal Education: Essays in Honour of Michael Coper*, ed. James Stellios (Annandale, NSW: Federation Press, 2018), 34.

[68] Morris Graham, "Piddington, Albert Bathurst," in *The Oxford Companion to the High Court of Australia*, eds. Tony Blackshield, Michael Coper and George Williams (South Melbourne: OUP, 2001), 533, 534.

[69] *New South Wales v Commonwealth* (1915) 20 CLR 54 ('*The Wheat Case*').

"adjudication." A majority of the High Court, jealous of its own jurisdiction,[70] held that the whole of Pt V was invalid on the ground that it attempted to confer federal judicial power on a body that was not a Ch III court.[71] There was a powerful dissent by Sir Edmund Barton which many consider to be one of his finest judgments.[72]

Although the Commission was to do important work on the tariff,[73] the High Court's decision, combined with the onset of the First World War, meant that the Inter-State Commission limped on into constitutional and historical obscurity and, when the seven-year terms of its first three Commissioners expired, there were no replacements and the Inter-State Commission passed into a constitutional graveyard.[74]

Just as he emerged, however, from the disappointments which no doubt surrounded his appointment to and then resignation from the High Court, Piddington emerged from the demise of the Inter-State Commission. In March 1919, though his commission as Chairman of the Inter-State Commission was still on foot, Piddington was appointed a Royal Commissioner again, this time charged with inquiring into the sugar industry. It was a sign of the decline of the Inter-State Commission that the inquiry was conducted as a Royal Commission, not under the auspices of the constitutional body.[75]

In December 1919, Piddington was given yet another commission by the Commonwealth, this time charged with leading a Royal Commission on the cost of living. In the *Harvester* decision of 1907, Justice Higgins, the President of the Commonwealth Conciliation and Arbitration Court, had decided that seven shillings per day was a "fair and reasonable" wage for an unskilled worker, sufficient to cover "the normal needs of the average employee, regarded as a human being living in a civilised community."[76] A wage defined in these terms came to be known as a "basic wage." The

[70] Bell, "The Missing Constitutional Cog," 69.

[71] *The Wheat Case*, 65 (Griffith CJ), 95 (Isaacs J), 107 (Powers J), 110 (Rich J); 75, 77 (Barton J, dissenting), 104 (Gavan Duffy J, dissenting).

[72] Oscar Roos, "Justice Barton and the Demise of the Inter-State Commission in the *Wheat Case* (1915)," in *Great Australian Dissents*, ed. Andrew Lynch (Cambridge: CUP, 2016), 20.

[73] Bell, "Inter-State Commission," 353.

[74] The Commission had a brief, and largely ineffective, second life between 1984 and 1990. See Michael Coper, "The Second Coming of the Fourth Arm: The Role and Functions of the Inter-State Commission," *ALJ* 63 (1989).

[75] Bell, "The Missing Constitutional Cog," 69.

[76] *Ex parte H V McKay* (1907) 2 CAR 1, 3 ("*the Harvester case*").

report penned by Piddington and his fellow commissioners pointed out, however, that:[77]

> while the Harvester Case laid down the doctrine that a basic wage should be at least adequate to cover the cost of living according to reasonable standards, the decision in the case was given without that cost of living having been ascertained by evidence except to a partial extent.

With the resources of a Royal Commission—and without the constraints of the litigious setting in which Higgins J formulated the *Harvester* standard—Piddington and his colleagues gathered data on the four key components of a living wage: rent, clothing, food, and "miscellaneous items," a capacious category that included everything from life insurance to school expenses. The Commission determined a concrete standard for each of these four categories of expenses, and so developed a more realistic basis for determining the cost of living than the *Harvester* standard had provided.[78] The Report effectively recommended that the basic wage should correspond to the actual cost of living, as calculated by the Commission. Implementing that recommendation, however, would be very costly for employers, and the Report was more or less dead in the water on publication.[79]

The Report had been drafted by Piddington,[80] and some persistent themes in his social thought are seeded through it. One that would come to have particular prominence was his advocacy of child endowment—that is, financial assistance from the state to help meet the costs of raising children.[81] Piddington mentioned this cause in an appendix to the 1920 Report,[82] and developed his thoughts more fully in a tract he published the following year, titled *The Next Step: A Family Basic Income*.[83] An admirable concern for the welfare of children clearly stood behind his support for child endowment. But his support for the cause also had a dark side to it.

---

[77] Commonwealth, Royal Commission on the Basic Wage, *Report* (1920) 9.

[78] Ibid., 57.

[79] Graham, *A. B. Piddington*, 86, 88–9.

[80] Commonwealth, Royal Commission on the Basic Wage, *Report* (1920) 63.

[81] Graham, *A. B. Piddington*, 87.

[82] Commonwealth, Royal Commission on the Basic Wage, *Report* (1920) 90.

[83] Ash, "Albert Bathurst Piddington," 51.

Together with his wife, Marion, Piddington had a keen interest in eugenics, the so-called science of improving the human species by selective breeding and, in particular, the "breeding out" of perceived undesirable characteristics. Piddington and his wife were both very much concerned about "race suicide" and "race decay"—that is, about the enfeeblement of White Australia as a result of factors such as women and children working in damaging factory conditions and young men dying in the Great War. Marion's advocacy was concerned with heredity; Albert, on the other hand, was more focused on the ways that material and institutional conditions—"an adequate living wage, healthy housing standards and a sound education"—might contribute to improvement in both quantity and quality of the population.[84] His support of eugenic ideologies did not, of course, irredeemably taint child endowment as a policy. Women's rights activists at the time lobbied for the adoption of child endowment as government policy, together with equal pay and motherhood endowment.[85] But like so many figures in Australia's history, there is no escaping the fact that Piddington, for all his virtues, also had what we now see clearly as vices.

After chairing the 1920 Royal Commission, Piddington attempted to return to politics. In 1922, he contested the seat of North Sydney. His opponent was none other than the prime minister, Billy Hughes. It was a bitterly fought campaign, with the skeletons of 1913 exhumed in the papers, and mudslinging on both sides. Hughes won the seat, though did not last long as prime minister.[86]

In 1926, the Labor Premier of New South Wales, Jack Lang, appointed Piddington to lead a newly formed body, the Industrial Commission which, in essence, existed until 1991, when it was replaced by the Industrial Relations Commission. The Industrial Commission was part of a new system of industrial conciliation in which industry-specific conciliation committees, composed of representatives of employers and employees and a chair appointed by the minister, had primary responsibility for resolving industrial disputes. The committees could make binding orders or awards. The role of the Commission was to resolve disputes referred to it by

---

[84] Graham, *A. B. Piddington*, 93.

[85] Marilyn Lake, "The Independence of Women and the Brotherhood of Man: Debates in the Labour Movement over Equal Pay and Motherhood Endowment in the 1920s" *Labour History* 63 (1992): 4.

[86] Graham, *A. B. Piddington*, 95–99.

8 WHAT ALBERT DID AND WHAT ALBERT DID NEXT: ALBERT BATHURST... 151

committees or by the Minister and, to deal with bigger-picture questions, such as determining the standard of living and fixing the basic wage accordingly.[87] Piddington was appointed to lead this powerful body amidst controversy: he was, by this time, perceived by employers as a radical. And it did not take long for his radicalism to come through in his decisions. Initially, his decisions only grated employers; but when he began to use his position to implement his then-idiosyncratic views on child endowment—in a manner that resulted in a lower basic wage than many expected, and one that was substantially lower than what employees on Commonwealth awards received—he managed to alienate both labour and capital.[88]

In January 1929, Piddington found time to visit Gandhi at Satyagraha Ashram, in the state of Gujarat in India.[89] In his memoir, *Worshipful Masters*, Piddington devoted a chapter to his recollections of Gandhi, calling him—in the style of his followers at the ashram—Bapu Gandhi, that is, Father Gandhi.[90] Piddington wrote admiringly of Gandhi, and was sympathetic to his core political aspiration—Indian Home Rule. In Gandhi, Piddington found someone who shared his conviction that political and social questions could not be divorced from questions of individual character. He describes Gandhi's insistence that Home Rule must "begin in the personal life of the individuals of the nation."[91] This was not a quietist prescription of gradualism, but rather, was a critical insight, recognising that governing requires virtues that need to be cultivated if government is to truly serve the people.

While at the ashram, Piddington told Gandhi about child endowment policies in New South Wales. At the end of their conversation, Gandhi asked, "And you have come all the way from Calcutta to tell me all this interesting news about the methods of your country?" Piddington described this, perhaps optimistically, as a "courteous observation"; one wonders if the truth was that he had chewed Gandhi's ear off.[92] Whatever the case, Gandhi later said that he was "greatly struck" by what Piddington

---

[87] Ibid., 123–4.
[88] Ibid., 124–134.
[89] Ash, "Albert Bathurst Piddington," 54; Piddington, *Worshipful Masters*, 160–1.
[90] Piddington, *Worshipful Masters*, 170.
[91] Ibid., 184.
[92] Ibid., 192–3.

152   A. S. BELL AND J. MONAGHAN

had told him.[93] And Piddington was clearly affected by his meeting with the man he described as the parens patriae of India.[94]

From the serenity of the ashram, Piddington was thrown back into the political tumble that was New South Wales under the Lang Government. In 1932, when the governor, Sir Philip Game, dismissed Lang, Piddington resigned from his position at the Industrial Commission, just weeks shy of the date at which he would have qualified for a pension.[95] He believed strongly that Game had acted unconstitutionally in dismissing Lang. A tract he wrote on the constitutional crisis, together with his personal correspondence with the governor, was published under the title *The King and the People and the Severing of their Unity.* The title gets to the heart of the complaint: he thought that Game's dismissal of Lang's government—which had a majority in both houses—"destroyed Responsible Government and was, in nature, a severing of the constitutional nexus between the Crown of England and the Parliament of New South Wales."[96] His resignation from the Industrial Commission signalled the end of his long string of high-profile legal offices. But yet again, other adventures lay ahead.

In 1934, Piddington was in his early 70s. Egon Erwin Kisch, a Czechoslovakian communist journalist and activist, was invited to Australia to speak at an event called the Congress Against War and Fascism. Accepting the invitation, he set sail from Europe aboard the SS Strathaird. The Lyons government did not welcome Kisch's visit and sought to deny him entry to Australia by various means. Kisch's local supporters sought legal assistance,[97] and Piddington was briefed by Christian Jollie Smith, a left-wing lawyer who was the second woman to be admitted to practice as a solicitor in New South Wales.[98]

Famously, Kisch was administered the dictation test in Scottish Gaelic and, refusing to take what he described, rightly, as a "stupid and unfair test,"[99] was arrested. Piddington took the case to the High Court, where

[93] Ibid., 194.

[94] Ibid., 199.

[95] Garran, "A. B. Piddington," 69.

[96] Albert Bathurst Piddington, *The King and the People and the Severing of their Unity* (Sydney: R. T. Kelly Ltd., 1932), 15.

[97] Kisch, *Australian Landfall*, 64.

[98] Joy Damousi, "Jollie Smith, Christian (1885–1963)," in *Australian Dictionary of Biography*, 11th ed. (Melbourne: MUP, 1988), http://adb.anu.edu.au/biography/jollie-smith-christian-8465

[99] Kisch, *Australian Landfall*, 73.

he argued that Scottish Gaelic was not a "European language" within the meaning of s 3(a) of the *Immigration Restriction Act 1901* (Cth); rather, it was a dialect. Consequently, the dictation test had been unlawfully administered. The High Court accepted this argument,[100] much to the chagrin of some, including Sir Mungo MacCallum, the rather conservative Scot who was Chancellor of the University of Sydney at the time. MacCallum wrote to the *Sydney Morning Herald* under the nom-de-plume "Columbinus," protesting that:

> Some of us may have supposed the Immigration Act was meant to provide a test whereby, even if in a quibbling and pettifogging way, undesirable aliens might be excluded, and that an alien forbidden to land in England might be considered undesirable here. Now we know better. It behoves us to bow down before the court's confident pronouncement: "We are dictators over all language and above linguistic facts."[101]

In his memoir of his time in Australia, Kisch gives a memorable description of Piddington, writing:

> Mr A. B. Piddington, K.C., could be a sketch by Dickens, a grey-haired old gentleman, thin as a rake, but inside him there burns a volcano, which soon will erupt and spit fire for four months. He will cause the judges a lot of trouble, although he was one himself not long ago. He resigned his position on the bench of the High Court, and also his position of Arbitration Court Judge, with their high salaries and high honours, the first because of a personal view regarding a point of duty, the second as a protest against an anti-democratic measure of the Governor. He is respected for his fidelity to his convictions, and as a sociologist, as an art-historian, as a Shakespearean scholar, and as a linguist.[102]

Having been a judge of the High Court, albeit briefly, and an advocate before the Court, towards the end of his life, Piddington also found himself an aggrieved party in that Court.[103] On 11 April 1938, by now 75 years of age, Piddington was knocked over in Phillip Street by a motorcycle and sidecar driven by a servant of Bennett and Wood Proprietary Limited. He

---

[100] *R v Wilson; Ex parte Kisch* (1934) 52 CLR 234.

[101] Quoted in Keith Mason, "The Saga of Egon Kisch and the White Australia Policy," *Bar News* (Summer 2014): 67.

[102] Kisch, *Australian Landfall*, 64.

[103] *Piddington v Bennett and Wood Pty Ltd* (1940) 63 CLR 533.

commenced negligence proceedings in the Supreme Court of New South Wales, claiming damages in the sum of £15,000. The jury returned a verdict for the defendant. Piddington applied to the Full Court for a new trial on the basis that inadmissible evidence had gone before the jury. The Full Court refused that application. Piddington appealed to the High Court where, by a narrow majority, he succeeded in obtaining orders for a new trial. Bennett and Wood unsuccessfully sought leave to appeal to the Privy Council.[104]

Whether the retrial went ahead is difficult to say: it seems the only record of it is a notice in the *Sydney Morning Herald* on Tuesday 15 October 1940, stating that the matter of *Piddington v Bennett and Wood Pty Ltd* was to be heard by the Prothonotary at 9:30 am "for writ of commission"—that is, the matter was to come before the Prothonotary for a procedural hearing to determine whether the Court should order the examination of witnesses on oath, whether they be in or out of the jurisdiction.[105]

On 5 June 1945, at the age of 82, Piddington died in Sydney. A headline in the *Sydney Morning Herald* the following day read "Noted Jurist Dead" and described him as "for many years ... prominent in the political and judicial life of New South Wales."[106] He was buried at St Thomas' Cemetery in Crows Nest, and was survived by his wife Marion, who died five years later, and their only child, Ralph, a social anthropologist.[107]

---

[104] "Privy Council: Applications for Leave to Appeal," *Sydney Morning Herald*, May 1, 1940.

[105] The power to issue such commissions was located in s 4(1)(b) of the *Witnesses Examination Act 1900* (NSW). "State Jurisdiction: Supreme Court Causes List," *Sydney Morning Herald*, Oct 15, 1940.

[106] "Noted Jurist Dead," *Sydney Morning Herald*, Jun 6, 1945.

[107] Ash, "Albert Bathurst Piddington," 57.

CHAPTER 9

# Path Dependency, the High Court, and the Constitution

*Jeremy Patrick*

## INTRODUCTION

Imagine that a lawyer jumped into a time machine with a copy of the Constitution and the newest constitutional law textbook. If she jumped back 60 years, or 100 years, she would find that our copy of the Constitution matches up almost perfectly with one from the past, barring a handful of amendments. But our constitutional law textbook would prove quite different, even astonishingly so, when compared to one from an earlier age. Certain elements and core concepts would certainly be recognisable, but

---

A version of this chapter was published as Jeremy Patrick, "Path Dependency, the High Court, and the Constitution," *Journal of Judicial Administration* 30, no 2 (2020): 49–63. This chapter is based on the author's original manuscript and complies with all relevant copyright laws and publishing agreements.

---

J. Patrick (✉)
School of Law and Justice, University of Southern Queensland,
Toowoomba, QLD, Australia
e-mail: Jeremy.Patrick@usq.edu.au

© The Author(s), under exclusive license to Springer Nature    155
Switzerland AG 2022
S. McKibbin et al. (eds.), *The Impact of Law's History*, Palgrave
Modern Legal History,
https://doi.org/10.1007/978-3-030-90068-7_9

156    J. PATRICK

could someone from 1910 or even 1950 have predicted the legal and political dominance of the Federal government, the application of doctrines like the implied freedom of political communication, or the roller-coaster ride of High Court jurisprudence on state excise taxes? The Constitution remains essentially the same, but constitutional law changes—sometimes dramatically.

Yet, to confuse and complicate the scenario, one can also easily find examples of High Court cases and doctrines that have remained in place, changing only cosmetically—if at all—throughout the decades. The High Court's interpretation of the grants power, for example, is almost the same today as it was in 1926[1] despite its contribution to the well-known problem of vertical fiscal imbalance. Continuity and change are both facets of constitutional law, but how could an observer explain (or predict) which will manifest in any strand? The concept of path dependence may hold some explanatory power.

Path dependence is a concept that originally arose in the field of economics before gaining currency with political scientists and historians. The essence of path dependency is that temporality matters: once a decision is made, it often becomes "locked-in" and persists despite the existence of more efficient or otherwise better alternatives that could become apparent later. A classic example in the literature is the QWERTY keyboard: almost all of us use a keyboard designed in 1873 to intentionally slow typing speed (to prevent typewriter jamming).[2] Despite the existence of alternative keyboard designs that could improve typing efficiency,[3] there is (practically speaking) no turning back from QWERTY. It persists a century and a half later because it was the first standard, not the best possible standard.

The tentative hypothesis advanced here is that the concept of path dependency is useful for understanding why some doctrines of Australian constitutional law have changed dramatically since first developed while others remain largely the same. The next section addresses path dependency in more detail. Section III provides an example of a High Court case that illustrates path dependency along with a second example that shows why path dependency is not inevitable. Section IV explores the role

---

[1] See *Victoria v Commonwealth* (1926) 38 CLR 399.

[2] See Paul A. David, "Clio and the Economics of QWERTY," *American Economic Review* 72, no. 2 (1985).

[3] A contested point in the economics literature. See S. J. Liebowitz and Stephen Margolis, "The Fable of the Keys," *Journal of Law and Economics* 33 (1990).

of path dependency in Australia's constitutional jurisprudence and discusses why particular features of its judicial system allow path dependency to have a stronger effect here than in countries like Canada or the United States. Section V offers some concluding thoughts.

## PATH DEPENDENCY

An excellent starting point to illustrate the concept of path dependency is a metaphor from Mark Roe that involves, quite literally, a path—a trail that eventually becomes a road:

> We are on a road and wonder why it winds and goes here instead of there, when a straight road would be a much easier drive. Today's road depends on what path was taken before. Decades ago, a fur trader cut a path through the woods, and the trader, bent on avoiding a wolves' den and other dangerous sites, took a winding indirect route. Were the fur trader a better hunter of wolves, the trader might have chosen a straighter path. Later travelers dragged wagons along the same winding path the trader chose, deepening the grooves and clearing away some trees. Travelers continued to deepen and broaden the road even after the dangerous sites were gone. Industry came and settled in the road's bends; housing developments went up that fit the road and industry. Local civic promoters widened the path and paved it into a road suitable for today's trucks.[4]

Roe continues the metaphor by asking what should be done with the road now. Its placement is inefficient because today there is no need to fear the wolves' den of centuries past: a new, simple straight road would no doubt shave minutes from everyone's driving time, and this benefit would last for future drivers in perpetuity. But to straighten the road would necessitate tearing out much of the old road, razing housing developments, altering intersections, and more. Under what Roe calls "semi-strong form path dependence," observers *know* the road is sub-optimal but decide it is better to leave it in place because the costs of doing anything about it outweigh the potential benefits.[5] Under "strong-form"

---

[4] Mark J. Roe, "Chaos and Evolution in Law and Economics," *Harvard Law Review* 109 (1996): 643.

[5] Ibid., 648 ("once a society has invested in its institutions, it has many reasons not to change them radically, or at all, because the costs of change might outweigh any advantages from change.").

158    J. PATRICK

path dependence, however, it *would* be worth it in the long run to straighten the road, but the sunk costs fallacy and behavioural inertia are enough to keep people from doing anything about it.[6]

The concept of path dependence arose in the field of economics to help explain why arguably inferior technologies, just like inferior roads, sometimes triumph over their better competitors: QWERTY keyboards over Dvorak keyboards, VHS videotapes over Betamax, and DOS-based computers over Macs.[7] The concept was eventually carried over to explain other seeming discrepancies, such as why (fairly homogeneous) American beers dominate the US market despite the existence of better-crafted alternatives, or why many physicians were slow to take up electronic medical record-keeping despite the obvious advantages it holds over paper records.[8] The reason why one narrow geographical location might receive the lion's share of a country's activity in a particular industry (like Hollywood for American movies, or Silicon Valley for technology) might be explained through path dependency,[9] as could questions of public policy such as the development of agricultural policy in the European Union or public housing reform in the United Kingdom.[10]

For path dependency to have robust application as an explanatory concept, it needs to be more than simply a vague proxy for the commonsense intuition that "history matters." A key part of path dependency is the idea of increasing returns processes. Political scientist Paul Pierson explains it well:

> In an increasing returns process, the probability of further steps along the same path increases with each move down that path. This is because the

---

[6] Ibid., 650. Roe also discusses "weak-form" path dependence in which one standard is adopted but that standard is not appreciably more or less efficient than its competitors. This type holds historical explanatory value but is not important in a present-day decision-making sense. See ibid., 647. A similar discussion of different types of path dependency can be found in Lawrence B. Solum, "Constitutional Possibilities," *Indiana Law Journal* 83 (2008) 313–14 (citing S. J. Liebowitz and Stephen E. Margolis, "Path Dependency, Lock-in, and History," *Journal of Law, Economics, and Organization* 11 (1995).

[7] See Paul Pierson, "Increasing Returns, Path Dependence, and the Study of Politics," *American Political Science Review* 94, no. 2 (2000) 254.

[8] See William Barnes et al., "Old Habits Die Hard: Path Dependency and Behavioral Lock-in," *Journal of Economics Issues* 38, no. 2 (2004): 374–76.

[9] See Pierson, "Increasing Returns, Path Dependence, and the Study of Politics," 255.

[10] See citations in Adrian Kay, "A Critique of the Use of Path Dependency in Policy Studies," *Public Administration* 83, no. 3 (2005): 558.

9 PATH DEPENDENCY, THE HIGH COURT, AND THE CONSTITUTION    159

*relative* benefits of the current activity compared with other possible options increase over time. To put it a different way, the costs of exit—of switching to some previously plausible alternative—rise. Increasing returns can also be described as self-reinforcing or positive feedback processes.[11]

Characteristics of an increasing return process include "nonergodicity" (small, even random or accidental events at the beginning of a path create consequences down into the future), inflexibility (it becomes increasingly harder to shift out of the path), and potential inefficiency compared to untaken alternatives.[12] To return to the road metaphor, the chance encounter of the fur trader with the wolves' den illustrates nonergodicity (his decision on what path to tread isn't cancelled out by other intervening events); the fact that the trail becomes increasingly smooth and well-marked through repeated use illustrates inflexibility (and eventually other infrastructure is built with the assumption that the trail is fixed in its current location); and the hypothetical possibility of a new, straight road that would be faster for travellers illustrates potential inefficiency.

A term often used in the context of inflexibility is "lock-in." Lock-in refers to the fact that once a single decision is made, a host of smaller choices can follow that have the cumulative effect of making the original decision very hard to change.[13] If a consumer buys a VHS videocassette player, every purchase they subsequently make of a movie on VHS makes it less likely they will switch to Betamax (even if persuaded it is a somewhat better system) because they need to not just replace the player but also (perhaps) each of the videocassettes. A related concept, "behavioural lock-in," draws on human psychology: "once consumers or users have invested time or money in learning a particular system or becoming comfortable with a traditional practice, they will be less likely to try a rival process, even if over time it proves superior."[14] For example, in the twenty-first century,

---

[11] Pierson, "Increasing Returns, Path Dependence, and the Study of Politics," 252.

[12] Ibid., 253 (drawing from W. Brian Arthur, *Increasing Returns and Path Dependence in the Economy* (Ann Arbor: University of Michigan Press, 1994) 112–3).

[13] See Taylor C. Boas, "Conceptualizing Continuity and Change: The Composite-Standard Model of Path Dependence," *Journal of Theoretical Politics* 19, no. 1 (2007): 37 (discussing the mechanisms of lock-in in greater detail).

[14] Barnes et al., "Old Habits Die Hard," 372. See also John Bell, "Path Dependence and Legal Development," *Tulane Law Review* 87 (2013): 794 ("[T]he basic idea is that we get used to something and organise the future, treating it as a fixed point. As a result, we compound the embeddedness of this feature of life. It becomes difficult to change direction.

160    J. PATRICK

most Americans still think in terms of yards instead of metres, and miles instead of kilometres. Old habits die hard.

But if path dependence is a "real" phenomenon, how can anything change? If increasing returns or behavioural lock-in, for example, tend to keep a standard in place even if more efficient alternatives exist, why is it that sometimes standards *do* change? Why are electric cars (slowly) becoming more viable and less expensive despite over a century of infrastructure built with the gasoline engine in mind, or, to return to the measurements example, why did *most* countries that used the Imperial system (perhaps for centuries) eventually shift to metric? A viable theory needs to be able to explain its own limits.

For path dependency, different explanations may apply in different fields. Political scientists studying the development of institutions and policies, for example, often discuss two different models of change: (1) a "punctuated equilibria" model where an opportunity to change a long-established institution or policy is created by a sudden or dramatic external event (a national emergency, a political shake-up, etc.)[15] and (2) a "layering and conversion" model where the cumulative effect of very small changes over time gradually remakes an institution or policy into something very different from what it was originally.[16] Pierson writes:

> [P]ath dependent analyses need not imply that a particular alternative is permanently locked in following the move onto a self-reinforcing path. Identifying self-reinforcing processes helps us understand why organizational and institutional practices are often extremely persistent—and this is crucial, because these continuities are a striking feature of the social world. Asserting that the social landscape can be permanently frozen is hardly credible, and that is not the claim. Change continues, but it is bounded change—until something erodes or swamps the mechanisms of reproduction that generate continuity.[17]

---

Both inertia and self-interest tend to lead to minimal change, even when, from an objective point of view, it becomes necessary.").

[15] See Ian Greener, "The Potential of Path Dependence in Political Studies," *Politics* 25, no. 1 (2005): 64.

[16] See Boas, "Conceptualizing Continuity and Change," 35 ("incremental changes in political institutions can cumulate into a fundamental transformation over time, even as increasing returns render an institution resistant to wholesale change at any given moment").

[17] Pierson, "Increasing Returns, Path Dependence, and the Study of Politics," 265.

## 9 PATH DEPENDENCY, THE HIGH COURT, AND THE CONSTITUTION   161

Until this point, this chapter has deliberately avoided any reference to how law could be impacted by path dependency, but the potential is clear. Constitutions are the most obvious example: once enacted, they become the legal foundation for everything else. Because constitutions are (usually) very difficult to change, mechanisms of governance or principles of legality that they set in place can persist for centuries even if later thought to be misguided or inefficient. The Electoral College created by the American Constitution, for example, is roundly criticised every four years as an undemocratic institution and has never been an influential model for the drafters of constitutions elsewhere in the world. The Electoral College, like the QWERTY keyboard, is not ideal: but it works *just* well enough that it's not replaced. They persist, despite the existence of better alternatives, because it is too difficult for people today to deviate from the path set by their long-dead ancestors.

The heart of the common law itself—the notion of precedent—is seen by some scholars in terms of path dependency.[18] Contrary to the evolutionary model favoured by many law and economics scholars, in which inefficient rules are eventually displaced by more efficient ones over time, a path-dependent view of precedent contests the idea that law inevitably "works itself pure." As Oona Hathaway explains:

> Applying path dependence theory to the law leads to both striking insights and troubling conclusions. It reveals, for example, that courts' early resolutions of legal issues can become locked-in and resistant to change. This inflexibility can lead to inefficiency when legal rules fail to respond to underlying conditions. Path dependence theory also indicates that final outcomes will be difficult to predict ex ante, because they are highly dependent upon early decisions, which are in turn difficult, if not impossible, to predict. The theory further suggests that the opportunities for significant change in a common law system are brief and intermittent, occurring during critical junctures when new legal issues arise or higher courts or legislatures intercede. Moreover, it leads to the unsettling conclusion that the order in which cases arrive in the courts can significantly affect the specific legal doctrine that ultimately results.[19]

[18] See especially Oona A. Hathaway, "Path Dependence in the Law: The Course and Pattern of Legal Change in a Common Law System," *Iowa Law Review* 86 (2001). See also Bell, "Path Dependence and Legal Development"; Roe, "Chaos and Evolution in Law and Economics"; Michael J. Gerhardt, "The Limited Path Dependency of Precedent," *University of Pennsylvania Journal of Constitutional Law* 7 (2005).
[19] Hathaway, "Path Dependence in the Law," 105.

## 162    J. PATRICK

If path dependence holds explanatory power in understanding common law doctrines, it will be even more robust in understanding constitutional jurisprudence: after all, the only thing that can overrule a constitutional precedent is changed thinking from the highest court in the land or an amendment to the constitution itself. The hypothesis examined in this chapter is that features of High Court jurisprudence in Australia are best explained through the theory of path dependence. In the next section, two well-known doctrines from Australian constitutional law are briefly examined with a discussion of why one of them displays path dependence and the other does not.

## Examples

### *Grants*

A clear example of the concept of path dependency at work in Australian constitutional law can be found in the doctrine surrounding s. 96, the grants power. The nearly limitless scope the High Court has given to the grants power has allowed the Federal government to offer money to the States: as much money as the Federal government wants, when it wants, and with whatever conditions it wishes to attach. In practice, this has significantly contributed to the well-known phenomenon of the "vertical fiscal imbalance":[20] although the States, constitutionally speaking, have plenary legislative powers while the Commonwealth has only enumerated ones, it is the latter that raises the bulk (80%) of the tax revenue[21] and thus makes the real policy decisions in any area it wishes, including vocational schools, health care, primary and secondary education, and housing.[22] Through the grants power and modern statutory mechanisms like the GST, the Commonwealth redistributes money to the States with strings

---

[20] See, e.g., Robert Dalton, "The Adverse Attributes of Specific Purpose Payments in Australia," *Southern Cross University Law Review* 10 (2006): 45 ("The inability of States to produce the revenue that they require, and their subsequent reliance on grants, has led to what is known as 'vertical fiscal imbalance', that is, minimal correlation between what governments earn and what they spend. In Australia's case, the federal government uses tied grants to influence State spending decisions").

[21] See Shipra Chordia, "Section 96 of the Constitution: Developments in Methodology and Interpretation," *University of Tasmania Law Review* 34 (2015): 54–5.

[22] See ibid., 56 ("the majority of [specific purpose grant] funding has the effect of influencing Commonwealth objectives in areas of State constitutional responsibility").

## 9 PATH DEPENDENCY, THE HIGH COURT, AND THE CONSTITUTION    163

attached, and the amount of money involved is so large that, realistically, no State can turn it down and forge its own course. A constitution designed with federalism in mind has instead turned towards centralisation, and a large part of the blame can be attached to the expansive interpretation that the High Court has given to the grants power.

Section 96 reads:

> During a period of ten years after the establishment of the Commonwealth and thereafter until the Parliament otherwise provides, the Parliament may grant financial assistance to any State on such terms and conditions as the Parliament thinks fit.

Section 96 is problematic in both conception and execution.[23] The first clause is simply a case of poor drafting, as it essentially states that Parliament can do a particular thing until it no longer wishes to do a particular thing; from a strictly legal perspective, everything before the comma could be omitted and the power given to Parliament would be exactly the same. As an aid to interpretation, however, those first words are vital: they show that the drafters assumed that s. 96 would be a sort of transitional or emergency provision, allowing the Commonwealth to help the States through the disruptive effects of Confederation and other crises that may arise thereafter.[24] If the provision is envisioned as a mechanism for cooperative federalism rather than as a lever that the Commonwealth could pull to get the States to do whatever it wants, its interpretation can change accordingly. One could, just at first glance, plausibly read the provision as applying in only a narrow set of circumstances: such as when the States demonstrably need "financial assistance" or when the "terms and

---

[23] See Cheryl Saunders, "Towards a Theory for Section 96: Part II," *Melbourne University Law Review* 16 (1988): 699 ("[S]ection 96 is conceptually flawed, and therefore sits uneasily with the constitutional principles on which the Constitution is based and with other provisions of the Constitution itself."); Greg Taylor, "On the Origin of Section 96 of the Constitution," *University of New South Wales Law Journal* 39 (2016): 1438 ("In so many ways Australian federalism has been a study in unintended consequences—never more so, perhaps, than in relation to section 96 of the federal *Constitution*.")

[24] See Enid Campbell, "The Commonwealth Grants Power," *Federal Law Review* 3 (1968): 225 ("When section 96 was drafted no attempt was made to fetter Parliament in its prescription of terms or conditions, but it was generally assumed that Parliament would use its discretion sparingly and that grants under section 96 would be exceptional").

164 J. PATRICK

conditions" set by Parliament relate directly to the assistance that is being given.[25]

The discussion above is familiar to students of constitutional law. My purpose here is to show how the High Court's interpretation of the grants power, and the problems it has caused for federalism in modern Australia, can all be traced back to a single case from almost a century ago in a classic instance of path dependency: the *Federal Roads Case*.[26] Two remarkable things about the case are how short the Court's opinion is (just 56 words!) and how it pays absolutely no attention to the problems that would result.

The case involved federal legislation designed to give States a certain amount of money, on the condition that they use it to build specific roads. Obviously, there is no "Roads" head of power in the Constitution, so unless another head of power is plausibly invoked the effort could be seen to fall outside the legislative competence of the Commonwealth and therefore be invalid. The plaintiffs, two States arguing for invalidity of the legislation, argued that s. 96 could not be used to "attach as conditions to its grant any conditions which amount in substance to the exercise of any legislative power which is not within s. 51 of the Constitution."[27] The Commonwealth defended itself by reference to the defence power (arguing that better roads meant the easier sell of exports, which in turn was needed to pay off war debts from World War I) and the immigration power (suggesting that better roads were needed to lure settlers from Great Britain in an explicit invocation of the White Australia policy, because otherwise "such policy will be difficult to maintain against outside pressure unless the population of Australia is largely increased by suitable migration").[28]

But the High Court did not want to hear about heads of power and even cut off the Commonwealth's barrister just one sentence into his oral argument.[29] According to the High Court in its per curiam opinion, the answer was easy:

[25] See, e.g., Taylor, "On the Origin of Section 96 of the Constitution," 1461–62; Campbell, "The Commonwealth Grants Power," 223.

[26] (1926) 38 CLR 399.

[27] Ibid., 405 (as summarised by headnote). The connection to the defence power seems tenuous, but a more plausible argument along the same lines could perhaps have invoked the interstate trade head of power (depending on where the road construction was in relation to state borders and the flow of commerce).

[28] Ibid., 404.

[29] See ibid., 406.

# 9 PATH DEPENDENCY, THE HIGH COURT, AND THE CONSTITUTION    165

The Court is of opinion that the *Federal Aid Roads Act* No. 46 of 1926 is a valid enactment. It is plainly warranted by the provisions of sec. 96 of the Constitution, and not affected by those of sec. 99 or any other provisions of the Constitution, so that exposition is unnecessary. The action is dismissed.[30]

Rarely in Australian legal history has such a momentous decision been communicated in such a pithy manner. There is no attempt to limit the decision to the precise facts in front of the court, to link the decision to the purported heads of power supporting the legislation (however dubious the defence and immigration rationales seem in isolation), or to acknowledge that although the decision may be justified on the bare words of s. 96, there will be serious consequences for the federal nature of Australia if the Commonwealth uses its "new" power without restraint.

However, the point here is not whether the *Federal Roads Case* was correctly decided, but instead (as will be seen) that every subsequent decision on the scope of the grants power followed along with the principle established in that case.

This first becomes apparent thirteen years later when the High Court next entertained a case involving s. 96.[31] Instead of building roads, in *Moran's Case* the Commonwealth sought to nationalise prices on flour and wheat in order to stabilise the markets and subsidise wheat farmers.[32] This was achieved by a tax on flour and wheat, which would then be redistributed to the States for disbursement to its farmers.[33] But because Tasmania was the only State that had to import wheat, special dispensation had to be made for it in the scheme.[34] Because the Commonwealth's power over taxation does not allow it to discriminate between States, a separate piece of legislation was passed under s. 96, enabling the Commonwealth to essentially refund all the money collected in Tasmania back to Tasmania.[35] In other words, this was constitutional formalism: each State was taxed to the same degree to satisfy the taxation head of power, but one State received more money back under the grants power.

---

[30] Ibid., 406.

[31] *Deputy Federal Commission of Taxation (New South Wales) v. W. R. Moran Proprietary Ltd.*, (1939) 61 CLR 735 (*Moran's Case*).

[32] See ibid., 752–73 (describing the scheme).

[33] See ibid.

[34] See ibid., 754–55.

[35] See ibid., 756–757.

166    J. PATRICK

The High Court, with Chief Justice Latham writing for the majority, found no constitutional impediment to this legislative manoeuvre. Regarding s. 96, Latham wrote:

> The words of this section show that Parliament may grant financial assistance to a single State under this power and may therefore discriminate between States in making grants. They also show that the Parliament has the fullest power of fixing the terms and conditions of any grant under the section. ... [T]he case of *Victoria v. The Commonwealth* (the *Roads Case*) is conclusive ... upon this point.[36]

Whether s. 96 allowed for discrimination between the States was an open question, and the High Court could have qualified the power it had given the Commonwealth. But already, the *Federal Roads Case*, despite its incredible brevity and failure to discuss its reasoning, had become a fixed point for judicial interpretation of s. 96. The path of unfettered federal power was set by the *Federal Roads Case*, and this case about taxation and a subsidy scheme on wheat would have to follow it.

The effect of path dependency in this context reaches its most visible and startling point with the *First Uniform Tax Case*.[37] Under this well-known case, the Commonwealth successfully gained total control over income taxation in Australia by making it practically impossible for the States to stay in the field.[38] It did this through a complex statutory scheme, but a key enabler was s. 96: the Commonwealth would levy income taxes and return some of it to a State as a grant, on the condition that the State abolish its own income taxes.[39] Here is the famous statement by Latham CJ that:

> The *Grants Act* offers an inducement to the State Parliaments not to exercise a power the continued existence of which is recognized—the power to impose income tax. The States may or may not yield to this inducement, but there is no legal compulsion to yield.[40]

[36] Ibid., 763 (Latham, C.J.). There was one dissenting opinion in the case, as Evatt J. attacked the "very thinly disguised ... breach of the provision against discrimination" and suggested that s. 96 should be interpreted to have expired. See ibid., 778, 803.

[37] (1941) 65 CLR 373.

[38] See ibid., 405 (Latham, C.J.) ("This Act, it is said, makes it practically impossible for any State to impose a State tax upon income").

[39] See ibid., 416.

[40] Ibid., 417.

## 9 PATH DEPENDENCY, THE HIGH COURT, AND THE CONSTITUTION   167

This "temptation is not compulsion"[41] rationale underlies everything the Commonwealth has done with the grants power ever since. There is never a *legal* requirement that the States give up income taxation or accept federal policy intervention in education, aged care, health care, and many other sectors. There is no stick, just a carrot so large and juicy that it cannot possibly be refused.[42] When the Commonwealth tells a State that every school must have a flag pole or it will lose out on all primary and secondary school funding for the year, those flag poles get built![43] When some States balked at the notion that all public school chaplains must have religious affiliations, those States fell in line quickly when the Commonwealth threatened to cancel chaplaincy grants altogether.[44] At least in the *First Uniform Tax Case*, the High Court acknowledged how the unrestricted scope it has given to s. 96 could distort, damage, and, ultimately, undermine the system of federalism envisioned by the Constitution.[45]

[41] Ibid.

[42] See Jonathan Crowe and Peta Stephenson, "Reimagining Fiscal Federalism: Section 96 as a Transitional Provision," *University of Queensland Law Journal* 33 (2014): 226 ("Conditional grants made by the Commonwealth to the states under s. 96 are theoretically 'consensual,' in that the states are under no legal obligation to accept them. However, in practice and as a result of Australia's vertical fiscal imbalance, the states have little choice but to accept these grants and the conditions attached"); Chordia, "Section 96 of the Constitution," 55–56 ("while the High Court has proscribed legal compulsion, it has not prohibited the Commonwealth from making s. 96 grants in practical circumstances, frequently of the Commonwealth's own design, that have left the States no real choice but to accept").

[43] See Dalton, "The Adverse Attributes of Specific Purpose Payments in Australia," 60–61 (discussing 2004's *Schools Quadrennial Funding Agreement*).

[44] See Chordia, "Section 96 of the Constitution," 56–7. School chaplaincy is a perfect example of the distortion caused by the Court's interpretation of s. 96. Twice, Ron Williams went to the High Court to have federal funding of school chaplaincy invalidated as unconstitutional. Twice, he won. See *Williams v. Commonwealth (No 1)*, [2012] HCA 23; *Williams v. Commonwealth (No 2)*, [2014] HCA 23. But in response to the defeats, the Commonwealth simply changed from directly funding school chaplaincy to indirectly funding it through a s. 96 grants scheme. Nothing has changed in practice. The words of A.J. Myers, although written fifty years ago, are on point: "But about the whole subject [of the grants power] there is an air of unreality. Not only are the legal powers of the Commonwealth ample, but as the dominant government of the federation it [can] now ensure the fulfilment of its policies in any event by extra-legal means." See A. J. Myers, "The Grants Power-Key to Commonwealth State Financial Relations," *Melbourne University Law Review* 7, no. 4 (1970): 566.

[45] See (1941) 65 CLR 373, 429 (Latham, C.J.) ("It is perhaps not out of place to point out that the scheme which the Commonwealth has applied to income tax of imposing rates

168   J. PATRICK

The *First Uniform Tax Case* was decided in 1941, during the darkest days of Australia's participation in World War II, and much of the discussion in the case centred around the defence power and the necessity of Commonwealth control over revenue and expenditure to aid in the war effort. In the middle of the 1950s, the scheme was challenged again by States hoping that a peacetime High Court would reach a different result. But instead, the *Second Uniform Tax Case*[46] reiterated the High Court's full support for an unrestricted interpretation of s. 96. Chief Justice Dixon's opinion is important for present purposes because it demonstrates how strong of a hold the *Federal Roads Case* had on the issue despite subsequent qualms by members of the High Court. Dixon CJ writes:

> There has been what amounts to a course of decisions upon s. 96 all amplifying the power and tending to a denial of any restriction upon the purpose of the appropriation or the character of the condition. The first case decided under s. 96 was [the *Federal Roads Case*]. The enactment there in question ... did not express its reliance on s. 96 either in terms or by reference to the grant of financial assistance. ... The validity of the legislation was upheld by this Court as authorised by s. 96. This means that the power conferred by that provision is well exercised although (1) the State is bound to apply the money specifically to an object that has been defined, (2) the object is outside the powers of the Commonwealth, (3) the payments are left to the discretion of the Commonwealth Minister, (4) the money is provided as the Commonwealth's contribution to an object to which the State is also to contribute funds.[47]

Crucially, Dixon CJ notes that:

> If s. 96 came before us for the first time for interpretation, the contention might be supported ... that the true scope and purpose of the power which s. 96 confers upon the Parliament ... did not admit of any attempt to influence the direction by the State of its legislative or executive powers. It may well be that s. 96 was conceived by the framers as (1) a transitional power, (2) confined to supplementing the resources of the Treasury of a State ... when some special or particular need or occasion arose, and (3) imposing

so high as practically to exclude State taxation could be applied to other taxes so as to make the States almost completely dependent, financially and therefore generally, upon the Commonwealth").

[46] (1957) 99 CLR 575.

[47] Ibid., 605–606.

## 9 PATH DEPENDENCY, THE HIGH COURT, AND THE CONSTITUTION 169

terms or conditions relevant to the situation which called for special relief or assistance[.] *But the course of judicial decision has put any such limited interpretation of s. 96 out of consideration.*[48]

The "course of judicial decision" Dixon CJ is referring to is later explicitly noted as starting with the *Federal Roads Case*,[49] and other members of the Court invoked it as decisive authority as well.[50]

In her examination of the grants power, Cheryl Saunders wrote about the *Federal Roads Case* that:

It has been relied upon as the first step on an inexorable path to a conclusion that a grant of financial assistance under section 96 can be used to induce a State to refrain from exercise its powers ... It has been the foundation case on which the edifice of argument has been built in relation to every issue.[51]

The High Court's interpretation of the grants power that started with the *Federal Roads Case* may not be the right one, but it is far too late now to change things.[52] This "cavalier and dismissive" opinion that "prematurely rigidif[ied] the development of the law concerning the grants power" cannot be easily undone.[53] It is safer to follow the "course of judicial decision." As with keyboards and QWERTY, it is often easier to keep going on the wrong path than to start over on the right one.

### *Interstate Trade and Commerce*

If path dependency in the High Court's constitutional law jurisprudence can be exemplified with its approach to the grants power, the mirror

---

[48] Ibid., 609.

[49] See ibid., 610.

[50] See ibid., 656 (per Fullagar J); 659 (per Taylor J.).

[51] Cheryl Saunders, "Towards a Theory for Section 96: Part I," *Melbourne University Law Review* 16 (1987): 29–30.

[52] See Crowe and Stephenson, "Reimagining Fiscal Federalism," 222 ("There is, of course, no real chance of either the Commonwealth Parliament or the High Court treating s. 96 as a spent provision. It is too deeply entrenched in federal arrangements."); Myers, "The Grants Power-Key to Commonwealth State Financial Relations," 559 ("It is settled law that section 96 is a permanent part of the Constitution. Equally well settled is that few, if any, limits can be set on the power of the Commonwealth to impose terms and conditions").

[53] Graham Fricke, "The Knox Court: Exposition Unnecessary," *Federal Law Review* 27 (1999): 125, *quoted in* Chordia, "Section 96 of the Constitution," 60 n. 42.

opposite situation can be found with its history of interpreting Section 92 of the Constitution. Section 92 provides in relevant part that "trade, commerce, and intercourse among the States ... shall be absolutely free." In the famous quote by Robert Garran, a hypothetical law student trying to understand the High Court's first several decades of caselaw on the meaning of Section 92 may as well "close his notebook, sell his law books, and resolve to take up some easy study, like nuclear physics or higher mathematics."[54] And to be clear, the reason is not because (like advanced physics and mathematics) the material requires high intellectual ability and rigorous logical reasoning skills, but instead because the Court's cases were, to put it kindly, an absolute mess. From the first case on Section 92 in 1909[55] until a landmark change of direction in 1988,[56] the cases involved "extraordinary twists and turns of legal doctrine"[57] that were "fraught with disagreement and instability"[58] became "a judicial labyrinth"[59] and "caused many a judge ... to give forth with a judicial *cri de coeur* that could not possibly be provoked by any other part of our body of law."[60] Indeed, the approximately 140 cases on Section 92 decided during this period[61] means that it was probably the most frequently litigated provision in the Constitution.[62]

Everything started off fine. The High Court was unanimous in finding a violation of Section 92 in its first case on the subject, 1909's *Fox v Robbins*.[63] The facts were about as simple as they could get: Western Australian legislation allowed vendors to sell liquor made with fruit grown

[54] Robert Garran, *Prosper the Commonwealth* (1958), 415, *quoted in Cole v Whitfield* (1988) 165 CLR 360, 392 (itself quoting LaNauze, *Absolutely Free*, 58).

[55] *Fox v Robbins* (1909) 8 CLR 115.

[56] *Cole v Whitfield* (1988) 165 CLR 360.

[57] Michael Coper, "Interstate Trade and Commerce, Freedom of," in Tony Blackshield et al., *The Oxford Companion to the High Court of Australia* (South Melbourne: Oxford University Press, 2001), 354.

[58] Amelia Simpson, "Grounding the High Court's Modern Section 92 Jurisprudence: The Case for Improper Purpose as the Touchstone," *Federal Law Review* 33, no. 3 (2005): 446.

[59] Gozalo Villalta Puig, "A European Saving Test for Section 92 of the Australian Constitution," *Deakin Law Review* 13 (2008): 100.

[60] Leslie Zines, *The High Court and the Constitution*, 5th ed. (Annandale, N.S.W.: Federation Press, 2008), 139.

[61] Andrew S. Bell, "Section 92, Factual Discrimination and the High Court," *Federal Law Review* 20 (1991): 240.

[62] P. D. Connolly, "*Cole v Whitfield*—The Repeal of Section 92 of the Constitution," *University of Queensland Law Journal* 16 (1991): 290.

[63] (1909) 8 CLR 115.

# 9 PATH DEPENDENCY, THE HIGH COURT, AND THE CONSTITUTION   171

in the state for a licence that cost two pounds a year, but a licence to sell liquor made with fruit grown outside the state cost a vendor *fifty* pounds a year.[64] All five members of the Court, writing seriatim, said the problem was the adverse differential treatment of interstate trade compared to intrastate trade. As Griffith CJ wrote, "This provision would be quite illusory if a State could impose disabilities upon the sale of the products of other States which are not imposed upon the sale of home products."[65] The other members of the Court agreed that this was the core defect in the law.[66]

If path dependency had taken root with *Fox v Robbins*, as it did regarding the grants power in the *Federal Roads Case*, the next several decades of Section 92 caselaw would be very different. The primary question in each case would have been whether there was adverse discriminatory treatment towards interstate trade that thus favoured local, in-state traders—in other words, protectionism. And as with any judicial "test" of validity, one could imagine occasional hard cases and interesting questions about the difference between a law having a discriminatory purpose and it having discriminatory effects. But the through-line would be the presence or absence of adverse discrimination, and one could expect the courts to gradually give content and meaning to that standard in various factual scenarios.

Unfortunately, for generations of Australian law students, this is not what happened, of course. Within a decade of deciding *Fox v Robbins*, the

---

[64] Ibid., 118.

[65] Ibid., 119–120 (per Griffith, C.J.).

[66] Ibid., 123 (per Barton J). ("To impose one charge on the sale of the wines of other States, while allowing the sale of Western Australian wines at another and a lower fee, is discrimination of a kind which if lawful in this case is lawful in a thousand others—for this is a question of power. By burdens of this kind and that, whether under the name of licence fees or under any other name, the operation of inter-state free trade could be so hampered and restricted as to reduce the Constitution in that regard to mere futility"); ibid., 126 (per O'Connor J.) ("It is clear that the Constitution does not permit a State by such discriminating charges to place at a disadvantage the goods of other States passing into it for sale"); ibid., 127 (per Isaacs J.) ("Sec. 92 of the *Constitution* ... prevents adverse discrimination from being lawful; so far as the Act can be effectively worked in conformity with the constitutional requirement it still stands; so far as it cannot it simply ceases to operate"); ibid., 131 (per Higgins J.) ("This [differential license fee] involves a discrimination in favour of Western Australian products, and an infringement of the provision of sec. 92 of the *Constitution*"). See also Coper, "Interstate Trade and Commerce, Freedom of," 354 ("The very early cases were consistent with the idea that a state should not erect protectionist barriers—whether in the form of monetary imposts or broader measures—against the trade of another state").

172 J. PATRICK

High Court fractured and lost sight of adverse discrimination as the test for Section 92.[67] In 1920's *McArthur's Case*,[68] for example, the Court invalidated a Queensland anti-profiteering law that set maximum prices for which certain products could be sold—and the maximum price was the same whether the goods were produced locally or imported from out of state. There was not, at least on the face of things, any attempt at protectionism at play, but a majority of the Court said the problem was simply that the law directly affected interstate trade (the movement of goods across state lines for sale) and that violated Section 92's command that interstate trade "be absolutely free."[69] The fact that local products and out-of-state products were treated in the same way could not save the law.[70]

This view of Section 92, often called the "individual rights" approach because it focused on whether an individual interstate trader was burdened by a state law,[71] was only one of several competing methods of interpretation that the Court and its various members would bounce back-and-forth between in succeeding years, with confusion only added by repeated interference from the Privy Council.[72] As one scholar explained, "The answer to the query as to which theory applie[d], was that no theory applied and all theories applied. No theory enjoyed majority support but behind majority outcomes all theories were used, from time to time, to support individual conclusions in particular cases."[73]

The High Court would not manage to extricate itself from this morass until the landmark decision in *Cole v Whitfield*[74] (1988) announced a new standard that every member of the Court agreed on: whether suspect legislation had discriminatory effects of a protectionist kind against interstate

---

[67] See Gerard Carney, "The Re-interpretation of Section 92: The Decline of Free Enterprise and the Rise of Free Trade," *Bond Law Review* 3 (1991).

[68] (1920) 28 CLR 530.

[69] See ibid.

[70] See ibid., 552 ( "[A] State cannot enact [a] prior restraint on inter-State trade, commerce and intercourse, whether it attacks inter-State trade, commerce and intercourse alone, or in company with its own domestic trade and commerce.... [T]he State cannot annul the protection given by sec. 92 by mingling the subject matter beyond its control with matter lawfully under its control").

[71] See Zines, *The High Court and the Constitution*, 141.

[72] The clearest history of this frankly exhausting morass is in Zines, *The High Court and the Constitution*.

[73] Richard Cullen, "Section 92: Quo Vadis," *University of Western Australia Law Review* 19 (1989): 109 (listing five different approaches).

[74] [1988] HCA 18.

trade. In many ways, the new standard is simply an elegant elaboration of the principle at work in *Fox v Robbins*,[75] but the decision has been (almost[76]) universally hailed as finally bringing clarity and order to a chaotic field of jurisprudence while simultaneously adhering to the framers' original intentions in including Section 92 in the Constitution.[77]

The natural question that arises from this narrative is why didn't *Fox v Robbins* stick. Why did it take almost eighty years of the High Court wandering in the juridical wilderness of Section 92 before returning very close to where it first started? If path dependency means anything, why did the Court so quickly and easily move on from the first case interpreting the section? The next section attempts to answer some of these questions.

## ANALYSIS

Earlier, this chapter summarised various facets of path dependency as articulated in the economics and political science literature. Here, in the context of the examples (Section 96 grants and Section 92 interstate trade) discussed above, two of these concepts will be examined: (1) opportunity and exit, and (2) lock-in and reliance. The reasoning that follows is necessarily tentative and speculative but will hopefully illustrate some of the factors that affect why path dependency is often, but not always, seen at play in Australian constitutional law.

### *Opportunity and Exit*

One of the hallmarks of a path-dependent process is that deviating from the originally chosen course is difficult because the costs of exiting the current paradigm and switching to an alternative usually become higher the longer the status quo continues. But in some path-dependent

---

[75] Cf. Simpson, "Grounding the High Court's Modern Section 92 Jurisprudence," 447 ("After many decades of disagreement, the Court has in relatively recent times cemented section 92's status as a non-discrimination norm").

[76] There have been some dissenters. For example, see the stringent opposition provided by Connolly, "*Cole v Whitfield*," 293.

[77] See, for example, Bell, "Section 92, Factual Discrimination and the High Court," 240 ("The High Court's bicentennial contribution of *Cole v Whitfield* was warmly received by constitutional commentators, descending, in the colourful language of one, as some sort of judicial deus ex machina") (quoting P. H. Lane, "The Present Test for Invalidity under s. 92 of the Constitution," *Australian Law Journal* 62 (1988): 614).

174   J. PATRICK

processes, exiting the current paradigm is not an option that is always available at any given time (even if desired). For example, if the Federal government suddenly decided every employee should start using a Dvorak keyboard, it is going to have to wait for a dramatic ramp-up in the production of those keyboards before it can make the switch. In other words, one cannot exit from a fixed path unless there is an opportunity to do so.

For Australian constitutional law, a part of understanding the effects of path dependency may involve these concepts of exit and opportunity. Specifically, the thesis here is that path dependency will be less likely to take hold in areas of constitutional law that are heavily and frequently litigated. The High Court cannot decide cases in the absence of adverse parties, and some provisions of the Constitution are naturally going to generate far less controversy than others. But each case the Court does have before it is an opportunity to exit the current paradigm; the more opportunities, the higher the likelihood of exit at some point in the course of jurisprudence.

This perhaps can be seen at work in the two examples discussed above. By 1988, there had been over 140 High Court and Privy Council cases discussing Section 92,[78] compared to a mere handful discussing Section 96. Every one of those 140 cases was an opportunity to "exit" from the discrimination standard used in *Fox v Robbins*, and every one of those cases was also an opportunity to propose, distinguish, and dissent from the variety of other theories that different members of the Court had as to what the guarantee in Section 92 meant. If true, the next logical question is why did Section 92 generate far more cases than Section 96. A possible argument is that Section 92 is a provision that, if invoked successfully, directly affects the bottom line of those businesses and corporations with the economic resources necessary to mount an expensive constitutional challenge. In contrast, Section 96 cases rarely generate standing for private interests, and the very same states receiving monetary grants from the Federal government are unlikely to challenge the constitutionality of those grants in court.

The reason that the sheer number of cases generated by a provision matters is that those provisions that generate future cases create fewer opportunities for the High Court to deviate from an established judicial standard; there are fewer opportunities for Justices to evaluate how the standard is working, fewer opportunities for dissenting judges to argue for

---

[78] See *Cole v Whitfield* (1988) 165 CLR 360, 386.

different judicial tests, fewer opportunities for persuasive barristers to make subtle factual distinctions and cleverly distinguish prior cases, and, perhaps most importantly, fewer opportunities for lower courts to make decisions in hard cases that the High Court then has to resolve. The old adage is that "hard cases make bad law," but hard cases also often generate *new* law. But without cases, the High Court cannot make law—and without opportunity, it cannot exit from its original course of action.

It may be useful in this context to contrast the High Court of Australia with the Supreme Court of the United States. The High Court decides only a handful of constitutional cases every year, and particular provisions of the Australian Constitution may go decades without being meaningfully discussed. In contrast, the Supreme Court decides dozens of constitutional cases every year, and the federal circuit and district courts (not to mention state courts) decide, quite literally, thousands more. There is going to be much, much more grist for the judicial mill in the United States and thus far more opportunities, if the Supreme Court wants them, to announce a change in direction. In Australia, by contrast, opportunities are sometimes few and far between.[79]

By understanding each new case as an opportunity for exit, one can also begin to consider, in a legal context, the discussion in the path dependency literature about how exit can take place through two very different methods: (1) punctuated equilibria, and (2) layering and conversion. When most people think of the classic common law, slowly changing and evolving over time to incorporate new problems into new understandings of legal rules, that paradigm follows the layering and conversion model. Observers might expect, over decades and centuries of cases on a particular topic, for the law to end up in a very different place than it started, even if each individual change was relatively small in itself. It might also be expected that constitutional provisions that are frequently litigated would also follow this layering and conversion model, but that provisions rarely litigated would be more likely to change (if they change at all) suddenly and dramatically. However, this is not what one sees with Section 92—the discrimination standard in *Fox v Robbins* did *not* gradually evolve through

---

[79] Compare, for example, the voluminous caselaw in the United States on the meaning of the Free Exercise and Establishment Clauses with the mere handful of cases in Australia on the same subjects. Although many have argued that the High Court's interpretation of Section 116 in the *DOGS Case* has rendered the establishment clause an almost meaningless standard, there have been no opportunities for the Court to exit from the rule announced in that case, even if it wanted to.

176    J. PATRICK

interpretation in dozens of cases over decades—instead, it was almost summarily abandoned, and a host of contested theories vied for dominance in a slew of confusing cases and shifting court majorities. If anything, the Section 92 jurisprudence followed the punctuated equilibria model when *Cole v Whitfield* "wipe[d] the slate clean."[80] This complication challenges a direct overlay of path dependency to constitutional law and invites further analysis of whether and to what degree the concepts developed in other contexts are applicable here.

### *Lock-in and Reliance*

One of the metaphors for a path-dependent process known as "lock-in" used at the beginning of this chapter was that as a trail becomes a path and a path becomes a road, development builds up around it. Eventually the burdens of changing the road's course become so high that, even if the realisation eventually comes that the current situation is not ideal, it is just too late to go back and start another route. This metaphor can be applied to the concept of a "reliance interest" that is sometimes invoked in judicial conversations about the importance of stare decisis: individuals, governments, and social groups have a right to know what the law "is" and to rely on its relative stability when making decisions.[81] This concern over the impact of overturning settled expectations sometimes manifests as a greater reluctance to depart from precedent when more than just the discrete parties before the court would be affected. Similarly, decisions that announce new standards that have only prospective effects on behaviour are usually viewed as less problematic than new standards that would have retroactive effects.

---

[80] Bell, "Section 92, Factual Discrimination and the High Court," 240.

[81] See, for example, Murray Gleeson, "The Centenary of the High Court: Lessons from History" (speech presented at the Australian Institute of Judicial Administration, October 3, 2003). For a more general overview, see Randy J. Kozel, "Precedent and Reliance," *Emory Law Journal* 62 (2013). A good example of perceived reliance interests affecting High Court decision making in the constitutional law context can be found in the lengthy debate over whether state "licensing schemes" for alcohol and tobacco sales ran afoul on the Section 90 prohibition on excise taxes. See, for example, Nicolee J. Dixon, "Section 90—Ninety Years On," *Federal Law Review* 21 (1993). Of course, the High Court seized the opportunity when the states themselves invited the issue to be revisited in *Ha v New South Wales* (1997) 189 CLR 465.

This concept of a reliance interest may help explain why path dependency takes hold in some lines of jurisprudence but not others. In the context of the two examples used throughout this chapter, one might argue that, although changing the interpretation of "absolutely free" in Section 92 creates some disruption for interstate traders and state legislatures, businesses large enough to afford litigation in the High Court are usually resilient enough to adapt to changing regulations and that states generally have a variety of methods at their disposal to attain their policy goals. In contrast, when talking about the grants power, imagine if the High Court suddenly announced that the *Federal Roads Case* was wrongly decided and that the Court was going to instead adopt the more constitutionally faithful but also more restrictive interpretation of Section 96 urged by many scholars critical of the vertical fiscal imbalance. There would be extreme and widespread disruption in sectors of the economy as crucial as health, education, social services, and more—not to mention the damage done to the current GST scheme. Such a result is almost unthinkable, which militates towards the idea that if change is ever to happen regarding the grants power it will come through gradual "layering and conversion"—not through the type of sudden change contemplated by the "punctuated equilibria" model.

But in any event, the larger point is that when courts discuss the reliance interest generated by stare decisis as a reason to stay the course, this can be understood, through the lens of path dependency, as a way of saying that lock-in is in effect. The costs of changing—which may be costs to the prestige, reputation, and political capital of the court—are just too high to be seriously contemplated.

## CONCLUSION

This chapter has argued that the concept of path dependency operative in economics and other social science literature may have value in explaining certain features of Australian constitutional law. Specifically, the concept helps illuminate why early cases are of such great importance in determining the future of a line of jurisprudence, while also clarifying when deviations are likely to occur. Characteristic facets of path dependency, including lock-in and exit, can be related to and complicate the law's own invocation of concepts like stare decisis and the reliance interest.

The concept of path dependency could potentially be fruitfully applied to other aspects of law. For example, one could apply the concept in a statutory context and query whether the persistent refusal of some states to adopt the well-regarded Uniform Evidence Bill is an instance of path dependency, with antiquated state legislation persisting due to the difficulty in getting judges and practitioners to adopt something new ("behavioural lock-in"), just like retraining employees is a bar to the widespread adoption of the Dvorak keyboard.[82] Similarly, one might apply the concept to legal education and ask whether the "Priestly 11" has created a situation of lock-in that results in the core curriculum of most Australian law schools looking substantially the same through decades of change in the society (and legal profession) around them.

The preliminary nature of the thesis that path dependency has explanatory power in constitutional law must be kept in mind. Surely, additional examples need to be generated that do and do not seem to fit the model to see if it remains plausible. If path dependency *is* at work in Australian constitutional law, the importance of careful positioning and presentation of early litigation is even more crucial: since the Constitution is so hard to change, the first decision on an issue, whether right or wrong, may become "locked-in" for generations to come, with ramifications for all of us.

---

[82] The author is grateful to Dr Andrew Hemming for this example.

CHAPTER 10

# The Use and Misuse of Legal History in the High Court of Australia

*Warren Swain*

## INTRODUCTION

Legal history is sometimes seen as little more than the study of "old, unhappy, far-off things" or, worse, as a kind of legal antiquarianism that has little to contribute towards the development of contemporary private law. As a result, as Paul Finn has observed, legal history has "for the most part ... been marginalised to the point of near extinction." To which he quite correctly adds that, "This is more than a matter for regret. It impoverished our legal imagination."[1] He is not alone in fearing for the future of the teaching of legal history in Australia.[2] In 2005, Wilfred Prest found

---

[1] *Historical Foundations of Australian Law: Institutions, Concepts and Personalities*, ed. J. T. Gleeson, J. A. Watson, R. C. A. Higgins (Alexandria, NSW: Federation Press, 2013), v.
[2] M. D. Kirby, "Is Legal History now Ancient History?," *Australian Law Journal* 83 (2009): 31.

---

W. Swain (✉)
The University of Auckland, Auckland, New Zealand
e-mail: w.swain@auckland.ac.nz

© The Author(s), under exclusive license to Springer Nature Switzerland AG 2022
S. McKibbin et al. (eds.), *The Impact of Law's History*, Palgrave Modern Legal History,
https://doi.org/10.1007/978-3-030-90068-7_10

that, at the ten Australian Law Schools established before 1982,[3] legal history was taught in only six of them.[4] There has been a small further decline in those universities teaching legal history since that time.[5]

The relative marginalisation of legal history in universities is not confined to Australia. Although the subject remains in good health in the United States,[6] the position of legal history in the United Kingdom is equally precarious. It is probably no coincidence that the four English law schools of genuine world standing at the University of Oxford, University of Cambridge, the London School of Economics and University College London run courses in the subject.[7] The reasons behind the decline are complex.[8] When taught properly, legal history makes heavy demands. It requires a level of intellectual engagement, broad knowledge and sheer persistence that put it beyond the reach of many students and academics alike. When there are easier, trendier or apparently more "relevant" alternatives, the path of least resistance is usually a more attractive one. Once a subject is no longer on the curriculum, usually because the person teaching it has left or retired, it can be very difficult to revive it.

Despite the prospects for legal history in Australian universities looking slightly gloomy, an analysis of the High Court's judgments tells a very different story. Bruce Kercher observed that the period since the 1960s has

---

[3] This includes all of the Group of Eight plus Macquarie and the University of Tasmania.

[4] Wilfrid Prest, "Legal History in Australian Law Schools: 1982 and 2005," *Adelaide Law Review* 27, no. 2 (2006): 272, http://www.austlii.edu.au/au/journals/AdelLawRw/2006/7.pdf

[5] In 2021 distinct courses in legal history in some form are offered at the following pre-1982 law schools: University of Adelaide, University of Melbourne, UNSW, University of Sydney, and University of Tasmania. It should also be noted however that other courses in all ten universities have some legal historical content. Legal history is also taught at some of the newer law schools, but they have not been systematically surveyed. For an impressionist view on this issue, see: Amanda Whiting and Ann O'Connell, *Legal History Matters: From Magna Carta to the Clinton Impeachment* (Melbourne: Melbourne University Publishing, 2020), 5.

[6] Joan Howland, "A History of Legal History Courses Offered in American Law Schools," *American Journal of Legal History* 53 (2013): 363, https://doi.org/10.1093/ajlh/53.4.363. There is an extraordinary variety of legal history taught in the United States. Some flavour of this can be gleaned from Robert M. Jarvis, *Teaching Legal History* (London: Wildy, Simmonds & Hill Publishing, 2014).

[7] The situation in Scotland is different with a strong focus on legal history albeit sometimes Civilian legal history at the University of Edinburgh, Glasgow and Aberdeen.

[8] For some suggestions, see Prest, "Legal History," 274–76.

seen a "rejection of the symbols of deference to English legal ideas."[9] As is well chronicled during the 1980s, the High Court began to shift Australian private law in new directions, which involved a departure from English law.[10] The precise manner in which the High Court has gone about this process, particularly through the use of historical sources, is less well documented.[11] At the heart of the process is a paradox. In reforming the common law arguments derived from English legal history, sometimes quite ancient history has played a pivotal role.

## THE ENGLISH LITERARY TRADITION IN AUSTRALIA

Law books have played a role in the development of the common law for centuries, but the nineteenth century was a golden age of the legal treatise.[12] Early New South Wales lawyers brought law books with them. What sort of works they saw as useful can be gathered from a request for books made by Deputy Judge Advocate Thomas Hibbins in 1796.[13] In addition to the *Statutes at Large,* he also asked to be sent Blackstone's *Commentaries*

---

[9] Bruce Kercher, *An Unruly Child: A History of Law in Australia* (Sydney: Allen and Unwin, 1995), 203.

[10] Discussions include Anthony Mason, "Future Directions in Australian Law," *Monash University Law Review* 13, no. 3 (1987), https://heinonline.org/HOL/P?h=hein.journals/monash13&i=159; Anthony Mason, "The Impact of Equitable Doctrine on the Law of Contract," *Anglo-American Law Review* 27 (1998), https://heinonline.org/HOL/P?h=hein.journals/comlwr27&i=19; J. W. Carter and Andrew Stewart, "Commerce and Conscience: The High Court's Developing View of Contract," *University of Western Australia Law Review* 23, no. 1 (1993), http://www.austlii.edu.au/au/journals/UWALawRw/1993/4.pdf; Paul Finn, "Common Law Divergences," *Melbourne University Law Review* 37, no. 2 (2013): 509, http://www5.austlii.edu.au/au/journals/MelbULawRw/2013/20.html

[11] For some discussion of this issue, see: Enid Campbell, "Lawyers' Uses of History," *University of Queensland Law Journal* 6 (1968–1969), http://www.austlii.edu.au/au/journals/UQLJ/1968/1.pdf; Rob McQueen, "Why High Court Judges Make Poor Historians: The Corporations Act Case and Early Attempts to Establish a National System of Company Regulation in Australia," *Federal Law Review* 19 (1990), http://classic.austlii.edu.au/au/journals/FedLawRw/1990/11.pdf

[12] A. W. B. Simpson, "The Rise and Fall of the Legal Treatise: Legal Principles and the Forms of Legal Literature," *University of Chicago Law Review* 48, no. 3 (1981), https://chicagounbound.uchicago.edu/cgi/viewcontent.cgi?article=4245&context=uclrev

[13] *Historical Records of New South Wales,* ed. F. M. Bladen, vol. 3, (Sydney: Charles Potter, 1895), 13.

182  W. SWAIN

*on the Laws of England*,[14] Hale's *Pleas of the Crown*,[15] Burn's *The Justice of the Peace*,[16] Reeves's *A History of English Law*,[17] Impey's *The New Instructor Clericalis*,[18] Buller's *Nisi Prius*,[19] Dogherty's *The Crown Circuit Assistant*,[20] Jacob's *Law Dictionary*,[21] Wood's *Conveyancing*,[22] Hawkins's *Treatise of Pleas of the Crown*[23] and Foster's *Reports and Discourses on Crown Law*.[24]

Blackstone's *Commentaries* were popular in the early colony. The four volumes contain a broad overview of the common law.[25] If the strength of the work was its brevity, then it was also a weakness. Some subjects like the law of contract barely receive a mention. The merit of the *Commentaries* to early judges (such as Judge Advocate Richard Atkins), who were not trained lawyers,[26] was that they were accessible to those without expert knowledge.[27] The *Commentaries* were portable in a society that travelled on horseback. From the 1820s[28] to the present day, the Australian courts continue to cite the *Commentaries* regularly. Whilst no distinctively Australian edition was produced,[29] the English versions of the *Commentaries*

[14] William Blackstone, *Commentaries on the Laws of England* (Oxford: Clarendon Press, 1765–69) ('*Commentaries*').

[15] Matthew Hale, *Pleas of the Crown* (London: E. & R. Nutt, 1736).

[16] Richard Burn, *The Justice of the Peace* (London: A. Millar, 1756).

[17] John Reeves, *A History of English Law* (London: T. Wright, 1783).

[18] John Impey, *The New Instructor Clericalis* (London: W. Strahan and W. Woodfall, 1784) which was usually referred to by the sub-title of *Practice in the Court of King's Bench*.

[19] Francis Buller, *Nisi Prius* (London: C. Bathurst, 1775).

[20] C. J. Dogherty, *The Crown Circuit Assistant* (London: P. Uriel, 1787).

[21] Giles Jacob, *Law Dictionary* (London: E. & R. Nutt, 1729).

[22] Edward Wood, *Conveyancing* (London: J. Worrall, 1749).

[23] William Hawkins, *Treatise of Pleas of the Crown* (London: J. Walthoe, 1721).

[24] Michael Foster, *Reports and Discourses on Crown Law* (Oxford: Clarendon Press, 1762).

[25] Wilfred Prest, "Antipodean Blackstone: The Commentaries Down Under," *Flinders Journal of Law Reform* 6, no. 2 (2003): 155–56, https://search.informit.org/doi/abs/10.3316/agispt.20033796

[26] J. M. Bennett, "Richard Atkins: An Amateur Judge Jeffreys," *Journal of the Royal Australian Historical Society* 52 (1966): 261.

[27] The lectures on which the *Commentaries* were based were delivered to an audience of young gentleman who paid a fee to attend. The common law was not taught as part of a degree at Oxford in the eighteenth century.

[28] Prest, "Antipodean Blackstone," 157–59.

[29] In America a home-grown edition first appeared in 1803. On the impact of Blackstone in America, see Dennis Nolan, "Sir William Blackstone and the New American Republic: A Study of Intellectual Impact," *New York University Law Review* 51 (1976), https://heinonline.org/HOL/P?h=hein.journals/nylr51&i=755. The original *Commentaries* also sold well

were given a radical re-working by Henry Stephen in the 1840s and continued to be published for a further 100 years.[30]

The value placed on iconic English writers was evident from the earliest days of the High Court. In *Delohery v Permanent Trustee Company of New South Wales*,[31] a decision about prescription and the right to light, Griffith CJ referred to a passage in Justinian's *Digest*,[32] alongside a quotation from *Coke on Littleton*, and cited Blackstone's *Commentaries* and *The Laws and Customs of England*, which was commonly called *Bracton*.[33] *Bracton* was the oldest of the English treatises mentioned[34] and concerned the Royal Court's practices of the early thirteenth century. However, it was more than just a work of procedure. The author developed substantive legal ideas and displayed a reasonable knowledge of Roman law. *Bracton* was the most sophisticated and comprehensive book about the common law before Blackstone.[35] The final work referred to Sir Thomas Littleton's *New Tenures*, known as *Littleton*, was written around 1460 and first published, in law French,[36] just after Sir Thomas's death in 1481.[37] Coke

in America: M. H. Hoeflich, *Legal Publishing in Antebellum America* (New York: Cambridge University Press, 2010), 131–34.

[30] The last edition was: Henry Stephen, *Commentaries on the Laws of England*, ed. L. Crispin Warmington (London: Butterworth, 1950).

[31] (1904) 1 CLR 283.

[32] *The Digest of Justinian*, ed. Alan Watson (Pennsylvania, United States: University of Pennsylvania Press, 1998), D 41.3.1.

[33] The standard modern version is: *On the Laws and Customs of England*, 4 vols., trans. Samuel E. Thorne (Cambridge, Mass.: Belknap Press, 1968).

[34] A number of theories have been put forward as to the date and authorship of Bracton: H. G. Richardson, *Bracton: The Problem of his Text* (London: Selden Society, 1965); J. L. Barton, "The Mystery of Bracton," *Journal of Legal History* 14, no. 3 (1993), https://doi.org/10.1080/01440369308553085; Paul Brand, "The Age of Bracton" in *The History of English Law. Centenary Essays on 'Pollock and Maitland'*, ed. John Hudson (Oxford: Oxford University Press, 1996), 65–89; J. L. Barton, "The Authorship of Bracton: Again," *Journal of Legal History* 30, no. 2 (2009), https://doi.org/10.1080/01440360903069742; Paul Brand, "The Date and Authorship of Bracton: a Response," *Journal of Legal History* 31, no. 3 (2010), https://doi.org/10.1080/01440365.2010.525913

[35] Which is not to say that some common law writers did not attempt to present the law in a systematic and coherent fashion, on which see: David Seipp, "Roman Legal Categories and the Early Common Law" in *Legal Record and Historical Reality*, ed. Thomas Watkin (London: Hambledon Press, 1989), 9–36.

[36] T. Littleton, *Tenores Noveli* (London: Lettou & Machlinia, 1481).

[37] Littleton also began writing a larger work on the laws of England, which was incomplete on his death, J. H. Baker, "The Newe Littleton," *Cambridge Law Journal* 30, no. 1 (1972): 145.

described *Littleton* as "the most perfect and absolute work that ever was written in any human science,"[38] and he produced his own version with a commentary. *Coke on Littleton*[39] is the version usually used today. Before the nineteenth century, it was commonly read by those learning the law of real property. It continues to be cited in recent times.[40] The fact that a cultured and intelligent man like Sir Samuel Griffith was perfectly at ease with such a diverse range of older English writers is unsurprising.[41] It might also be said to be characteristic of a time when the English common law still dominated Australian private law. Yet Griffith was far from unique in his own time or later. As recently as 2020, Nettle J cited *Bracton* in two High Court judgments.[42]

It is easy enough to look at citations of the iconic English legal texts in the judgments of the High Court beginning with *The Treatise on the Laws and Customs of the Realm of England Commonly Called Glanvill*,[43] which was a work on the procedures of the Royal Courts from the late 1180s. The sample size includes all the decisions of the High Court as reported in the Commonwealth Law Reports between 1903 and 2019. The methodology for counting the citations is that adopted by Russell Smyth in his studies of citation practice.[44] If the source received repeat citations, it is counted only once unless on a different point. Where a citation appears in

---

[38] Edward Coke, *First Part of the Institutes of the Laws of England or a Commentary on Littleton* (London: Society of Stationers, 1628), v.

[39] Ibid.

[40] For example, in *Andrews v Australian and New Zealand Banking Group* (2012) 247 CLR 205 discussed below.

[41] For a life of Griffith, see Roger Joyce, *Samuel Walker Griffith* (St Lucia, Queensland: University of Queensland Press, 1984).

[42] *Pickett v Western Australia* (2020) 379 ALR 471, 498 [98]; *Love v Commonwealth of Australia* (2020) 375 ALR 597, 653–5 [246]–[247].

[43] The best modern translation is: *The Treatise on the Laws and Customs of the Realm of England Commonly Called Glanvill*, trans. G. D. C. Hall (Oxford: Oxford University Press, 1965).

[44] Russell Smyth, "Other than Accepted Sources of Law: A Quantitative Study of Secondary Source Citations in the High Court," *University of New South Wales Law Journal* 22 (1999), http://www.unswlawjournal.unsw.edu.au/wp-content/uploads/2017/09/22-1-20.pdf; Russell Smyth, "What do Intermediate Appellate Courts Cite—A Quantitative Study of the Citation Practices of Australian State Supreme Courts," *Adelaide Law Review* 21 (1999), http://classic.austlii.edu.au/au/journals/AdelLawRw/1999/3.pdf; Russell Smyth, "The Authority of Secondary Authority—A Quantitative Study of Secondary Source Citations in the Federal Court," *Griffith Law Review* 9 (2000), https://heinonline.org/HOL/P?h=hein. journals/griffith9&i=29

a joint judgment, the number of citations is calculated by multiplying by the number of judges. Where a judge simply concurs, a citation is not attributed twice. For convenience, the citations are divided up into roughly twenty-year blocks in order to identify trends across time.

The main conclusion to be gathered from this exercise is that the practice of citing English legal classics and secondary historical literature continues to be healthy. Despite other evidence that the High Court is keen to jettison the past as represented by English law, the number of historical citations has in fact greatly increased in recent decades. One reason might be changes in the nature of judgments. Ex tempore judgments are rarely delivered in the High Court. Judgments are also much longer than they used to be and can include more material, including legal literature.[45] The process of writing judgments has changed too.[46] Since the 1970s, the role of judicial associates has altered from providing secretarial support to carrying out research work.[47] Even if associates do not enjoy the level of influence of their counterparts in the Supreme Court of the United States, the reliance on associates may encourage greater use of earlier authority.[48]

As shown in Table 10.1, the most cited of the iconic English treatises by the High Court is Blackstone's *Commentaries*. It makes up 66.8% of the total citations. Hale's *The History of the Pleas of the Crown* is a distant second, making up for 16.1% of the total citations. The oldest treatise in the sample, *Glanvill*, is cited a mere five times over the same period. Blackstone's *Commentaries* will be more familiar to modern Australian lawyers than the other works. It has an established pedigree in Australia. Other studies of the High Court have produced very similar findings,[49] although it may be that Blackstone appears less frequently in other courts.[50]

[45] Matthew Groves and Russell Smyth, "A Century of Judicial Style: Changing Patterns in Judgment Writing on the High Court 1903–2001," *Federal Law Review* 32, no. 2 (2004): 258–66, https://doi.org/10.22145/flr.32.2.4

[46] For some discussion of the process, see M. D. Kirby, "On the Writing of Judgments," *Australian Law Journal* 64 (1990). For some insight into the process in earlier times, see Phillip Ayers, *Owen Dixon* (Melbourne, Australia: The Miegunyah Press, 2003), 262–63.

[47] Andrew Leigh, "Associates" in *The Oxford Companion to the High Court of Australia*, eds. Tony Blackshield, Michael Coper and George Williams (Oxford: Oxford University Press, 2001), 34–35.

[48] On this phenomenon in the United States, see Artemus Ward and David Weiden, *Sorcerers' Apprentices* (New York: New York University Press, 2006), 231.

[49] Smyth, "Other than Accepted Sources," 48; Prest, "Antipodean Blackstone," 161–62.

[50] Smyth, "Other than Accepted Sources"; Smyth, "The Authority of Secondary Authority," 43.

186   W. SWAIN

The fact that Blackstone's *Commentaries* remain so popular is something of a puzzle as they were, after all, first published in the 1750s. It is difficult to see how it can have all that much relevance in the modern world. Yet citations from Blackstone in the High Court are far from receding. Instead, they have increased, along with historical citations as a whole, in the period since 1981. Curiously, this is also the period in which Australian private law has undergone the most rapid period of change. It can hardly be likely that Blackstone was part of the legal education of the current High Court Bench or those appearing before them. Perhaps it is simply a case of citation begets citation and Blackstone remains at the forefront of the legal consciousness. Another explanation is that the work captures the law at a particular time or put another way Blackstone can be used as a convenient shorthand for the history of English law.

Some of the secondary works on legal history are also commonly referred to by the High Court and are listed in Table 10.2. Sir William Holdsworth is the most cited author by a very large margin. The first volume of *A History of English Law* was published in 1903.[51] Sixteen further volumes followed, the last of which appeared posthumously in 1966.[52] This work is cited nearly 400 times by the High Court. However, compared to Sir Frederic Maitland, it is fair to say that Holdsworth is not held in such high regard by contemporary legal historians.[53] In part, this may be because Maitland built his reputation on his use of manuscript sources. Holdsworth wrote only using secondary sources or printed reports. But judges are not usually legal historians of the specialist kind, and Holdsworth's *History of English Law* is nothing if not comprehensive. It was a singular achievement for one man. The citation of the two books by Australian authors is puny by comparison. For many decades, Victor Windeyer's *Lectures on Legal History*[54] was the primary introduction to the subject in Australia. Windeyer almost exclusively focused on English legal

---

[51] William Holdsworth, *A History of English Law* (London: Methuen, 1903).

[52] J. H. Baker, "Holdsworth, Sir William Searle" in *Biographical Dictionary of the Common Law*, ed. A. W. B. Simpson (London: Butterworths, 1984), 247–49.

[53] Maitland is widely seen as the finest legal historian who ever lived. For biographies see, C. H. S. Fifoot, *Frederic William Maitland: A Life* (Cambridge, Mass.: Harvard University Press, 1971); G. R. Elton, *F W Maitland* (London: Weidenfeld and Nicholson, 1986); S. F. C. Milsom, "Maitland," *Cambridge Law Journal* 60, no. 2 (2001), doi:https://doi.org/10.1017/S0008197301000113

[54] W. J. V. Windeyer, *Lectures on Legal History* (Sydney: Law Book Company, 1938). This is the first edition. A second edition appeared in 1957.

history. Between 1958 and 1972, the author sat in the High Court of Australia[55] and would unsurprisingly make prominent use of historical sources. Alex Castles's *An Australian Legal History*[56] is a very different book. It was the first major attempt to treat Australian legal history as a serious and sustained subject for study.[57] Between the authors, Windeyer and Castles are cited thirty-three times in total. Admittedly Castles's book is only just over thirty years old. The first edition of Windeyer's text appeared as long ago as 1938, and he may have gained some kudos from the fact that he was a senior judge even if the substance of the work adds little to Holdsworth's more extensive *History of English Law*.

Raw citation scores tell only part of the story. The works referred to are only a sample. The secondary literature included are the main works of those authors. Some of these writers, especially Maitland, wrote a great deal more besides. There is considerable variation between different judges. In Table 10.3, Windeyer J had the greatest number of citations of the English legal classics. For a judge of that era, he made heavy use of sources beyond the law reports.[58] During his thirteen years on the High Court, he cited the English legal classics thirty-eight times. Kirby and Gummow JJ come a close second with thirty-two citations each. Isaacs CJ follows with thirty citations and Dixon CJ with twenty-nine citations. When averaged out by years on the Bench, Windeyer J also has the second highest score of 2.92 citations per year. Of this group, Dixon CJ has the lowest average of 0.82 citations per year in the very long period in which he sat on the High Court. Some more recent High Court judges have notched up a considerable number of citations. French CJ cited the English legal classics in the sample twenty times, or 3.33 citations per year, before he retired in 2017—just ahead of Windeyer J.

Over the last thirty years the trend is towards more individual and collective citation of the English legal classics. But this does not tell the whole story. Variations are not always generational. Of the earliest High Court judges, Griffith CJ was the most prolific user of the legal classics. In contrast, Barton and O'Connor JJ rarely cited any of these works. Equally,

---

[55] Bruce Debelle, "Windeyer, Sir William John Victor (Vic) (1900–1987)," Australian Dictionary of Biography, accessed 16 February 2021, http://adb.anu.edu.au/biography/windeyer-sir-william-john-victor-vic-15867

[56] Alex Castles, *An Australian Legal History* (Sydney: Law Book Co., 1982).

[57] For this shift, see Rosemary Hunter, "Australian Legal Histories in Context," *Law and History Review* 21, no. 3 (2003), https://www.jstor.org/stable/3595121

[58] Smyth, "Other than Accepted Sources," 36.

188    W. SWAIN

there are contrasting citation rates within the modern High Court. Whilst Kirby J cited the legal classics thirty-two times in twelve years, Gleeson and Heydon JJ, in just two years fewer, cited these sources eleven and thirteen times, respectively. No citation count alone, even broken down in quite a fine graded fashion, can tell us anything about the importance of work referred to in the actual decision itself. Undoubtedly, historical sources appear in some High Court decisions that changed the law in fundamental ways. Bracton and Blackstone were both cited in *Mabo v Queensland [No 2]*,[59] with Holdsworth, Windeyer and Castles also featuring in the decision. The views expressed by Sir Matthew Hale in *The History of the Pleas of the Crown*, on whether or not a husband could rape his wife, were central to the High Court's deliberations in *PGA v The Queen*.[60] Like *Coke on Littleton*, Hale's *Pleas of the Crown* was, until the nineteenth century, a standard work which has enjoyed a long afterlife.[61]

## A CASE STUDY

The main conclusions from the raw citation figures are that the English legal classics and, to a lesser extent, secondary legal historical literature (Table 10.4) remain a feature of the High Court of Australia's judgments into modern time. For more insight into this influence, it is necessary to undertake case studies from some leading High Court cases. A good illustration is provided by two recent decisions on the doctrine of penalties, *Andrews v Australia and New Zealand Banking Group Ltd*[62] and *Paciocco v Australian and New Zealand Banking Group Ltd*.[63] Space limits discussion to two decisions, but other subjects could have been chosen just as easily. Legal history has, for example, played a key role in the debates around the basis and scope of a doctrine of unjust enrichment in Australia.[64]

[59] (1992) 175 CLR 1.

[60] (2012) 245 CLR 355.

[61] The edition usually cited by the High Court is, George Wilson, *The History of the Pleas of the Crown*, ed. Sir Matthew Hale (London: T. Payne, 1800). For a discussion of the treatise in context see, Lindsay Farmer, "Of Treatises and Textbooks: the Literature of the Criminal Law in Nineteenth-Century Britain," in *Law Books in Action Essays on the Anglo-American Legal Treatise*, eds. Angela Fernandez and Markus Dubber (London: Hart, 2012), 145, 147–48.

[62] (2012) 247 CLR 205 ('*Andrews*').

[63] (2016) 258 CLR 525 ('*Paciocco*').

[64] For example, *Roxborough v Rothmans of Pall Mall Australia Ltd* (2001) 208 CLR 516. See Warren Swain, "Unjust Enrichment and the Role of Legal History in England and

In recent years, the scope of the penalty doctrine has been the subject of lengthy debate in both the United Kingdom Supreme Court[65] and the High Court of Australia. Two recent academic monographs have also considered the subject in detail.[66] The appellants in *Andrews* were bank customers who had found themselves subject to bank charges for various transactions, including honour and dishonour fees when there were insufficient funds to meet cheques drawn on an account, late payment fees and fees for exceeding an agreed overdraft. The main point of contention was whether the penalty doctrine ought to apply only in cases of breach of contract or whether it had wider application to cases like the present, in which a fee was payable without a breach. The Federal Court had concluded that the penalty doctrine only applied in instances of breach of contract.[67] This view was consistent with existing practice and reflected in a number of earlier High Court decisions.[68] A key feature of how the High Court came to a different conclusion was by using legal history, to the extent that it was even said that "an understanding of the penalty doctrine requires more than a brief backward glance."[69]

The High Court had already considered the history of penalties nearly twenty years ago in *AMEV-UDC Finance Ltd v Austin*,[70] where some of the same precedents were discussed. On that occasion, Mason and Wilson JJ had warned that "The doctrine of penalties has pursued such a tortuous path in the course of its long development that it is a risky enterprise to construct an argument on the basis of the old decisions."[71] A majority of the High Court in *Austin* came to two conclusions. First, that the penalty

---

Australia," *New South Wales Law Journal* 36, no. 3 (2013), https://ssrn.com/abstract=2378154

[65] *Cavendish Square Holding BV v Talal El Makdessi* [2016] AC 1172 ('*Cavendish*').

[66] Roger Halson, *Liquidated Damages and Penalty Clauses* (Oxford: Oxford University Press, 2018); Nicholas A. Tiverios, *Contractual Penalties in Australia and the United Kingdom History, Theory and Practice* (Sydney: The Federation Press, 2019).

[67] *Andrews v Australia and New Zealand Banking Group Ltd* (2011) 211 FCR 53.

[68] *Ringrow v BP Australia Pty Ltd* (2005) 224 CLR 656, 662–63. For a discussion of the earlier High Court authority, see J. W. Carter et al., "Contractual Penalties: Resurrecting the Equitable Jurisdiction," *Journal of Contract Law* 30 (2013): 102–103, http://hdl.handle.net/2440/81558

[69] *Andrews* (2012) 247 CLR 205, 218 [14].

[70] (1986) 162 CLR 170 ('*Austin*').

[71] *Austin* (1986) CLR 170, 186.

190   W. SWAIN

doctrine only applied in cases of breach of contract.[72] Second, as Mason and Wilson JJ made clear, although there was once a separate equitable doctrine that applied to penalties, it had been subsumed into the common law[73] or, at best, marginalised, for example, in situations in which specific performance is ordered as a remedy.[74]

The point at issue in *Paciocco* was different. There was undoubtedly a breach of contract,[75] and the High Court was merely asked to determine whether late payment fees imposed by a bank fell within the definition of a penalty. Nevertheless, there were some important obiter comments on *Andrews*. Until recently, *Dunlop Pneumatic Tyre Co v New Garage & Motor Co Ltd*,[76] especially the speech of Lord Dunedin, was regarded as the established English position on whether or not a clause was a penalty.[77] This was something to be determined, he said, as a matter of construction at the time that the contract was made rather than at the time of the breach.[78] Rather than simply applying *Dunlop*, the High Court in *Paciocco* chose instead to adopt a test which more closely resembled the one favoured by the UK Supreme Court in *Cavendish*: whether or not a late payment fee or other clause could be enforced depended on whether the party seeking to enforce it had a "legitimate interest" in enforcing the obligation. This process remains an exercise in construction, but the inquiry is a broader one than suggested by Lord Dunedin's analysis. Once again, this conclusion was partly justified by reference to the penalty doctrine's historical foundation in equity.[79]

In *Cavendish*, Lords Neuberger and Sumption observed that "The penalty rule in England is an ancient, haphazardly constructed edifice

---

[72] *Austin* 176 (Gibbs CJ), 184 (Mason and Wilson JJ), 211 (Dawson J), contrary on this point Deane J 199.

[73] *Austin* 191 (Mason and Wilson JJ).

[74] *Austin* 195 (Deane J).

[75] *Paciocco* (2016) 258 CLR 525, 605 [253] (Keane J).

[76] [1915] AC 79 ('*Dunlop*'). Discussed for other purposes in *Andrews* (2012) 247 CLR 205, 234–36 [69]–[77].

[77] In *Cavendish* [2016] AC 1172, 1199 [22], Lords Neuberger and Sumption described Lord Dunedin's speech has having "achieved the status of a quasi-statutory code."

[78] [1915] AC 79, 86–87. This was in line with earlier authority: *Public Works Commissioner v Hills* [1906] AC 368, 376.

[79] *Paciocco* (2016) 258 CLR 525, 545 [22] (Kiefel J), 577 [155] (Gageler J). For a more sceptical view of the continued relevance of the equitable history see: *Paciocco* (2016) 258 CLR 525, 605 [252] (Keane J).

which has not weathered well."[80] The history is difficult to unravel. Agreements with a penalty for non-performance attached have been used in a wide variety of situations since the Middle Ages.[81] One significant application was a money bond with a condition attached.[82] The conditional bond was a flexible device and a useful means of securing performance. Take a simple example: A agrees to loan B £100. B will execute a bond in A's favour for a larger sum, say £200, to be repaid on a certain day. The bond will be subject to a condition of defeasance so that if £100 is repaid before that day the bond is void. The basis of the obligation was the bond itself. Failure to perform the condition cannot be equated with breach of contract in the modern sense. Performance merely provides the condition of defeasance. Chancery began to grant relief from the sixteenth century in exceptional cases.[83] By the seventeenth century, relief was granted in equity as a matter of course when the sum in the bond did not reflect the size of the debt.[84]

In *Andrews*, it was suggested that the common law developed a doctrine of relief against penalties in the 1670s, which was regulated by statute at the time.[85] However, recent scholarship shows that the common law courts applied a penalty doctrine before the legislation was passed using a process in which the defendant paid the principal interest and cost into court, which could then be taken as full satisfaction of the debt.[86] Nevertheless, the default rule was still that the bond was enforceable at common law irrespective of the size of the actual debt. The scope of

---

[80] *Cavendish* [2016] AC 1172, 1192 [3] (Lords Neuberger and Sumption). In *Paciocco* (2016) 258 CLR 525, 603 [247], Keane J said that, "The penalty rule is of ancient but somewhat uncertain origin."

[81] Joseph Biancalana, "Contractual Penalties in the King's Court 1260–1360," *Cambridge Law Journal* 64, no. 1 (2005): 213–15, https://www.jstor.org/stable/25166350

[82] A. W. B. Simpson, "The Penal Bond with Conditional Defeasance," *Law Quarterly Review* 82 (1966).

[83] E. G. Henderson, "Relief from Bonds in the English Chancery: Mid-Sixteenth Century," *American Journal of Legal History* 18, no. 4 (1974), https://www.jstor.org/stable/845168

[84] D. E. C. Yale, *Lord Nottingham's Chancery Cases* (London: Selden Society, 1961), 15–16.

[85] *Andrews* (2012) 247 CLR 205, 229–30 [53].

[86] For details of the process, see P. G. Turner, "*Lex Sequitur Equitatem* Fusion and the Penalty Doctrine" in *Equity and Law Fusion and Fission*, ed. John C. P. Goldberg, Henry E. Smith and P. G. Turner (Cambridge: Cambridge University Press, 2019), 258–60. There are even earlier statements disapproving of penalties in the common law, but these do not add up to a regular stand against penalties, for example *Umfraville v Lonstede* YB 2 Edw II; (1308) 19 SS 58.

exceptions to the strict common law position significantly increased under the statutory procedure because it covered performance bonds[87] and common money bonds,[88] whereas the existing practice covered only money bonds. On payment of the principal, interest and costs into court, the debt was deemed to be discharged. The sum paid then acted as a security pending the action. At the trial, the question of loss was put to a jury who came up with a sum that reflected the actual loss suffered instead of the amount stated in the bond and that might be different. Whilst formally an action of debt and therefore resting on an entitlement to a fixed sum, the claim had become in substance an action for damages reflecting the loss suffered.[89] Where the transaction was covered by the statutes it was compulsory to proceed under this process. In many cases it was no longer necessary to seek an injunction in equity and then ask for a *quantum damnificatus* (to assess the actual loss) before a jury.[90] This was obviously a more efficient process and also cheaper.

The High Court in *Andrews* insisted that the equitable jurisdiction survived in the face of a regular intervention from the common law courts. This analysis was necessary because equitable relief was not confined to cases of breach of contract.[91] Still, the relationship between the equitable and common law jurisdictions over penalties was not static. By the early nineteenth century, other means of raising credit were becoming popular.[92] The action of assumpsit had taken the place of debt. The courts began applying the same technique as they had used in actions of debt to claims in assumpsit for damages.[93] It was said that, otherwise, the statute could be evaded.[94] A clause that fixed a sum in advance payable on breach and which was not deemed a penalty was enforceable, whereas a penalty

---

[87] *Administration of Justice Act 1696*, 8 & 9 Wm 3, c 11, s 8.

[88] *Perpetuation and Amendment of Acts 1704*, 4 Anne, c 16, ss 12–13. For a discussion of its application see *Murray v Earl of Stair* (1823) 2 B & C 82; 107 ER 313.

[89] For a discussion of this important point see D. J. Ibbetson, *A Historical Introduction to the Law of Obligations* (Oxford: Oxford University Press, 1999), 150–51.

[90] *Roles v Rosewell* (1794) 5 TR 538; 101 ER 302; *Hardy v Bern* (1794) 5 TR 636; 101 ER 355.

[91] Hence in *Paciocco* which was a breach case it was unnecessary to rely on equity on this point, see *Paciocco* (2016) 258 CLR 525, 605 [253] (Keane J).

[92] Notably through negotiable instruments and changes in banking practice, see James Rogers, *The Early History of the Law of Bills and Notes* (Cambridge: Cambridge University Press, 1995), 112–16.

[93] *Davies v Penton* (1827) 6 B & C 216; 108 ER 433.

[94] *Astley v Weldon* (1801) 2 B & P 345; 126 ER 1318, 1322 ('*Astley*').

# 10 THE USE AND MISUSE OF LEGAL HISTORY IN THE HIGH COURT... 193

was not. In the latter, the damages awarded reflected the actual loss. Distinguishing between the two types of clauses was difficult. Lord Eldon would concede, having reviewed the authorities, that he was "much embarrassed in ascertaining the principle upon which those cases were founded."[95] His judgment shows the earlier cases in equity were still of some relevance in addressing this question.[96] The common law was soon developing a doctrine of penalties. The assertion in *Andrews* that, prior to the *Judicature Acts*, the common law penalty doctrine did "not somehow supplant the equity jurisdiction"[97] was technically correct. However, it does not reflect practice in which equity, by this stage, had a more peripheral role. One of the leading writers on classical contract law, Frederick Pollock, conceded that the equitable doctrine still existed but thought it was mainly confined to mortgage transactions.[98] Whatever the scope of the original equitable doctrine and its influence on the common law, it was smothered both by the statutes and developments within the common law itself. The new orthodoxy was reflected in the remarks of Lord Eldon, who said, "it appears to me extremely difficult to apply with propriety the word 'excessive' to the terms in which the parties choose to contract with each other."[99] In *Kemble v Farren*, Tindal CJ had stressed that, "For we see nothing illegal or unreasonable in the parties, by their mutual agreement, settling the amount of damages, uncertain in their nature, at any sum upon which they may agree."[100]

In *Dunlop,* having briefly discussed the history of the subject at common law and in equity, Lord Dunedin said that it was "probably more interesting than material."[101] A few years earlier, Lord Halsbury had stated that he saw no difference between common law and equity in relation to penalties beyond an administrative one.[102] In *Cavendish*, Lords Neuberger and Sumption explained at some length why they rejected the position in

---

[95] *Astley*, 1321 (Lord Eldon).

[96] *Astley*, 1321–2.

[97] *Andrews* (2012) 247 CLR 205, 232 [61].

[98] Frederick Pollock, *Principles of Contract at Law and in Equity* (London: Stevens and Sons, 1876), 417.

[99] *Astley*, 1321.

[100] (1829) 6 Bing 141; 130 ER 1234, 1237.

[101] [1915] AC 79, 87.

[102] *Clydebank Engineering and Shipping Co Ltd v Don Jose Ramos Yzquierdo y Castaneda* [1905] AC 6, 10, albeit that was a Scottish case and therefore different considerations applied, see Lord Dunedin in *Public Works Commissioner v Hills* [1906] AC 368, 375.

*Andrews* that there was a broader equitable penalties doctrine that had survived fusion.[103] By doing so, they underplay the extent to which the common law relating to penalties grew out of equitable doctrine before the nineteenth century. Focusing on the law post-fusion[104] ignores the older history of the subject. They are hardly the first to be sceptical about the continued importance of equity in shaping the development of the penalties doctrine as applied in the common law courts of the nineteenth century. In the 1880s, Jessel MR, having examined the common law cases on penalties, said: "The ground stated by the Judges in two or three of the cases is this—they say it was an extension to the Common Law of the well-known doctrine of Equity. I do know a little of Equity, but I am sorry to say I cannot assent to the accuracy of the statement that it is an extension to the Common Law of the well-known doctrine."[105] The implication here seems to be that it was wrong to suggest that the common law doctrine of penalties was transplanted from equity.

In *Andrews,* there is no doubt that the High Court took a different view of the importance of the history of the penalties doctrine from the English Supreme Court. *Paciocco* also accepted the continued existence of an equitable jurisdiction over penalties. Simultaneously, the High Court applied the same test of a penalty as used by the Supreme Court in *Cavendish.* In *Cavendish,* this approach was unproblematic because the Supreme Court was clear that there was a single jurisdiction over penalties which only applied to a breach of contract.[106] Any of the pre-fusion equitable doctrine was irrelevant. Only Gageler J in *Paciocco* explicitly addressed the relationship between law and equity. He seems to suggest that there are two penalty doctrines, one at law and one in equity.[107] In the absence of clear guidance, it is also possible that the High Courts in *Andrews* and *Paciocco* were engaged in an even more ambitious project of arguing that the whole doctrine of penalties was, in essence, equitable in character. There are, after all, other examples of the High Court doing

---

[103] *Cavendish* [2016] AC 1172, 1208–1209 [42].

[104] Ibid.

[105] *Wallis v Smith* [1882] 21 Ch D 243, 256.

[106] More specifically where the term was a secondary obligation to pay a sum of money rather than a primary obligation to perform, *Cavendish* [2016] AC 1172, 1196 [14] (Lords Neuberger and Sumption), 1240 [129]–[130] (Lord Mance), 1274 [242], 1279 [258] (Lord Hodge), 1285 [291] (Lord Clarke).

[107] *Paciocco* (2016) 258 CLR 525, 569 [125]–[126].

just that in other contexts.[108] It is difficult to come to any firm conclusions, though Gageler J did talk about the "equitable root of the penalty doctrine."[109]

All of this still leaves unclear what test would be applied to determine whether a clause is a penalty where there was no breach of contract and, therefore unarguably, the equitable doctrine applies. In a discussion of *Dunlop* in *Andrews*, it seems to be hinted that a version of the "legitimate interest" test is appropriate in an equity case as well as at common law.[110] Yet, it is very difficult to see how the "legitimate interest" test reflects historical practice in equity. Kiefel J explained that "The aim of the equity courts was to compensate in the event of a default, not to punish."[111] The basis of equity's intervention was to allow compensation and no more.[112] This is a perfectly correct summary of the position in equity. More problematic is how Kiefel J gets from this position to one in which she argues that the appropriate test of enforcement is whether the innocent party had a legitimate interest in enforcing the clause. She does this by suggesting that the reason that equity intervened was because "it would not tolerate individuals exacting punishment."[113] From this position, it is then assumed that a clause that punishes is one where there is no legitimate interest.[114] The problem with this reasoning is that whether the amount claimed was more than compensatory and whether the clause was a punishment are not precisely overlapping concepts. It is possible to imagine a clause which the sum exceeds the loss suffered but is not penal or in the modern language where there is a legitimate interest in enforcing the clause. To trace the legitimate interest test into equity does not reflect the nature of equity's original jurisdiction over penalties, which was to ensure proper compensation rather than to stop the enforcement of a clause because it was a punishment.

---

[108] Notably in the development of estoppel in *Waltons Stores (Interstate) Ltd v Maher* (1988) 164 CLR 387.

[109] *Paciocco* (2016) 258 CLR 525, 577 [155].

[110] *Andrews* (2012) 247 CLR 205, 236 [75].

[111] *Paciocco* (2016) 258 CLR 525, 577, 544 [21].

[112] *Paciocco*, 577, 544 [21].

[113] *Paciocco*, 577, 544 [21].

[114] *Paciocco*, 77, 545 [22].

Relief in Chancery was premised on the legitimacy of recovering actual loss suffered along with some interests and costs. This was why a *quantum damnificatus* was used so that a common law jury could assess the damage suffered. The legitimate interest test is different. It looks at the clause before the breach has occurred. It does not involve an inquiry into the extent of the loss caused by the breach. This explains why in England, clauses for sums much larger than the loss suffered might be legitimate, for example because the clause in question acts as a deterrent.[115] At best, whether the sum is commensurate is one factor of a number in determining whether the clause is legitimate.[116] If, as the High Court seems to accept, there is an equitable doctrine of penalties and one at common law, then the implication as far as one can make out is that the same test of enforcement applies to both, namely whether there is a legitimate interest in enforcing the clause. There will be other differences in whether the equitable or common law doctrine applies because the former can be used without a breach of contract. The remedies may also be different. But this leaves us with the confusing position of a penalty doctrine said to be derived from equity with a test for enforcement that is difficult to square with the historical scope of Chancery jurisdiction over penalties.

## The Importance of History

It is evident from the analysis of citations and the analysis of recent decisions on penalties that the High Court continues to make significant use of historical sources, whether in the form of classic legal texts, secondary literature or old English precedents. One might expect this practice to decline as Australian private law moves further away from its English roots. However, this has not happened. All the evidence shows that, far from declining, the use of historical sources is increasing. An understanding of

---

[115] Hence a parking fine which is not commensurate with the loss suffered might be perfectly legitimate and enforceable: D. Campbell and R. Halson, "By Their Fruits Shall Ye Know Them," *Cambridge Law Journal* 79, no. 3 (2020).

[116] For a recent example, see *ST Investment Pty v Geng* [2020] NSWSC 329 at [46]. A number of cases have continued to emphasise this element: *Melbourne Linh Son Buddhist Society v Gippsreal* [2017] VSCA 161.

the history of legal doctrine is useful. It can explain why doctrine has evolved in a particular way, but some care needs to be taken.

History can be used creatively to reach a particular outcome. The High Court in *Andrews* was perfectly correct to claim that Chancery would intervene beyond breach of contract. The authorities concern conditional bonds and not contracts. At the same time, Roscoe Pound once observed that "Law must be stable and yet it cannot stand still."[117] There are dangers in taking the history of a legal doctrine at a particular point in time and transplanting it into another period. Lord Thurlow LC in *Sloman v Walter*[118] said that "The rule, that where a penalty is inserted merely to secure the enjoyment of a collateral object, the enjoyment of the object is considered as the principal intent of the deed, and the penalty only as accessional, and, therefore, only to secure the damage really incurred, is too strongly established in equity to be shaken."[119] Put another way, it was perfectly valid to insert a term to secure performance. This was, after all, how conditional bonds worked. The focus of the penalty doctrine in both equity and at common law before the nineteenth century was on whether the sum reflected the agreed performance; hence the importance of the loss suffered. Yet, the modern penalty doctrine has a quite different emphasis—whether there is a "legitimate interest" protected by the clause. The problem with the two High Court cases is one of consistency. History is used for one purpose—to allow the penalty doctrine to apply outside of breach of contract—and not another—in determining how a court properly characterises a clause as penal. The result has been some uncertainty at the expense of doctrinal purity.[120] Looking to the future, it may well be that "statutory law reform offers more promise than debates about the true reading of English legal history" in this area.[121] But one thing is certain: legal history continues to shape the modern private law in Australia.

[117] Roscoe Pound, *Interpretations of Legal History* (Cambridge: Cambridge University Press, 1923), 1.

[118] (1783) 1 Bro CC 418; 28 ER 1213.

[119] Ibid. 1214.

[120] *Arab Bank Australia Ltd v Sayde Developments Pty Ltd* (2016) 934 NSWLR 231 at [10].

[121] *Paciocco* (2016) 258 CLR 525, 540–41 [10] (French CJ).

APPENDIX

**Table 10.1**   Total citations of English legal classics by the High Court from 1903 to 2019

| Author | 1903–1920 | 1921–1940 | 1941–1960 | 1961–1980 | 1981–2000 | 2001–2019 | Total of the author |
|---|---|---|---|---|---|---|---|
| Glanvill | 3 | 0 | 1 | 0 | 0 | 1 | 5 |
| Bracton | 2 | 4 | 9 | 5 | 10 | 20 | 50 |
| Littleton | 18 | 6 | 11 | 7 | 12 | 24 | 78 |
| Hale | 4 | 7 | 1 | 21 | 43 | 50 | 126 |
| Blackstone | 24 | 33 | 32 | 45 | 191 | 197 | 522 |
| Total citations | 51 | 50 | 54 | 78 | 256 | 312 | 781 |

**Table 10.2** Total citations of secondary legal historical literature by the High Court from 1903 to 2019

| Author | 1903–1920 | 1921–1940 | 1941–1960 | 1961–1980 | 1981–2000 | 2001–2019 | Total of the author |
|---|---|---|---|---|---|---|---|
| Pollock and Maitland | 0 | 6 | 9 | 10 | 22 | 5 | 52 |
| Holdsworth | 0 | 33 | 55 | 47 | 114 | 150 | 399 |
| Windeyer | N/A | 0 | 0 | 0 | 11 | 5 | 16 |
| Castles | N/A | N/A | N/A | N/A | 15 | 2 | 17 |
| Total citations | 0 | 39 | 64 | 57 | 162 | 162 | 484 |

**Table 10.3** Citation of English legal classics by High Court judges of ten or more

| Judge | Number of citations | Years on the Bench (rounding down) to the end of 2019 | Average number of citations per year |
|---|---|---|---|
| Windeyer | 38 | 13 | 2.92 |
| Gummow | 32 | 17 | 1.88 |
| Kirby | 32 | 12 | 2.66 |
| Isaacs | 30 | 24 | 1.25 |
| Dixon | 29 | 35 | 0.82 |
| Brennan | 27 | 17 | 1.58 |
| McHugh | 26 | 16 | 1.62 |
| Mason | 25 | 22 | 1.13 |
| Deane | 25 | 13 | 1.92 |
| Gaudron | 25 | 15 | 1.66 |
| Hayne | 24 | 17 | 1.41 |
| Crennan | 20 | 9 | 2.22 |
| French | 20 | 6 | 3.33 |
| Toohey | 19 | 10 | 1.9 |
| Dawson | 17 | 15 | 1.13 |
| Rich | 14 | 37 | 0.37 |
| Kiefel | 14 | 7 | 2 |
| Bell | 14 | 5 | 2.8 |
| Griffith | 13 | 16 | 0.81 |
| Heydon | 13 | 10 | 1.3 |
| Callinan | 12 | 9 | 1.33 |
| Murphy | 11 | 11 | 1 |
| Gleeson | 11 | 10 | 1.1 |
| Kitto | 10 | 20 | 0.5 |
| Gibbs | 10 | 16 | 0.62 |

**Table 10.4** Citations of historical secondary literature by High Court judges of ten or more

| Judge | Number of citations | Years on the Bench (rounding down) to the end of 2019 | Average number of citations per year |
|---|---|---|---|
| McHugh | 27 | 16 | 1.68 |
| Brennan | 25 | 17 | 1.47 |
| Dixon | 24 | 35 | 0.68 |
| Windeyer | 19 | 13 | 1.46 |
| Deane | 17 | 13 | 1.30 |
| Toohey | 16 | 10 | 1.6 |
| Kirby | 14 | 12 | 1.16 |
| Gummow | 13 | 17 | 0.76 |
| Mason | 11 | 22 | 0.5 |
| Gaudron | 11 | 15 | 0.73 |
| Callinan | 11 | 9 | 1.22 |
| Starke | 10 | 29 | 0.34 |
| Stephen | 10 | 10 | 1 |
| Dawson | 10 | 15 | 0.66 |

CHAPTER 11

# Did the Early British Colonists Regard the Indigenous Peoples of New South Wales as Subjects of the Crown Entitled to the Protection of English Law?

*Gavin Loughton*

## INTRODUCTION

In his reasons for decision in *Mabo v Queensland [No. 2]*, Justice Brennan explained how (and why) the common law recognises and protects "native title rights", the traditional rights in relation to land and waters of the Indigenous peoples of Australia. The explanation required his Honour to go into some legal history. He traced how the law of England came to

---

Gavin Loughton is a solicitor with the Australian Government Solicitor in Canberra. The views expressed herein are his personal views only. I am grateful to Robert Orr for his helpful comments on an earlier draft of this essay.

---

G. Loughton (✉)
Constitutional Litigation Unit of the Australian Government Solicitor,
Canberra, ACT, Australia
e-mail: gavin.loughton@ags.gov.au

© The Author(s), under exclusive license to Springer Nature Switzerland AG 2022
S. McKibbin et al. (eds.), *The Impact of Law's History*, Palgrave Modern Legal History,
https://doi.org/10.1007/978-3-030-90068-7_11

201

New South Wales with the First Fleet and became the law of all the people living here, European and Indigenous:

> [T]he theory which underpins the application of English law to the Colony of New South Wales is that English settlers brought with them the law of England and that, as the indigenous inhabitants were regarded as barbarous or unsettled and without a settled law, the law of England including the common law became the law of the Colony ...The common law thus became the common law of all subjects within the Colony who were equally entitled to the law's protection as subjects of the Crown.

Thus, on the coming of the British the Indigenous peoples "became British subjects owing allegiance to the Imperial Sovereign entitled to such rights and privileges and subject to such liabilities as the common law and applicable statutes provided".[1]

That is what today's legal doctrine supposes the early colonists thought—or should have thought. Is it what they really thought? There is reason to doubt it. It is now over 20 years since Professor Kercher drew attention back to the remarkable trilogy of NSW Supreme Court cases, *R v Lowe* (1827), *R v Ballard* (1829) and *R v Murrell* (1836),[2] in which, some 40 years after the First Fleet arrived, we see lawyers and judges in the Supreme Court of New South Wales perplexed and embarrassed by the question of the legal status of the Indigenous peoples.[3] What, then, had

---

[1] *Mabo v Queensland [No. 2]* (1992) 175 CLR 1, 37–38 (Mason CJ and McHugh J agreeing at 15). See also to similar effect 80 (Deane and Gaudron JJ) and 182 (Toohey J).

[2] *R v Lowe* [1827] NSWKR 4; [1827] NSWSupC 32; [1827] Sel. Cas. (Kercher) 859; *R v Ballard or Barrett* [1829] NSW SupC 26 sub nom *R v Dirty Dick* (1828) NSW Sel Cas (Dowling) 2; *R v Murrell* (1836) 1 Legge 72; [1836] NSWSupC 35. As to the latter case, the report in Legge is very imperfect. The report at law.mq.edu.au is far better.

[3] Bruce Kercher, "Recognition of Indigenous Legal Autonomy in Nineteenth Century New South Wales," *Indigenous Law Bulletin* 4 (1998); Bruce Kercher, "The Recognition of Aboriginal Status and Laws in the Supreme Court of New South Wales under Forbes CJ, 1824–1836," in *Land and Freedom: Law, Property Rights and the British Diaspora*, ed. Andrew Buck, John McLaren and Nancy Wright (Aldershot: Ashgate, 2001), 83 ff; Bruce Kercher, "Native Title in the Shadows: the Origins of the Myth of *Terra Nullius* in Early New South Wales Courts," in *Colonialism and the Modern World*, ed. Gregory Blue, Martin Bunton and Ralph Crozier (New York: ME Sharpe, 2002), 100 ff. There had been earlier discussion: Barry Bridges, "The Aborigines and the Law: New South Wales 1788–1855," *Teaching History* (December 1970): 40, 45–46; Barry Bridges, "The Extension of English Law to the Aborigines for Offences Committed Inter Se, 1829–1842," *Journal of the Royal Australian Historical Society* 59 (1973). However, Bridges's writings present a dilemma to

## 11 DID THE EARLY BRITISH COLONISTS REGARD THE INDIGENOUS... 203

the colonists who preceded these lawyers and judges thought? How did things go during those first four decades of the colony such that the legal position of Indigenous peoples still appears to the colonists in the 1820s and 1830s as a *vexata quaestio*? And when and how was that question resolved?

## THE STATE OF THE UNDERSTANDING OF THE LAW IN 1788

When we look at the Royal Instructions given to Governor Phillip a few weeks before the First Fleet set sail, we find no clear sign that the Indigenous inhabitants of New South Wales were conceived of as His Majesty's subjects. If anything the drafter of the Instructions, whether consciously or unconsciously, appears to have erected in his language a distinction between "our subjects" and "the natives" (in what follow the italics are mine)[4]:

> You are to endeavour by every possible means to open an intercourse with *the natives*, and to conciliate their affections, enjoining all *our subjects* to live in amity and kindness with *them*. And if any of *our subjects* shall wantonly destroy *them*, or give *them* any unnecessary interruption in the exercise of their several occupations, it is our will and pleasure that you do cause such offenders to be brought to punishment according to the degree of the offence. You will endeavour to procure an account of the numbers inhabiting the neighbourhood of the intended settlement, and report your opinion to one of our Secretaries of State in what manner our intercourse with *these people* may be turned to the advantage of this colony.

There is no trace here of the "Our Indian and Our other Subjects resident in Our settlement" found in the not-much-earlier (1767) Royal Commission to Robert Hodgson appointing him Commander in Chief of

---

the historian. His archival work has not been bettered, but on occasion one finds him expressing sentiments of a kind that they seem completely foreign to us and, indeed, highly objectionable. Presumably in consequence of this his work is little discussed today.

[4] Frederick Watson, ed. *Historical Records of Australia* (Sydney: Library Committee of the Commonwealth Parliament, 1914–1925) (hereafter "*HRA*"), Series I, vol 1, 13–14 (italics mine). This distinction was noticed by Rath J in *R v Wedge* [1976] NSWLR 581, 585. He supposed that "there may well have been both uncertainty and ambivalence in the official attitude".

204    G. LOUGHTON

the Mosquito Shore in the Caribbean.[5] Phillip's Instructions refer to "the natives" in terms which seem to convey an expectation that they were to be treated not so much as subjects as strangers to whom a kind of cautious friendliness was due. On the one hand, Phillip had been provided with merchandise to barter with them; on the other he was directed immediately upon landing to take "measures for securing yourself and the people who accompany you as much as possible from any attacks or interruptions of *the natives* of *that* country".[6] And yet, nor did the Instructions actually refer to the natives as "aliens" or say anything definite to indicate this was regarded as their status. Perhaps this vagueness was the drafter deliberately skirting around an obscure legal question. Or perhaps his masters had simply not given it much thought—perhaps indeed had decided they did not need to give it much thought. Parliament had specifically empowered His Majesty to establish a bespoke Court of Criminal Judicature for New South Wales, to be presided over by a Judge-Advocate and "with authority to proceed in a more summary way than is used within this realm, according to the known laws thereof".[7] In consequence, the King by letters patent had established a Court of Civil Jurisdiction and a Court of Criminal Jurisdiction for the colony. The latter had the power to hear, determine and punish all crimes committed "within the Settlement and Colony", with punishment "so to be Inflicted being according to the Laws of that part of Our Kingdom of Great Britain called England, as nearly as may be, considering and allowing for the Circumstances and Situation of the place and Settlement aforesaid and the Inhabitants thereof".[8] Both the act of

[5] Cited in William Sorsby "The British Superintendency of the Mosquito Shore 1749–1787" (PhD thesis, University College London, 1969), 157–158 n 3. Such a Commission had been preceded by decades of interaction between the British and the indigenous peoples there, including a treaty in 1740, Article II of which provided "That he [King Edward of the Mosquitos] and his People do hereby become Subjects of Great Britain and desire the same Protection and to be instructed in the same Knowledge and to be governed by the same Laws as the English who shall settle among them": ibid., 20. I am indebted to Alan Atkinson, *The Europeans in Australia. Volume One: The Beginning* (Sydney: NewSouth Publishing, 1997, 2016 ed), 212, for being put on the trail of this reference. At one point (212) Atkinson reads Phillip's Instructions as regarding the Indigenous inhabitants as aliens. As will be evident from follows, I think the better view is that the Instructions were simply vague (and cf. Atkinson 219–220).

[6] *HRA*, Series I, vol 1, 12, 11 (italics mine).

[7] *An Act to enable his Majesty to establish a Court of Criminal Judicature on the Eastern Coast of New South Wales, and the Parts* adjacent, 27 Geo. III c.2 (1787).

[8] "Warrant for the Charter of Justice," April 2, 1787, *HRA*, Series IV, vol 1, 6 at 10.

parliament and the letters patent evince some thought being given to the question of how the machinery of English law was to operate in the new colony. Neither of them mentions the Indigenous peoples. Against these two documents, the Instructions to Phillip to live in amity and kindness with the natives, and that any colonists who gave them unnecessary interruption should be punished according to the degree of the offence, seem to amount to little more than Phillip being told to use his common sense.[9]

Had our drafter sought legal advice on status of the Indigenous inhabitants of "our territory called New South Wales",[10] what might that advice have been? In the eyes of British law, either His Majesty had acquired sovereignty over New South Wales in 1770 (on Captain Cook purporting to take possession) or would acquire it on the establishment of the colony (which, in the event, occurred at Port Jackson in 1788).[11] Whichever of those two be the correct date, the territory in question was already inhabited at the critical date. That is, many or all of the Indigenous peoples inhabiting New South Wales when the First Fleet arrived had been born in a land that was, *when they were born,* outside of the dominions of the King. Such Indigenous peoples were therefore not natural-born subjects of the King. This is because, according to the rules derived from *Calvin's Case,* the status of a place *at the time of the person's birth* is crucial. A person born within the dominions of the King was a natural-born subject. A person born without those dominions was an alien.[12]

But when the King acquired sovereignty over New South Wales, did that act automatically transform the Indigenous peoples already living there from aliens into subjects of the King? It was certainly arguable. There existed case law that was not exactly on point, but close enough to provide a good analogy. Fourteen years earlier, in the case of *Campbell v*

---

[9] Whatever we might think about Bridges's other conclusions, it is difficult to deny the correctness of his observation that "[i]n the planning of the settlement at Botany Bay very little thought was given to the Aborigines...": Barry Bridges, "The Aborigines and the Law: New South Wales 1788–1855," *Teaching History* (1970): 40.

[10] *HRA*, Series I, vol 1, 2.

[11] *Mabo v Queensland [No. 2]* (1992) 175 CLR 1, 77–78.

[12] (1608) 7 Co Rep 1a, 18a, 18b [97 ER 379, 399]: "The time of birth is chiefly to be considered; for he cannot be a subject born of one kingdom that was born under the ligeance of a King of another kingdom, albeit afterwards one kingdom descend to the King of another...the time of his birth is of the essence of a subject born; *for he cannot be a subject of the King of England, unless at the time of his birth he was under the ligeance and obedience of the King*" (italics mine).

*Hall*,[13] the Court of King's Bench in London had been required to consider the question of what laws were then in force on the island of Grenada in the West Indies. The island had been captured by British forces from the French during the Seven Years War and formally ceded to Britain by the peace treaty that concluded that war. Lord Mansfield CJ, in the course of delivering the unanimous opinion of the Court, laid down a number of what his Lordship regarded as elementary propositions about overseas dominions of the King. These were propositions "in which both sides seem to be perfectly agreed; and which, indeed are too clear to be controverted" (208). The second and fourth propositions were as follows:

> The 2nd is, that the conquered inhabitants once received under the King's protection, become subjects, and are to be universally considered in that light, not as enemies or aliens.
>
> ...
>
> The 4th, that the law and legislative government of every dominion, equally affects all persons and all property within the limits thereof; and is the rule of decision for all questions of law which arise there. Whoever purchases, lives, or sues there, puts himself under the law of the place. An Englishman in Ireland, Minorca, the Isle of Man, or the plantations, has not privilege distinct from the natives.

Of course, New South Wales had not, in the eyes of English law, become "our territory" by conquest. (Just how New South Wales had become British territory was, as we know now, to become one of the thorny questions of Australia's legal history. But that was a problem for the future: at the time, the British conceived of what was planned for Botany Bay as a "settlement".[14]) Reasoning by analogy in a manner that is orthodox to lawyers: if all the inhabitants of places obtained by *conquest* become British subjects, then should not all inhabitants of places obtained by other means (such as *settlement*) become British subjects too? Further, Lord Mansfield stated the fourth proposition as a general one, not just one applicable to

---

[13] (1774) 1 Cowp. 204.

[14] In the letter (dated on its face) 18 August 1786 from Lord Sydney (Secretary of State for the Home Department) to the Lords Commissioners of the Treasury announcing to them his Majesty's command that "measures should immediately be pursued" for the transportation of convicts to Botany Bay, the word "settlement" appears nine times to describe what is intended; the people to go are described as "the new settlers": Frank Bladen, ed., *Historical Records of New South Wales* (Sydney: Charles Potter, Government Printer 1892–1901) (hereafter *HRNSW*), vol 1, part 2, 14–16.

conquered places. If "the law…of every dominion equally affects all persons and all property within the limits thereof; and is the rule of decision for all questions of law which arise there" then would not that mean that the English law that the colonists supposed that they had brought with them should apply to colonists and "natives" alike? These were available conclusions of law to draw.

That the British had sufficient precedents to hand to be able to work out the probable legal position is one thing; that they had actually worked it out is another. As we shall see, it seems closer to the mark to say that in 1788 the question of the legal position of the Indigenous inhabitants of New Holland had been insufficiently anticipated and prepared for.[15]

Probably it was not regarded as a pressing problem. As is now well known, the British had expected to find some "natives" in the vicinity of Botany Bay, but not a large Indigenous population. When one reads the diaries of the colonists and the official dispatches from the early days and months of the penal colony at Sydney, one thing that is striking is the number of times a remark of is made to the effect of, *there are many more natives here than we had expected*.[16] In 1785, Joseph Banks had told a Committee of the House of Commons that the few natives there were would speedily abandon the country to the newcomers.[17] Faced with that

---

[15] Prince says that "there should have been no question" that at the acquisition of sovereignty the Indigenous inhabitants became subjects of the King: Peter Prince, "Aliens in their Own Land. 'Alien' and the Rule of Law in Colonial and Post-Federation Australia" (PhD thesis, The Australian National University, 2015), 64–65. However, he relies here on writers on international law and nationality law from the twentieth century. This tends to mask the novelty and obscurity of the issue in the eighteenth century. It was only during the course of the nineteenth century, when numerous annexations by the British Crown occurred, that the British government worked out its position on the issue (which was, in any event, often in particular cases governed by treaty): see Daniel O'Connell, *State Succession in Municipal Law and International Law* (Cambridge: CUP, 1967), 519; see also 502. The perceived difficulty of these issues in the nineteenth century can be seen in the opinions reproduced in Arnold McNair, *International Law Opinions Selected and Annotated, vol II* (Cambridge: CUP, 1956), 20–26.

[16] I have summarised the primary evidence on this point in "Truth and Fictions: Lying and the Law," in *An ABC of Lying*, eds. Livo Dobrez, Jan Lloyd Jones and Patricia Dobrez (Melbourne: Australian Scholarly Publishing, 2004), 170.

[17] "Minutes of Committee of the House of Commons respecting a plan for transporting felons to the island of Leemaine in the River Gambia," Public Records Office (London) HO 7/1, Minutes of 10 May 1785 (Lord Beauchamp in the chair), examination of Sir Joseph Banks, f.71 ff at f.75: "Do you think that 500 Men being put on Shore there would meet with that Obstruction from the Natives which might prevent them settling there? Certainly

## 208   G. LOUGHTON

evidence, what official would devote time and resources to the pursuit of a legal problem that seemed largely hypothetical? This was an age of "ultra-small government" in Britain.[18] The official who was chiefly responsible for the establishment of the penal settlement in New South Wales was the Secretary of State for the Home Department.[19] In his entire department one would have found at work on any given working day between 1784 and 1789 a total of about 16 people—provided one includes the office porter and the housekeeper but does not count the four additional officials who worked in the sub-department known as the Planation Office.[20] To these handful of men fell a list of duties that to us "seems so wide that it is difficult at first sight to understand how they were discharged by so few people".[21] The establishment of the colony in New South Wales was but one of these duties. If no evidence has yet come to light of officials turning their minds to nice questions of law concerning those few "natives" in the vicinity of Botany Bay, who were expected to speedily abandon the country to the newcomers, that should not be a surprise.

But "the natives" were numerous and did not speedily abandon the country to the newcomers. Worse, sporadic acts of violence soon began to occur between colonists and Indigenous inhabitants. As the pale of British settlement expanded over the following decades, these hostilities intensified rather than subsided. As the colonists occupied more and more land,

---

not—from the Experience I have had of the Natives of another part of the same Coast I am inclined to believe they would speedily abandon the Country to the New Comers".

[18] David Neal, *The Rule of Law in a Penal Colony* (Cambridge: Cambridge University Press 1991), 8.

[19] Arthur McMartin, *Public Servants and Patronage. The Foundation and Rise of the New South Wales Public Service, 1786–1859* (Sydney: Sydney University Press, 1984), 8. This leaves aside the immediate practical task of the "hiring, fitting-out, assembling, provisions and stationing of the ships", which was the responsibility of the Admiralty and the Treasury: 17.

[20] Ronald Nelson, *The Home Office, 1782–1801* (Durham, NC: Duke University Press 1969), 46.

[21] Austin Strutt, "The Home Office: An Introduction to its Early History," *Public Administration* 39 (1961). See also McMartin, *Public Servants and Patronage. The Foundation and Rise of the New South Wales Public Service, 1786–1859*, 8: "[T]he administration of those colonies that remained after the loss of the thirteen in North America; the establishment and administration of the first colony in Australia; the maintenance of communication between the governments in London and Dublin; the preservation of law and order throughout the kingdom; and until 1794…the control of troop movements at home and abroad".

the more they came up against "a fundamental Aboriginal hostility to settlers".[22] So, a new problem must arise: where, in the eyes of the colonists' law, did "the natives" stand?

## THREE LEGAL QUESTIONS FOR THE COLONISTS

We are reminded of Milsom's warning: "[p]erhaps more than in any other kind of history, the historian of law is enticed into carrying concepts…back into periods to which they do not belong".[23] Guided by this warning, our first task is to abandon the assumption that, for those involved with the First Fleet, the legal status of the Indigenous inhabitants was something about which they had already thought out a definite answer—or had even recognised it as a significant question.

So far as we can tell, the planners of the First Fleet possessed some scant information—to a significant extent wrong, and in any event hopelessly incomplete—and some opinions, perhaps we might better call them "prejudices", about "the natives" of New South Wales.[24] We may also accept that there were circulating among the educated classes in Britain competing political theories or doctrines that from time to time shaped British

---

[22] Grace Karstens, *The Colony. A History of Early Sydney* (Sydney: Allen & Unwin, 2010), 493. Stephen Gapps says that serious consideration should be given to characterising the state of relations in the Sydney region between the Indigenous Inhabitants and the Europeans from 1788 to 1817 as "warfare": Stephen Gapps, *The Sydney Wars* (Sydney: NewSouth Publishing, 2018), 263–265, 271–273. That problem, being essentially a question of historical fact, is one which this essay—which is principally concerned with the history of a legal doctrine—is only tangentially concerned. However, there might be an interesting question (not pursued further here) as to the extent to which the law, and even the lawyers, of that time might have been capable of entertaining such a characterisation (albeit that it was never the official line).

[23] Stroud Milsom, *Historical Foundations of the Common Law*, 2nd ed. (London: Butterworths, 1981), vi.

[24] Summarised well in Stuart Banner, *Possessing the Pacific* (Cambridge: Harvard University Press, 2007), 16–20. Or, if we may take an example from slightly after 1788, here is Jeremy Bentham writing c.1796 in his essay "Anarchical fallacies": "We know what it is for men to live without government…for instance, among the savages of New South Wales, whose way of living is so well known to us: no habit of obedience, and thence no government—no government, and thence no laws—no laws, and thence no such things as rights—no security—no property…". Reprinted in Jeremy Waldron, ed. *Nonsense upon Stilts. Bentham, Burke and Marx on the Rights of Man* (London: Methuen & Co, 1987), 53.

Imperial policy towards Indigenous peoples throughout the Empire.[25] But what we do not find as at 1788 is clear evidence of any thought-out *legal doctrine* concerning the position of Indigenous peoples of New South Wales, or any interest in articulating one. (By "legal doctrine" I mean definite rules of law, specifically spelled-out rules which would be expected to be followed by officials and applied by courts when called upon to do so.) The assumption that there existed an articulated legal doctrine concerning the Indigenous peoples of New South Wales tends to create the impression that there were answers that the authorities knew and applied from the outset and no great questions arose. The truth is the other way round. The great questions arose, and answers had to be found for them. What came to be the orthodox theory was worked out in Australia only very gradually and in a very fumbling way. If this is not grasped we miss the fact that it was in haphazard stages that British law was applied to events involving the Indigenous inhabitants.

Confining ourselves in this essay to the criminal law—for it is within the sphere of the criminal law that the most immediate practical problems arose—there were three basic legal questions for the colonists to confront: (1) did English criminal law apply to the colonists in their dealings with the Indigenous people? (2) Did English criminal law apply to Indigenous people in their dealings with the colonists? And (3) did English criminal law apply to Indigenous people in their dealings between each other? It is useful to keep the three questions separate, for they are to a significant degree distinct. I have stated them in ascending order of difficulty. Question (1) was, in principle, the easiest. If one thing was clear to the colonists, it was that they were bringing English law with them. The colonists at least were British subjects, subject to English law, in a land under British sovereignty and in which British courts had been established with power to hear, determine and punish all crimes, with punishment to be inflicted according to English law or as nearly as may be.[26] It would therefore be an anomalous conclusion if English criminal law applied to some of the colonists' conduct, but not to violence perpetrated against "the natives". By contrast questions (2) and (3), if and when one took notice of them, posed harder problems. Did the Indigenous peoples have any laws of their own? If so, were the Indigenous people allowed to keep

---

[25] See, for example, Banner, *Possessing the Pacific*, 14–18; Paul McHugh, *Aboriginal Societies and the Common Law* (Oxford: Oxford University Press, 2004), 130–131.

[26] See nn 9 and 10 above, and accompanying text.

them? If not, could the Indigenous peoples fairly be subjected to English law? In connection to these problems, where the Indigenous peoples British subjects, and did that make any difference? These questions would take the colony into unchartered waters. How the colonists coped with the far easier question (1) will begin to give us some measure of the situation. It is therefore with question (1) that the remainder of this essay is concerned. To use the words of Brennan J to formulate the question, did the colonists regard the Indigenous peoples as people who "were equally entitled to the law's protection as subjects of the Crown"?

## GOVERNOR PHILLIP'S "POLICY"

In February 1832 Dowling J of the Supreme Court of New South Wales, writing in his judicial notebook at some point during the course of the criminal trial in *R v Boatman*, gave this summary of the law on what I have called "question (1)" (the italics are mine):

> The general principle acted upon, I believe, with respect to these people *since the foundation of this as a British colony*, is to regard them [ie "the Aboriginal natives"] as being entirely under the protection of the law of England for offences committed against them by the white settlers.[27]

When Dowling J wrote these words—there is a significant doubt in my mind that he ever pronounced them in court[28]—the colony had been in

[27] "Proceedings of the Supreme Court from 23 February to 14th March 1832. Vol. 64," State Archives of NSW 2/3247, numbered page 11. There is a report: *R v Boatman or Jackass and Bulleye* (1832) NSW Sel. Cas. (Dowling) 6, 7.

[28] It is here particularly important to proceed by reference to the detailed contemporary newspaper account of the trial in the *Sydney Gazette* of 25 February 1832 (which can be found online at law.mq.edu.au in the report for *R v Boatman or Jackass and Bulleye* [1832] NSWSupC 4). That newspaper account, which is very full, does not record Dowling J making any statement of the law in the terms quoted above. The newspaper account merely records counsel making an objection to jurisdiction "on the ground that the aboriginal natives of the colony were not subject to the British laws" and Dowling J in response taking the objection on notice "for the consideration of the full court, should it be necessary". In the event neither accused was convicted, so that consideration was not necessary. My suspicion is that the relevant passage in Dowling J's notebook is the draft of a ruling that was prepared in advance, in anticipation of the point arising, but which never needed to be made. (The passage cannot, I think, be a transcription of something that was first said orally. The handwriting is too neat when compared to that found in the surrounding pages in the note-

212   G. LOUGHTON

existence for 44 years. Dowling J had been a resident of it for only the last four of them. As a statement of legal history it is far from correct but nor is it completely wrong either. The true position is more obscure, confused and inconsistent.

There are a small number of documents written in the months prior to the First Fleet setting sail that show Governor Phillip turning his mind to the question of what approach he should take to "the natives". In April 1787 he commented on a draft of his Instructions, "Any man who takes the life of a Native, will be put on his trial as if he had kill'd one of the Garrison. This appears to me not only just, but good policy".[29] This language—"just", "good policy"—is ambiguous. Was Phillip describing a "principle" (to use Dowling J's later word) that he thought the law required? Or did Phillip think this was merely a policy that was subject to his discretion? We have no evidence of him, or anyone, pondering this in any fundamental way. In another document, an *aide memoire* from February 1787, Phillip remarked in a context that does not involve the natives that the laws of England "will, of course, be introduced in [New] South Wales".[30] The "of course" is suggestive. It suggests to me that Phillip did not suppose that he needed to think much about it. When in the same document Phillip turns specifically to the question of "the natives", he does not seem to be thinking in terms of the law. He addresses the issue with the practical mind of a governor. On the one hand, he needs a "small cannon" for defence, just in case. On the other hand, Phillip hopes to "proceed in this business without having any dispute with the natives", and he expressed a vague thought that he might be able to "civilize" a few of them.[31]

When the First Fleet arrived, we find Phillip endeavouring to implement his "good policy". David Collins records that as early as March 1788 (italics mine):

---

book. The latter appears as an untidy scrawl, a hurried attempt to get down evidence as nearly as possible verbatim.)

[29] Michael Pembroke, *Arthur Phillip. Sailor Mercenary Governor Spy* (Melbourne, Hardie Grant Books, 2013) 159, citing a document at the National Archives, London CO 201/2, fol.131.

[30] *HR NSW*, vol 1, part 2, 53.

[31] *HR NSW*, vol 1, part 2, 53.

## 11 DID THE EARLY BRITISH COLONISTS REGARD THE INDIGENOUS... 213

it had been declared in public orders early in the month, that in forming the intended settlement, any act of cruelty to the natives being contrary to his Majesty's most gracious intentions, *the offenders would be subject to a criminal prosecution.*[32]

It turned out to be far easier said than done. Collins notes that when some convicts denied having given any provocation for injuries done to them by the natives, it was "difficult to believe them", but "they well knew that the natives themselves, however injured, could not contradict their assertions".[33] For this kind of practical reason Phillip's policy ran hopelessly into the sand. The Governor was in command of a small penal settlement in a large and largely unknown continent: no trained lawyers, hardly any law books, mutual linguistic and cultural incomprehension between settlers and Indigenous people; a place thinly populated where events might occur away from the eyes of competent (or any) witnesses; and no police force to speak of (no modern police force existed even in England before the 1820s).[34] If the Governor felt the security of the colony was threatened, all he had was a blunt instrument: marines. This was to be the state of affairs for decades. A rudimentary administration of the law amongst the colonists was hard enough. There was no realistic possibility of dealing with hard legal problems concerning the position of the

---

[32] David Collins, *An Account of the English Colony in New South Wales*, ed. Brian Fletcher (Sydney: AH&A Reed, 1975), 18.

[33] Collins, 18.

[34] On arrival in New South Wales Phillip appointed Henry Brewer "Provost-Marshall of the Colony", that is, a military policeman. (The statute 27 Geo. III c.2 (1787) had provided for such an official.) This was in place of the man who had originally been designated for the role, but who had not sailed with the First Fleet. In February 1788 Phillip also appointed one "Mr J Smith" as "headborough", that is, the head man of the borough, an ancient office which had evolved into that of a local constable. The mysterious Mr Smith—who may have been either the most eccentric or the most optimistic man in Australian history—was a free man who, for reasons unknown, had somehow contrived to smuggle himself or inveigle his way on board the Lady Penrhyn without attracting notice. In this way Phillip, by a kind of *bricolage*, assembled for himself some meagre resources for what might be called "policing" the convicts. But the real work of the enforcement of the law was in the hands of the Judge-Advocate and justices of the peace. (For Brewer see *HRA*, Series I, vol 1, 722 note 31 and also the entry by AJ Gray on "Brewer, Henry" in *Australian Dictionary of Biography, volume 1: 1788–1850, A–H*, ed. Douglas Pike, 149 (Melbourne: Melbourne University Press, 1966). For Smith see Arthur Bowes Smyth, *The Journal of Arthur Bowes Smyth: Surgeon, Lady Penrhyn 1787–1789*, ed. A Paul Fidlion and RJ Ryan (Sydney: Australian Documents Library, 1979), 72 (entry for 15 Feb 1788).

Indigenous peoples in any satisfactory way. On this matter we see in Phillip (to borrow the words of Hugh Trevor-Roper from a different context) the predicament of a man challenged by a problem too large for his resources.

The difficulties are illustrated by an incident that occurred only a few months after the First Fleet arrived. Lieutenant Bradley's diary for 23 May 1788 records some Indigenous people in canoes landing at a property "at Major Ross' Garden up the Harbour; they stole a jacket and several other things". Some convicts followed them along the shore "to the next cove where they landed and we have reason to suppose that one of the Natives was murdered by them but the proof could not be got, they were dismissed without coming before a Criminal Court".[35] Phillip must have been desperate to get evidence to support a prosecution here. Only a couple of days earlier, on 21 May 1788, two convicts had been attacked by Indigenous people. One of the two had crawled back to camp with a severe spear wound. The other, Peter Burns, did not return; all that was found of him later were his clothes, torn, bloody and pierced with spears. Peter Burns is the first white man at Sydney Cove who is known, with tolerable certainly, to have been killed by the Indigenous inhabitants.[36] And now, a convict had wounded, perhaps killed, an Indigenous man. Phillip may have sensed that the future of his "good policy" was in the balance. He offered what must have been a tempting reward. It was to no avail. As Collins recounts:

> It having been reported, that one of the natives who had stolen a jacket from a convict had afterwards been killed or wounded by him in an attempt to recover it, the governor issued a proclamation, promising a free pardon, with remission of the sentence of transportation, to such male or female convict as should give information of any such offender or offenders, so that he or they might be brought to trial, and prosecuted to conviction; but no discovery was made in consequence of this offer.[37]

We have even better evidence of the attempt to gather proof for a prosecution in the case. In a volume kept in the NSW State Archives, which

---

[35] William Bradley, *A Voyage to New South Wales. The Journal of Lieutenant William Bradley of HMS Sirius 1786–1792* (Sydney: Trustees of the Public Library of New South Wales in association with Ure Smith Pty Ltd, 1969), 108.

[36] AJ Gray, "Peter Burn. The First Convict Officially Presumed Killed by Natives at Sydney Cove," *Journal of the Royal Australian Historical Society* 45 (1959).

[37] Collins, *An Account of the English Colony in New South Wales*, 27.

## 11 DID THE EARLY BRITISH COLONISTS REGARD THE INDIGENOUS... 215

volume now bears on the cover the label "Archives Office of New South Wales. Bench of Magistrates Sydney. Minutes & Proceedings. Feb 1788 to Jan 1792" (available to me only on microfiche[38]), we find depositions about the events in question. They are handwritten, possibly in the hand of David Collins himself in his role as Deputy Judge-Advocate. (Collins's name appears at the bottom of the depositions.) I have attempted a transcription below in an Appendix.[39]

Three people were deposed: two convicts and a marine.[40] The first two deponents could give only hearsay. The story each had heard—in both cases traceable back to one Jesse Molock,[41] a convict who had seen the events close-up—is as follows. A few days previous, the natives had come down to Major Ross's farm and stolen some things from there, including a jacket belonging to a convict, Humphrey Lynch. The next day two natives, a man and a woman, returned in a canoe. Lynch saw his jacket in the canoe and went down to the water to retrieve it. The Indigenous man was unwilling to part with it. A struggle ensued. The man beat Lynch with a paddle. Lynch had a knife and with it "ripped him [the Indigenous man] across the lower Parts of his Belly".

Here were the makings of a prosecution. But then, we come to the crucial final deponent, Molock himself, the only one of the three deponents who had witnessed the events. Molock says that he went with Lynch to help him retrieve his jacket. Molock made signs for the native to come ashore. When the native did, Lynch held the canoe and Molock took out the jacket and tossed it ashore. But, on reaching the crucial point in the narrative—the alleged wounding, possibly killing, of the Indigenous man—Molock squibs. Or perhaps we should say he takes the side of his fellow-convict. In any event, Molock gives an evasive account: "Lynch had

---

[38] NSW State Archives Item No SZ765 at page 47; INX-1-61. For being alerted to this record I am indebted to Victoria Gollan's index of "Indigenous Colonial Court Cases," available online at the website of NSW State Archives: https://www.records.nsw.gov.au/archives/collections-and-research/guides-and-indexes/indigenous-colonial-court-cases

[39] This evidence is also made use of in John Cobley, *Sydney Cove 1788* (Sydney: Angus & Robertson 1980) 157. However, Cobley's attempted reconstruction of events is not sufficiently detailed or reliable for present purposes. His index also misidentifies the man at the centre of events as "Morty Lynch" (a marine), rather than "Humphrey Lynch" (a convict).

[40] For reasons unknown, Major Ross was not among them, though he is mentioned in the depositions. May we infer that he did not witness the crucial events?

[41] I give the name as rendered in the depositions, although the correct spelling is apparently "Mulcock": Mollie Gillen, *The Founders of Australia. A Biographical Dictionary of the First Fleet* (Sydney: Library of Australian History, 1989), 256.

## 216   G. LOUGHTON

a Knife in his Hand", but "he thinks he dropped it on his going into the Water". Molock then deposes to the native beating Lynch with a paddle and then paddling away.

Suppose the events in question had occurred in England. The fate of the man whom Lynch allegedly "ripped up" would probably have been either notorious or readily ascertainable. Further, aside from Lynch there would have been at least two eyewitnesses to the crucial events who might have been deposed—the Indigenous woman and Molock—three, if the wounded man had lived or had lived long enough. And there would have been no risk of a jury being prejudiced in favour of Englishmen over threatening and barbarous natives. By contrast, at Port Jackson there was no knowledge of what became of Lynch's alleged victim. Molock was the only practicable eyewitness aside from Lynch himself,[42] and Molock had deposed that no stabbing had occurred. Furthermore, as later history would repeatedly demonstrate, the juries of the colony were notoriously slow to convict colonists of crimes against Indigenous people. It was as Bradley put it: "the proof could not be got".[43] So far as I know, this is the last we hear of Phillip trying to invoke in a concrete way the ordinary machinery of English criminal law to protect the Indigenous inhabitants. After that, he fell back on far more rudimentary and ad hoc methods. It is true that, overall, he showed a determination (at least, compared with what was to come at the hands of his successors) to adhere to the scanty terms of his Instructions. It may even be, as Clendinnen suggests, that Phillip never abandoned the "determined optimism" that supported his "dream of a unitary commonwealth of whites and blacks living peaceably

---

[42] There is perhaps an interesting question as to why Lynch himself was not deposed. As part of the pre-trial procedure in England at the time it appears to have not been uncommon for a Justice of the Peace to take a deposition from the suspect: see John Langbein, *The Origins of Adversary Criminal Trial* (Oxford OUP 2003), 41–42.

[43] William Bradley, *A Voyage to New South Wales. The Journal of Lieutenant William Bradley of HMS Sirius 1786–1792*, 108. A note to the electronic catalogue of the State Library of NSW (www.sl.nsw.gov.au), where the "original" of Bradley's journal is kept, says that the journal was probably compiled some years after the events it records. This is apparently on the basis that one of the physical pages in the volume bears a watermark for the year 1802. The journal entry described above demonstrates that the journal is a reconstructed account: Bradley's entry is dated 23 May 1788. Upon this day Bradley might conceivably have learned about the altercation between Lynch and the Indigenous man, but Bradley could not have known that "the proof could not be got" until a week or so later.

## 11 DID THE EARLY BRITISH COLONISTS REGARD THE INDIGENOUS... 217

under British law".[44] But after the affair of Humphrey Lynch's jacket we do not find Phillip resorting anymore to the ordinary forms of the criminal law in furtherance of that dream.

Stanner is our best guide for colonist-Indigenous relations during Phillip's governorship. As we read his account of the way Phillip's "mentality veered" in the various phases of his dealings with the Indigenous peoples, we find a strange mixture of courage, self-control, perplexity, vexation, and punitiveness: taken together, "methods [that] were very untactical, on occasions slightly crazy".[45] Here we see Phillip, exasperated at his lack of progress in opening friendly communications with the Indigenous people, twice ordering the kidnapping (!) of one or more of them with a view to trying to "attain their language, or teach them ours" and generally win them over.[46] There we see Phillip trying to demonstrate British justice by having white offenders flogged extra-judicially, in the presence of (appalled) Aboriginal spectators.[47] Here again we see Phillip eventually deciding to order a punitive expedition against the Indigenous people, and then another when the first failed: "[h]e did not intend to hold a trial; he wanted some natives, and any would do".[48] Phillip's original policy had been based on a more strict conformity with the law. It had been abandoned in the face of overwhelming practical obstacles.

---

[44] Inga Clendinnen, *Dancing with Strangers* (Melbourne: Text Publishing 2003), 29, 258.

[45] William Stanner, "The History of Indifference Thus Begins," in *The Dreaming and Other Essays*, ed. Robert Manne, 92, 107, 122 (Melbourne: Black Inc. Agenda 2009).

[46] *HR NSW*, vol 1, part 2, 298, 300. Phillip reports to London, without a trace of irony, that one of his motives in ordering a "native" to be "taken" was so that "the means of redress might be pointed out to them if they are injured". As to the "means of redress" that Phillip had in mind, and the effects on the Indigenous people of his demonstration of it, see the next sentence in the text above.

[47] Watkin Tench, *1788*, Tim Flannery, ed. (Melbourne: The Text Publishing Company, 1996), 184; see also 101–102.

[48] William Stanner, "The History of Indifference Thus Begins," 114–115. A fairly full account is given in Watkin Tench, *1788*, 164–176; see also Collins, *An Account of the English Colony in New South Wales*, 118–119. Clendinnen, *Dancing with Strangers* 172–178, takes a relatively benign view of the two punitive expeditions under the command of Tench: they came to nothing and perhaps were intended to. Clendinnen sees them as warnings, "theatrical statements". They were certainly that, but it is hard to read the sources and conclude they were intended as *nothing* but that. Lt Dawes at least, who initially refused to serve on the mission and then regretted it when ultimately he did participate, must have thought them to have been more in earnest: see *HRA*, Series I, vol 1, 292, 293–294. Gapps also takes a more serious view of the expeditions: Gapps, *The Sydney Wars*, 85–90.

## After Phillip, up to Macquarie

Phillip sailed from the colony in December 1792. His (generally) determined restraint went with him. In the years immediately following the colony appears to a modern eye as a place that has largely given up on English law as a means of governing relations between the colonists and the Indigenous inhabitants—yet never quite completely. The picture is inconsistent and confusing. It is, in its essentials, correctly described by Neal: "[t]he truth of it is that for the first fifty years the colonial legal system had trouble deciding whether the Aborigines should be treated as subjects of the Crown or foreign enemies who could be hunted down in reprisal raids and shot".[49]

In April 1794, Acting Lieutenant-Governor Grose reported to London that "I have settled on the banks of the Hawkesbury twenty-two settlers".[50] Collins records that very soon "an open war seemed...to have commenced between the natives and the settlers" there.[51] Intermittent hostilities on the Hawkesbury lasted for decades. Take two examples from near the beginning of this "open war". Collins records that in late September 1794, in response to an attack by the natives on settlers on the Hawkesbury, "the sufferers collected what arms they could, and following, them [ie the Indigenous attackers], seven or eight of the plunderers were killed on the spot".[52] The same incident is recorded in the contemporaneous journal of Richard Atkins.[53] One modern historian has characterised this incident as

---

[49] David Neal, *The Rule of Law in a Penal Colony. Law and Power in Early New South Wales*, 17. See also Alex Castles, *An Australian Legal History* (Sydney: The Law Book Company, 1982), 520: "For many years the situation of the Aborigines in relation to European law seems to have been largely a matter of chance". To the extent to which there was a lacuna in the operation of English law in the colony, this left room for the operation of other legal systems, in particular Indigenous ones. Thus some scholars speak of the existence of a kind of legal "pluralism" in the first decades of the colony: Bruce Kercher, "Native Title in the Shadows: The Origins of the Myth of *Terra Nullius* in Early New South Wales Courts," 167–168, 184–193; Lisa Ford, *Settler Sovereignty* (Cambridge, Mass: Harvard University Press 2010), 3, 50 (although it will be evident from this essay that I would place limits on Ford's claim that "[t]his multiplicity did not equate to confusion").

[50] *HRNSW*, vol 2, 210.

[51] Collins, *An Account of the English Colony in New South Wales*, 348.

[52] Collins, 326.

[53] Journal of Richard Atkins, National Library of Australia MS 4309, hand numbered page 54, entry for 26 September 1794: "The Settlers at the Hawkesbury have kill'd 6 of the Natives, since what time they have not seen them".

"the first massacre carried out by the colonists".[54] There was apparently no suggestion that the machinery of the law should be invoked, or even that thought was given to the possibility. The assessment of Collins was only, "[t]his mode of treating them had become absolutely necessary, from the frequency and evil effects of their visits". At this time, Collins was the most senior judicial officer in the colony. Atkins was even more brief: "how far this is justifiable I cannot say".[55] He was a Justice of the Peace, himself two years short of being appointed acting Deputy Judge-Advocate.[56] (In 1805 Atkins was to issue a now well-known legal opinion in which he concluded, that "[t]he Natives are within the Pale of HM protection", albeit that they were incapable of being brought before a criminal court, either as witnesses or as accused criminals.[57])

Not long afterwards (December 1794) William Patterson, a soldier, became Lieutenant-Governor. He treated the situation on the Hawkesbury as a soldier might. Collins records Patterson directing that a party of marines to be sent from Parramatta "[t]o check at once, if possible, these dangerous depredators" who had been plundering the settlers. He instructed the marines "to destroy as many as they could meet with of the wood tribe…and, in the hope of striking terror, to erect gibbets in different places, whereon the bodies of all they might kill were to be hung".[58] There is no sign here of the natives being regarded as subjects under the protection of British law. In the result, Patterson wrote to the Secretary of State for the Home Office that "seven or eight natives were killed".[59] Collins records a baby amongst the casualties and generally laments the state of affairs on the Hawkesbury. The stationing of soldiers there became

[54] Stephen Gapps, *The Sydney Wars*, 109.

[55] Journal of Richard Atkins, National Library of Australia MS 4309, hand numbered page 54, entry for 26 September 1794.

[56] *HRA*, Series I, vol 1, 602 and 761 n 194. See also Alan Atkinson, "Richard Atkins: the Women's Judge," *Journal of Colonial History* 1 (1999): 124, 126.

[57] *HRA*, Series I, vol 5, 502–504. On how the early courts dealt with the issue of the evidence of Indigenous people see Brent Salter, "'For Want of Evidence': Initial Impressions of Indigenous Exchanges with the First Colonial Superior Courts of Australia," *University of Tasmania Law Review* 27 (2008): 146.

[58] Collins, *An Account of the English Colony in New South Wales*, 348.

[59] *HR NSW*, vol 2, 307. Patterson's account appears self-serving. London responded that his steps "for instilling into the minds of the natives a proper degree of respect and regard for the colony, appear to have been highly proper": *HR NSW*, vol 3, 52.

permanent, "distributed among the settlers for their protection; a protection, however, that many of them did not merit".[60]

On the other hand, we also find in Collins's narrative evidence of the machinery of the criminal law attempting to stir itself at around this time, albeit ineffectually. Collins records another event on the Hawkesbury, the possible torture and killing of "a native boy" in October 1794. The incident is also evidenced in the archival record. It shows a Bench of Magistrates assembling, for the purposes of "[e]xamination of the persons supposed to have murdered a Native Boy at the Hawkesbury, and the Evidence against them".[61] We see three witnesses being examined (giving improbable, self-exculpating testimony) before the record peters out without reporting the outcome. Collins's narrative fills the gap: "No person appearing to contradict this account, it was admitted as a truth; but many still considered it as a tale invented to cover the true circumstance, that a boy had been cruelly and wantonly murdered by them". Thus, once more the practical problem of lack of evidence stood in the way of further legal proceedings. Collins observed that, in consequence, the problems on the Hawkesbury could be expected to multiply. The settlers there, "finding themselves freed from bondage, instantly conceived that they were above all restrictions; and, being without any internal regulations, irregularities of the worst kind might be expected to happen".[62]

In September 1795, John Hunter assumed the office of Lieutenant-Governor. During his administration Pemulwuy's campaign of violent resistance to the colonists intensified.[63] Yet we also see the authorities again publicly affirming, or at least purporting to affirm, that Indigenous peoples were entitled to the protection of English criminal law. By a general "order"[64] dated 22 February 1796 the Governor referred to "[t]he frequent attacks and depredations to which the settlers situated on the

---

[60] Collins, *An Account of the English Colony in New South Wales*, 348, 349.

[61] *Murder of Native Boy case* [1794] NSWKR 2; [1794] NSWSupC 2 (the original source being "Bench of Magistrates, Minutes of Proceedings Fed 1788–Jan 1792, State Records NSW, SZ765"). This proceeding is evaluated in John Nagle, *Collins, the Courts & the Colony. Law & Society in Colonial New South Wales 1788–1796* (Sydney: UNSW Press 2006), 243–247.

[62] Collins, *An Account of the English Colony in New South Wales*, 329–330.

[63] See, for example, the fine little book by Jonathan Lim, *The Battle of Parramatta, 21 to 22 March 1797* (Melbourne: Australian Scholarly Publishing Ltd., 2016).

[64] Jeremy Bentham of course raised grave doubts about the legality of gubernatorial "orders" generally: *HRA*, Series IV, vol 1, 883 ff.

banks of the Hawkesbury and other places are liable from the natives" and enjoined the settlers to "mutually afford their assistance to each other by assembling without a moment [sic] delay whenever any numerous body of the natives are known to be lurking about the farms." It was apparently hoped this would deter attacks. Then he added a warning:

> it is his Excellency's positive injunction to the settlers and others who have firearms that they do not wantonly fire at or take the lives of any of the natives, as such an act would be considered a deliberate murder, and subject the offender to such punishment as (if proved) the law might direct to be inflicted.[65]

It took more than a year for this warning to be acted upon. In late 1797, we have the first instances of colonists being tried for killing Aboriginal people. The trials were in October 1797[66] and March and October 1799.[67]

---

[65] *HR NSW*, vol 3, 25–26. Sometimes cited in the literature is a later copy of this document, different from the version reproduced in *HR NSW* only in one small respect: the date that appears on the later copy is 22 February 1797, that is, one year later than the date of the version reproduced in *HR NSW*. The later copy is to be found in Bruce Kercher and Brent Salter, Original Documents on Aborigines and Law, 1797–1840 at law.mq.edu.au, under the title "Extracts from Orderly Books 11th Sept 1795 to 31st December 1797: 22 February 1797" (from the State Records NSW file called "Miscellaneous Correspondence Relating to Aborigines, 1797–1840" (SRNSW: NRS 13696, [5/1161]). Kercher and Salter suppose this to be a copy made by Burton J. That would mean the copy was made at least three decades after the original entry was made in the orderly book itself. Assuming the theory is to be rejected as improbable that the identical order was separately published twice one year apart (i.e. in 1796 and 1797), the date of 22 February 1796 is to be preferred because it is closely corroborated by Collins: Collins, *An Account of the English Colony in New South Wales*, 382.

[66] *R v Millar and Bevan* (1797) Sel. Cas. (Kercher) 147. The two accused were acquitted for "want of evidence".

[67] The first case from 1799, presided over by Atkins, was *R v Hewitt* (1799) Sel. Cas. (Kercher) 154. The accused was acquitted. This was principally due to the fact that the main witness to the killing, the widow of the deceased Aboriginal man, "was not capacitated to give sufficient testimony" (the difficulty of obtaining evidence from Aboriginal witnesses was later the subject of an opinion in 1805 by Atkins: see n 57 above). In this case there was a partial workaround: the accused was convicted on the alternative charge of "being an incorrigible rogue and vagabond" (for which there was admissible evidence, from the district constable) and was sentenced "to receive 300 lashes in public and at a time when the greatest number of natives can be assembled together to witness his punishment after which he is to work in the gaol gang for the space of 12 calendar months from this day".

The second of the two cases from 1799, *R v Powell*,[68] is the subject of a detailed report.[69] The evidence given by the witnesses in *R v Powell* confirms the great extent to which frontier violence on the Hawkesbury went unnoticed by the legal system. The colonists attested to a belief that they were free to kill the natives, at least in self-defence or in retaliation (!), and indeed that their understanding of official expectations was that they would.[70] Perhaps this evidence was self-serving. The jury was prepared to accept it. Though the five accused were found guilty by the jury (of, in the words of some of the jury members "murder" and of others "killing" two "natives") one of the members of the jury added that "by his opinion he means not to affect their lives, because it is the first instance of such an offence being brought before a criminal court and therefore the prisoners were not aware of the consequences of the law".[71] The jury by majority reserved by special verdict the question of sentence "until the sense of his Majesty's Minister is known upon the subject".[72]

Pemulwuy's campaign continued. On 1 May 1801, Acting Governor-King himself directed that "a large body of natives, resident about Parramatta, George's River, and Prospect Hill", some of whom had committed violence against settlers and livestock, "to be driven back from the settlers' habitations by firing at them".[73] In November 1801 the Governor offered a reward for anyone who might bring in, "dead or alive", any or all of the trio of Pemulwuy, William Knight and Thomas Thrush. The latter two were convicts who had taken up with Pemulwuy. Both of these convicts had "by regular form been outlawed", or so government and general orders asserted.[74] One sometimes reads that Pemulwuy too had been outlawed.[75] This is, I believe, not correct. It would be notable if

[68] (1799) Sel. Cas. (Kercher) 209.

[69] The proceedings are also reproduced (in substantially similar, but not identical, form) in *HRA*, Series I, volume 2, 403–422.

[70] *R v Powell* (1799) Sel. Cas. (Kercher) 209, 213, 216, 217, 218, 225, 227, 231–232.

[71] *R v Powell*, 232.

[72] *R v Powell*, 232–233.

[73] *HRA*, Series I, vol 3, 250. The caution was added, "But this order does not extend to the natives in any other district; nor is any native to be molested in any part of the harbour, at Sydney, or on the road leading to Parramatta".

[74] *HRA*, Series I, vol 3, 251, 466.

[75] See, e.g., Karstens, *The Colony. A History of Early Sydney*, 474, 480; also the entry on "Pemulwuy," in *Australian Dictionary of Biography Supplement 1580–1980*, ed. Christopher Cunneen, 318 (Melbourne: Melbourne University Press, 2005).

Pemulwuy *had* been outlawed, but he was not so carefully treated.[76] The Governor simply "gave orders for every person doing their utmost to bring Pemulwye in either dead or alive"[77] and offered a reward. In consequence, in June 1802 Pemulwuy was shot and killed.

In the meantime (by now former) Governor Hunter's account of *R v Powell* had reached London. In January 1802 Lord Hobart, the Secretary of State for the Colonies, wrote to (by then) Governor King agreeing to pardon the five defendants in that case. Lord Hobart added, with nice understatement, that he could not help "lamenting that the wise and humane instructions of my predecessors, relative to the necessity of cultivating the good-will of the natives, do not appear to have been observed in earlier periods of the establishment of the colony with an attention corresponding to the importance of the object". His Lordship wished it to be "clearly understood that on future occasions, any instance of injustice or wanton cruelty towards the natives will be punished with the utmost severity of the law".[78] King in his reply of October 1802 assured Hobart that he had immediately caused a proclamation to that effect to be published[79] and the natives to be made sensible of it. ("They expressed much

[76] If Pemulwuy had been "outlawed" (an elaborate, formal process known to law: see n 94 below) that would carry the necessary implications that the authorities had (a) regarded Pemulwuy as prima facie subject to British law and therefore entitled to the ordinary protections of it and (b) further thought it proper to invoke the ordinary criminal process against Pemulwuy to exclude him from those ordinary protections. However, the order of 17 November 1801 reproduced at *HRA*, Series I, vol 3, 466–467, distinguishes between "William Knight and Thomas Thrush (outlaws) and the native, Pemulwoy". In any event, it should not be supposed that in 1801 being "outlawed" meant being exposed to the risk of being peremptorily killed by anyone and everyone. It may once have meant that in English law but, if so, had long ceased to do so by 1801: Sir Frederick Pollock and Frederick Maitland, *The History of the English Law Before the Time of Edward I* (Cambridge: CUP, 1898): see vol 1, 476–477, vol 2, 449–450. Blackstone writing in 1769 said of the consequences of being outlawed for treason or felony, "no man is entitled to kill him wantonly or wilfully; but in so doing is guilty of murder, unless it happens in the endeavour to apprehend him": William Blackstone, *Commentaries of the Laws of England*, ed. Ruth Paley (Oxford: OUP, 2016), 207 (being 314–315 in the first edition of 1769).

[77] *HRA*, Series I, vol 3, 582; see also 466–467, 800.

[78] *HRA*, Series I, vol 3, 366–367.

[79] The Proclamation (dated 30 June 1802) is at *HRA*, Series I, vol 3, 592–593. The language of the proclamation continues (whether consciously or not) the practice of drawing a distinction between "the Natives" and "His Majesty's subjects". The Proclamation forbade cruelty and injustice towards "the Natives", "on pain of being dealt with in the same manner *as if* such act of Injustice or wanton Cruelty should be committed against the Persons and Estates of any of *His Majesty's Subjects*" (emphasis added). See also the Port Regulations

224   G. LOUGHTON

joy and are now on more friendly terms than ever".[80]) There was an even stronger statement to the same effect—the most thoroughgoing to date—included in a general order published in the new "settlement" at Hobart Town in January 1805.[81]

Yet the more often and emphatic such statements appear, the more they seem to be protesting too much. In fact, after *R v Powell* prosecutions of settlers for crimes against Indigenous persons apparently ceased for a decade,[82] though the cycle of waxing and waning hostilities between colonists and Indigenous inhabitants at the expanding frontiers of the settlement continued. The Governor treated this as a military or "diplomatic" problem, not a legal one.[83] So, for instance, in mid-1804 Governor King sent a detachment of marines to assist some farmers on the Hawkesbury who had unsuccessfully sought to take matters into their own hands. A party of armed settlers (led by the local magistrate!) had marched off to confront "the hostile savages" and ended being driven back "by a flight of spears". The marines were "sent to their relief" and shot two Indigenous men before a negotiated peace was concluded.[84]

Examples of this divergence between what one might call the "official" position and the actual practice might be multiplied into Governor Macquarie's time. Indeed, it seems that no significant further thinking had taken place in London on the issue in the 20 years that elapsed between the First Fleet and the appointment of Macquarie. The Instructions given to Macquarie in 1809 are, in the relevant respect, essentially what we would now call a "cut and paste" of the Instructions given to Phillip in

---

issued on 10 October 1802, reg XVII: "If any of the Natives are killed, or Violence offered to their Women, the Offenders will be tried for their Lives": *HRA*, Series I, vol 3, 714.

[80] *HRA*, Series I, vol 3, 583.

[81] *HRA*, Series III, vol 1, 529: "He [the Lieutenant-Governor] has received it in command from His Majesty to place the Native Inhabitants of whatever place, he should settle at, in the King's Peace, and to afford their Persons and Property the Protection of the British Laws."

[82] The next case was apparently *R v Luttrell* [1810] NSWKR 1; (1810) Sel. Cas. (Kercher) 419 (a settler was found not guilty of assault for the shooting of an Aboriginal man, the jury apparently accepting he acted in self-defence). And after that, there was not another prosecution for an offence against an Indigenous person for years. See the table set out in Barry Bridges, "The Aborigines and the Law: New South Wales 1788–1855," *Teaching History* (December 1970): 48.

[83] On this point I follow the analysis of Lisa Ford, *Settler Sovereignty*, 44–45, 47–48.

[84] *Sydney Gazette*, 17 June 1804 and 1 July 1804 (under the heading "Natives"), and the corresponding account in King's despatch to Lord Hobart of 14 August 1804, *HRA*, Series I, vol 5 at 17–18.

# 11 DID THE EARLY BRITISH COLONISTS REGARD THE INDIGENOUS... 225

1787.[85] In the event, things kept repeating themselves, but on a more terrible scale. Macquarie fell into the same basic pattern laid down by Phillip, described above, but with the telling qualification that Macquarie was far more hardened and ruthless in his attitude towards the Indigenous people and had more effective military resources at his disposal. First, there was the announcement that all Indigenous people were entitled to the protection of British law. Then there was the failure of that approach. Then there was the abandonment of it and resort to military force with no serious attempt universally to afford the Indigenous peoples the protections of British law.

As to the first stage, within a year of his arrival we see Macquarie promulgating "Port Regulations and Orders" to be observed at Port Jackson, reg 27 of which provided (again ambiguous as to whether "the natives" really were British subjects[86]):

> The natives of this territory are to be treated in every respect as Europeans; and any injury or violence done or offered to the men or women natives will be punished according to law in the same manner and in equal degree as if done to any of his Majesty's subjects or foreigners residing here.[87]

Then the second stage. The four years of relative peace that followed Macquarie's arrival ended with in May 1814. There was an outbreak of violence between settlers and Indigenous people on a farm in the southwest of the colony. An attempted taking of maize by Indigenous people spiralled into "a chain of revenge attacks and atrocities".[88] There was an investigation by a bench of magistrates into these events. That investigation, announced Macquarie after it had concluded, had been "enough to convince any unprejudiced Man that the first personal Attacks were made on the Part of the Settlers, and of their Servants". However, "it was not sufficiently clear and satisfactory to warrant the Institution of Criminal Prosecution". Macquarie affirmed that "the Natives" are, in like manner

---

[85] *HR NSW*, vol 7, 135 (para 6).

[86] For a similar ambiguity see Macquarie's announcement published in the *Sydney Gazette* of 18 June 1814: "should Outrages be further committed by the Natives, on Information being given to the Magistrate of the District, the Most active Measures will be taken for their Apprehension and Punishment, in like Manner as under similar Circumstances would take Place *when British subjects only were concerned*" (italics mine).

[87] *HR NSW*, vol 7, 418.

[88] Karstens, *The Colony. A History of Early Sydney*, 492–493, 498–499.

as "the Settlers", "under, and entitled to the Protection of British Laws". But he then added an ominous rider that could not be found in any law book: "so long as they conduct themselves conformably to them".[89]

Then the third stage: when hostilities continued, the ominous rider was invoked. Macquarie ordered out, in the words of Karstens, "his first reprisal party".[90] So far as we know, that party seems to have achieved nothing on that occasion. However, when a large and organised group of Indigenous men began raiding farms in the west in February and March 1816 Macquarie tried harder.[91] On 10 April 1816, he sent out to the west three military detachments with instructions to detain all Aborigines they met with; and that any who "showed fight" or tried to run away were to be shot and their bodies hung from trees, "in order to strike the greater terror into survivors"[92] (shades of Patterson in 1794). Two of the detachments encountered few Indigenous people, but the third surprised a camp of Indigenous people on 17 April 1816 and killed 14 men, women, and children (and wounded others) by shooting them or driving them over a cliff.[93] Obviously, there is no serious attention paid here to affording these people the protections of British law.[94] In Macquarie's schema, there were those "Natives as may wish to be considered under the Protection of the British Government" on the one

[89] *Sydney Gazette*, 18 June 1814 ("Government and General Orders" on the first page).

[90] Karstens, *The Colony. A History of Early Sydney*, 494.

[91] In his subsequent report to the Secretary of State for War and the Colonies of 8 June 1816 Macquarie described his actions in terms of "the necessity of resorting to Military Force": *HRA*, Series I, vol 9, 140.

[92] *HRA*, Series I, vol 9, 854 (note 36); Karstens, *The Colony. A History of Early Sydney*, 507.

[93] Karstens, *The Colony. A History of Early Sydney*, 494, 510–513; *HRA*, Series I, vol 9, 139–140.

[94] Later in the course of his campaign, in July 1816, Macquarie purported, by his own proclamation, to outlaw "Ten Natives...well known to be the principal and most violent Instigators of the late Murders": Proclamation of 20 July 1816: *HRA*, Series I, vol 9, 362. However, to borrow some evocative language from Ford (*Settler Sovereignty*, 43) this was "a pageant of law", not the substance of it. In fact, Macquarie had no power to outlaw anyone. In English law it was never part of the powers of the executive branch of government to pronounce people outlaws. Outlawry occurred by judgment of a court, after a lengthy and elaborate judicial procedure: see John Archbold, *The Practice of the Crown Office of the Court of Queen's Bench* (London: Shaw and Sons, 1844), 47–52; William Hawkins and John Curwood, *A Treatise of the Pleas of the Crown*, 8th ed. (London: S. Sweet, A. Maxwell and R. Stevens and sons, 1824), vol II, 422–433.

hand and those manifesting "a strong and sanguinary Spirit of Animosity and Hostility towards the British Inhabitants" on the other. The latter were subject to "unavoidable" measures that Macquarie hoped would "eventually strike Terror amongst the surviving Tribes, and deter them from the further Commission of such sanguinary Outrages and Barbarities".[95] Ford and Salter also show Macquarie at around this time apprehending and incarcerating significant numbers of Indigenous people. However, as Ford and Salter demonstrate, this was not for the purposes of making these people available for the courts to deal with; they were held in jail as hostages and were released when Macquarie found it expedient to do so.[96] In short, Macquarie was not treating the Indigenous peoples universally as subjects; he was involved in the anterior step of reducing them more completely to subjection.[97]

Eventually, with order having been restored to Macquarie's satisfaction, we see him turn to the regular machinery of the law again. In 1818 he referred to a bench of magistrates for investigation (in the event, ineffectual) of suspected offences against Indigenous people in the Illawarra.[98] In 1820 we have the earliest known record of a European being tried, convicted and executed for the murder of an Indigenous man.[99] In 1822 there is another trial for a colonist for the murder of an Indigenous man.[100]

---

[95] Proclamation of 4 May 1816, *HRA*, Series I, vol 9, 141–145.

[96] Lisa Ford and Brent Salter, "From Pluralism to Territorial Sovereignty: the 1816 Trial of Mow-watty in the Superior Court of New South Wales, "*Indigenous Law Journal 7* (2008): 81–82. See also Lisa Ford, *Settler Sovereignty*, 51–52.

[97] "Quelling and Subduing the hostile spirit of Violence and Rapine, which the black Natives or Aborigines of this Country had for a Considerable time past Manifested": despatch from Macquarie to Bathurst, 3 April 1817: *HRA*, Series I, vol 9, 342 (para 4).

[98] Lisa Ford, *Settler Sovereignty*, 105–107. Against the primary evidence she unearths, the information contained in the "Bench of Magistrates, County of Cumberland, Minutes of Proceedings: Bench Book 1815–1821," 24 October 1818, p. 146 (NSW State Archives 7/2691; SZ775, reel 659) seems laconic to the point of being suspicious.

[99] *R v Kirby and Thompson* [1820] NSWKR 11; [1820] NSWSupC 11.

[100] *R v Hawker* [1822] NSWKR 4; [1822] NSWSup C 4 (acquitted). The presiding Judge-Advocate is reported as saying that he "wished it to be properly and lastingly impressed upon the minds of all, that the aboriginal natives have as much right to expect justice at the hand of the British Law, as Europeans" (although the editorial note to this case at "Decisions of the Superior Courts of New South Wales, 1788–1899," at law.mq.edu.au says that the record of the trial suggests partiality on the part of his Honour in his leading questioning of the witnesses).

## The Permanent Supreme Court of NSW and After

In 1824 a permanent Supreme Court was established. The locus of authority for deciding questions about the legal position of the Indigenous inhabitants shifted to the new court. However, we must not suppose that once trained lawyers had turned their mind to this issue it was quickly or easily cleared up. This is so even for the easiest of the three questions we have identified. In what follows I take another look at ground previously gone over by Professor Kercher with a view to adding something to the picture.[101]

The case that has attracted the most attention in this regard is *R v Lowe* [1827] NSWKR 4.[102] By the 1820s, the pale of British settlement had expanded. The resistance formerly encountered on the Hawkesbury River was now being encountered further north on the Hunter. In June 1826, Governor Darling sent Lieutenant Lowe, in command of a detachment of Mounted Police, to support the colonists there. Lowe was subsequently charged with murder for the extra-judicial execution of an Indigenous man who had been taken into custody for the suspected of killing a colonist. The Indigenous man was alleged to have been chained up to a tree and shot. Lowe's counsel made objection—Professor Kercher calls it "audacious",[103] I am tempted to call it mischievous—to the jurisdiction of the Court "to try a British subject for an alleged offence committed against that Aboriginal native".[104]

On one view, this was not a hard question. There had already been a string of trials in the permanent Supreme Court between 1824 and 1827

---

[101] See Bruce Kercher, "The Recognition of Aboriginal Status and Laws in the Supreme Court of New South Wales under Forbes CJ, 1824–1836," 83 ff.

[102] Over the past 20 years, *R v Lowe* has attracted significant scholarly attention from many directions. In addition to the texts cited at n 3 above see: Laura Benton, *Law and Colonial Cultures. Legal Regimes in World History, 1400–1900* (Cambridge: CUP, 2002), 187–191; Lisa Ford, "Empire and Order on the Colonial Frontiers of Georgia and New South Wales," *Itinerario* 30 (2006): 103–106; Kelly Chaves, "'A solemn judicial farce, the mere mockery of a trial': the Acquittal of Lieutenant Lowe, 1827," *Aboriginal History* 31 (2007); Andrew Tink, *William Charles Wentworth* (Sydney: Allen & Unwin 2009), 98–99; Lisa Ford, *Settler Sovereignty*, 120–128.

[103] Bruce Kercher, "The Recognition of Aboriginal Status and Laws in the Supreme Court of New South Wales under Forbes CJ, 1824–1836," 87.

[104] *R v Lowe* [1827] NSWKR 4; [1827] Sel. Cas. (Kercher) 859, 860.

for offences against Indigenous people.[105] In those cases it had apparently been uncontroversial that Aborigines were entitled to the protection of English criminal law. One of those trials, *R v Ridgway, Chip, Colthurst and Stanly*, had even resulted in a guilty verdict for a charge of murder. The reported summing up of Forbes CJ in that case is representative:

> The Chief Justice…observed, it was hardly necessary for him to say that his Majesty's white subjects in this colony were as amenable to the laws, for violence committed on the persons of the natives as if it were perpetrated on any other of the inhabitants.

Indeed, the mere fact that Lieutenant Lowe had been charged with murder already demonstrates a certain practical acceptance of the same principle. It was a principle that had been struggling to articulate itself since Phillip's time. Now that the permanent Supreme Court had begun to act upon it with some kind of regularity, now that a judge had said it, it could properly be taken to be a principle of the law.

But what was the legal basis for the principle? That nettle had not yet been grasped. That is the significance of the objection to jurisdiction in *Lowe's case*. Spurious as it was, the objection nonetheless forced the Court (comprised in that case of Forbes CJ and Stephen J) to justify what it had hitherto assumed. Strange as it might seem to us, a thoroughly persuasive justification was not readily forthcoming.

It was orthodox common law that all persons are either subjects or aliens; if aliens, they are either friendly aliens or enemy aliens.[106] Lowe's counsel submitted that an "Aboriginal native" fell into none of these categories. He was not a subject ("because his tribe had not been reduced under His Majesty's subjection, and because there has been no treaty"); nor was he an enemy alien ("because his tribe is not in hostilities with the British sovereign"); nor was he a friendly alien ("because his tribe may be, and in fact is in a state of public hostility with individual subjects of the British sovereign"). An Aboriginal native was therefore not to be dealt

---

[105] *R v Johnston, Clarke, Nicholson, Castles and Crear* [1824] NSWSupC 8 (verdict of not guilty for manslaughter); *R v Ridgway, Chip, Colthurst and Stanly* [1826] NSWSupC 62 (verdict of guilty for murder); *R v Stanley* [1827] NSWSupC 12 (verdict of not guilty for murder); *R v Jamieson* [1827] NSWSupC 31 (verdict of not guilty for manslaughter).

[106] *Calvin's Case* (1608) 7 Co Rep 1a, 17a [97 ER 379, 397]: "Every man is either *alienigna*, an alien born, or *subitus*, a subject born. Every alien is either a friend that is in league, &c, or an enemy that is in open war, &c".

230    G. LOUGHTON

with by forms of British law ("of which he had not sense to comprehend"), but by "divine law". That is, in shooting the Indigenous man Lieutenant Lowe had been acting in accordance with "divine law" and that law was not within the purview of the Supreme Court.[107]

The decision in *Campbell v Hall* (discussed above) offered one easy way out of this specious reasoning. Neither judge mentioned the case. Perhaps Stephen J had it in mind. He held that there were no facts before the Court from which it could infer "but that he [the accused] was a subject of his Majesty". However, this very cursory reasoning is contingent and opaque. The Chief Justice gave longer reasons. For Forbes CJ, it seems to have been a sufficient answer that the *New South Wales Act 1823* (4 Geo IV c. 96) operated to confer jurisdiction on the Supreme Court and that it was implicit in that statute that the Crown has sovereignty over New South Wales and that British law applied here. One might object that this does not answer the essential question so much as re-state it. The basic question remained: what did British law say about the legal position of the Aboriginal people? Forbes CJ address it. The report of the case edited by Kercher and Salter reproduces the very full account given in the *Australian* newspaper of 23 May 1827. This reports Forbes CJ speaking as follows:

> The offence charged against him [Lowe] is that of having taken away the life of a native; now, this native must be considered, whatever be his denomination, a British subject. If not to be an alien friend, or an alien ami, in any case he is entitled to lex loci, and it is only under peculiar circumstances he can be excluded from that right.

These two sentences present a challenge for the reader. Read literally, as a statement of the law they seem not so much incorrect as nonsensical. They seem to have Forbes CJ saying, first, that the Indigenous man is a British subject irrespective of his "denomination" (even this is not easy to follow[108]), and then, second, the man is entitled to the *lex loci* even if he were not a friendly alien (but the man had just been held to be a subject).

---

[107] *R v Lowe* [1827] NSWKR 4; [1827] Sel. Cas. (Kercher) 859, 860–861.

[108] What does "denomination" mean here? Dr Johnson's 1755 definition of the word was: "[a] name given to a thing, which commonly marks some principal quality of it". In context then, the "denomination" of a "native" would seem to denote his classification for the purposes of the law of alienage, that is, his place in the taxonomy of persons laid down by the law for the purpose (as to which, see n 106 above). That would mean that Forbes CJ as reported by the *Australian* was saying that, no matter what the classification of the "native"

## 11 DID THE EARLY BRITISH COLONISTS REGARD THE INDIGENOUS... 231

We can grasp the basic conclusion: the native is entitled to the protection of British law. But the reasoning seems to fall into incoherence.

A possible solution begins with recalling that the *Australian* was not quoting written reasons. The report makes it clear that the *Australian* was publishing a transcription, made by someone who was in court at the time, of an ex tempore judgment—of oral reasons delivered on the spot, right after argument had concluded. Every litigator knows the foibles of ex tempore judgments. Judges can make grammatical stumbles. Even when they do not, spoken English does not always have the same syntax as written English; the person making the transcription must do his or her best to supply the correct punctuation. In addition, a person who trying to get down a hurried note of oral reasons can easily make a slip. If we may make allowance for all these possibilities we might contemplate adjusting the *Australian*'s punctuation slightly as follows, remembering all the while that this is the Chief Justice *speaking* not writing:

> now, this native must be considered, whatever his denomination—a British subject, if not, to be an alien friend or an alien *ami*—in any case, he is entitled to lex loci, and it is only under peculiar circumstances he can be excluded from that right.

If we were permitted to re-write the reasons in order to spell out the point, we might gloss Forbes CJ's reasoning it this way:

> now, this native, whatever be his denomination, must be considered to be entitled to the *lex loci*, ie the law in force in the colony of NSW, ie English law. This is the case whether the native be a British subject or, if he is not a British subject, then an alien friend (to use the legal jargon, an alien *ami*[109]). It is only under peculiar circumstances that he can be excluded from the right to the protection of the *lex loci*, eg if he is an enemy alien in open war with the King (and there is no proof of that before the Court).

This reading is of course speculative, but we find a kind of rough corroboration of it in the alternate report of *R v Lowe* that appeared in another newspaper, the *Sydney Gazette* of 21 May 1827. The *Sydney Gazette*'s

---

for the purposes of the law of alien status, he is nevertheless a British subject. But that is a non-sequitur.

[109] From the Latin, *amicus*, friend.

232    G. LOUGHTON

reporter was not quite as fastidious in trying to get down the Chief Justice's actual words, but he may have come closer to capturing the gist:

> The offence charged against him, is taking away the life of an aboriginal native, who must be either a friend or foe; and, taking him as either, he is entitled to the benefit of the *lex loci*, unless put out of it by some circumstance made to appear in the course of proof before the Court.

So Forbes CJ evaded deciding whether Indigenous peoples are subjects or not.[110] This was on the basis that aliens are generally entitled to the benefits of the local law anyway.

So, when did the courts definitively settle the question of the legal status of the Indigenous people who were already living here when the First Fleet arrived? Not in the later and even more remarkable case of *R v Murrell* (1836). The reasons of Burton J (i.e. the reasons in his original hand preserved in the State Archives of NSW, as opposed to the truncated newspaper report that is reproduced at (1836) 1 Legge 72) can be read as essentially following the same reasoning as Forbes CJ in *R v Lowe* and thereby evading the question in the same way.[111] Kercher contends that, at least as far as the executive branch of government was concerned, the question was settled by Imperial fiat. In July 1837 after surveyor-general Thomas Mitchell had, in the course of a journey of exploration along the Murray, shot and killed a number of Indigenous people, the Secretary of

[110] But compare Forbes CJ's later, bolder statement *R v Jackey* [1834] NSWSupC 94, as reported by the *Sydney Gazette*. In the trial of an Indigenous man for murder of a colonist, Forbes CJ told the jury that he would "put the case of the prisoner at the bar to them in the same manner so against any of his Majesty's subjects, because he knew of nothing to prevent these people being considered as such".

[111] "5thly, This Court has repeatedly tried and even executed aboriginal natives of this Colony for offences committed by them upon subjects of the King, ever since the opening of the Court in May 1824; and there is no distinction in law in respect to the protection due to his person between a subject living in this Colony under the Kings Peace and an alien living therein under the Kings Peace": State Archives of NSW, 5/116, p. 214. A transcription appears in the report of *R v Murrell and Bummaree* (1836) [1836] NSWSupC 35 on the website of the "Decisions of the Superior Courts of New South Wales, 1788-1899". The archival papers include what appears to be more detailed draft reasons prepared by Burton J in anticipation of being in dissent. Kercher, "The Recognition of Aboriginal Status and Laws in the Supreme Court of New South Wales under Forbes CJ, 1824–1836," 97, draws attention to "curious" reasoning in this draft. That is, the draft (at p. 241) seems to be premised on the proposition that Indigenous people are aliens unless and until they submit to the Crown.

State for War and the Colonies wrote to Governor Bourke to impress upon him "the general principles to be observed in your conduct towards the Aborigines". It was that they "must be considered as Subjects of the Queen, and within HM's Allegiance", and not "Aliens with whom a War can exist".[112] Professor Kercher concludes that the judges of the Supreme Court "soon fell into line, accepting the government's view of the law".[113] Perhaps they did.[114] But if so, no more great cases on this point arose in which they could show it.[115]

It may be that the problem of whether Indigenous peoples were subjects simply faded away as a significant question. For the purposes of the criminal law, *R v Lowe* and *R v Murrell* had between them established that whether or not Indigenous people were subjects did not matter, because even aliens were entitled to the protection of the criminal law. In the unlikely event that the question whether an Indigenous person was a subject arose for any other purpose then, by 1836 there were presumably few Indigenous people still alive who had been born in New South Wales before 1788 (let alone 1770). Any Indigenous person born after 1788 clearly fell within the principle derived from *Calvin's Case*, that any person born within the dominions of the King is a natural-born subject. Over time, this class grew to include all living Indigenous people. The question

---

[112] *HRA*, Series I, vol 9, 48; see also *HRA*, Series I, vol 18, 590, 656.

[113] Bruce Kercher, "The Recognition of Aboriginal Status and Laws in the Supreme Court of New South Wales under Forbes CJ, 1824–1836," 98.

[114] Although it cannot be said that the justices of the Supreme Court of the 1820s and 1830s lacked independence from the executive branch: Neal, *The Rule of Law in a Penal Colony. Law and Power in Early New South Wales*, 108–113.

[115] There is a cursory statement by Dowling CJ, summing up for the jury in *R v Billy* [1840] NSWSupC 78, a case of an Aboriginal defendant tried for murder. The Chief Justice observed, with a sort of mordant irony, that the defendant was "by fiction of law a British subject, and as such was entitled to be tried by his peers". The prosecution of an Indigenous man for the murder of another Indigenous man in *R v Bonjon* (1841) (the decision is most readily accessible at "Decisions of the Superior Courts of New South Wales, 1788–1899," at law.mq.edu.au under "Port Phillip District Cases") certainly had the makings of a great case on these issues. However, the prosecution collapsed for want of evidence so Willis J did not need to give a final ruling on the legal position of the Indigenous people for crimes inter-se. Further, it seems that if there had been any wider appetite for the radical analysis set out by Willis J in *R v Bonjon* ("the aborigines must be considered and dealt with, until some further provision be made, as distinct though dependent tribes governed among themselves by their own rude laws and customs"—similar to the position that had by then been taken in the United States by the Supreme Court there), the decision in *Murrell* extinguished it: *HRA*, Series I, vol 21, 656–657.

## 234 G. LOUGHTON

of the status of those who were already living here when the First Fleet arrived became moot. When, in 1961, Professor Sawer provided an opinion on the "National Status of Aborigines in Western Australia" it was sufficient for him to cite the rule in *Calvin's case* and say that "[i]t is clear that on these principles every aboriginal native of Australia born in Australia after 1829 (by which date the whole of the continent was part of the dominions of the Crown) became a British subject by birth". (He added: "As far as I can ascertain these questions have never been the subject of judicial decision".)[116]

If we return to the passage from Brennan J in *Mabo [No 2]* cited at the beginning of this chapter and examine the authorities he relied on for that passage, we find this footnote[117]:

> As the subjects of a conquered territory (*Calvin's case* (1608), 7 Co. Rep. 1a, at p. 6a. [77 ER 377, at p. 384]); *Campbell v Hall* (1774) Lofft, at p. 741 [98 ER, at p. 895] and of a ceded territory (*Donegani v Donegani* (1835), 3 Knapp 63, at p. 85 [12 ER 571, at p. 580]) became British subjects (*Lyons (Mayor of) v East India Co.* (1836), 1 Moo. P.C., at pp. 286–287 [12 ER, at p. 823]; 1 Moo. Ind. App. 175, at pp. 286–287 [18 E.R. 66, at pp. 108–109]), a fortiori the subjects of a settled territory must have acquired that status. And see *Reg. v Wedge*, [1976] 1 NSWLR 581, at p. 585.

---

[116] Geoffrey Sawer, "National Status of Aborigines in Western Australia," in House of Representatives, Report of the Select Committee on Voting Rights of Aborigines (1961), Appendix III.

[117] Of the principal cases cited by Brennan J in this footnote, *Calvin's case* and *Campbell v Hall* have already been discussed. The other two were succession cases which raised questions concerning the legal status of inhabitants, and the applicable law, of territories obtained by the British Crown by conquest or cession. *Donegani v Donegani* was a dispute over the estate left by a man who had died in Montreal in 1809, that is, after it had been ceded to Britain by the French. In the passage referred to by Brennan J, it was (relevantly) held that "[w]hen the King of England became the King of Canada the natives of Canada became his subjects; Canada became part of his dominions subject to be governed by its local laws". *Mayor of Lyons v East India Co* was a dispute over the will of a French citizen who had died in India in the employ of the East India Company. In the first-mentioned passage referred to by Brennan J, Lord Brougham said that "the argument maintained by the Crown requires the proposition to be carried thus far, that upon a conquest or a cession, all the inhabitants continue aliens after the change of dominion unless and until the conqueror or the purchaser grants their naturalization. But this position seems wholly untenable; for all the authorities lay it down, that upon a conquest, the inhabitants, *ante nati* as well as *post nati*, of the conquered country, become denizens of the conquered country".

Which is to say, here is Brennan J working it out for himself, from first principles. He was doing something that the early colonists and their Imperial masters did not manage to do; indeed, he needed to do it because they had not. If, therefore, we want to know when it was authoritatively resolved in Australian law that the Indigenous peoples who were encountered by the first colonists were subjects of the King entitled to the protection of English law, we might consider that the answer is: 3 June 1992.

## CONCLUSION

Maitland famously said that the ambition of the historian is to recover, to make thinkable once more, the "thoughts of our forefathers, their common thoughts about common things".[118] When it comes to the early history of the colony in New South Wales it is a little different. Our hope is instead to recover their common thoughts about *uncommon* things. For those men and women who arrived with the First Fleet, for the men and women who were already here when the First Fleet arrived, almost everything that happened after that was uncommon. As David Collins said of the First Fleet leaving the Cape of Good Hope, "we were leaving the world behind us, to enter on a state unknown".[119] We might go so far as to say that, so far as relations with the Indigenous peoples were concerned, the colonists were making a leap into the dark. We might also wonder whether they were prepared for it. We must also remember, however, that our questions were not their questions.

If we therefore find it difficult to tell whether or not the early colonists believed that the Indigenous people were subjects of the King entitled to the protection of English law, that may be because the colonists did not know themselves. For them it was a new and difficult question. At first, they did not care about it; when eventually circumstances required them to care, they found they were unsure of the answer. Eventually the Supreme Court came to a view. That view was incomplete but, it seems, was for a long time regarded as sufficient unto the day.[120]

---

[118] Frederic Maitland, *Domesday Book and Beyond* (Cambridge: CUP, 1897; Fontana Library edition, 1960), 596.

[119] Collins, *An Account of the English Colony in New South Wales*, lxxxvi.

[120] In February 2020 the High Court held, by 4-3 majority, that it is beyond the power of the Commonwealth Parliament to treat "Aboriginal Australians" as aliens for constitutional purposes (even if born in a foreign country): *Love v Commonwealth, Thoms v Commonwealth* [2020] HCA 3, esp. at [81]. This was on the basis that Aboriginal Australians have such a

## 236 G. LOUGHTON

### APPENDIX: TRANSCRIPTION OF DEPOSITIONS TAKEN ON OR ABOUT 1 JUNE 1788 AT SYDNEY COVE BEFORE THE MAGISTRATES

The following is taken from the microfiche copy of a bound volume held at the NSW State Archives, item SZ765. That volume now bears on its cover the title "Archives Office of New South Wales. Bench of Magistrates Sydney. Minutes & Proceedings. Feb 1788 to Jan 1792" and the reference "1/296". The pages transcribed below are pages 47–48. They are hand-written. Where the deciphering of the handwriting has required some conjecture on my part, the words in question are in square brackets. Where a significant amount of conjecture was required, the words are in square brackets with a question mark at the end.

> Depositions taken before [Magistrates?]
> Sydney Cove
> 1st [June?] 1788
> James Strong deposes that J Molock told him that on a Day in the last [week], the Natives came down to Major Ross's Farm, & stole a Jacket & some other things from [thence] – that the next Day, they came again, and that Ross (at the Farm) fired at them– that Humphrey Lynch seeing his jacket in the Bow of the Canoe, went down to take it out – that the Native in the Canoe was unwilling to part with it – that Lynch [hauled] the Canoe ashore – that the Native struck him on the [limbs] with a Paddle – that Lynch struck him with a Knife [across] the Belly.
>
> Elias [Bishop], Soldier, deposes that the night before last James Strong told him that Lynch seeing his Jacket in the Bow of a Canoe, he went to it to get it again – that the Native struggled with Lynch, struck him over the [limbs] with a Paddle, & that Lynch then [ripped] him across the lower Parts of his Belly with a Knife – he also [mentioned?] a [Musquet] having been [fired] amongst the Natives by [Maj] Ross. That a Woman was in the Canoe with the Man who was wounded – who was taken out of the Canoe, upon the Man's falling back when his Belly was ripped up, and she was put into another Canoe.
>
> Jesse Molock deposes that H. Lynch seeing his Jacket in a Canoe [pointed?] it out to the Deponent, [asking] him to assist him in getting it

unique connection with the land of Australia that, applying the settled constitutional test for the scope of the "aliens" power laid down by Gibbs CJ in *Pochi v Macphee* (1982) 151 CLR 101, 109 (Gibbs CJ), such people "cannot possibly answer the description of 'aliens' in the ordinary understanding of the word". Much has changed since 1788.

## 11 DID THE EARLY BRITISH COLONISTS REGARD THE INDIGENOUS...   237

again, which he [assented] to – that he made Sign to the Native to come ashore – that after some time, he did come – that Lynch went into the ~~Canoe~~[121]Water, & took hold of the Canoe – that then this Deponent took the Jacket out of the Canoe & [tossed] it onshore – that Lynch had a Knife in his [Hand] when he took out the Jacket – that he thinks he [dropped] it on his going [into] the Water – that the Native beat Lynch very much on his Hand and Arm with his Paddle. That when Lynch got hold of the Canoe from one Side, the Native got out at the other – that when they left the Canoe, the Native got into it again – and [paddled] away.

    David Collins

    JA

---

[121] The strike-through is in the original.

CHAPTER 12

# Land, the Social Imaginary, and the *Constitution Act 1867* (Qld)

*Julie Copley*

## INTRODUCTION

At separation from New South Wales in 1859, the use of land (and wealth from land) was essential to the idea of order in the colony of Queensland. Queensland was established as an experiment in imperialism. The spectrum of land ownership interests, quasi-ownership interests, and non-ownership proprietary interests was essential to the "modern social imaginary" in Queensland.[1] One consequence was sections 30 and 40 of the *Constitution Act 1867* (Qld), enacted to make specific provision for the legislature to govern the "wastelands" of the Crown.[2] Despite an extensive programme of constitutional consolidation and repeal enacted as the *Constitution of Queensland 2001*, sections 30 and 40 remain on foot.

---

[1] Charles Taylor, *Modern Social Imaginaries* (Durham: Duke University Press, 2004), 23.
[2] *Constitution Act 1867* (Qld) s. 4.

---

J. Copley (✉)
University of Southern Queensland, Ipswich, QLD, Australia
e-mail: Julie.Copley@usq.edu.au

© The Author(s), under exclusive license to Springer Nature
Switzerland AG 2022
S. McKibbin et al. (eds.), *The Impact of Law's History*, Palgrave
Modern Legal History,
https://doi.org/10.1007/978-3-030-90068-7_12

239

240    J. COPLEY

An analysis of legal and social theories of property and justice establishes that the "contextual considerations" of land and the early colonial modern social imaginary continue to enter the legislative equation about private property interests related to land and individual freedom. These social and legal incidents of the institution of property are the prologue to every contemporary contestation of use of and wealth from land in Queensland.

## COLONIAL QUEENSLAND AND PROPERTY AS WEALTH

Harris explains that property institutions are "instrumentalities for controlling the use of things and for the allocation of wealth". In legal and non-legal understandings, they have a dual function that may be stated as "property as things" and "property as wealth".[3] The salient features of property institutions "build upon the twinned and mutually irreducible notions of trespassory rules and the ownership spectrum", incorporating transmission freedoms and the consequential opportunity to build wealth in the form of money and cashable rights.[4] From the time of Aristotle to the present day, instrumental benefits of property have been recognised as increases in aggregate social wealth from incentives and markets, and political and cultural advantages associated with individual independence from the state.[5] Accordingly, states acting in the public interest establish and refine property institutions and allocate property as wealth,[6] as occurred in the early years of the colony of Queensland when wealth was built from Crown allocations of ownership interests relating to an apparent abundance of land.[7]

Under the common law of England brought to the Australian colonies by the European settlers, the Crown's sovereignty gave it title to land and the power to appropriate land to itself or to alienate it to others.[8] And under the law, "when validly made, a grant of an interest in land binds the Crown and the Sovereign's successors. The courts cannot refuse to give

---

[3] J. W. Harris, *Property and Justice* (New York: Cambridge University Press, 1996), 140.

[4] Harris, *Property and Justice*, 141.

[5] Harris, *Property and Justice*, 279.

[6] Charles A. Reich, "The New Property". *The Yale Law Journal* 73, no. 5 (April 1964): 746–55.

[7] Paul Babie, "Completing the Painting: Legislative Innovation and the 'Australianness' of Australian Real Property Law" *Property Law Review* 6, no. 3 (2017): 161.

[8] Brendan Edgeworth, *Butt's Land Law* (Sydney: Lawbook Co, 2017), 450.

## 12 LAND, THE SOCIAL IMAGINARY, AND THE *CONSTITUTION ACT...* 241

effect to a Crown grant."[9] Accumulations of wealth were built upon the security of real property interests because "an interest validly granted by the Crown, or a right or interest dependent on an interest validly granted by the Crown cannot be extinguished by the Crown without statutory authority".[10] Further, the effect of a grant of an estate in fee simple, for example, is that the holder may remove from the control of the state indefinitely and even in perpetuity the land subject to the interest. A person holding an estate in fee simple may during his or her life dispose of the estate as desired—by sale or other disposal, in whole or in part, subject to the prohibitions on waste. The fee simple entitlements, moreover, survive a person's death and form part of his or her estate, subject to "the enjoyment by anyone else of any right or interest ... conferred by statute, by the owner of the fee simple or by a predecessor in title".[11]

In the colonial era—when large corporations and other wealth-generating institutions were yet to be established and thus the "liberty of the individual was secured by traditional forms of property such as land or a house"—the discovery of the area that would become Queensland quickly led to European settlement of that land.[12] In 1768, James Cook departed Plymouth Dockyard for the South Pacific, with instructions that he should "with the consent of the Natives ... take possession of Convenient Situations in the country in the Name of the King of Great Britain; or, if [he should] find the Country uninhabited take Possession for his Majesty by setting up Proper Marks and Inscriptions, as first discoverers and possessors".[13] In 1770, Cook charted the east coast of the Australian mainland and in August took "possession" at "Possession Island" known to Torres Strait Islanders as Bedanug or Bedhan Lag.[14] Matthew Flinders explored the future Queensland region in 1799, and in 1819, the east coast was hydrographically surveyed. In 1823, shown the Brisbane River by Aboriginal people and timber-getters, Surveyor-General Oxley thought

---

[9] *Mabo v Queensland [No 2]* (1992) 175 CLR 1, 47 (Brennan J).

[10] *Mabo v Queensland [No 2]*, 74 (Brennan J).

[11] *Fejo v Northern Territory* (1998) 195 CLR 96, 126 [43].

[12] Charles A. Reich, "The Liberty Impact of the New Property," *William and Mary Law Review* 31, no. 2 (Winter 1990): 295.

[13] "Secret Instructions to Lieutenant Cook 30 July 1768 (UK)," Museum of Australian Democracy: Documenting a Democracy, 2011, accessed July 26, 2021, https://www.foundingdocs.gov.au/item-did-34.html

[14] Gerard Carney, *The Constitutional Systems of the Australian States and Territories*, (Cambridge: Cambridge University Press, 2006), 37.

it an entrance to an inland sea.[15] At separation, the colony of Queensland comprised 22.5 per cent of Australian land, but its boundaries were then extended to the west, and to the north to incorporate the islands in the Torres Strait.[16]

In 1784, New South Wales—all the continent east of the 135th meridian, with "adjacent islands"—had been declared a penal settlement under an Imperial Act.[17] In 1824, a penal station was established near the mouth of the Brisbane River, relocated upstream in 1825, and in 1842, closed by proclamation. At that time, the Crown Land Commissioner and the Police Magistrate jointly assumed authority for the colony of Moreton Bay.[18] Already, pastoralists had moved up through New England, substantial building activity had occurred, and the coast and hinterland had been explored. Until 1859, individualised land grants were made under the law of the New South Wales colony.[19]

Exercises of the prerogative power of the Crown and then legislative power established the property institution, including its transmission freedoms and the consequential opportunity to build wealth, but powers were exercised in contravention of the instructions provided to Cook by the British government and the Royal Society who had sponsored Cook's voyage. Those instructions were to treat residents of populated lands as owners.[20] Recording Aboriginal and Torres Strait Islander peoples to be "the most wretched people on earth" and living without government or property, Cook provided foundation for a disregard of both British policy and the laws, customs, and relationships of First Nations peoples with land.[21]

---

[15] Raymond Evans, *A History of Queensland* (Port Melbourne: Cambridge University Press, 2007), xvi.

[16] R. D. Lumb, "The Torres Strait Islands: Some Questions Relating to Their Annexation and Status," *Federal Law Review* 19, no. 2 (1990): 155.

[17] P. M. Lane, "Australian Land Law," in *Historical Foundations of Australian Law: Volume I – Institutions, Concepts and Personalities*, eds. J. T. Gleeson, J. A. Watson and R. C. A. Higgins (Sydney: The Federation Press, 2013), 219.

[18] Carney, *The Constitutional Systems*, 55.

[19] Queensland Law Reform Commission, *A Working Paper of the Law Reform Commission on a Bill in Respect of an Act to Reform and Consolidate the Real Property Acts of Queensland: WP 32* (Brisbane: Queensland Government Printer, 1989); Enid Campbell, "Crown Land Grants: Form and Validity," *Australian Law Journal* 40 (June 1966): 36–8. The Governor had power to make and withhold grants of land, a power exercisable by him alone. Until 1820, grants of fee simple in land were made; thereafter the fee simple was sold.

[20] Stuart Banner, *Possessing the Pacific: Land, Settlers, and Indigenous People from Australia to Alaska* (Cambridge: Harvard University Press, 2007), 14.

[21] Lisa Ford, *Settler Sovereignty: Jurisdiction and Indigenous People in America and Australia, 1788–1836* (Cambridge: Harvard University Press, 2011), 205; Banner, *Possessing*

Indeed, European settlers generally "treated all land which had not been the subject of a grant from the Crown as unoccupied and having no other proprietor".[22]

Aboriginal peoples and Torres Strait Islanders were entitled in law only to "such rights and privileges and subject to such limitations as the common law and applicable statutes provided".[23] The colonial courts found it "unquestionable" that "the Crown [was] the absolute beneficial owner of all of the land in New South Wales from the time of settlement in 1788",[24] as "when Governor Phillip received his first Commission from King George III on 12th October 1786 the whole of the lands of Australia were already in law the property of the King of England".[25] Any rights in respect of any land were "derived either directly or indirectly from the Crown, or not at all".[26] Nevertheless, when contestations arose between "avaricious settlers and indigenous peoples" in Queensland,[27] settlers called for legislation asserting rights to territory and legitimising their settlement.[28] They sought a clear statement of "the idea of territorial jurisdiction and the authority of the state to exercise it".[29]

At the opening of the first Queensland Parliament on 29 May 1860, Governor George Bowen advised the legislature that it was called to administer "the control and disposal of the whole" of the land as a "gigantic patrimony". He stated that the legislators must be "deeply impressed with the responsibility involved in such a trust", for the mode in which the duties connected with it were acquitted would "in all human probability, affect materially the interests of generations yet unborn". In short, the "Land Question" would be "at once the most comprehensive and the most important" question for the legislature.[30]

---

*the Pacific*, 11, 56.

[22] *New South Wales Aboriginal Land Council v Minister Administering the Crown Lands Act* (2016) 260 CLR 232, 277 [111] (Gageler J).

[23] *Mabo v Queensland [No 2]*, 59–61 (Brennan J).

[24] *New South Wales Aboriginal Land Council Case*, 277 [111] (Gageler J).

[25] *Williams v Attorney-General (NSW)* (1913) 16 CLR 404, 439 (Isaacs J).

[26] T. P. Fry, "Land Tenures in Australian Law," *Res Judicatae* 42, no. 3 (1946–7): 158.

[27] Paul McHugh and Lisa Ford, "Settler Sovereignty and the Shapeshifting Crown," in *Between Indigenous and Settler Governance*, eds. Lisa Ford and Tim Rowse (Abingdon: Routledge, 2012), 23.

[28] PA Keane, "The 2009 W A Lee Lecture in Equity: The Conscience of Equity," *Australian Law Journal* 84, no. 2 (2010): 106.

[29] Ford, *Settler Sovereignty*, 40–6.

[30] *Record of the Proceedings of the Queensland Parliament, Legislative Council, extracted from the third-party account as published in the Moreton Bay Courier*, May 29, 1860, accessed

## A New Venture in Imperialism

In the establishing of a modern constitutional state, Taylor explains, the social imaginary means "the ways people imagine their social existence, how they fit together with others, how things go on between them and their fellows, the expectations that are normally met, and the deeper normative notions and images that underlie these expectations". The social imaginary "is shared by large groups of people, if not the whole society" and "is that common understanding that makes possible common practices and a widely shared sense of legitimacy".[31] When rules such as the trespassory rules for a property institution are made, they are tailored to the idea of order within that state, reflecting "what was happening on the ground … the rise of merchants, of capitalist forms of agriculture, the extension of markets".[32] In Australasian colonies, Jeremy Waldron refers to a public commitment to a common political life, characteristics of which included the diffusion of property rights and broad economic equality.[33] In *Fejo v Northern Territory*, Australia's High Court observed that in real property institutions, "An estate in fee simple is, 'for almost all practical purposes, the equivalent of full ownership of the land' and confers 'the lawful right to exercise over, upon, and in respect to, the land, every act of ownership which can enter into the imagination'".[34]

The new colony's idea of order is manifest in the real property institution formed at the creation of Queensland. The State's establishment was at a time when rural land was the most important source of individual wealth. Ownership interests in land were "virtually the only form of investment available to a Christian capitalist".[35] Therefore, while "the amount of the trade at the ports gave promise of rapid and vigorous development" and migration schemes "provided the bone and sinew of economic

July 26, 2021, https://www.parliament.qld.gov.au/work-of-assembly/hansard

[31] Taylor, *Modern Social Imaginaries*, 23.

[32] Taylor, *Modern Social Imaginaries*, 31.

[33] Jeremy Waldron, *The Rule of Law and the Measure of Property* (Cambridge: Cambridge University Press, 2012), 31.

[34] *Fejo v Northern Territory*, 126 [43].

[35] Queensland Law Reform Commission, *A Bill to Consolidate, Amend, and Reform, The Law Relating To Conveyancing, Property, and Contract and To Terminate The Application of Certain Imperial Statutes: Report No 16* (Brisbane: Queensland Government Printer, 1973) 1–2.

growth", the prospect of land ownership brought many to Queensland.[36] As the only Australasian colony never to pass through the preliminary stages of colonial government, Queensland was described by Governor Bowen as a most peculiar colony, "exceptional beyond precedent in the history of colonization". In other colonies, autocratic powers were conferred, supported by military force, guided by English officials, and funded from the Imperial Treasury. Queensland, however, represented "a new venture in imperialism". Colonisation was on the cheap and at arm's length from Great Britain, and the colony commenced with full-blown parliamentary self-government.[37]

Section 51 of the *Australian Constitutions Act 1842* (Imp) made provision for a separate colony in the north, but the power was not exercised at that time. Nor was a new colony created under a power in the *Australian Constitutions Act (No 2) 1850* (Imp). One reason was protracted disagreement about the boundary between the colonies: in the 1850s, the placement of "the border between New South Wales and Queensland aroused more controversy and debate than any other Australian land border", including because the British government sought to ensure a sufficiency of settled land within Queensland to provide revenue for its public administration.[38] When section 7 of the *New South Wales Constitution Act 1855* (Imp) once more allowed for the formation of a colony "in [a] manner as nearly resembling the form of government and legislature established in New South Wales as the circumstances of the new colony would permit", in 1859 an Imperial Order in Council was made finally. Letters Patent also issued in 1859 provided for separation, a government, a colonial legislature, and a constitution closely following New South Wales provisions.[39] Governor Bowen had "full power and authority by and with the advice of the said Executive Council to grant in Our name and on Our behalf any

---

[36] Edward Jenks, *A History of the Australasian Colonies: From their Foundation to the Year 1911* (Cambridge: Cambridge University Press, 2012), 112; Evans, *A History of Queensland*, 83.

[37] Evans, *A History of Queensland*, 78.

[38] Carney, "A Legal and Historical Overview," 598.

[39] "Order-in-Council establishing Representative Government in Queensland 6 June 1859 (UK)," Museum of Australian Democracy: Documenting a Democracy, 2011, accessed July 26, 2021, https://www.foundingdocs.gov.au/item-sdid-48.html; Carney, *The Constitutional Systems*, 56.

waste or unsettled lands in Us vested within Our said colony", and public records were to be kept of land grants.[40]

Parliamentary elections were held, the legislature sat for the first time in May 1860, and its Upper and Lower Houses acted quickly to meet responsibilities as guardians and administrators of the "gigantic patrimony". Indeed, a real property institution was the first substantive, non-procedural issue addressed by the Legislative Assembly. The Colonial Secretary said the government intended to introduce measures to amend the law relating to real property,[41] and the Attorney General said "the Government were fully alive to the importance of the question".[42]

The early legislation of the Queensland legislature created a property institution built upon the mutually irreducible notions of trespassory rules and the ownership spectrum, but "designed to provide for conditions unknown in England and to meet local wants in a fashion unprovided for in England". One feature was the early adoption of the Torrens statutory system of title by registration "whereby statute makes the certificate of title conclusive evidence of its particulars and protects the registered proprietor from actions to recover the land, except in specifically described cases".[43] Another was the creation by statute of new forms of tenure characterised by, first, annual payment of rent and, second, conditions placed on occupation and development to ensure full use and development of land.[44] During debate on the bill for the *Crown Lands Alienation Act 1860* to open land for selection, the Colonial Secretary said, "The object of any land bill must be the settlement of the country, and in order to induce people to leave England and come and settle here, the land system of the colony must be based on liberal principles, and made as attractive as

---

[40] "Letters Patent erecting Colony of Queensland 6 June 1859 (UK)," Museum of Australian Democracy: Documenting a Democracy, 2011, accessed July 26, 2021, https://www.foundingdocs.gov.au/resources/transcripts/qld1i_doc_1859.pdf

[41] *Record of the Proceedings of the Queensland Parliament, Legislative Assembly, extracted from the third-party account as published in the Moreton Bay Courier*, 29 May 1860, accessed July 26, 2021, https://www.parliament.qld.gov.au/work-of-assembly/sitting-dates/dates/1860

[42] *Record of the Proceedings of the Queensland Parliament, Legislative Assembly, extracted from the third-party account as published in the Moreton Bay Courier*, 1 June 1860, accessed July 26, 2021, https://www.parliament.qld.gov.au/work-of-assembly/sitting-dates/dates/1860

[43] *Wik Peoples v Queensland* (1996) 187 CLR 1, 174 (Gummow J).

[44] Babie, "Completing the Painting," 163.

# 12 LAND, THE SOCIAL IMAGINARY, AND THE *CONSTITUTION ACT*... 247

possible".[45] In this context, the *Real Property Act 1861* establishing the Torrens system "did not become a political issue in Queensland". The bill passed through Parliament "virtually without any opposition from the legal profession or anyone else".[46] Similarly other statutes, such as the *Agricultural Reserves Act 1863* establishing a scheme for land in agricultural reserves to be purchased and leased, were passed quickly.

The deeper normative notions and images that underlie that early legislation are seen also in the *Constitution Act 1867*, key provisions of which assert the authority of the legislature over the real property institution. Section 2 confers "Her Majesty" with "power by and with the advice and consent of the ... Assembly to make laws for the peace welfare and good government of the colony in all cases whatsoever". Sections 30 and 40 gave, and continue to give, the legislature responsibility for turning the wastelands of the Crown into land from which public and private wealth may be generated.

## CONSTITUTIONAL PROVISION

In 1975, in *Cudgen Rutile v Chalk*, the Privy Council accepted as "fully established" the proposition that, "in Queensland, as in other States of the Commonwealth of Australia, the Crown cannot contract for the disposal of any interest in Crown Lands unless under and in accordance with power to that effect conferred by statute". The legal basis for the legislative power, and limitations on that power, is "found in the *Constitution Act of 1867*, of which s.30 provides for the making of laws regulating the sale, letting, disposal and occupation of the waste lands of the Crown, and s.40 vests the management and control of the waste lands of the Crown in the Legislature". The Privy Council noted that, "[n]umerous pronouncements in the Courts in Australia have given effect to this principle".[47]

For a Queensland legislature called to be guardian and administrator of a grand patrimony of a real property institution, sections 30 and 40 are of

---

[45] *Record of the Proceedings of the Queensland Parliament, Legislative Assembly, extracted from the third-party account as published in the Moreton Bay Courier*, 28 August 1860, accessed July 26, 2021, https://www.parliament.qld.gov.au/work-of-assembly/sitting-dates/dates/1860

[46] Douglas Whalan, *The Torrens System in Australia* (Sydney: Law Book Company, 1962), 8–9; A. A. Preece, "Reform of the Real Property Acts in Queensland," *QUT Law Journal 2*, no. 2 (1986), 41.

[47] *Cudgen Rutile (No. 2) Ltd v Chalk* (1975) AC 520, 533–4.

great significance, marking "the real birth of Queensland as a political entity with the substantial responsibility for the peace, order and good government of the people of the colony".[48] The sections withdraw from the Crown—whether represented by Imperial authorities or the Executive Government of Queensland—significant elements of Crown prerogative. Responsibility is vested instead in the legislature which, by virtue of section 40, has authority over the "entire management and control of the waste lands … the appropriation of the gross proceeds of the sales of such lands and all other proceeds and revenues … including all royalties, mines, and minerals".

There are three vital and enduring aspects of the grand patrimony. First, control of immense land revenue allowed the setting of "priorities in terms of the expenditure of public moneys". Second, "the power to pursue the internal development of the new colony" has become power over development for the peace, welfare, and good government of the State.[49] Third, exercise of the Crown's title "so as to control the exercise of an individual's rights in relation to land", including as held under one of the forms of tenure created by legislation, ensures that land is "preserved for the public good".[50] Thus, the entire ownership spectrum of real property interests remains subject to compulsory acquisition by statute.[51]

For the colony of Queensland, legislative responsibility for Crown land was integral to the idea of order. As it was "[p]enniless at its inception and not blessed with an endowment from Sydney or London, Queensland was born to debt",[52] and creation of wealth from territory became a pillar of the colony (and then State). Legislation put in place measures "best calculated to advance the policies and thought … to be appropriate for the purpose of ensuring the safety and prosperity of the realm".[53] These included, on the one hand, a vast body of ownership interests in land created by way of an array of statutory tenures unknown to the English law; Fry refers to the Crown perpetual leasehold tenure as "the zenith of the

---

[48] Keane, "The Conscience of Equity," 122.

[49] Keane, "The Conscience of Equity," 122–3.

[50] Babie, "Completing the Painting," 163.

[51] *R & R Fazzolari Pty Limited v Parramatta City Council* (2009) 237 CLR 603, 619 [40]–[41] (French CJ).

[52] Paul Finn, *Law and Government in Colonial Australia* (Melbourne: Oxford University Press, 1987), 114.

[53] Fry, "Land Tenures," 170

Australian system of Crown leasehold tenures".[54] On the other, the *Real Property Act 1861* required a clear, public record of the ownership spectrum in the State-backed Torrens system of title. In each case, public revenue from land defrayed the cost of carrying on colonial government and subsidised emigration to the colony.[55] Although New South Wales pushed for apportionment of public debt relating to the costs of administration and public works in the northern colony,[56] Queensland failed to meet the debt claimed. Relevantly, parliamentary and public debate in Queensland evidences strong expectation of revenue from land and its use for Queensland's safety and prosperity.[57]

The Queensland legislature's constitutional authority diverged from the constitutional arrangements in other non-Australasian British colonies where land acquisition tended to be ad hoc rather than the subject of significant explicit constitutional provision.[58] The specific authority in the Queensland Constitution was due to an earlier fight conducted by New South Wales parliaments for the right to that colony's own land revenue. The *Australian Constitutions Act 1842* (Imp) conferred New South Wales with a representative parliament, as long as the parliament did not make any law interfering with the sale of Crown lands in the colony or the revenue from that land. The proviso was influenced by "social theorist Edward Gibbon Wakefield, who advocated that colonial land should be sold at a substantial price and that the proceeds of its sale should be used to fund further emigration to the colonies".[59] The proviso was retained in the *Australian Constitutions Act 1850* (Imp), but the Legislative Council conveyed its deep dissatisfaction to the Imperial Parliament, indicating the importance of an institution of property in land in the colony, including revenues from that land. The Legislative Council declared "the Revenue arising from the Public Lands, derived as it is 'mainly' from the value

---

[54] Fry, "Land Tenures," 167.

[55] *Williams v Attorney-General for New South Wales*, 408 (Barton ACJ).

[56] *Queensland Debt Act 1862* (NSW).

[57] *Record of the Proceedings of the Queensland Parliament, Legislative Assembly, extracted from the third-party account as published in the Moreton Bay Courier*, July 4, 1860, accessed July 26, 2021, https://www.parliament.qld.gov.au/work-of-assembly/sitting-dates/dates/1860; Supplement to the Moreton Bay Courier, "Moreton Bay Public Debt," *The Moreton Bay Courier*, December 1, 1857.

[58] Tom Allen, *The Right to Property in Commonwealth Constitutions* (Cambridge: University of Cambridge Press, 2000), 1–2.

[59] *New South Wales Aboriginal Land Council Case* [103] (Gageler J).

imparted to them, by the labour and capital of the people of this Colony, is as much their property as the ordinary Revenue, and ought therefore to be subject only to the like control and appropriation". Thus, "plenary powers of Legislation should be conferred upon and exercised by the Colonial Legislature, for the time being".[60] Subsequently, section 2 of the *New South Wales Constitution Act 1855* (Imp) vested in the legislature the entire management and control of the unoccupied lands belonging to the Crown and power to appropriate the proceeds of sale. That section operated in Queensland until enactment of the *Constitution Act 1867*.

The constitutional withdrawal of Crown prerogative has an important consequence; although "Canadian legislation created the possibility of a fiduciary obligation on the Crown" regarding land interests and First Nations peoples, that avenue was unavailable in Queensland as "radically different legislative regimes in Australia denied that possibility".[61] Importantly, while it was open for the legislature to affirm the interests in the land held by Aboriginal peoples and Torres Strait Islanders "subject only to the new paramount title of the Crown", the institution of property created in Queensland preferenced the interests of European settlers.[62]

The continuing relevance of early constitutional provision was laid bare during constitutional review at the turn of the twenty-first century. Recommendations for consolidation of the various Constitution Acts supported repeal of sections 30 and 40 of the *Constitution Act 1867*.[63] However, the Queensland Parliament's Legal Constitutional and Administrative Review Committee found that, beyond repealing a proviso in section 40(2) regarded in law as spent, sections 30 and 40 of the *Constitution Act 1867* should continue. In the committee's view it was important to leave undisturbed "the constitutional status quo surrounding land ownership and native title", as "re-enactment of these sections would affect native title holders differently than it would affect freehold

---

[60] New South Wales Legislative Council, *Votes and Proceedings of the Legislative Council,* May 1, 1851, accessed July 26, 2021, https://www.parliament.nsw.gov.au/hansard/pages/first-council.aspx#

[61] Keane, "The Conscience of Equity," 109.

[62] Fry, "Land Tenures," 158.

[63] Electoral and Administrative Review Commission, *Report on Consolidation and Review of the Queensland Constitution* (Brisbane: Queensland Government Printer, 1993); Queensland Constitutional Review Commission, *Report on the Possible Reform of and Changes to the Acts and Laws that Relate to the Queensland Constitution* (Brisbane: Queensland Government Printer, 2000).

## 12 LAND, THE SOCIAL IMAGINARY, AND THE *CONSTITUTION ACT...* 251

title holders and would therefore not be a valid future act under the *Commonwealth Native Title Act 1993*".[64] Upon referral of a specific question from the legislature, the Committee recommended enactment of a preamble to the State's constitution that included a reference to the relationships of Aboriginal peoples and Torres Strait Islanders to land.[65]

The legislature adopted each of the Committee's recommendations. First, sections 30 and 40 were preserved by the *Constitution of Queensland 2001*. The Explanatory Notes to the draft Constitution draw attention to a concern that "native title might remain over some Crown land" and, therefore, "re-enacting these sections would permit dealings with land in respect of which there may be native title but not ordinary title. The re-enactment may affect native title holders whereas ordinary title holders would not be affected because the legislation has no effect on them".[66] Second, in 2010, the legislature enacted a preamble to the *Constitution of Queensland 2001*, reciting that the people of Queensland "honour the Aboriginal peoples and Torres Strait Islander peoples, the First Australians, whose lands, winds and waters we all now share; and pay tribute to their unique values, and their ancient and enduring cultures, which deepen and enrich the life of our community; and ... resolve ... to nurture our inheritance, and build a society based on democracy, freedom and peace".[67]

The committee's thoughtful analysis of the historical evolution of the property institution and the subsequent parliamentary actions evidences the vital importance for real property questions of a full appreciation of Queensland's bespoke property institution and the instrumental values of property it entails. As explained by Taylor, answers to property questions must be tailored to the social imaginary shared by the society: the common understanding that makes (and has made) possible "common practices and a widely shared sense of legitimacy".[68] The "ancient" sense of the constitutional provisions—the deeper normative notions and images that

---

[64] Legal Constitutional and Administrative Review Committee, *Review of the Queensland Constitutional Review Commission's Recommendations Relating to a Consolidation of the Queensland Constitution (Report No. 24)* (Brisbane: Queensland Government Printer, 2000).

[65] Law, Justice and Safety Committee, *A Preamble for the Constitution of Queensland 2001 (Report No. 70)* (Brisbane: Queensland Government, 2009).

[66] Queensland Constitution Bill 2001, Explanatory Notes, accessed July 26, 2021, https://www.legislation.qld.gov.au/view/html/bill.first/bill-2001-755/lh#creationhistory, 33–4.

[67] *Constitution of Queensland 2001*, Preamble.

[68] Taylor, *Modern Social Imaginaries*, 23.

drew Queensland's colonial community together "into a common political life"—must work together with the "modern universal logic of rights protection".[69] As modelled by the committee and the legislature, and as examined in the final section of this chapter, these deeper norms are within the foundations of the State's property institution.

## ANSWERING CONTEMPORARY PROPERTY QUESTIONS

To operate a property institution intelligently, Waldron says, often "we need to justify in order to understand" because "there are a number of issues that make little sense unless debated with an awareness of the point of property rules".[70] Harris defines a property institution as the "social and legal institution which constitutes the background for conventional property-talk among both laymen and lawyers", building on conceptions of property as both "property as things" and "property as wealth".[71] As such, a property institution incorporates transmission freedoms and consequential authority to build financial wealth,[72] the background to contemporary contestation about property and individual freedom.[73]

For contemporary questions then, a state's property institution and the instrumental values inherent in the community's idea of order have continuing significance. First, the institution's trespassory rules and ownership spectrum continue to maintain "independence, dignity and pluralism in society by creating zones in which the majority has to yield to the owner", even if, with the growth and reach of the modern constitutional state there is no longer the same scope to secure independence from the state via accumulated wealth in the form of private property interests as to land, goods, or money.[74] Second, it is necessary to appreciate that at its simplest the "constitutional logic that puts a concern for communities at the heart of the constitutional project" can facilitate "groups as sites of

---

[69] Benjamin L. Berger, "Freedom of Religion," in *The Oxford Handbook of the Canadian Constitution*, eds. Peter Oliver, Patrick Macklem and Nathalie Des Rosiers (New York: Oxford University Press, 2017), 755.

[70] Jeremy Waldron, "Property Law," in *A Companion to Philosophy of Law and Legal Theory*, ed. Dennis Patterson (Oxford: Blackwell Publishing, 2010), 15.

[71] Harris, *Property and Justice*, 141.

[72] Harris, *Property and Justice*, 304.

[73] Harris, *Property and Justice*, 284.

[74] Reich, *The New Property*, 771.

repression and discrimination".[75] As in the past, holdings of wealth in the form of private property may secure independence, but holders of wealth are able to dominate the lives of others, particularly when wealth is consolidated in the form of large corporate holdings.[76] Third, even in a post-colonial context, often there is a mismatch between real property rights recognised by the community and rights recognised by a state legal system.[77]

Analysis of the historical evolution of a property institution promotes appreciation that "an argument from independence is distributionally blind".[78] When the property institution in Queensland was being established, there was on foot a "global recasting of discourses of statehood", as colonies on the periphery sought to govern by way of local institutions of state and in their own right.[79] In *Mabo v Queensland [No 2]*, Justice Brennan refers to a "fiction" enabling the rights and interests of First Nations peoples to be treated as non-existent, "justified by a policy which has no place in the contemporary law of this country".[80] In *Western Australia v Commonwealth*, a majority of the High Court said, "The title of Aboriginal peoples in land was ignored because, at that time, there was a common opinion (which *Mabo (No.2)* holds to be erroneous) that the Aborigines had no legal interest in land".[81] And, in *Love v Commonwealth*, Justice Gordon states that the recent case law recognises the continuation of native title rights and interests after European settlement, and acknowledges:

> the fragility of those rights and interests and their susceptibility to extinguishment. The subsequent enactment of the Native Title Act and the many cases that have been brought about the nature and extent of native title rights and interests in respect of particular parts of this country should not obscure ... the deeper truth recognised by Mabo [No 2]: that the Indigenous peoples of Australia are the first peoples of this country, and that the connec-

---

[75] Berger, "Freedom of Religion," 769.

[76] Harris, *Property and Justice*, 149; Reich, *The New Property*, 746–55.

[77] Brian Z. Tamanaha, *A Realistic Theory of Law* (New York: Cambridge University Press, 2017), 55.

[78] Harris, *Property and Justice*, 306.

[79] Ford, *Settler Sovereignty*, 4.

[80] *Mabo v Queensland [No 2]*, 42 (Brennan J).

[81] *Western Australia v Commonwealth* (1995) 183 CLR 373, 432 (Mason CJ, Brennan, Deane, Toohey, Gaudron and McHugh JJ).

tion between the Indigenous peoples of Australia and the land and waters that now make up the territory of Australia was not severed or extinguished by European settlement.[82]

When a contemporary property question arises then independence remains one of the instrumental justifications for a property institution, and the domination potential of a property institution remains an important objection.[83] Waldron illustrates compellingly with a description of a speech to New Zealand Federated Farmers. Perceiving that farmers were "facing a number of irksome environmental statutes"; the representative group sought "some philosophical vindication of their rights in their land" in order to set up "natural entitlements" against legislative incursions. Waldron explains, however, that even in Robert Nozick's version of John Locke's account, "the importance of respecting a current property right presupposes that it is the culmination of an unbroken series of consensual transactions stretching back to the dawn of time". In New Zealand—as in other Australasian colonies—"the land seems to have been governed by social and public legal arrangements from start to finish".[84] This analysis finds "law-making oriented explicitly to the policy needs of New Zealand as an economy and to what was for a long time a public commitment to the diffusion of property rights and broad economic equality". And, "at every stage modifications to the conveyancing laws, in farmers' ability to alienate government leaseholds, in the laws of trusts and bankruptcy, and in the laws of inheritance, family provision and intestacy ... all took place not through some inexorable logic endogenous to private law (let alone natural law), but by statute (mainly)".[85]

According to these deeper norms, therefore, "the community does not treat its owners unjustly where it imposes property-limitation or expropriation rules uniformly for the good of all (as in environmental and planning regulations)", nor does a political community do so where rules are imposed selectively "to counter illegitimate domination".[86] As property

---

[82] *Love v Commonwealth of Australia; Thoms v Commonwealth of Australia* [2020] HCA 3, [498] (Gordon J).

[83] Harris, *Property and Justice*, 150, 303.

[84] Waldron, *The Rule of Law*, 30–1.

[85] Waldron, *The Rule of Law*, 32.

[86] Harris, *Property and Justice*, 306.

questions lead to different answers in different states,[87] to work towards trespassory rules and an ownership spectrum allocating "property as wealth" on just and principled lines, each state must act in accordance with its own, established idea of order.

As modelled by the Queensland parliamentary committee in its thoughtful analysis of the enduring relevance of sections 30 and 40 of the *Constitution Act 1867* and the legislature's adoption of the committee's recommendations, historical evolution of the State's property institution continues. In the past, allocation of property as wealth made possible the founding of modern constitutional states, each according to a bespoke idea of order. The Queensland example—of land, social imaginary, and constitutional provisions—provides clear evidence that the deeper normative notions and images underlying the social imaginary of a state and its property institution remain foundational.

[87] Harris, *Property and Justice*, 29; JW Harris, "Is Property a Human Right?" in *Property and the Constitution*, ed. Janet McLean (Portland: Hart Publishing, 2010), 67.

CHAPTER 13

# The Good, the Bad and the Ugly: A Short History of Biosecurity Regulation in Australia

*Noeleen McNamara*

## INTRODUCTION

Although rabbits arrived on the First Fleet in 1788, they were brought for purely utilitarian reasons as a food supply and given the parlous state of the first settlement in its early days, one can only assume some were consumed rather quickly. By the mid-nineteenth century, however, an idea took hold amongst the colonial elite that was formulated around a more-or-less romantic remembrance of the flora and fauna on the European continent, and only partially by the question of gaining a food supply. Food supply, however, was a strong reason for the introduction of commercial crops and animals. This idea resulted ultimately in the importation and distribution of new animals and new flora which had a totally different ecological base. In 1857 and 1858, for example, the biologist Ferdinand von Mueller

---

N. McNamara (✉)
School of Law and Justice, University of Southern Queensland,
Ipswich, QLD, Australia
e-mail: Noeleen.McNamara@usq.edu.au

© The Author(s), under exclusive license to Springer Nature    257
Switzerland AG 2022
S. McKibbin et al. (eds.), *The Impact of Law's History*, Palgrave
Modern Legal History,
https://doi.org/10.1007/978-3-030-90068-7_13

distributed 7120 living plants and 22,438 packets of seed throughout the gardens of the colonies.[1] Although a biologist, Mueller seems to have been ignorant of the potential deleterious effect of these introductions on the local ecology.

Unfortunately for the Australian environment, Mueller's example was taken up enthusiastically by groups of soi-disant naturalists, who eventually coalesced under the rubric of various colonial acclimatation societies. Acclimatisation in the nineteenth century was scientifically understood to mean the process by which animals and plants gradually adapt to climatic and environmental conditions different to those that prevailed in their original habitats.[2] By way of some examples, the Victorian Acclimatisation Society was founded in 1861 by Edward Wilson, a private collector whose motto was "if it lives, we want it".[3] The Society was primarily responsible for the introduction of starlings, sparrows, Sambar Deer and European carp in the Murray River. Acclimatisation society gardens in each of the capital cities in Australia imported plants and animals, propagating and distributing them to their members all over the continent. As Rolls points out: "there was never a body of men so foolishly, so vigorously, and so disastrously wrong".[4] To use the theme of this chapter, this had both "good" and "bad" consequences. The Queensland society imported and experimented with many plants that are now important agricultural crops in the state.[5] These included sugar cane, bananas, cotton, apples, pineapples, pasture grasses, maize, olives, and mangoes. However, it also released rabbits on several Moreton Bay Islands and sparrows into the Brisbane Botanical Gardens.[6]

The purpose of this chapter is to illustrate, by use of a number of case studies, examples where biosecurity policy and legislation has protected an industry and where lessons have been learnt that have resulted in the strengthening of biosecurity measures. (In all but one of these case

---

[1] Deborah Tout-Smith, "Acclimatisation Society of Victoria," Museums Victoria Collection, last modified 2003, https://collections.museumsvictoria.com.au/articles/1803

[2] Peter Osborne, "Queensland Acclimatisation Society," last modified October 14, 2010, https://qhatlas.com.au/content/queensland-acclimatisation-society

[3] Tout-Smith, "Acclimatisation Society of Victoria".

[4] Eric C. Rolls, *They All Ran Wild: the Animals and Plants That Plague Australia* (Sydney: Angus & Robertson, 1984) cited by Tout-Smith, ibid.

[5] Osborne, "Queensland Acclimatisation Society".

[6] Ibid.

studies, the "pests" have been deliberately introduced and have proven worse than the problem they were seeking to fix.) Indeed, the invasion of exotic species is among the most important global-scale problems experienced by natural ecosystems.[7] Despite the current legislative and policy controls in place in Australia, mistakes continue to be made and vigilance is needed. Examples of both flora and fauna will be considered in an Australian context.

## THE HISTORICAL LEGISLATION

Before reviewing these case studies, it is important to understand the roles that the Commonwealth and the states and territories have in relation to biosecurity in Australia. "Biosecurity", in the contemporary understanding of the word, is the modern equivalent of the much older term, "quarantine". In 1908, the federal government passed the *Quarantine Act*, which sought to control the importation of fauna and flora which could have deleterious effects if released into a relatively pristine Australian environment. In his second reading speech, Senator Keating stated:

> This is a measure which Parliament is called upon to consider, not merely because it is invested with power to legislate in regard to quarantine, but also because of the manifest duty which devolves upon a central authority, as soon as convenient after it's [sic] establishment, to institute a uniform system of quarantine for the whole of the territory under its control. That power is specifically intrusted to this Parliament under section 51 of the Constitution. There has been in existence in each State, as in other countries, a system of quarantine; but those systems; although perhaps they have been more or less moulded on one original plan, have in them many divergences.[8]

The Australian Constitution, which in sections 51 and 52 allocates legislative responsibilities to the Commonwealth and States within a federal system, refers in s 51(ix) to the power of the Commonwealth to make laws with respect to quarantine. Gray[9] notes that the constitutional validity of

---

[7] Gyan P. Sharma, Akhilesh S. Raghubanshi, and Jamuna S. Singh, "Lantana Invasion: An Overview," *Weed Biology and Management* 5, no. 4 (December 2005): 157.

[8] Senate, *Hansard*, September 6, 1907.

[9] Anthony Gray, "The Australian Quarantine and Biosecurity Legislation: Constitutionality and Critique," *Journal of Law and Medicine 22*, no. 4 (2015): 793–94.

this Act has not been confirmed by the High Court—although s 51(ix) was also relied on as the head of power in the *Biosecurity Act 2015* (Cth). This power is concurrent with the States and Commonwealth legislation prevails where there exists a clear difference to a state legislative enactment.[10]

The *Quarantine Act 1908* (Cth) emerged from ongoing policy considerations around the demonstrable threats to Australia, in terms of both ecology and public health. As enacted, it represented a sophisticated approach to biosecurity and was in advance of the *Public Health Act 1896* (UK). Equally, despite considerable amendment, it served the interests of the country until it was repealed in 2015. Impetus for the change arose from several reviews (the Nairn Report and later Beale Review) into Australia's biosecurity system. These identified "systemic flaws that were causing the country to be vulnerable to incursions of foreign pests and diseases through the administration of an archaic regulatory regime".[11]

The 2015 Act is "An Act relating to diseases and pests that may cause harm to human, animal or plant health or the environment, and for related purposes".[12] The fact that the Bill received bipartisan support is testament to the generalised concern about the need to update the legislation. It provides a legislative framework to manage the risk of pests and diseases entering Australian borders and causing harm to human, plant and animal health, as well as to the environment and the economy. That is, it takes a risk-based rather than a zero-risk approach, which is not feasible due to expense and likelihood of success. It is administered by two federal departments: the Department of Health and the Department of Water and the Environment. As recommended by the Beale Review in 2008, a statutory office of Inspector-General of Biosecurity was also established pursuant to the *Inspector-General of Biosecurity Act 2015* (Cth). The Department of Health is charged with the oversight and control of biological threats to people and industries, including those that involve biopandemic diseases and bioterrorism. The Department of Water and the Environment is more concerned under its regulations in stopping undesirable organisms from entering the country, which is the focus of this chapter.

---

[10] *Biosecurity Act 2015* (Cth), s. 8.

[11] Sam Durant and Thomas Faunce, "Analysis of Australia's New Biosecurity Legislation," *Journal of Law and Medicine* 25, no. 3 (2018): 647.

[12] *Biosecurity Act 2015* (Cth), long title.

The case studies which follow are taken from the period both prior to federation and after the enactment of the *Quarantine Act*. They are illustrative of the historical factors which eventually gave rise to the body of state and Commonwealth legislation which constitute the regulatory biosecurity apparatus, which applies today.

## THE GOOD

A "good" example (indeed, best practice example) of government and industry working together to achieve biosecurity outcomes is the policy and legislation which has kept phylloxera out of the South Australian vineyards for over 100 years. Phylloxera is a tiny yellow aphid-like root louse that destroys grapevines. Working underground, the insect eats away at the vines, and damage is not visible until the vines become yellow, then shrivel and die. The insect originated in America, where the roots of local vines (*Vitis labrusca*) were at least partially resistant to its predations. It was introduced into old-world wine regions when specimens of American vines were taken to England in the 1850s and devastated vineyards before moving to Europe. By the end of the 1800s, it had caused the devastation of a great number of vineyards, "generating a deep crisis in the European wine production and trade industries".[13] The nature of the problem was graphically described by a report of the Phylloxera Board in 1885:

> It has been stated by some of the best authorities that a nymph or single unwinged phylloxera produces in less than 12 months at least 25 million eggs, which will give birth to as many more insects with the same devastating power. It will thus be seen that the underground insect, like its winged relative, though diminutive in size, is gigantic in procreative power, and that its multiplication, if not successfully arrested, must soon end in the total destruction of the vine, or that its subtle and rapid ravages will make vine-culture unprofitable.[14]

---

[13] Javier Tello, Roswitha Mammerler, Marko Čajić and Astrid Forneck, "Major Outbreaks in the Nineteenth Century Shaped Grape Phylloxera Contemporary Genetic Structure in Europe," *Scientific Reports* 9 (November 26, 2019): [17540], https://doi.org/10.1038/s41598-019-54122-0

[14] Phylloxera Board, Geelong Vine Disease District Report (1885), iv, http://parliament.vic.gov.au/papers/govpub/VPARL1996Np33.pdf

Phylloxera was first discovered in Australia around 1875 and officially documented at Fyansford (near Geelong), Victoria, in 1877. Once several vineyards in Victoria were found to be infested, legislation was passed—the *Vine Diseases Act 1879* (Vic). This legislation was based on the French experience that eradication of the insect was best achieved by the wholesale destruction of vineyards and leaving them fallow for many years. It applied to affected vineyards in the Geelong and Bendigo areas and also prohibited the transportation of vine stock.

Unfortunately, this early attempt at eradication was unsuccessful, and phylloxera was later detected in other parts of central and north-eastern Victoria. The first detection in New South Wales was in 1884 at Camden, and further infestations were subsequently found nearby. Phylloxera was first found in Queensland at Enoggera, Brisbane, in 1910. So serious was the phylloxera problem that it featured as a topic of conversation in the intercolonial conference of 1880 between New South Wales, Victoria, and South Australia, one of the early fora that set the agenda for Federation. "A federal court of appeal for all Australia, intercolonial railways, intercolonial free trade, a uniform tariff, the eradication of the phylloxera, the Chinese question, the rabbit pest etc" were all discussed as potential reasons for federation.[15]

It is noteworthy that vignerons in South Australia were at the forefront of acting in a bid to protect their industry. Even before the discovery of phylloxera in Victoria, they lobbied legislators to act, the result of which was the *Vines Protection Act 1874*. The object of this Act was "to prevent the introduction of certain vine cuttings or rooted vines". The Act provided that the "Governor may prohibit the introduction of any vine cuttings prohibition, or rooted vines, either absolutely or from any countries therein named whose vineyards are infected, or may be suspected of being infected, by any kind of disease, whether such disease shall be caused by an insect named *Phylloxera Vastatrix*, or from any other cause or causes whatsoever".[16] An Inspector of Vineyards was appointed to administer the Act. Any person breaching the prohibition was liable to a penalty of between 10 and 100 pounds, and the plant matter was seized and destroyed by fire. No other grape vines could be planted for five years after the

---

[15] South Australian Register, December 11, 1880 as quoted by Andrew Calliard, "Hidden Menace," last modified August 9, 2018, https://app.gourmettravellerwine.com/editions/2018-08-09/articles/caillard.html

[16] *Vines Protection Act 1874* (SA), s. 1.

removal of affected vines. In discussing amendments to the Act in 1878, the *Adelaide Observer* reported "it is open to question whether these provisions will be found sufficiently stringent" due to the requirement to only destroy the vines actually affected, rather than the requirement to destroy nearby plants: "if any portion of a vineyard is condemned as unfit for the growth of grapevines the prohibition should extend also to the adjoining land".[17]

The *Phylloxera Act 1899* established the Phylloxera Board of South Australia, a statutory authority dedicated to the protection of vineyards from phylloxera infestation. Again, industry (the South Australian Vinegrowers' Association) was champions of this legislation. Delegates from the various vine-growing districts held a conference in Adelaide on May 16, 1899, to discuss the introduction of a proposed Phylloxera Bill. Chief amongst the concerns was the establishment of a compensation scheme if vines had to be removed. The *Adelaide Chronicle* reports:

> When in 1897 phylloxera was making its presence felt in New South Wales, and was spreading in Victoria, the vignerons of South Australia rose to the occasion and without any paltry parochial quibbling treated the matter in a statesmanlike fashion. They began an immediate agitation in favour of a measure to establish an insurance fund ... [as well to pay] an expert systematically to inspect and report upon the vineyards throughout the State.[18]

At this meeting, they proposed a compensation scheme of six pounds per acre to be paid to growers whose vineyards were required to be destroyed under the Act, although "in the case of persistently neglected vineyards there would be destruction without compensation".[19] "Police troopers in the various districts [were] instructed to collect the necessary information from which to compile the vignerons' roll".[20] Growers were required to pay one shilling per acre towards a compensation fund, "which was practically an insurance fund in the event of the disease making its appearance".[21]

This Act continued to prevent the importation of vine stock material for 70 years, although by the late 1960s it was recognised that the import of new virus-free vines and new varietals should be permitted under strict

---

[17] "The Protection of Vines," *Adelaide Observer*, September 7, 1878, 10.

[18] "Guarding against phylloxera," *The Adelaide Chronicle*, July 20, 1907, 11.

[19] "The Phylloxera Crusade," *Adelaide Observer*, May 27, 1899, 6.

[20] "The Phylloxera Board," *The Express and Telegraph*, January 25, 1900, 2.

[21] "The Phylloxera Tax," *Weekly Times*, November 17, 1906, 42.

supervision. In 1995 the Act was repealed and replaced with the *Phylloxera and Grape Industry Act 1995*. The Phylloxera Board now trades as "Vinehealth Australia". Every vineyard owner with 0.5 hectares or more under vine in South Australia (approximately 3360 vineyards) makes an annual contribution of $9.50 per hectare (minimum of $50) to enable Vinehealth Australia to perform its functions under the *Phylloxera and Grape Industry Act 1995*.[22]

Each state now has legislation and regulations which restrict or prohibit the movement of "phylloxera risk vectors". These include grapevine material, grape products and vineyard or winery equipment and machinery.[23] Additionally, there is an industry-led National Phylloxera Management Protocol 2009, which has been developed by the National Vine Health Steering Committee to reduce the risk of spread of grapevine phylloxera. The purpose of the National Protocol is to provide a basis from which legislation and regulations for the movement of phylloxera risk vectors can be developed by each state and territory government, and to which the regulations can be aligned, creating a consistent set of requirements across Australia.[24]

In terms of the prevention of phylloxera and other diseases in the wine industry, particularly in South Australia where there is an imperative to protect not only the $2.15 billion wine industry[25] but also some of the oldest vines in the world, vigilance needs to continue. For example, the June 2021 South Australia's Plant Quarantine Standard version 17.2 is the result of extensive consultation by government with industry (3300 stakeholders) and implements a "risk-based approach to strengthen the conditions under which items that can pick up and spread phylloxera, may enter the State".[26] The review process noted that "Phylloxera is on the move in the Yarra Valley, Victoria, and the risk of pick up and spread of this pest into SA has never been higher".[27]

---

[22] Vinehealth Australia, "A Visionary Legacy," last modified 2018, https://vinehealth.com.au/who-we-are/

[23] National Vine Health Steering Committee, "National Phylloxera Management Protocol" (October 2009): 4.

[24] Ibid., 2.

[25] Vinehealth Australia, "SA Plant Quarantine Standard," last modified July 2021, http://vinehealth.com.au/regulation/sa-pqs

[26] Ibid.

[27] Ibid.

This case study illustrates both the importance of historical regulation, but also the need for the industry to be invested in the regulatory solutions. While the pest remains an ongoing threat, education is needed to ensure community awareness of the problem (e.g. signs warning the public who visit cellar doors not to enter the vineyard plantings) as well as inspections to prohibit the transfer of vine cuttings and machinery that has been used in a phylloxera-affected area.

## THE BAD AND THE GOOD: THE PRICKLY PEAR CACTUS

The introduced Prickly Pear cactus, and its subsequent control, is an example of both "bad and good" biosecurity in Australia. Whilst phylloxera caused great economic harm to the affected vineyards, the prickly pear cactus had a more generalised catastrophic impact by rendering thousands of acres of agricultural and grazing land unproductive. Rather than providing a specific legislative solution, as was illustrated by the phylloxera case study, government intervention took the form of funding and cooperation by affected states and the Commonwealth for a dedicated body to be established to investigate solutions.

As Stiling states:

> When the first ships carrying British convicts landed on the site that is now Sydney, Australia, in 1788, the human passengers were not the only newcomers on board. A type of prickly pear, *Opuntia monacantha*, also made the voyage. Collected in Rio de Janeiro, the cactus – or, more precisely, the cochineal insects that feed on it and yield a red-purpose stain when crushed – were to be the basis of a dye industry. The dye enterprise never took off, but the prickly pear did.[28]

The red dye was essential for the red coats of British soldiers, so Britain was keen to establish their own supplies of cochineal—as the trade was monopolised by Mexico.[29] Other species of cactus were later imported. Whilst the genus *Opuntia* contains about 400 species, which are indigenous to the northern prairies of the United States through to Argentina, the two that became serious pests in Australia are natives of the southern

---

[28] Peter Stiling, "A Worm that Turned: Exemplars of Biological Control," *Natural History* 109, no. 5 (June 2000): 40.
[29] Leonie Seabrook and Clive McAlpine, "Prickly Pear," *Queensland Historical Atlas: Histories, Cultures, Landscapes* (2009–2010).

coastline of the United States.[30] They are *Opuntia inermis*, which is the common prickly pear of Queensland and New South Wales and *Opuntia stricta*, which overran several million acres in Central Queensland.[31] Prickly pear was also introduced by early settlers for use as hedges and as pot plants.[32] For example, *inermis* was brought into Australia around 1839, where it was taken to Scone in New South Wales and used as hedging on several properties in the period 1840–1860.[33] Likewise, *stricta* was recorded as being used as a hedge in Rockhampton in 1870.[34] Hence the spread "radiated from a number of initial focal points".[35]

By 1925, at the height of the problem, 94,000 square miles in Queensland and New South Wales were covered with *Opuntia*.[36] The cactus averaged from 4 to 6 feet wide and over 20 feet high, presenting a significant portion of the best farming and dairy land.[37] Hundreds of settlers were driven off the land, pastoral properties were abandoned and homesteads deserted.[38]

A quarter of a century prior, the Queensland government was aware of this growing problem, as evidenced by their offering a £5000 reward in 1901 to anyone who could provide a practical solution to the spread of cactus. This was doubled in 1907; however, it was never collected.[39] Another financial incentive—this time to stop the spread of pricky pear seeds—saw the introduction of a bounty on certain birds in 1924 in Queensland, including emus (2s.6d), currawongs (4d) and crows (6d).[40]

Further steps were taken to address the problem in Queensland. In 1912, the Queensland Prickly-Pear Travelling Commission was established to investigate biological controls. Over the next three years, it

---

[30] A. P. Dodd, "The Conquest of the Prickly Pear," *Journal of the Royal Historical Society of Queensland* 3, no. 5 (1945): 351.

[31] Ibid., 352.

[32] Colin Ward, "Prickly Pear Control," CSIRO, last modified February 9, 2011, http://csiropedia.csiro.au/prickly-pear-control

[33] Ibid.

[34] Dodd, "The Conquest of the Prickly Pear," 352.

[35] Ibid., 352.

[36] Stiling, "A Worm That Turned: Exemplars of Biological Control," 42.

[37] Terry Domico, "The Great Cactus War," *Natural History* (October 2018): 17.

[38] Dodd, "The Conquest of the Prickly Pear," 353.

[39] Department of Agriculture and Fisheries, Queensland, "The Prickly Pear Story," last modified June 2020, https://www.daf.qld.gov.au/__data/assets/pdf_file/0014/55301/prickly-pear-story.pdf

[40] Leonie Seabrook and Clive McAlpine, "Prickly Pear".

13 THE GOOD, THE BAD AND THE UGLY: A SHORT HISTORY... 267

conducted a world survey, and various insects, and fungus species, were trialled. In 1920, the Commonwealth and New South Wales joined with the Queensland government to address this problem and established the Prickly Pear Board to "study the possibilities of the control of the prickly-pear pest in Australia by means of biological agencies".[41] The choice of biological agents was made because previous investigations had established that in its native home, America, prickly pear is attacked by various insects and fungus disease that appears to be confined to plants of the cactus family.[42] One of the Board's first steps was to send entomologists to the United States, Mexico and Argentina to find other insects that naturally fed on *Opuntia*.

About 50 insect species were trialled, with the most effective being the Argentinian moth, *Cactoblastis cactorum*, which was imported into Australia in 1925. Notably, and in contrast to the cane toad importation, before insects were shipped to Australia, tests were carried out with each insect to "ascertain the possibility of its being able to develop on other plants".[43] These tests were repeated against economic plants and native trees once the insects arrived in Australia. As it transpired, only one shipment of 2750 Cactoblastis eggs, which arrived in Brisbane as half-grown larvae, were needed, and they were used as the initial breeding stock. Half were kept at quarantine facilities in Brisbane and half were sent to the Chinchilla Prickly Pear Experimental Station. By March 1927, more than ten million eggs were released. As soon as 1930, vast tracts of eastern Australia had been cleared of dense prickly pear.[44]

Whilst the use of the cactoblastis is regarded as probably the world's most famous case of one introduced species being controlled by another,[45] there is still a need for vigilance in the control of cactus. For example, The *Courier-Mail* reported a new "cactus [Hudson pear] so tough that its spines can penetrate boots and car tyres, has been found growing at Mundubbera, Queensland".[46] A Queensland biosecurity officer is reported

---

[41] A.P. Dodd, "The Campaign against Prickly-Pear in Australia: Work of the Commonwealth Prickly-Pear Board," *Nature* 117 (1926): 625.

[42] Ibid., 625.

[43] Ibid., 625.

[44] Stiling, "A Worm That Turned: Exemplars of Biological Control," 44.

[45] Peter Kevan and Les Shipp, Comprehensive Biology (2011, 2nd ed): para 4.61.2, last modified 2011, https://www.sciencedirect.com/referencework/9780080885049/comprehensive-biotechnology

[46] Brian Williams, "Deadly Cactus Invades," *The Courier-Mail*, February 27, 2008, 10.

268  N. MCNAMARA

to have said that its spread was aided by opal miners who deliberately grew them around their diggings to keep prowlers and thieves away.[47]

Whilst this case study has proven the value of "good" biosecurity control, Raghu and Walton caution that governments cannot assume that such controls will always be effective. They cite the example of *lantana camara*, a "modern-day equivalent of Opuntia in Australia that infests a comparable area".[48] Lantana is a woody flowering bush and was introduced as an ornamental plant in 1841.[49] By 1897, it was recognised as one of the most troublesome weeds.[50] Lantana now covers more than four million hectares along eastern Australia,[51] particularly in coastal areas between Cairns in northern Queensland and Sydney, New South Wales.[52] Sharma reports research by Julien and Griffiths that, internationally, biological control trials started in 1902, and since then 41 agents have been released in around 50 countries.[53] In Australia, 26 species of insects have been released since 1914.[54] However, no biocontrol agent has satisfactorily controlled the spread or reduced the density of Lantana due to unfavourable climatic conditions, parasitism, predation, and cultivar preferences.[55]

[47] Ibid., 10.

[48] S. Raghu and Craig Walton, "Understanding the Ghost of Cactoblastis Past: Historical Clarifications on the Poster Child of Classical Biological Control," *BioScience* 57, no. 8 (September 2007): 701–02.

[49] Ibid., 702.

[50] Sharma, Raghubanshi, and Singh, "Lantana Invasion: An Overview," 157.

[51] Raghu and Walton, "Understanding the Gosh of Cactoblastis Past: Historical Clarifications on the Poster Child of Classical Biological Control," 701–02.

[52] Sonya Broughton, "Parasitism and Predation of the Lantana Leafmining Beetles Octotoma scabripennis Guerin-Meneville and Uroplata Girardi Pic (Coleoptera: Chrysomelidae: Hispinae) in Australia," *Australian Journal of Entomology* 40, no. 3 (July 2001): 286.

[53] Sharma, Raghubanshi, and Singh, "Lantana Invasion: An Overview," 158.

[54] Broughton, "Parasitism and Predation of the Lantana Leafmining Beetles," 287.

[55] Sonya Broughton, "Review and Evaluation of Lantana Biocontrol Programs," *Biological Control* 17 (2000): 272.

## THE BAD—AND THE UGLY: THE CANE TOAD
### (*BUFO MARINUS*)

Like lantana, another introduced species that has proven intractable is the cane toad. Cane toads easily qualify as both "bad" and "ugly" in terms of their impacts on native fauna. They are indiscriminate feeders and out-compete native species for habitat and food. They poison animals that ingest them, so therefore kill many native predators.[56] Their introduction to Australia was also "bad" in terms of an illustration of government policy and oversight as there was no mandated requirement to conduct tests to ensure that the toads would eat the insects that they were to predate in a controlled environment. It is also a story of political pressure being exerted by the Queensland government and industry on anyone (even the Commonwealth government) who cautioned against the release of the toad.

One parallel with the phylloxera experience was that the Queensland government established the Queensland Bureau of Sugar Experiment Stations ("Bureau") in 1900 to work on the beetle problem. The Bureau was established due to lobbying by cane farmers. Of particular concern was the grey-back beetle, as well as cane weevils, army worms and mole crickets.[57] One of the foremost issues that the Bureau was dealing with was that the larvae of native beetles ate the roots of the sugar cane.[58] The report in *The Queenslander* stated: "Every practicable mechanical method has been tried, with varying degrees of success, but it is believed that complete control of the pest may be gained by biological means. Experience with the giant toad in other cane-growing countries has proved its definite value in pest reduction … it is not likely to develop pernicious habits, nor become in any way a pest itself, in a new environment".[59]

In 1932 Bureau plant pathologist, Arthur Bell, represented Queensland at an international conference of sugar cane technologists at Puerto Rico, where "the usefulness of the toad" in reducing populations of cane beetles

---

[56] Centre for Invasive Species Solutions, "How Did the Cane Toad Arrive in Australia. Factsheet," last modified 2012, https://pestsmart.org.au/toolkit-resource/how-did-the-cane-toad-arrive-in-australia

[57] "An Ally to Beat the Beetle: Giant Toads Imported for the Cane Fields," *Queenslander*, July 27, 1935, 17.

[58] National Museum Australia, "Introduction of Cane Toads," last modified July 16, 2021, https://www.nma.gov.au/defining-moments/resources/introduction-of-cane-toads

[59] "An Ally to Beat the Beetle: Giant Toads Imported for the Cane Fields," 17.

in America was "brought directly under his notice".[60] In June 1935, Bureau entomologist, Reginald Mungomery was sent to Honolulu by the Queensland government to see the toads living under their new conditions (having been introduced from Puerto Rico), with the idea of "bringing a consignment back to Queensland to attack the grey-back beetle in the cane field".[61] It was reported that in Hawaii, the toads not only kept down cane beetles but had decimated the insect enemies of cultivated plants, such as roses and lettuces. Mungomery captured 102 toads and returned to Gordonvale, Queensland, and placed them in a special enclosure. Two months later, the toads had successfully reproduced. Two thousand, four hundred toads were released in the Gordonvale area, the area where the grey-back beetle was causing the greatest havoc.[62] "Remarkably, no studies of the potential impact on the environment had been carried out. Nor had the Bureau of Sugar Experiment Stations even determined whether the toad would actually eat the cane beetles".[63] However, the beetles that the toads were supposed to control were native Australian species, different to those causing problems in Hawaii and Puerto Rico.[64] Historian Peter Griggs has speculated that scientists' success in controlling prickly pear with biological, rather than chemical means, may have led to the misguided decision by the Bureau to try the cane toad.[65]

Nevertheless, even at the time, there was opposition to this first release of cane toads. Another Australian entomologist, Walter Froggatt, the President of the New South Wales Naturalist Society, stated prophetically "this great toad, immune from enemies, omnivorous in its habits, and breeding all year round, may become as great a pest as the rabbit or cactus".[66] He lobbied the federal government to exercise caution, and the Commonwealth Director-General of Health banned any further release of toads in December 1935.[67] Unfortunately, the Queensland Agriculture

---

[60] Ibid., 17.

[61] "Toad Army Lands," *Courier-Mail*, June 21, 1935, 16.

[62] Centre for Invasive Species Solutions, "How Did the Cane Toad Arrive in Australia. Factsheet".

[63] National Museum Australia, "Introduction of Cane Toads".

[64] Ibid.

[65] Centre for Invasive Species Solutions, "How Did the Cane Toad Arrive in Australia. Factsheet".

[66] David Dall, "A Catastrophe of Cane Toads," *Outlooks on Pest Management* 22, no. 5 (2011): 226.

[67] "Giant Toads: Federal Ban Imposed," *Sydney Morning Herald*, November 29, 1935, 11.

## 13 THE GOOD, THE BAD AND THE UGLY: A SHORT HISTORY... 271

Minister Frank Bulcock and Premier William Forgan Smith pressured the Commonwealth government and Prime Minister Joseph Lyons to overturn the ban a few months later. Frank Bulcock was a strong defender of the cane toad, writing in the *Courier-Mail* in 1938: "careful inquiries [were] made before the introduction of giant toads into Northern cane fields ... it had been closely observed in Hawaii and South America ... one of the department's own officers was sent overseas to study it, and his inquiries did not reveal any objectionable features".[68] Once the restrictions were removed, further releases of toads were made as far south as the Isis District, some 1400 kilometres south of the first release site.

Within two years, a report by the Director of the Bureau of Sugar Experiment Stations (Dr H. W. Kerr) revealed that they had continued "to increase in numbers in a highly satisfactory manner".[69] However, by 1940, massive beetle infestations were still occurring in places where toads were well established.[70] In 1947, Arthur Bell was reported as saying that:

> the toad had been very successful against the cane beetle borer, but had not been of much use in attacking the cane beetles. It also attacked a number of garden pests, and was sudden death to cockroaches in North Queensland. Its most unsuspected virtue, however, was as a snake killer. By killing vast numbers it had reduced the snake population considerably – generally at the sacrifice of its own life.[71]

Despite the obvious problems with the cane toad, various residents of Byron Bay apparently intentionally introduced the cane toad into the area as late as 1965. Van Beurden and Grigg surveyed the community while studying the population of cane toads in northern New South Wales and received responses to their questionnaires that led them to believe that residents introduced the toads as they thought that the toads would control their garden pests.[72]

---

[68] "Giant Toad Not a Menace," *Courier-Mail*, January 26, 1938, 16.

[69] "Giant American Toad: Favourable Queensland Reports," *Sydney Morning Herald*, September 22, 1937, 15.

[70] Dall, "A Catastrophe of Cane Toads," 226.

[71] "The Toad has his Defenders," *Daily Mercury*, February 10, 1947, 3.

[72] Eric K. van Burden and Gordon Grigg, "An Isolated and Expanding Population of the Introduced Toad *Bufo marinus* in New South Wales," *Australian Wildlife Research 7*, no. 2 (1980): 308.

The toad has had no appreciable impact on cane beetles, which are today controlled by chemical pesticides. Shine et al. have confirmed that sugar production did not significantly increase after the cane toads were released. They suggest that "this is because the toads reduced rates of predation on beetle pests by consuming some of the native predators of these beetles (ants), fatally poisoning others (varanid lizards) and increasing the numbers of crop-eating rodents (that can consume toads without ill-effect)".[73]

Cane toad control was not raised as a national issue until the 1980s. In 1986, the Commonwealth provided funding and established a cane toad Research Management Committee. The biological effects, including lethal toxic ingestion caused by cane toads, are listed as a key threatening process under the *Environment Protection and Biodiversity Conservation Act 1999* (Cth) ("EPBC Act"). This listing triggers the requirement to prepare a threat abatement plan. This plan sets out the research, management and other actions necessary to reduce the key threatening process to an acceptable level in order to maximise the chances of long-term survival of native species and ecological communities affected by cane toads. Research is focusing on finding methods to protect the most vulnerable native species and on gaining a better understanding of how other species are adapting to the toad's presence.[74] There is unlikely to ever be a broadscale method available to control cane toads across Australia.[75] The toads reached the Kakadu National Park in March 2001, crossed into the northern part of Western Australia from the Northern Territory in February 2009 and continue their spread at westwards at a rate of 40–60 kilometres per year.[76]

[73] Richard Shine, Georgia Ward-Fear and Gregory P. Brown, "A Famous Failure: Why Were Cane Toads an Ineffective Biocontrol in Australia," *Conservation Science and Practice*, no. 2 (2020), e296, https://doi.org/10.1111.csp2.296

[74] Department of Agriculture, Water and the Environment, "Threat Abatement Plan for the Biological Effects, Including Lethal Toxic Ingestion, Caused by Cane Toads: The Plan," http://www.environment.gov.au/biodiversity/threatened/publications/tap/threat-abatement-plan-biological-effects-including-lethal-toxic-ingestion-caused-cane-toads

[75] Department of Sustainability, Environment, Water, Population and Communities, "Threat Abatement Plan for the Biological Effects, Including Lethal Toxic Ingestion, Caused by Cane Toads: The Plan," (2011): 10.

[76] Department of the Environment, Water, Heritage and the Arts, "The Cane Toad (Bufo Marinus): Fact Sheet," last modified 2010, https://www.environment.gov.au/biodiversity/invasive-species/publications/factsheet-cane-toad-bufo-marinus

## "Bad" with Some Good News: Rabbits (*Oryctolagus cuniculus*)

Like the cane toad, the European rabbit has had devastating consequences for native fauna and flora, and apart from dingoes, the rabbit has no natural predator in Australia. Rabbits can survive on a diet as various as leaves, bark and grass, and their overgrazing of pastures and the warrens that they dig can be catastrophic for both agriculture and livestock farming.[77] Whilst a limited number were passengers on the First Fleet, and there are records of their release on various Islands in the Bass Strait to provide food for shipwrecked sailors,[78] they were released widely in 1859 in Victoria and hunted for sport. Coman reports that "on Christmas day 1859 Thomas Austin, a self-made wealthy settler, released 13[79] European wild rabbits on his estate, Winchelsea, Barwon Park, Victoria. They had been specially collected and sent to him by a relative in England".[80]

The rabbits bred most successfully in their new environment, with a hunter recording bagging 14,000 rabbits on one sheep property in Victoria in 1866.[81] By 1880 rabbits had entered NSW, by 1886 Qld and by 1894 had crossed what would have been assumed to have been an impassable barrier and entered WA.[82] With the exception of the feral cat in Australia, it is considered to be the fastest rate of any colonising mammal in the world.[83] One estimate put the rabbit population in the early part of the twentieth century at 250 million.[84]

---

[77] Department of the Environment and Energy, "Threat Abatement Plan for Competition and Land Degradation by Rabbits," (2016): 6–7.

[78] Department of Sustainability, Environment, Water, Population and Communities, "Feral European Rabbit (Oryctolagus cuniculus)," (2011):1.

[79] Other reports suggest that this number was 24: Centre for Invasive Species Solutions, "Key Facts About Rabbit Control in Australia. Factsheet," last modified 2015, http://pestsmart.org.au/toolkit-resource/key-facts-about-rabbit-control-in-australia

[80] Brian Coman, "Rabbits Introduced," National Museum Australia, last modified August 3, 2021, https://www.nma.gov.au/defining-moments/resources/rabbits-introduced

[81] Ibid.

[82] Ibid.

[83] Department of the Environment and Energy, "Threat Abatement Plan for Competition and Land Degradation by Rabbits," 6.

[84] Tarnya Cox, Tanja Strive and Greg Mutze et al., "Benefits of Rabbit Biocontrol in Australia," PestSmart Toolkit publication, Invasive Animals Cooperative Research Centre (Canberra, 2013): 13.

Faced with what appeared to be a virtually insurmountable problem, the first serious attempt in terms of regulation and control by the colonies was fencing. By the time of the passage of the *Quarantine Act 1908* (Cth) 320,000 km of fencing had been built. The Western Australian/South Australian fence alone stretched for 3256 km.[85] Unfortunately, a fence is only as good as it is maintained, and its maintenance was substantially reduced between World Wars I and II. Hence, with the cost of construction and maintenance, fencing as a remedy to rabbit inundation became unsupportable.

Advances in scientific knowledge, particularly in the fields of virology and immunology, led to a search for a virus which could be used via a vector. A rabbit-specific virus was eventually found in myxomatosis, which was released in the rabbit population of Victoria in 1949–50. It had astonishing results. Provided sufficient mosquitoes were present (the virus vector), early results showed up to a 90 per cent kill rate. The residual populations, however, created a problem as they developed an immunity to the virus and passed this immunity on to successive generations. Consequently by 1995, a new virus, calicivirus, was released with initially good results. Over time, however, the population developed immunity to this virus as well.[86]

Like the cane toad, the Commonwealth's legislative response to the problem has been to list the rabbit as a key threatening process under the EPBC Act. This has also triggered the preparation of a threat abatement plan. The latest is the *Threat Abatement Plan for Competition and Land Degradation by Rabbits*, released in 2016. Scientific advice received in preparing the plan is that "rabbits have reached their ecological limit within Australia".[87] Whilst this is positive, the economic impact of rabbits is estimated to be around $200 million a year.[88] Like other pests discussed in this chapter—cane toads, phylloxera and lantana—there is a recognition that eradication is impossible, so a variety of controls—biological,

---

[85] Coman, "Rabbits Introduced".

[86] Tarnya Cox, Tanja Strive and Greg Mutze et al., "Benefits of Rabbit Biocontrol in Australia," 8.

[87] Department of the Environment and Energy, "Threat Abatement Plan for Competition and Land Degradation by Rabbits," 5.

[88] Department of the Environment and Energy, "Threat Abatement Plan for Competition and Land Degradation by Rabbits," 6.

chemical and mechanical—need to be used.[89] One interesting aberration is that Queensland is the only state in Australia where there is a prohibition against keeping a rabbit as a pet.[90]

## CONCLUSION

This chapter has, by necessity, only addressed a snapshot of biosecurity concerns in Australian legal history to illustrate lessons that can be learnt in regulating this area going forward. It has also just dealt with flora and fauna examples that have impacted the environment—arguably the aim that Australia remains "free from diseases that affect ... people in other parts of the world"[91] has taken on a graphically important meaning in recent years. The "good" examples presented in the case studies are the product of both industry and government co-operation—especially where industry has led the initiative. The spirit of co-operation and shared responsibility between the Commonwealth and states, together with relevant stakeholders, is embedded in the latest Intergovernmental Agreement on Biosecurity 2019, despite the acknowledgement that "in practical terms, zero biosecurity risk is unattainable".[92]

Lessons have been learnt from the cane toad example, and it is hopefully now unthinkable that trials would not be conducted to see if insects or other animals that were providing useful biological controls overseas would translate to Australian conditions. Indeed, the Centre for Invasive Solutions has noted that it is likely that "the lessons learnt from the cane toad debacle have influenced the strict quarantine laws and risk assessment procedures Australia has in place today".[93] At the very least, risk assessments of potential harm from the introduced species would be undertaken. Even where direct impacts can be assessed (such as whether the introduced species will kill or compete with native wildlife), indirect impacts may be harder to predict and may only become apparent once the

---

[89] Tarnya Cox, Tanja Strive and Greg Mutze et al., "Benefits of Rabbit Biocontrol in Australia," 3.

[90] The Rabbit is a declared pest under the *Land Protection (Pest and Stock Route Management) Act 2002* (Qld).

[91] Department of Agriculture, Water and the Environment, "Intergovernmental Agreement on Biosecurity," (January 3, 2019): recital 2.

[92] Ibid., clause 13.

[93] Centre for Invasive Species Solutions, "How Did the Cane Toad Arrive in Australia. Factsheet".

species has been introduced.[94] It should be noted, however, that the examples of prickly pear's continued survival in spite of Cactoblastis and the ability of the rabbit to "out survive" various biosecurity controls "serve to remind [us] of one of evolution's most persistent conundrums: you have to continually 'out-evolve' your enemy".[95]

[94] Richard Shine, Georgia Ward-Fear and Gregory P. Brown, "A Famous Failure: Why Were Cane Toads an Ineffective Biocontrol in Australia," e296.
[95] Domico, "The Great Cactus War," 21.

CHAPTER 14

# Legal Pluralism Past and Present: Magna Carta and a First Nations' Voice in the Australian Constitution

*Jason Taliadoros*

## INTRODUCTION

Scholars, most prominently Megan Davis and Shireen Morris, have endorsed the Uluru Statement from the Heart's call for constitutionally entrenched recognition of Indigenous Australians, by means of a First Nations Voice enshrined in the Constitution.[1] Such a project involves reconciling very different sources of law: on the one hand, the common law system that exists in Australia and, on the other, an Indigenous conception of law that represents Aboriginal and Torres Strait Islander peoples. In

[1] Megan Davis and Marcia Langton, *It's Our Country: Indigenous Arguments for Meaningful Constitutional Recognition and Reform* (Carlton: Melbourne University Press, 2016); Shireen Morris, *A First Nations Voice in the Australian Constitution* (Oxford: Hart Publishing, 2020).

J. Taliadoros (✉)
Deakin University, Melbourne, VIC, Australia
e-mail: jason.taliadoros@deakin.edu.au

© The Author(s), under exclusive license to Springer Nature Switzerland AG 2022
S. McKibbin et al. (eds.), *The Impact of Law's History*, Palgrave Modern Legal History,
https://doi.org/10.1007/978-3-030-90068-7_14

277

other words, there is a need to deal with different legal sources within the one legal system that is the Australian state. Scholars such as Dani Larkin and Kate Galloway have conceived of a means of approaching this issue by envisioning the Uluru Statement as 'the opportunity to embrace legal pluralism ... as an expression of a truly Australian public law'.[2]

This chapter takes such a conception further by asking whether, and to what extent, legal pluralism is helpful in conceptualising constitutional recognition of Indigenous rights in Australia today. It does so by recourse to precedent—not the precedent of case law but the precedent of historical example, in particular Magna Carta. This chapter suggests that Magna Carta, well-known as a foundational document in English legal history and the history of law and government, was itself a product of legal pluralism. Accordingly, conceptions of legal pluralism may inform a deeper and more historically informed context for dealing with different legal systems within a single geographic space. The purpose of this provocation is to illustrate how unsatisfactory the explanation is that considers law in society as monistic or unitary, when a conception based on legal pluralism accommodates multiple legal orderings. To cite Larkin and Galloway, this chapter is 'an allegory ... to illustrate the importance for the wider polity of understanding that we live in a pluralistic legal system'.[3]

## *What Is Legal Pluralism?*

Legal pluralism is usually defined, according to Margaret Davies, as 'the co-existence of multiple systems or forms of law within one geographical space'.[4] For Davies, this means that, first, the idea of law is not tied to a state, in contrast to a 'statist' or 'monist' (i.e. singular) understanding of law; and, second, that 'non-state based forms of law ... exist alongside state law'.[5] This is at the same time a challenge to legal positivism, which is a corollary of a monist or singular conception of law.[6]

In one of the first attempts to define the term, John Griffiths described legal pluralism as a 'sociological fact' and 'an empirical state of affairs

---

[2] Dani Larkin and Kate Galloway, 'Uluru Statement from the Heart: Australian Public Law Pluralism,' *Bond Law Review* 30, No. 2 (2018) 1–11, 1.

[3] Larkin and Galloway, 2.

[4] Margaret Davies, *Asking the Law Question* (Pyrmont, NSW: Thomson Reuters, 2017, 4th ed.), 410.

[5] Davies, 410.

[6] Davies, 411.

## 14  LEGAL PLURALISM PAST AND PRESENT: MAGNA CARTA AND A FIRST...   279

attaching to human relations'.[7] It exists, Griffiths continues, when 'in a social field more than one source of "law", more than one "legal order", is observable'.[8] As can be seen, legal pluralism begins with understanding law from its social structure, or its 'social field', an approach taken from anthropology. On this understanding, law is described (by Sally Moore) as a 'semi-autonomous field', a reference to the fact that social change can be brought about by that society itself making rules and customs internally but also by being subjected to rules and decisions emanating from outside.[9]

Legal pluralism has been criticised for its vagueness. It 'can seem to turn everything into law, or just include too many things in the category of law'.[10] For this reason, legal pluralism itself has become pluralistic. Davies describes four kinds of legal pluralism. The first kind is the 'classic' approach of legal pluralism, which has been used mostly to analyse 'customary law' in colonial and post-colonial contexts.[11] A second type, 'new' legal pluralism, translated this into Western legal cultures; it was based on the insight that all societies, whether or not formerly colonised, comprised 'semi-autonomous' fields of normative control.[12] A third type of legal pluralism takes the concept beyond the boundaries of the nation state and looks at the multiplicity of laws and legal systems across the globe, that is 'the sources of normativity beyond and between states'.[13] A fourth kind of legal pluralism is critical legal pluralism, which, unlike the preceding three forms, does not treat law as a social fact; it is, rather, a construction of

---

[7] Davies, 413, citing John Griffiths, 'What is Legal Pluralism?,' *The Journal of Legal Pluralism and Unofficial Law* 24 (1986) 1–55, 39.

[8] Griffiths, 38.

[9] Sally F. Moore, 'Law and Social Change: The Semi-Autonomous Social Field as an Appropriate Subject of Study,' *Law and Society Review* 7 (1973) 719–746, republished in Sally F. Moore, *Law as Process: An Anthropological Approach* (London: Routledge & Kegan Paul, 1978), 54–81, 55–56.

[10] Davies, 416.

[11] Davies, 417–418, citing scholars such as Lauren Benton, *Law and Colonial Cultures: Legal Regimes in World History, 1400–1900* (Cambridge and New York: Cambridge University Press, 2002), 134.

[12] Davies, 418, citing Sally Falk Moore, *Law as Process: An Anthropological Approach* (London: Routledge and Keegan Paul, 1978) and Sally Falk Moore, 'Certainties Undone: Fifty Turbulent Years of Legal Anthropology, 1949–1999,' *Journal of the Royal Anthropological Institute* 7 (2001) 95.

[13] Davies, 420.

human beings and cannot be understood outside the subjective experiences and imaginings of human subjects.[14]

But such neat categorisations of legal pluralist methodologies are misleading among scholars of pre-modern legal history. Although ostensibly a proponent of the third approach, Thomas Duve, an early modern legal historian of south-west Europe, prefers the term 'multinormativity',[15] since legal pluralism 'suffers from such vagueness that one may doubt its heuristic power'.[16] For Duve, multinormativity serves as an appropriate term for attempts at understanding law 'in the environment of other modes of normativity not structured by our idea of law.'[17] This multinormativity is 'transcultural',[18] since it can be deployed in respect of 'cultural translations', namely 'transformations that occur in the process of reproducing normative options stemming from one context in a different context'.[19] Accordingly, for Duve, such concepts can encompass 'non-state normativity that transcends cultural boundaries'.[20] The term 'multinormativity', Duve argues, 'forces us to look far beyond the circle of legal sources that make up the conventional circle of primary or secondary norms in the sense of HLA Hart'.[21]

Caroline Humfress adopts 'institutional legal-pluralist perspectives' in her work on the late Roman Empire.[22] That is, appreciating the social insights to be gained from legal pluralist approaches to law, she notes its limitations in dealing with 'local-level orderings' and the 'integral plurality' of state law, namely its simultaneous and contradictory convergence

---

[14] Davies, 420, citing Marta-Marie Kleinhans and Roderick Macdonald, 'What is a Critical Legal Pluralism?,' *Canadian Journal of Law and Society* 12 (1997) 25, 37–39.

[15] Thomas Duve, 'Was ist "Multinormativität"? Einführende Bemerkungen' ['What is Multinormativity? Introductory Remarks'] *Rechtsgeschichte/Legal History* 25 (2017) 88, 90, 91.

[16] Duve, 'Multinormativität', 91.

[17] Thomas Duve, 'European Legal History–Concepts, Methods, Challenges', in *Entanglements in Legal History: Conceptual Approaches*, ed. Thomas Duve (Frankfurt-am-Main: Max Planck Institute for European Legal History, 2014), 29–66, 58.

[18] Duve, 'European Legal History', 58.

[19] Duve, 'German Legal History' 38–39. See also Gunther Teubner, 'Global Bokowina: Legal Pluralism in the World Society,' in *Global Law without a State*, ed. Gunther Teubner (Dartmouth, Aldershot, 1996) 3–28.

[20] Duve, 'German Legal History', 40.

[21] Duve, 'Multinormativität', 96.

[22] Caroline Humfress, 'Thinking through the Lens of Legal Pluralism: "Forum Shopping" in the Later Roman Empire,' in *Law and Empire: Ideas, Practices, Actors*, ed. J. Duindam, Jill Harries, Caroline Humfress, and N. Hurvitz (Leiden: Brill, 2013), 225–250, 250.

with and opposition to other social forms.[23] She instead advocates an approach that 'explores the socially constructed nature of Roman legal institutions', by approaching legal procedures as 'situated practices' rather than static legal rules.[24]

Brian Tamanaha arguably adopts Davies's second type of legal pluralism in an article that advocates the universality of legal pluralism as exemplified in the Middle Ages.[25] Although a legal theorist rather than a legal historian, his article is an important intervention for both legal theorists and legal historians in respect of understanding legal pluralism in the pre-modern period.

For the purposes of this chapter, which attempts to link the pre-modern with the modern, I adopt Tamanaha's framework in the next part. This choice of legal pluralism is not because Tamanaha's is demonstrably superior to others; the above review of the different kinds of legal pluralism suggests that his notion of legal pluralism is open to many of the same criticisms aimed at others. It is rather that his understanding of legal pluralism applies a taxonomic structure that is transparent, thus enabling its application to the provisions of Magna Carta to be made relatively clear.

## Magna Carta and Legal Pluralism

This part illustrates the applicability of legal pluralism in the context of the Middle Ages, the period recognised as occurring after the Roman Empire and before the Renaissance, spanning the years of approximately 400–1400 CE. The very term the Middle Ages, or the medieval period, connotes a period in the 'middle' or between two other more significant periods; many refer to it misleadingly as the 'Dark Ages'. Within this millennial time span, the period after 1000 CE is referred to as the 'High' Middle Ages, because of the emerging features of modernity that began to appear across Western Europe in that time. It is this period of the high Middle Ages that witnessed the first issue of Magna Carta in 1215, less than a century after the emergence of the common law in England. Despite the centralising normative tendencies of this early common law in England,

---

[23] Humfress, 230–231.

[24] Humfress, 233.

[25] Brian Z. Tamanaha, 'Understanding Legal Pluralism: Past to Present, Local to Global,' *Sydney Law Review* 30 (2008) 375–411.

282     J. TALIADOROS

paradoxically we also see the diverse, overlapping, and sometimes adverse features of law in this period—what we might call legal pluralism.

Was there legal pluralism in the Middle Ages? According to Tamanaha, the answer is yes. He observes that there was a 'rich legal pluralism that characterised the medieval period',[26] especially the 'mid through late Middle Ages', namely the high Middle Ages.[27] Tamanaha's conception of legal pluralism, as noted above, followed the second understanding of that concept as comprising 'in every social arena ... a ... multiplicity of legal orders'.[28] To this, Tamanaha added a taxonomy of legal pluralism as comprising six *systems*: (1) 'official legal systems', (2) 'customary/cultural normative systems', (3) 'religious/cultural normative systems', (4) 'economic/capitalist normative systems', (5) 'functional normative systems', and (6) 'community/cultural normative systems'.[29] Added to this were three major *axes* within each of the systems identified above: (a) 'coexisting, overlapping bodies of law with different geographical reaches'; (b) 'coexisting institutionalised systems'; and (c) 'conflicting legal norms'.[30]

I note that, in more recent work, Tamanaha has found a definition of legal pluralism more evasive; he deals with that problem by rejecting the idea that law has the same properties everywhere and adopts a 'conventionalist' approach: how is law conventionally understood in different contexts? Accordingly, this definition of legal pluralism 'involves different phenomena going by the label "law", whereas legal pluralism usually involves a multiplicity of one basic phenomenon, "law" (as defined)'.[31]

Tamanaha applied these six systems and three axes to the medieval period. The first, official legal systems, comprised *ius commune, lex mercatoria*, and ecclesiastical law, which featured elements of axis (a) in their 'transnational' nature, that is by extending beyond geographical and political regions and co-existing 'with codified German customary law, feudal law, municipal law and unwritten local customary laws on the local level'.[32] They, too, exhibited features of axis (b), 'coexisting institutionalised systems', namely those identified by van Caenegem as the 'vertical dividing

---

[26] Tamanaha, 'Understanding Legal Pluralism,' 376.

[27] Tamanaha, 'Understanding Legal Pluralism,' 378.

[28] Tamanaha, 'Understanding Legal Pluralism,' 412.

[29] Tamanaha, 'Understanding Legal Pluralism,' 397.

[30] Tamanaha, 'Understanding Legal Pluralism,' 377–378.

[31] Brian Tamanaha, *General Jurisprudence of Law and Society* (Oxford: Oxford University Press, 2001), 194.

[32] Tamanaha, 'Understanding Legal Pluralism,' 378.

# 14 LEGAL PLURALISM PAST AND PRESENT: MAGNA CARTA AND A FIRST... 283

lines between legal systems: those which separated townsmen from countrymen, churchmen and students from laymen, members of guilds and crafts from those not so affiliated', and manifest in the 'distinct networks of law courts' by which individuals faced trial before their peers.[33] Tamanaha also refers to axis (c), 'conflicting legal norms', noting the example of the existence of several different and conflicting customary laws in existence in the same place.[34]

Tamanaha relies on the work of several well-known scholars on medieval law and society in making these assertions of legal pluralism, namely Raoul van Caenegem, Frederic W. Maitland, Harold Berman, and Walter Ullmann. Although these scholars observed a multiplicity of legal forms within individual legal systems in the medieval West, they did not evoke the term 'legal pluralism'. A notable exception is the study and edition by a team of scholars comprising Basile, Bestor, Coquillette, and well-known legal historian Charles Donahue, Jr, on a thirteenth-century 'mercantile law' text, which they characterised as an instance of legal pluralism.[35] Basile and others took an essentialist definition of legal pluralism, borrowed from Greenhouse and Strijbosch, as 'the presence or coincidence in a certain social field of more than one legal order'.[36] The authors applied this concept of legal pluralism explicitly to this late-thirteenth-century text and its English and continental contexts.

### Magna Carta

One document from the thirteenth century exceeds all others in its mythical and iconic status—the first issue of Magna Carta in 1215.[37] The

---

[33] Tamanaha, 'Understanding Legal Pluralism,' 378.

[34] Tamanaha, 'Understanding Legal Pluralism,' 378.

[35] Mary Elizabeth Basile, Jane Fair Bestor, Daniel R. Coquillette, and Charles Donahue, Jr., *Lex Mercatoria and Legal Pluralism: A Late Thirteenth-Century Treatise and Its Afterlife* (Cambridge, MA: Ames Foundation 1998), 139–146.

[36] Basile et al., 15 and 181.

[37] It is beyond the scope of this chapter to provide a detailed analysis of the chapters of Magna Carta and the context in which it was drafted. The standard account of Magna Carta, with facing-page translation, by Sir James Holt is authoritative, although somewhat inaccessible to the non-specialist: J. C. Holt, *Magna Carta* (Cambridge: Cambridge University Press, 2015, 3rd ed.), 378–398. Equally authoritative is David Carpenter's accessible account with a facing-page Latin to English translation of each chapter: David Carpenter, *Magna Carta* (London: Penguin, 2015), 22–34, 36–69. The chapter-by-chapter commentary by William Sharp McKechnie, *Magna Carta: A Commentary on the Great Charter of King John*

provisions of Magna Carta were drafted by royal officials, churchmen, and representatives of the barons, setting out new measures to be taken by King John and his royal administration to deal with perceived injustices, especially towards the earls and barons of the kingdom, often referred to as the 'Northerners'. This group had long been in conflict with John and his royal predecessors over feudal rights and fines. Magna Carta was intended to bring an end to hostilities, although within months it was abandoned by both parties and quashed by the pope.

Popular perceptions of Magna Carta have characterised it as either 'a fundamental protection against arbitrary and tyrannical rule' or 'a selfish document in which the baronial elite looked after its own interests'.[38] The truth lies somewhere in between, as it was both more, and less, than this. David Carpenter has described the provisions of Magna Carta in more practical, pragmatic, and political terms:

> The Charter was above all about money. Its overwhelming aim was to restrict the king's ability to take it from his subjects. Another major thrust was in the area of law and justice. The Charter wanted to make the king's dispensation of justice fairer and more accessible, while at the same time preventing his arbitrary and lawless treatment of individuals. Overlapping with both these agendas was the issue of local government. Here the Charter sought to deal with the malpractices of the king's local officials, above all his sheriffs and foresters. There were also chapters on London, and towns and trade, while the first chapter was on the church .... It was about redressing the injustices committed in the past. .... The chapters of the Charter set out the 'liberties' being granted by the king to his subjects.[39]

Magna Carta, therefore, had a strong emphasis on law and justice, including the exaction of fines and dues, the administration of justice and legal process at all levels, and political relations between a ruler and his subjects.

The importance of Magna Carta lies in its influence on English and, in turn, Australian law on ideas of due process and on constitutionalism more

---

(Glasgow: J. Maclehose & Sons, 1914) has been superseded in its substance by myriad scholarship and in its form by the online commentaries of the Magna Carta Project team: Henry Summerson, commentaries on the chapters of the 1215 Magna Carta, Magna Carta Project website: http://magnacarta.cmp.uea.ac.uk.

[38] Carpenter, vii.

[39] Carpenter, 24.

generally—that is, on notions of public law. It has become one of the most famous documents in world constitutional history, regarded as a fundamental protection against arbitrary and tyrannical rule.[40] This is due in part to several of its provisions that asserted the rule of law: chapter 40 provided that the king was not to sell, deny, or delay justice, and chapter 39 specified that no free man was to be imprisoned or dispossessed except 'by the lawful judgment of his peers' or 'by the law of the land'. These two provisions still stand on the statute book of the United Kingdom and in Australia.[41] The fame of Magna Carta is also due to its iconic status, however, which has arguably surpassed its substantive normative content.[42] In these two respects we can draw some tentative parallels between Magna Carta and the proposed Indigenous Voice in the Commonwealth Constitution: both are creatures of constitutional, or public law, and are therefore normative; further, both are, or likely to be, supra-normative in the sense that their influence goes beyond the written law itself. Further, we can see in both documents evidence of legal pluralism. I turn to this aspect of Magna Carta in the next section.

### Applying Tamanaha's Pluralism to Magna Carta

Tamanaha exemplified his model of legal pluralism with the six systems and three axes outlined above, as they applied to the myriad of normative systems in the 'high' Middle Ages of Western Europe. The project of this chapter is to test that model by applying it to a case study, namely the provisions of Magna Carta. Does it reveal pluralism within that document and in the normative orderings in which that document existed, namely thirteenth-century England?

Beginning with Tamanaha's system (1), official or 'positive' legal systems, he defines it as 'characteristically ... linked to an institutionalised

---

[40] Carpenter, vii–viii. The scholarship in this area is vast, for example Nicholas Vincent, *Magna Carta: The Foundation of Freedom* 1215–2015 (London: Third Millennium Publishing, 2015); Randy J. Holland, ed., *Magna Carta: Muse and Mentor* (St Paul, MN: Reuters, 2014); Roy E. Brownell, II, ed., *Magna Carta and the Rule of Law* (American Bar Association, 2015).

[41] David Clarke, 'The Icon of Liberty: The Status and Role of Magna Carta in Australian and New Zealand Law,' *Melbourne University Law Review* 24, No. 3 (2000) 866–892; David Clarke, 'Magna Carta in Australia 1803–2015: Law and Myth,' *Australian Law Journal* 89 (2015) 730–738.

[42] Clarke, 'Icon of Liberty'.

legal apparatus ... manifested in legislatures .... [that] give rise to powers, rights, agreements, criminal sanctions, and remedies'.[43] Magna Carta contains, predictably enough, frequent references to the civil and criminal law remedies that existed in the common law of England at the time, for example chapters 17 (common pleas), 18 and 19 (the 'possessory assizes': *novel disseisin*, *mort d'ancestor*, and *darrein presentment*), and 24 (crimes or 'pleas of the Crown') and 36 (writ of inquisition 'of life and limb'), and the right to legal process (chapter 40). According to accounts by Paul Brand and John Hudson, the nascent English common law in the twelfth and thirteenth centuries was characterised by the expansion of the operation of the king's royal courts across the realm, the operation of these courts by officials who were trained and experienced in the law of the realm, the application in these courts of a law that increasingly used writs (especially in actions concerning land), and the recording of decisions so that precedent and consistency became a feature of these courts.[44] It is noteworthy that custom was a fluid concept in the early thirteenth century because much of the 'official legal system', the English common law, was itself custom.[45]

Tamanaha's system (2), 'customary/cultural normative systems' are 'shared social rules and customs, as well as social institutions and mechanisms, from reciprocity, to dispute resolution tribunals, to councils of traditional leaders'; typically, such systems characterise the 'indigenous law' or 'traditional law' in colonial and post-colonial contexts, rather than the transplanted systems of the colonisers.[46] Although the concept of colonialism is a modern one and most commonly associated with Western European powers in the seventeenth, eighteenth, and nineteenth centuries, the term has been invoked in numerous studies of the medieval period and, in the English context, most often in relation to the Normans' invasion of the indigenous Anglo-Saxon kingdoms in 1066.[47] In the thirteenth

---

[43] Tamanaha, 'Understanding Legal Pluralism,' 397.

[44] Paul Brand, *The Origins of the English Legal Profession* (Oxford: Blackwell, 1992); John Hudson, *The Formation of the English Common Law: Law and Society in England from the Norman Conquest to Magna Carta* (London: Longman, 1996).

[45] David Ibbetson, 'Custom in Medieval Law', in *The Nature of Customary Law*, ed. Amanda Perrau-Saussine and James Bernard Murphy (Cambridge: Cambridge University Press, 2007) 154.

[46] Tamanaha, 'Understanding Legal Pluralism,' 397.

[47] For example, Brian Golding, *Conquest and Colonisation. The Normans in Britain, 1066–1100* (Basingstoke: Palgrave Macmillan, 2013, 2nd rev. ed.).

century, several instances of these 'indigenous' legal systems still remained, and their traces stand in marked contrast to the common law provisions of Magna Carta. For example, Kent, formerly part of the Anglo-Saxon heptarchy, retained the twelfth-century gavelkind form of tenure, which was peculiar to that place.[48] Gavelkind differed in several important respects from the knight service that characterised non-Kentian tenures at common law and featured in the chapters of Magna Carta on inheritance and relief (chapter 2); inheritance of minors (chapter 3); wardships (chapter 4); maintenance of wardships (chapter 5); and the dower, inheritance, and marriage portion of widows (chapter 7).

A quite different illustration of Tamanaha's system (2) customary normative systems are other unwritten conventions and traditions, or customs. These, in contrast to the Kent customs (*consuetudines Kanci*), do appear in Magna Carta. For instance, several chapters refer to prise or purveyance, the king's right to compulsorily purchase goods, such as castle guard (chapter 29), commandeering of horses and carts (chapter 30), or commandeering of timber (chapter 31). Further, other extant customs are referred to in chapter 23, which limited the obligation to build bridges to ancient and established usage. Chapters 23, 44, 47, and 48 deal with features of forest law, a law that prevailed to the exclusion of the common law, demonstrated by the subsequent Forest Charter of 1217.[49] Forest law was one of the several 'evil customs' (*males consuetudines*) referred to in chapter 48 that were to be investigated and then abolished. Magna Carta also refers to various feudal incidents that existed as custom, such as scutages and aids (chapter 12), aids imposed by lords (chapter 15), amercements or fines (chapter 20), and county farms and increments (chapter 25).

System (3), 'religious/cultural normative systems', for Tamanaha, are usually distinct from, but may contain norms that are recognised by, the official legal system; alternatively, such norms may be recognised 'on their own terms'.[50] The provisions of Magna Carta make clear reference to religious normative systems in chapters 1 and 63, which refer to the freedom of the English Church, namely the freedom to elect prelates free from lay influence. Other references abound: the lay tenements of clerics in chapter

---

[48] *Consuetudines Cantiae* [Customs of Kent], in *The Statutes of the Realm* (London, 1810), vol. 1, 223–225; N. Neilson, 'Custom and the Common Law in Kent,' *Harvard Law Review* 38, No. 4 (1925) 482, 487–489.

[49] David Crook, 'The Forest Eyre in the Reign of King John', in *Magna Carta and the England of King John*, ed. Janet S. Loengard (Woodbridge, UK: Boydell Press, 2010), 63–82.

[50] Tamanaha, 'Understanding Legal Pluralism,' 398.

288    J. TALIADOROS

22; the entitlement of the church to administer the chattels of a deceased's estate in chapter 27; and the crusader's respite in chapters 52, 53, and 57. Other related aspects were succession and wardship, which were matters dealt with in chapters 2 to 8, but could be heard in the ecclesiastical courts where they concerned marriage, bastardy, ecclesiastical lands, breach of faith, or testamentary succession.[51] Hence, these were areas where forum shopping occurred between ecclesiastical courts and secular courts.

System (4) comprises 'economic/capitalist normative systems', which 'consist of the range of norms and institutions that constitute and relate to capitalist production and market transactions within social arenas', one example being the *lex mercatoria*.[52] It seems that a separate and identifiable law of *lex mercatoria* did not exist in the thirteenth century, but only subsequently from the seventeenth.[53] Although a treatise from the late thirteenth century, called *Lex mercatoria* (1275–1286), gathered together a number of mercantile customs, 'those customs, however, did not add up to a body of customary law'.[54] Nevertheless, its author was at least self-consciously attempting to differentiate mercantile legal procedures from the English Common Law of the day.[55] Chapters 20 and 41 in Magna Carta, dealing with merchants' freedom to trade, the removal of fish weirs (chapter 33), and the standardisation of weights and measures (chapter 35), point to a specific interest in local and international trade matters that operated on a transnational basis.

Tamanaha's category (5) of 'functional normative systems' are those 'organised and arranged in connection with the pursuit of a particular function, purpose or activity that goes beyond purely commercial pursuits', such as universities, schools, and hospitals, and possess 'some degree of autonomy and self-governance aimed at achieving the purpose for which they are constituted'; further, they 'all have regulatory capacities'.[56] The nascent mercantile law referred to above is an example of this functional system within the Magna Carta provisions, although arguably purely

[51] John Hudson, *The Oxford History of the Laws of England. Volume 2: 871–1216* (Oxford: Oxford University Press, 2012) 566.

[52] Tamanaha, 'Understanding Legal Pluralism,' 398.

[53] Charles Donahue, Jr., 'Medieval and Early Modern *Lex Mercatoria*: An Attempt at the *Probatio Diabolica*', *Chicago Journal of International Law* 5, No. 1 (2004) 21–37, 26–27; Basile et al., 124, 179.

[54] Basile et al., 30.

[55] Basile et al., 15.

[56] Tamanaha, 'Understanding Legal Pluralism,' 399.

commercial in nature. A further example is the municipal privileges or franchises granted by the king to cities, such as London (chapter 13 and 32), and other major towns, provided autonomy to those communities and a sphere of freedom from royal control.[57] It is clear that these privileges were attractive to the relevant communities not just for the trade and commercial opportunities presented, but also for the ability to self-govern and administer such aspects as the sheriff's office, local custom, and other roles.

The final system (6), systems concerning 'community/cultural normative systems' are the 'vaguest' of Tamanaha's six systems and represent 'an imagined identification by a group of a common way of life, usually tied to a common language and history and contained within geographical boundaries of some kind'.[58] Magna Carta reveals the existence of normative measures linked to separate identifiable communities within English society in the first decades of the thirteenth century, such as the chapters that deal with the forest law justiciable in the forest eyres at that time[59] (chapters 23, 44, 47, 48) and those on inherited debts owed to Jewish people (chapter 11). Yet other chapters deal with the need to deal with foreign hostages in England, namely Welsh hostages (chapters 56–58) and Scottish hostages (chapter 59), while foreigners such as 'alien' officers and mercenaries were to be dismissed from the realm (chapter 50).

Alongside these six 'systems' are Tamanaha's three vertical 'axes' of coexisting and overlapping bodies of law, with features of (a) 'different geographical reaches', (b) 'coexisting institutionalised systems', and (c) 'conflicting legal norms within a system'.

Axis (a) of overlapping law is evident in the Magna Carta provisions on church law. For example, chapter 22 deals with amercement by the Crown of real property held by clerics. This is despite the operation of the assize *Utrum*, by which a justiciar of the common law courts determined the question whether (*utrum*) the land in dispute was lay fee or alm, and so ascertain whether the land was exigible or not.[60] A number of other provisions dealing with ecclesiastical affairs, which are referred to above in

---

[57] Holt, chapter 3; Hudson, 'Oxford History,' 562–565, 849.

[58] Tamanaha, 'Understanding Legal Pluralism,' 399.

[59] Crook, 1.

[60] Hudson, 'Oxford History,' 607–609; Samuel E. Thorne, 'The Assize "Utrum" and Canon Law in England,' *Columbia Law Review* 33 No. 3 (March 1933) 428–436.

respect of a religious system, involved potential overlap with the secular jurisdiction and the potential for forum shopping.

Axis (b), describing 'coexisting institutionalised systems', is also evident from these provisions on church law. Under the Constitutions of Clarendon of 1167, matters involving clergy were to be heard in ecclesiastical, not secular courts. This was a law of 'persons', which had no regard to the fact that the subject matter of the dispute could include property, crime, and other matters, which were equally justiciable in secular courts.[61] Another example of this axis of co-existence is evident from chapter 11, which deals with inherited debts to Jewish money lenders. This evidences the special relationship that Jewish businesspeople had with the Crown during the time of King John. On the one hand, matters of money lending between Christians and Jews were subject to the jurisdiction of the Crown and the royal courts, including the Exchequer of the Jews; on the other, intra-communal matters between Jews were dealt with according to Jewish law and wrongs emended and justice done within the community.[62]

Axis (c), which deals with 'conflicting legal norms within a system', is also exemplified in the overlap and co-existing ecclesiastical law and English common law and courts identified above. Chapters 52, 53, and 57 illustrate how the canon law 'exception' of the 'crusader's respite' conflicted with the substantive requirement of those provisions requiring John to return confiscated lands and to disafforest lands afforested by John's predecessors. In this instance, the difference was not merely institutional: the law applied by these ecclesiastical courts, in respect of the crusader's respite, was the substantive canon law derived from the precepts of the Church, based on papal decretals, Gratian's *Decretum*, and other sources.[63] This could often conflict with secular understandings of law. The chapters that deal with Welsh hostages (chapter 58), restoration of disseised Welsh lands (chapter 57), and restoration of disseised Welsh lands, liberties, and things (chapter 56), anticipate a conflict of laws in case of dispute by stipulating both the law that must apply and the place that it must be heard. In addition, forest law, although confined by chapter 44 to those who live in the forest, existed side-by-side with the English common

---

[61] Hudson, 'Oxford History,' 566.

[62] Paul Brand, 'Jews and the Law in England, 1190–1290', unpublished paper in the possession of the author. I am grateful to Professor Brand for providing me with a copy of this paper and the permission to cite it here.

[63] James A. Brundage, *Medieval Canon Law* (London: Routledge, 2016).

14  LEGAL PLURALISM PAST AND PRESENT: MAGNA CARTA AND A FIRST...    291

law, yet was far harsher in its penalties. For instance, blinding and emascu-lation was the penalty for trespass to movables, such as killing a deer.[64]

## Limitations of Tamanaha's Approach

The above analysis provides a striking illustration of the pluralistic nature of the provisions of Magna Carta, as revealed by one type of legal pluralist theory propounded by Brian Tamanaha. It is not contended that this is an unproblematic project. As well as the vagueness of legal pluralism that has been adverted to earlier in this chapter, the limits of Tamanaha's taxo-nomic analysis are also evident. A few examples illustrate the point.

One feature that evades clear categorisation into any of Tamanaha's six systems and three axes is what we might call 'public' or constitutional law or, less anachronistically, laws relating to rulership and governance. For instance, what of the prerogative entitlements in chapters 28, 30, 31 on royal purveyances, chapter 32 on confiscation of felons' lands, or chapter 37 on prerogative wardship? On a related note, the chapters that deal with privileges/franchises (e.g. chapters 33, 35, 41 regarding merchants and chapters 13 and 32 dealing with towns such as London) do not neatly fit the description of a normative ordering either. Further, the fundamental 'constitutional' entitlement envisaged by chapter 39, which required a person to be subject to legal process as a precursor to imprisonment or penalty, is also difficult to classify as a normative ordering. Yet further, those provisions of Magna Carta that took measures against the malprac-tices of the king's local officials, such as chapters 23 to 31 on sheriffs, bailiffs, and constables of castles, and chapter 50, on named officials, stand outside Tamanaha's categories. Such wrongdoing we might, in modern legal terms, label 'abuse of power' or 'abuse of office' find no easy place among the six types of systems of normative ordering.

A related feature that is similarly difficult to reconcile as a law or a nor-mative ordering in Tamanaha's systems is the exercise of political power. This is exemplified by the kingly power of mercy in chapter 49 regarding the restoration of English hostages and charters, which is also evident in chapters 56 to 58 on the return of Welsh hostages, possessions, and lands, and chapter 59 on the restoration of Scottish hostages, liberties, and rights. Chapter 62 deals with the royal pardon and amnesty granted to barons by way of resolution of the former *discordia* between them.

[64] Crook, 68.

292    J. TALIADOROS

Enforcement of the law sits somewhere between procedure and sub-stantive law and finds no place in Tamanaha's taxonomy either. Chapter 61, the 'security clause', which gives the 'court of Twenty Five', a group of barons, authority to enforce the concessions and grants in the provisions of Magna Carta against the king, is an example of this kind of enforcement provision that is difficult to classify.[65]

Yet another aspect of Magna Carta that defies clear categorisation using Tamanaha's hermeneutic, yet a clear example of an additional normative ordering existing within a single area, is Roman law. Although the long-standing debate as to whether Roman law influenced the drafting of the Magna Carta provisions no longer favours Richard Helmholz's 'maximal-ist' position,[66] but instead would prefer John Hudson's 'minimalist' position, even the latter's concession of Roman law influence, even if only in a general way, is evidenced in provisions such as chapter 28 on purveyance and chapter 63 on the freedom of the Church.[67]

Accordingly, while illustrative, the taxonomic approach of Tamanaha is, ironically, also limiting in its evocation of a medieval legal pluralism applicable to Magna Carta. Of note is the absence of Tamanaha's taxonomy to include notions of public law, or to the medieval precursors to such notions, outlined above. This is explicable on the basis that the divide between public and private laws was not yet clear or institutionalised in the common law of the early thirteenth century when Magna Carta came into being, as Horowitz has noted.[68]

## A First Nations Voice in the Constitution and Legal Pluralism

### *Uluru Statement and a First Nations Voice in the Constitution*

This part turns from the Middle Ages to the present day, and to consider-ations of how legal pluralism can play a role in understanding normative

---

[65] Richard Helmholz, 'Magna Carta and the Ius Commune,' *University of Chicago Law Review* 66 (1999) 297–371.

[66] Helmholz.

[67] John Hudson, 'Magna Carta, the Ius Commune, and the English Common Law', in *Magna Carta and the England of King John*, ed. Janet S. Loengard (Woodbridge, UK: Boydell Press, 2010), 99–119.

[68] Morton J. Horwitz, 'The History of the Public/Private Distinction,' *University of Pennsylvania Law Review* 130 (1982) 1423–1428.

## 14 LEGAL PLURALISM PAST AND PRESENT: MAGNA CARTA AND A FIRST... 293

orderings then and now. We are not familiar with understanding the contemporary Australian legal system as one that is 'pluralist', yet that is arguably one means by which Australians can make sense of the perceived dissonance between the Uluru Statement from the Heart and the Commonwealth Constitution in respect of recognising constitutionally entrenched rights for Indigenous Australians.

The Uluru Statement from the Heart is the declaration made at the National Indigenous Constitutional Convention on 26 May 2017. That convention, undertaken by the Referendum Council, was an Indigenous-led and Indigenous-designed consultation process. For that reason, it arguably represents a consensus view among Indigenous people on how to deal with the historical disadvantage of the erroneously applied legal doctrine of *terra nullius*, which led to significant deprivation of land and other rights among Australian First Nations peoples.[69] Relevantly, it reads as follows[70]:

> Our Aboriginal and Torres Strait Islander tribes were the first sovereign Nations of the Australian continent and its adjacent islands, and possessed it under our own laws and customs. This our ancestors did, according to the reckoning of our culture, from the Creation, according to the common law from 'time immemorial', and according to science more than 60,000 years ago.

> This sovereignty is a spiritual notion: the ancestral tie between the land, or 'mother nature', and the Aboriginal and Torres Strait Islander peoples who were born therefrom, remain attached thereto, and must one day return thither to be united with our ancestors. This link is the basis of the ownership of the soil, or better, of sovereignty. It has never been ceded or extinguished, and co-exists with the sovereignty of the Crown.

> How could it be otherwise? That peoples possessed a land for sixty millennia and this sacred link disappears from world history in merely the last two hundred years?

---

[69] Morris, 12–13.

[70] 'Uluru Statement from the Heart', issued 26 May 2017, https://www.referendum-council.org.au/sites/default/files/2017-05/Uluru_Statement_From_The_Heart_0.PDF (emphasis in original).

With substantive constitutional change and structural reform, we believe this ancient sovereignty can shine through as a fuller expression of Australia's nationhood.

Proportionally, we are the most incarcerated people on the planet. We are not an innately criminal people. Our children are aliened from their families at unprecedented rates. This cannot be because we have no love for them. And our youth languish in detention in obscene numbers. They should be our hope for the future.

These dimensions of our crisis tell plainly the structural nature of our problem. *This is the torment of our powerlessness.*

We seek constitutional reforms to empower our people and take a *rightful place* in our own country. When we have power over our destiny our children will flourish. They will walk in two worlds and their culture will be a gift to their country.

We call for the establishment of a First Nations Voice enshrined in the Constitution.

Makarrata is the culmination of our agenda: *the coming together after a struggle.* It captures our aspirations for a fair and truthful relationship with the people of Australia and a better future for our children based on justice and self-determination.

We seek a Makarrata Commission to supervise a process of agreement-making between governments and First Nations and truth-telling about our history.

This Uluru Statement, therefore, captures three aspirations: first, a First Nations Voice in the Commonwealth Constitution; second, a treaty or agreement between governments and First Nations people; and, third, a process of 'truth-telling'.[71] This chapter focuses on the first of these, the Voice.

Following the Uluru Statement, the Final Report of the Referendum Council detailed the nature of what a First Nations Voice in the Constitution entailed. First, it argued that the notion of a Voice in the Constitution was consistent with both international law and domestic law.

[71] Larkin and Galloway, 34.

The right to self-determination existed at international law for persons to 'freely pursu[e] their economic, social and cultural development', as outlined in Article 1 of the *International Covenant on Economic, Social and Cultural Rights* and Article 1 of the *International Covenant on Civil and Political Rights*.[72] It was also consistent with domestic Australian law insofar as that Voice played 'a role when Parliament and government make laws and policies about Indigenous affairs'.[73] Specifically, in relation to domestic law, the nature of the Voice was 'not by way of proposed alteration to the Constitution, but as guidance for associated legislation, that one of the specific functions of the body is to monitor the head of power section 51(xxvi) and section 122'.[74] Megan Davis, one of the prominent figures from the Referendum Council, confirmed this understanding of the Voice to Parliament to[75]:

> monitor the use of the race power and the territories power. And, more practically, the voice could have multiple functions, the most important being direct input into decisions that are made about law and policy that affect Aboriginal and Torres Strait Islander peoples.

The Prime Minister's Response in late October 2017 was outright rejection of the proposal for a Voice to Parliament. This was on the basis that it 'would inevitably become seen as a third chamber of Parliament'.[76] This is, on any measure, not only an inaccurate representation of the Voice, but a misleading one as well.[77] The above wording from the Uluru Statement refers to a 'spiritual' sovereignty that 'co-exists' with the sovereignty of the Crown.[78] Anne Twomey has also proposed a constitutional

---

[72] Final Report of the Referendum Council, Report (30 June 2017), 37.

[73] Final Report, 37.

[74] Final Report, 37.

[75] Megan Davis, 'To Walk in Two Worlds', *The Monthly* (online), July 2018, https://www.themonthly.com.au/issue/2017/july/1498831200/megan-davis/walk-two-worlds#mtr.

[76] Prime Minister Malcolm Turnbull, Media Release, 'Response to Referendum Council's report on Constitutional Recognition', 26 October 2017, https://pmtranscripts.pmc.gov.au/release/transcript-41263.

[77] Morris, 292–294.

[78] The wording is a paraphrasing from the *Western Sahara (Advisory Opinion)* [1975] ICJ Rep 12, 85–86 (Vice-President Ammoun). See also *Mabo v Queensland (No 2)* (1992) 175 CLR 1, 41.

clause effecting this, which does not impact on sovereignty.[79] Nevertheless, the perception of an Indigenous Voice having a veto power in Parliament was writ large in public perception, and remains. The issue of the Australian Commonwealth's parliamentary sovereignty being limited in any way was seen as a fundamental threat to the nation's parliamentary and legal systems.[80]

In the next part, I suggest that regarding the Voice as an instance of legal pluralism in this contemporary Australian discourse can be a means of alleviating perceptions of a challenge to Commonwealth sovereignty and as having historical precedent in Magna Carta.

## A First Nations Voice in the Constitution: An Application of Legal Pluralism

This chapter is not novel in suggesting the relevance of legal pluralism in the context of rights for Indigenous Australians. This part will briefly outline the views of some scholars who have suggested the relevance of the concept in dealing with the historical injustices facing Indigenous Australians. Further, this part will analyse Shireen Morris's arguments for a First Nations Voice in the Constitution, in particular observing the role of legal pluralism in her thesis.

As noted above, Larkin and Galloway observe that legal pluralism is an expression of 'a truly Australian public law'.[81] This is consistent with the views of Margaret Davies and others, who have deployed the notion of legal pluralism in Australian law regarding the issue of legal self-determination for Indigenous peoples.[82] Applying Griffiths's notion of legal centrism as a myth and pluralism as a social fact, Davies observed that 'the co-existence of state law, Indigenous law, and various religious laws in Australia is a fact but … this plurality of laws has been obscured by the myth of positivism, which only sees *state* law as law'.[83] For Davies, native title land entitlement is a 'weak' form of legal pluralism, as it recognised

---

[79] Morris, 39; Anne Twomey, 'Putting Words to the Tune of Indigenous Constitutional Recognition', *The Conversation* (20 May 2015), https://theconversation.com/putting-words-to-the-tune-of-indigenous-constitutional-recognition-42038.

[80] See Morris, 277, and the references cited therein to academics and populist commentators, such as Andrew Bolt and Greg Sheridan.

[81] Larkin and Galloway, 1.

[82] Davies, 412.

[83] Davies, 413.

14 LEGAL PLURALISM PAST AND PRESENT: MAGNA CARTA AND A FIRST... 297

aspects of indigenous law on this issue but strictly within the framework of colonial recognition.[84] According to Griffiths, 'weak' forms of pluralism do not challenge the doctrine of centralism but are subsumed within it; in contrast, 'strong' legal pluralism means that such difference cannot be reduced to the singular authority of a state, and there is no dominant or overarching system that orders relations between the different laws.[85] The legal and constitutional model of the Voice arguably also presents a form of 'soft' legal pluralism.

Constitutional lawyer and legal academic Shireen Morris, in her 2020 book, forcefully argues for a First Nations Voice in the Constitution, as advocated in the Uluru Statement.[86] Her arguments adopt the reasoning of legal philosopher Jeremy Waldron, among other legal theorists, as well as notions of legal pluralism.

In considering the historical context, Morris acknowledges the historical injustices visited on Indigenous peoples in Australia from colonialism to the present day, but agrees with Waldron that a mere 'first come, first served' or 'we were here first' approach to dealing with this injustice is inappropriate, without 'a practical focus on fair and balanced distribution of resources'.[87] In considering the political context, Morris notes Waldron's notion of participation being the 'right of all rights'.[88] Consonant with this, she notes Waldron's thesis that Australians have an 'embedded respect for the political process as the best mechanism for the defence and adjudication of rights', rather than judicial adjudication.[89] Next, turning to the 'theoretical' context, Morris notes that the proposition that a fair liberal democracy should constitutionally recognise Indigenous peoples 'is not self-explanatory and needs to be unpacked'.[90]

In unpacking the argument, Morris notes that 'the argument for Indigenous constitutional recognition proceeds from an understanding that Indigenous peoples are a legitimately distinct "constitutional entity", or constitutional constituency, within a plural legal order'.[91] Here Morris

---

[84] Davies, 414–415.

[85] Davies, 415.

[86] Morris.

[87] Morris, 56.

[88] Morris, 58 n 247, citing Jeremy Waldron, 'Participation: The Right of Rights,' *Proceedings of the Aristotelian Society* 98, No. 3 (1998) 307.

[89] Morris, 58.

[90] Morris, 66.

[91] Morris, 72.

explicitly acknowledges the scholarship on legal pluralism as it relates to colonial contexts, by scholars such as Benedict Kingsbury, Alexander Reilley, John Griffiths, and James Tully. Further, Morris notes the relevance to legal pluralism arguments of Will Kymlicka's understanding of minority group recognition within liberal democracies as grounded on the observation that many of these are multinational, thus accommodating distinct yet co-existing nations or peoples with a shared sense of patriotism—which she labels a 'middle way' of 'accommodation and recognition of co-existing domestic nations within states'.[92] Morris suggests that Kymlicka's middle way of accommodation and recognition is compatible with Waldron's notion that the fundamental purpose of democratic constitutions is political empowerment[93]:

> The Uluru Statement's request for a voice in Indigenous affairs, in my view, accords with Waldron's conception of the fundamental purpose of democratic constitutions in this respect: in contrast to autocratic regimes which maintain the power of elites, the constitution of a democracy 'involves empowering *those who would otherwise be powerless*, the ordinary people who in most polies are the subjects not the agents of political power'.

But Morris notes the tension between recognition and equality. Rawlsian arguments advocate that a liberal democracy requires a system of government in which citizens are free and equal, have an equal say through their equal vote, and have free and equal participation in the democratic system.[94] This is not the case if there is specific recognition for Indigenous Australians in the Constitution. Yet, as she correctly observes, the Constitution does not treat all Australian equally, specifically Indigenous people. Accordingly, Morris observes that the 'individualistic non-discrimination paradigm' does not suffice here in the context of recognising collective Indigenous rights and interests.[95] She argues that 'appropriately formulated, constitutional recognition of Indigenous peoples, accommodating and allowing for Indigenous survival as distinct

---

[92] Morris, 74, citing Will Kymlicka, *Multicultural Citizenship* (Oxford: Clarendon Press, 1995).

[93] Morris, 75, citing Jeremy Waldron 'Constitutionalism: A Skeptical View' Philip A. Hart Memorial Lecture, Georgetown University Law Centre (2010) https://scholarship.law.georgetown.edu/hartlecture/42010, 20, 24–25.

[94] Morris, 78.

[95] Morris, 78.

peoples and enabling their voices to be heard in their distinct affairs, would be a modest, if careful and appropriate characterisation in a federal liberal democracy like Australia'.[96]

Morris prefers constitutional change to mere legislative change. The basis for this, she explains, is Waldron's notion of 'participation', or right to political participation, which, as noted above, he calls the 'right of rights', and fundamental in a liberal democracy. On this basis, Morris argues for 'a non-justiciable, political process-centred' solution: 'a constitutionally guaranteed Indigenous representative body, to ensure Indigenous peoples fairer participation in political decision-making with respect to their rights'.[97] Morris observes that the Australian Constitution, according to Cheryl Saunders, already recognises distinct political collectives, since it has at its essence federalism, which 'involves multiple overlapping political communities, each with a degree of constitutional autonomy'.[98] That is, Morris continues, the Constitution could explicitly recognise Indigenous peoples as 'a distinct constitutional constituency', albeit not geographically constrained as the States and Territories are. These co-existing constitutional constituencies can peacefully disagree, co-operate and collaborate'.[99] Such a notion is also consistent, Morris argues, with Duncan Ivison's conception of post-colonial liberalism, which accommodates a 'complex co-existence' between Indigenous peoples and the state via mechanisms for ongoing dialogue.[100]

In short, Morris's vision for constitutional recognition of a First Nations Voice is premised on the recognition of legal pluralism or multiple normativities in Australian law. As observed above, the notion of a Voice in the Constitution arguably constitutes a form of public law pluralism. We are yet to see exactly what form this Voice might take, but Anne Twomey suggests a new chapter 1A in the Constitution after chapter 1, which deals with the legislature. This new chapter would comprise provisions that recognise an advisory Indigenous Australian body, provide for the tabling of that body's advice to the Houses of Parliament, and then require Parliament to have regard to the advice 'in debating proposed laws with respect to

---

[96] Morris, 82.

[97] Morris, 97, citing Waldron, 'Participation', 307, 308.

[98] Morris, 99, citing Cheryl Saunders, 'Protecting Rights in a Federalism,' *Adelaide Law Review* 25, No. 2 (2004) 177, 182.

[99] Morris, 99.

[100] Morris, 100, citing Duncan Ivison, *Postcolonial Liberalism* (Cambridge: Cambridge University Press, 2002) 22–23.

Aboriginal and Torres Strait Islander peoples'.[101] Although advisory in its role, such a body is constitutionally entrenched, and its advice must be listened to, even if not binding. It is, therefore, arguably more than merely 'political' in its nature; it is legal. Further, it is likely that any advice from such a body would create such an important source of normative guidance that the body's statements would practically have the effect of law (in that Parliament would be extremely reluctant to contravene it).

## CONCLUSION

This chapter is a provocation to traditional conceptions of understanding law and normative systems in the current Australian legal, constitutional, and political environment. One of the most iconic documents of the English common law that we inherited, Magna Carta, emerged from a culture of legal diversity and pluralism. The provisions of Magna Carta still bear the palimpsest traces of this pluralism if only we consider that document and its context in new ways. These new ways of perceiving, of seeing the law, provide lessons for our own times as to how we might consider the co-existence of an Indigenous First Nations Voice, as an instantiation of a spiritual sovereignty, alongside the traditional parliamentary sovereignty established in our Constitution. Further, the legal pluralism that this chapter has argued was present in Magna Carta resonates directly with the legal pluralism that a constitutionally entrenched Voice implicitly entails—specifically, a pluralist public law—in the contemporary Australian legal context.

[101] Twomey; Morris 269–273.

# Index[1]

**A**

Acclimatisation Society, 258
  Queensland, 258
  Victoria, 258
Anderson, Sir John, 30–32
Animals OR Fauna
  bounties on, 266
  cane toads, vii, 267, 269–275
  native wildlife, 275
  rabbits, 257, 258, 262,
    270, 273–276
  threat abatement plans, 272, 274
Arbitration, 86, 134, 136–139
Atkin, Lord, v, 3, 25–46
Atkins, Richard, 78, 182, 218,
  219, 221n67
Attorney general, v, 3, 5–21, 40, 58,
  72, 141, 246
*Australian Constitutions Act 1842*,
  245, 249

*Australian Constitutions Act 1850*, 249
Autonomy, 19, 53, 55, 288, 289, 299

**B**

Barristers, vi, 9, 10, 12, 13, 65, 66,
  68–73, 75–82, 92, 139, 141,
  164, 175
Blackstone, Sir William, 17, 181–183,
  185, 186, 188, 223n76
Brennan, Sir Gerard, 201, 234,
  234n117, 235, 253
Brexit, v, 3, 49–63, 51n7, 63n30, 79

**C**

*Calvin's Case 1608*, 205, 229n106,
  234, 234n117
*Campbell v Hall 1774*, 205, 230,
  234, 234n117

---

[1] Note: Page numbers followed by 'n' refer to notes.

© The Author(s), under exclusive license to Springer Nature
Switzerland AG 2022
S. McKibbin et al. (eds.), *The Impact of Law's History*, Palgrave
Modern Legal History,
https://doi.org/10.1007/978-3-030-90068-7

301

302 INDEX

Carroll, Lewis, 40
*Case of Thorns 1466*, 107, 110
Coke, Sir Edward, 67, 93, 100, 183
Collins, David, 212–215, 218–220, 235
Commonwealth Constitution, 136, 142, 285, 293, 294
Commonwealth Law Reports, 184
*Constitution Act 1867 (Qld)*, 4, 239–255
*Constitution of Queensland 2001*, 239, 251
Constitution, Australian
    Section 92, 170–177
    Section 96, 163, 163n23, 163n24, 173, 174, 177
Constitutional law, v, vi, 155, 156, 162, 164, 169, 173, 174, 176–178, 176n81, 291
Corporate social responsibility, 84, 98
Crown law officers, 6–8, 10, 12, 20

**D**

*Darnel's Case 1627*, 40
Decorum, 25, 26, 30, 35, 37–46
    indecorous, 26, 45, 46
Defamation, 125–127, 126n67, 126n70
Detention, 25, 26, 28, 29, 31, 33–35, 37, 40, 294
*Donoghue v Stevenson 1932*, 29, 30, 105

**E**

*Emergency Powers (Defence) Act 1939*, 33
Enterprise risk, 120
Executive, v, 18, 25–27, 30, 32–37, 39–41, 51, 52, 52n9, 56, 58, 60, 63, 101, 168, 226n94, 232, 233n114
Executive discretion, v, 25, 27, 30, 33–37

**F**

Fault, vi, 105–128, 138
Federation, 136–139, 145, 167n44, 261, 262
Fee simple, 241, 242n19, 244
First Fleet, 202, 203, 205, 209, 212, 213n34, 214, 224, 232, 234, 235, 257, 273
First Nations Voice, 277–300
Flora
    lantana, 268, 269, 274
    Phylloxera Board, 261, 263, 264
    prickly pear, 265–268, 270, 276
    Prickly Pear Board, 267
    Prickly Pear Travelling Commission, 266
    Queensland Bureau of Sugar Experiment Stations, 269
    Vinehealth Australia, 264
    weed control, 268
Forbes, Francis, 5

**G**

Gandhi, Mohandas, 151
*Garrow's Law*, 66, 67, 70–73, 78, 82
Garrow, William, 67, 71–73, 75, 77, 78, 80
*Gay News blasphemy trial*, 71
Grants, 33, 91, 156, 162–169, 171, 173, 174, 177, 191, 234n117, 240–243, 242n19, 245, 246, 292

**H**

Habeas corpus, 32
Hale, Sir Matthew, 113, 182, 185, 188, 188n61
High Court of Australia, vi, 3, 131, 175, 179
Holdsworth, Sir William, 6n1, 86, 186–188

INDEX 303

Home Department (UK), 208
Home Office (UK), 57n19, 219
House of Lords (UK), 7, 15, 28, 40,
  51, 53, 55, 56, 100, 117, 118, 126
Humpty Dumpty, 26, 38–46
Hunter, John, 220, 223

**I**

Indigenous Australians, 277, 293,
  296, 298, 299
  massacre, 219
Interstate Trade &
  Commerce, 169–173

**J**

Judiciary/judicial, 6, 8, 9, 11, 16, 18,
  19, 25–27, 29, 30, 30n24,
  32–34, 37–40, 43–46, 51, 52,
  52n9, 56, 58, 59, 63, 88, 89,
  100, 101, 113, 118, 132, 143,
  144, 147, 148, 154, 157, 166,
  169–171, 173n77, 174–176,
  185, 211, 219, 226n94, 234, 297

**K**

Kusch, Egon, 145n61, 152, 153

**L**

Legal advertising, 83, 94–95
Legal pluralism, vii, 2, 277–300
Legal service promotion, 84
Legal treatises, 181
Liability, 111
Liberty, 7, 25–27, 29, 32, 34, 36–39,
  41, 42, 46, 75, 79, 91, 241, 284,
  290, 291
Littleton, Sir Thomas, 183
*Liversidge v Anderson 1942*, v, 25

Lock-in and reliance, 173, 176–177
Lord Atkin's dissent, 3, 25–46
Lynch, Humphrey, 215–217, 216n42,
  216n43, 236, 237

**M**

*Mabo v Queensland [No 2] (1992)*,
  188, 201, 253
Macquarie, Lachlan, 218–227,
  225n86, 226n91,
  226n94, 227n97
Magna Carta, vii, 4, 29, 77,
  79, 277–300
Maintenance and champerty,
  93–94, 102
Maitland, F. W., 85, 87, 114, 186,
  186n53, 187, 223n76, 235, 283
Marshall Hall, Sir Edward, 65, 67,
  71–75, 77, 78, 80, 81
Maugham, Lord, 28, 30, 33,
  34, 38, 40
Modern social imaginary, 239, 240
Moyock, Jesee, 215, 216, 236
Mortimer, Sir John, 71, 75, 76, 80
Mulcock, Jesse, *see* Molock, Jessee

**N**

Native title, 250, 251, 253, 296
Negligence, 3, 105, 106, 108–111,
  110n15, 115–118, 121, 122,
  124–126, 125n60, 125n62,
  126n67, 126n68, 154
New South Wales
  Court of Criminal Judicature for
    New South Wales, 204
  Supreme Court of New South
    Wales, 134, 135, 154, 202,
    202n3, 211, 232n111
Nuisance, 109, 118, 119, 124, 125,
  125n60, 125n62, 127

304   INDEX

## O
Old Bailey, 67, 69, 70, 72, 81n34
Opportunity and exit, 173–176

## P
Parliament, 7, 8, 10, 18, 19, 33,
    49–52, 55, 56, 58, 60, 72, 79,
    115, 137, 146, 163, 163n24,
    164, 166, 168, 204, 205, 247,
    249, 259, 295, 296, 299, 300
Path dependency, vi, 3
Pemulwuy, 220, 222, 222n75,
    223, 223n76
Penalty clauses, 190, 195
Phillip, Arthur, 2, 3, 203–205, 204n5,
    211–227, 229, 243
Piddington, Albert, v, 131–154
Promotional methods, 84
Property as wealth, vi, 240–247,
    252, 255
Property institutions, 240, 242, 244,
    246, 247, 251–255
Property questions, 251–255
Public law, 26, 285, 292, 299, 300

## Q
Quarantine
    commonwealth legislation, 260, 261
    compensation schemes, 263
    intergovernmental co-operation, 275
Queensland, vi, 4, 29, 141, 172,
    239–253, 255, 266–270, 275
    colonial, 240–247, 252

## R
*R v Ballard 1829*, 202, 202n2
*R v Boatman 1832*, 211,
    211n27, 211n28
*R v Lowe 1827*, 202, 202n2, 228,
    228n102, 230n107, 231–233

*R v Murrell 1836*, 202, 202n2, 232,
    232n111, 233
*R v Powell 1799*, 222–224
*R v Ridgway 1826*, 229, 229n105
*Rake*, 81, 82
*Real Property Act 1861*, 247, 249
Regulation 18B' 'reasonable cause to
    believe,' 26, 33–35, 38
Roman law, 90, 107, 113, 183, 292
Royal Commissioner, 139, 146, 148
Rule of law, 19, 26, 37, 46, 56, 79,
    116, 285
*Rumpole of the Bailey*, 66–68,
    70, 76, 82
Ryder, Sir Dudley, v, 5–21
*Rylands v Fletcher 1868*, 116–119

## S
*Shadow of the Noose*, 66, 67, 74, 75, 82
Shorthand, 11, 12, 12n16, 21, 186
Solicitor general, 6, 7, 9, 10, 12, 14,
    15, 18, 19
Strict liability, vi, 3, 106–109, 111–128

## T
Television, vi, 3, 65–82
*Terra nullius*, 293
Torts, vi, 3, 105–106, 140
Trespass, 109, 110, 112, 126–128,
    127n71, 291

## U
Uluru Statement from the Heart, 4,
    277, 278n2, 293, 293n70

## W
*Weaver v Ward 1616*, 110
Windeyer, Victor, 135, 186–188
Word of mouth, 84, 102